SIGNIFICANT SISTERS

Margaret Forster is the author of many successful
novels, including *Lady's Maid*, *The Memory Box*,
Diary of an Ordinary Woman, two memoirs, *Hidden
Lives* and *Precious Lives*, and several acclaimed
biographies, including *Good Wives*.

ALSO BY MARGARET FORSTER

Fiction

Dame's Delight
Georgy Girl
The Bogeyman
The Travels of Maudie Tipstaff
The Park
Miss Owen-Owen is At Home
Fenella Phizackerley
Mr Bone's Retreat
The Seduction of Mrs Pendlebury
The Battle for Christabel
The Bride of Lowther Fell
Marital Rites
Private Papers
Have the Men Had Enough?
Lady's Maid
Mothers' Boys
Shadow Baby
The Memory Box
Mother Can You Hear Me?
Diary of an Ordinary Woman

Non-Fiction

The Rash Adventurer:
The Rise and Fall of Charles Edward Stuart
William Makepeace Thackeray:
Memoirs of a Victorian Gentleman
Elizabeth Barrett Browning
Daphne du Maurier
Hidden Lives
Rich Deserts & Captain's Thin:
A Family & Their Times 1831–1931
Precious Lives
Good Wives:
Mary, Fanny, Jennie & Me 1845–2001

Poetry

Selected Poems of
Elizabeth Barrett Browning (Editor)

Margaret Forster

SIGNIFICANT SISTERS
The Grassroots of Active Feminism
1839–1939

V

VINTAGE

Published by Vintage 2004

4 6 8 10 9 7 5

Copyright © Margaret Forster 1984

First published in Great Britain in 1984 by
Secker & Warburg

Vintage
Random House, 20 Vauxhall Bridge Road,
London SW1V 2SA

www.rbooks.co.uk

Addresses for companies within
The Penguin Random House Group can be found at:
global.penguinrandomhouse.com

The Random House Group Limited Reg. No. 954009
www.randomhouse.co.uk/vintage

A CIP catalogue record for this book
is available from the British Library

ISBN 9780099455578

Penguin Random House is committed to a sustainable future for
our business, our readers and our planet. This book is made from
Forest Stewardship Council® certified paper.

Printed and bound in Great Britain by Clays Ltd, Elcograf S.p.A.

for

ALISON HOOPER
who has fought the feminist fight
throughout her life

List of Contents

	Laws	Employment	Education
1839	**Infants Custody Act**		
1840			
1841	.		**Governesses' Benevolent Inst.**
1842	Mines Act		
1844	Factory Act		
1845			
1846	Repeal of Corn Laws		
1847			**E. Blackwell to med. school** (US)
1848	**Married Women's Property Bill, NY** (US)		**Queens College**
1849			**Bedford College**
			Blackwell qualifies (US)
1850			**North London Collegiate**
1851			
1852			**American Women's Educ. Assoc.** (US)
1854			**Cheltenham Ladies' College**
1855			
1856			
1857	**Matrimonial Causes Act**		
1858			**Iowa admits women to univ.** (US)
1859			
1860		**Soc. for Promoting Employ-ment of women**	
		Nightingale Training School	
1861		**Female MC Emigration Soc.**	
1863			**Cambridge Local Exams opened to girls**
1864	**1st Contagious Diseases Act**		
1865		**E. Garrett Anderson medical licence**	**Vassar Coll. for Women** (US)
			Taunton Commiss. includes girls' schools
1866	**2nd Contagious Diseases Act**		
1867	2nd Reform Act		**N. Eng. Council for Promoting Higher Educ. of Women**
1868			

* Specifically feminist issues are indicated **thus**; titles in *italic*. Unless otherwise stated all political acts, laws, unions, etc., are for Great Britain: it is not possible on a chart of this limited scope and size to list all the important counterparts in America because of the way progress developed from State to State. Only major events mentioned in the text are shown.

Social	Political	Publications	
Intro patents for gas cookers	Anti Corn Law League		**1839**
Penny post			1840
Anti-slavery Convention London			
		C. Fourier: *Theory of Four Movements*	1841
			1842
			1844
Start of railway mania			
		M. Fuller: *Women in the 19th Century*	1845
Electrical Telegraph Co.			1846
			1847
	Seneca Falls Declaration		1848
	Revolutions in Paris, Berlin, etc.		
		The Lily: **A. Bloomer's mag.**	**1849**
			1850
Great Exhibition			1851
1st wearing Bloomer costume			1852
	Crimean War	**C. Norton:** *Eng. Laws for Women in 19thC*	1854
		B. Leigh-Smith: *Brief Summary of Laws Relating to Women*	1855
		C. Norton: *Letter to the Queen*	
		B. Leigh-Smith: *Women & Work*	1856
NY Infirmary for Women & Children (US)	Indian Mutiny		1857
Nat. Assoc. Promotion Social Science			
			1858
		Englishwoman's Journal	**1859**
		E. Davies: *Letters to Daily Newspaper*	1860
	American Civil War		1861
			1863
			1864
Kensington Society			1865
	1st petition to GB Parlt for female suffrage	**E. Davies:** *The Higher Educ. of Women*	1866
	Nat. Soc. for Women's Suffrage		1867
	Nat. Women's Suffrage Assoc. (US)		
		The Revolution: **Stanton/Anthony newspaper**	1868

	Laws	Employment	Education
1869	**3rd Contagious Diseases Act**		**Women's coll. at Hitchin**
1870	Forster's Education Act		
1871	Army Reform Acts		
1872			**Girls' Public Day School Trust**
1873	Comstock Law (US)		**Girton College**
1874	Factory Act	**Women's Provident & Protective League**	**London Sch. of Medicine for Women**
1875	Public Health Act		**Newnham Hall: Smith Coll. (US)**
1876		Royal Commiss. on Factories & Wkshops	
1877	Univs. of Oxford & Cambridge Act		**M. Grey Training Coll. for Women**
1878			**Nat. & Union Training School** / **London Univ. admits women**
1879			**Somerville Coll; Lady Mgt Hall**
1881			**Cambridge degrees open to women**
1882	**Married Women's Property Act**		
1883			
1884	Franchise Reform Act		
1885	Criminal Law Amendment Act		**Bryn Mawr (US)**
1886	**Repeal of CD Acts**		
1887			**A. Ramsay heads 1st Class Hons (Classics), Cantab.**
1888	Local Govt Act		
1889		**Women's Trade Union League**	Board of Educ. estab.
1890			
1893	**New Zealand Woman Suffrage Act**	Royal Commiss. on Employment of Labour	**Radcliffe College (US)**
1898			
1899		**1st woman memb. Inst. Elec Engineers**	
1900			
1901			
1902	Balfour's Education Act		
1903		**Women's Trade Union League (US)**	
1906	**Finland Woman Suffrage Act**		
1907	**Qualification of Women Act**		
1908	Old Age Pensions Act / Children's Act		

Social	Political	Publications	
Ladies' Nat. Assoc. v CD Acts	**Wyoming gives women vote** **American WS Assoc.**	**J. S. Mill:** *Subjection of Women* **J. Butler:** *Women's Work & Culture*	**1869**
			1870
Royal Commiss. Contagious Diseases		**J. Butler:** *Constitution Violated* **G. Eliot:** *Middlemarch*	1871
			1872
			1873
Women's Christian Temperance Union (US)			1874
Remington start manuf. typewriter			1875
			1876
			1877
		H. Auclert: *Droit politique des femmes* **H. Ibsen:** *A Doll's House*	1878
(circa) **Invention Mensinga Diaphragm**		**A. Bebel:** *Woman & Socialism*	**1879**
A. Jacobs' birth control clinic (Holland)			1881
Internat. Gas & Elec Exhibit.			1882
Women's Co-op. Guild			1883
	Fabian Society	**F. Engels:** *Origin of the Family*	1884
Invention 'safety' bicycle			1885
			1886
Rational Dress Campaign			1887
			1888
1st public elec. supply, London			**1889**
Gas cooker wider domestic use			1890
	Independent Labour Party		1893
		C. P. Gilman: *Women & Economics*	1898
1st free milk for poor mothers	Boer War		**1899**
Manufacture electric cookers & irons			1900
Invention vacuum cleaner	Death Queen Victoria		1901
		J. Addams: *Democracy & Soc. Ethics*	1902
Car manufacture: Ford Motor Co.	**Women's Soc. & Polit. Union –** **Pankhursts**		1903
	Women's Freedom League	*Mother Earth:* Goldman's mag.	1906
	County & Borough Councils **open to women**		1907
		A. Kollontai: *Soc. Basis of the Woman Question*	1908

	Laws	Employment	Education
1909 1911	Parliament Act; Nat. Insurance Act		
1912		**Com. to open legal profess. to women**	
1913	**Norway Woman Suffrage Act**		
1914			
1915 1916			
1917			
1918	**GB Woman Suffrage Act** **Maternity & Child Welfare Act**		
1919	19th Amend. US Constitution: women to vote **Sex Disqualification Removal Act**	**Women's Engineering Soc.**	Oxford admits women as full members
1920 1921		**1st woman bar student**	
1922		**1st woman barrister**	
1923			
1924		**Women's Electrical Assoc.**	
1925	Guardianship of Infants Act	**Civil Service Exams (Admin.) admit women**	
1926	Electricity Supply Act		
1927			
1928			
1929 1932			
1933			
1934	Unemployment Act		
1935			
1936			
1939			

Social	Political	Publications	
			1909
		O. Schreiner: *Woman & Labour*	1911
		E. Goldman: *Anarchism & Other Essays*	
			1912
	Congressional Union for Women's Suffrage (US)		1913
	1st World War	*The Woman Rebel*: Sanger newspaper	1914
Nat. Birth Control League (US)			1915
Brownsville Birth Control Clinic, NY (US)			1916
(circa) Intro. elec. washing machine (US)	1st woman in Hse of Reps (US)		1917
	Russian Revolution		
	USA enters war		
	Armistice	M. Stopes: *Married Love*	1918
	1st woman MP takes seat		1919
			1920
1st World League Sexual Reform Cong.			1921
Marie Stopes Birth Control Clinic			
Radio broadcasting begins	Union of Ireland ends		1922
		A. Kollontai: *Love of Worker Bees*	1923
			1924
Intro. short skirts			1925
BBC gets charter	General Strike	S. Lafollette: *Concerning Women*	1926
Talking pictures: Eton crop			1927
		R. Strachey: *The Cause*	1928
The Depression begins	1st woman Cabinet Minister	V. Woolf: *A Room of One's Own*	**1929**
	Disarmament Conference		1932
	1st woman Cabinet Minister (US)	V. Brittain: *Testament of Youth*	1933
			1934
		M. Mead: *Sex & Temperament in 3 Primitive Societies*	1935
TV begins transmitting	Spanish Civil War		1936
Family Planning Association	2nd World War		**1939**

List of Illustrations

Acknowledgements

I should like to acknowledge first and foremost the enthusiastic and efficient assistance of the staff of the Fawcett Library, and in particular of David Doughan, the Reference Librarian. This home of priceless feminist history archive material is in Calcutta House, City of London Polytechnic. It closely resembles the Black Hole of Calcutta. Scholars come in increasing numbers from all over the world and find they have to work in a small basement, with no natural light, at a mere dozen cramped old school desks and tables. The library deserves better premises but has to remain grateful for what it has.

I should also like to thank the ever helpful, well-informed staff of Sisterwrite, the feminist bookshop in Upper Street, Islington. It may seem unusual to acknowledge the help of a commercial concern, but tracking down feminist tracts, pamphlets and books is a difficult business even today and finding many of them stocked at Sisterwrite, or obtainable through them, has greatly assisted me. It is quite remarkable, for example, to find there a modern paperback reprint of works such as Elizabeth Blackwell's *Pioneer Work in Opening the Medical Profession to Women*, written in 1895, and for so long unattainable.

In addition, and no less sincerely, I am indebted to several libraries: the British Library, especially the Department of Manuscripts; the Wellcome Institute for the History of Medicine; the Royal Free Hospital Library; the Library of Congress, Washington, especially the Manuscript Collection; Girton College; and the International Institute of Social History, Amsterdam. The General Medical Council and the Equal Opportunities Commission have readily supplied me with statistics.

There are also thanks due to the following individuals: Nancy Sahli, for permission to quote from her definitive thesis on Elizabeth Blackwell; Joyce Prince, for allowing me to read her unpublished thesis on Florence Nightingale; Theodora Ooms, for photostating enormous numbers of manuscript letters and documents in the Library of Congress and mailing them to me; John Carrier (London School of Economics) for helping me to locate certain printed sources; Richard Evans (University of East Anglia) and James Macmillan (University of York) for so generously encouraging me at the start of this project when it must have been obvious to them that, as a complete beginner in a field they both know so well, I hardly knew what I was taking on; Carmen Callil for her vigorous encouragement at every stage; and lastly but vitally my publisher Tom Rosenthal and my editor Alison Samuel from whose painstaking attention I have greatly benefited.

Introduction

Feminism is full of riddles. One of the most intriguing is why it has not attracted an enormous rank-and-file following among women themselves, why it is still as necessary as it was in the nineteenth century to have to ask a woman if she *is* a feminist. The plain truth is that not only do large numbers of women feel apathetic but many more actively hate feminism. This is because right from the invention of the word[1] it has been both misrepresented and misunderstood. Undeniably, this was the fault of men, because men controlled the outlets for the spreading of new ideas, but it was also the fault of the feminists themselves. They were too honest, expressed too openly and fully their fears and worries and, most of all, their resentments. The result was that feminism became frightening in its implications.

But in fact there is nothing to be frightened of. Feminism, both for men and women, is the most attractive and peaceful of doctrines. It is quite wrong to see it as an aggressive, destructive movement which aims at making neuters of us all. It is not really one movement at all. Its history, which has been until recently greatly neglected and is still far too little known, shows clearly enough that there has been no one movement progressing steadily throughout the decades. Sometimes feminists did indeed group together to achieve a particular goal but these groupings were always episodic. When that goal was achieved, the "movement" disappeared. Feminism, because of this, is not like a political belief. You cannot join the feminist party, for example, as you can join the Labour party (although you can join all kinds of women's organizations) and you cannot say you are a feminist in the same way that you can say you are a Socialist. Nor is feminism a religion, like Christianity. There is no church, no visible structure.

You cannot say you are a feminist in the same way you can say you are a Catholic or a Methodist. The only way to clear away the utter confusion surrounding the meaning of feminism is to start regarding it first of all as a kind of philosophy, as a way of looking at and thinking of life for all women.

It will immediately be obvious that this produces a problem: life for one woman is not the same as life for another. Even further, life in one place for one woman is not the same as that life in another place. An English feminist was never the same (and still is not) as a German feminist. All feminists think they want "self-fulfilment" for women but since that "self" changes dramatically from country to country, from class to class, and from age to age, this ambition is almost meaningless. What *is* "self-fulfilment"? Are there certain fundamental principles upon which all feminists can agree regardless of social, cultural and political differences? The history of feminism shows that there are but that it took a long time for them to be recognized. The trouble was that feminists did not know where to begin. They had the greatest difficulty in deciding *why* woman's lot was so much worse than man's even before they moved on to deciding how it could be improved. Long before active feminism arose, the theorists debated the situation and came to different conclusions. Some thought education was the key: women were not educated for anything but subordination. Change their education and their expectations in life would change. Others thought it was a matter of biology, that nature was the real enemy, and these were the most depressed theorists of all, for what could be done about nature? But while all this intellectual debate was going on, while the tracts and pamphlets on the condition of woman were appearing throughout the eighteenth century, the first stirrings of *active* feminism were being felt. At last, at the start of the nineteenth century, feminists were beginning to do something to change how women were obliged to live their lives instead of merely fretting about their position. Why feminism became active when it did is still not entirely explained (the main theories lay heavy emphasis on economic changes) but what can be very precisely explained is how this activity proceeded.

The history of feminism has appeared to be one of stops and starts. It seems to resemble a sequence of parallel lines, with all the different strands forging ahead, often quite separate from each other. The element of separation was to some extent deliberate.[2] It was considered dangerous to one cause to mix it with another and so Emily

Davies kept out of politics until her educational aims were achieved and Josephine Butler dropped out of the front line in the educational field in case it became tarnished by her prominence in the battle to get the Contagious Diseases Acts repealed. Because of this concentration on keeping different issues "clean" the leaders became even more significant than they would otherwise have been. If, early in its history, feminism had become one international movement fighting on many fronts but with some central control, then the cult of personality would never have been so strong. As it was, all the different causes were firmly linked with particular women, each an inspiring figurehead looked up to and relied upon and thought of as absolutely indispensable, however efficient and hardworking the committees and organizations behind her. Feminism seems to have needed this kind of identification with heroines and the heroines themselves had no illusions about their importance. Josephine Butler reckoned, without false modesty, that if she had not led her particular cause *nobody* else would have done so and, for all the sterling worth of all those others equally interested, it would have foundered. Florence Nightingale despaired at her own uniqueness. *Nobody*, she vowed, would have undertaken what she undertook and she despised her own sex for its cravenness. She simply could not contemplate dying because she was so vital. Elizabeth Blackwell wasted no time wondering why no one had gone before her. It was obvious to her that the way was too hard and *nobody* but she could have blazed that particular trail at that particular time. Caroline Norton loathed putting herself through what she had to endure and swore *nobody* else would have had the guts. Emily Davies, driven to distraction by the sheer tediousness of her task, stuck to it because, she said bitterly, *nobody* else would have the patience. And so on. Each woman saw herself and was seen by others as extremely significant and their claims need hardly be disputed.

But even more significant for feminist history than the actual leadership these women gave was their approach to feminism. All their approaches were different, all made their own way, none of them would have agreed that their goal was the same. Four of the women in this book claimed at one time or another in their lives they were not feminists (Caroline Norton, Florence Nightingale, Elizabeth Blackwell, Josephine Butler); one (Emily Davies) acknowledged only a limited feminism; only three (Margaret Sanger, Elizabeth Cady Stanton, Emma Goldman) were proudly feminist. They all meant different things by the word. Each had her own particular brand of feminism even if it went by other names and each forged it through direct personal experience. None of them was an abstract theorist. They were all activists brought to active feminism by the way they lived their lives. In every case they were reacting violently against particular circumstances. Neither class nor money made the kind of difference it might be expected to make: being a woman transcended other differences. Caroline Norton, brought up at Hampton Court, raged against her lot as a woman just as much as Margaret Sanger, brought up in poverty in a New York suburb. Elizabeth Cady Stanton, daughter of a wealthy judge, felt as humiliated by her sex as Emma Goldman, daughter of a poor Jewish-Russian inn-keeper. As women, they had things in common from which they suffered and which they wanted to change for all women.

Yet it is another aspect of the history of feminism that solidarity among women, in spite of their common experience, was never really embraced. The concept of solidarity has indeed caused more trouble than any other single factor. What made so many women think they were *not* feminists was their hostility to the idea of being against men. If feminism meant being anti-male then they had no time for it. Not a single one of the women in this book believed in uniting against the male sex. None of them saw men as monsters, only some men; none of them wanted a society without men, even if it were possible, nor a society in which men were made the subordinates as women had been for so long. All of them wanted better relationships with men, all of them wanted a better deal for *both* sexes. It panicked Elizabeth Blackwell to hear that men had been excluded from some meetings about suffrage in America. She thought it a dangerous precedent and cautioned her sister to have nothing to do with it. Josephine Butler preferred mixed audiences even when she was talking about the most intimate details of prostitution. She thought men as involved in and as concerned with reform as women. Elizabeth Cady Stanton said she was constantly reprimanded for being too friendly towards men and Margaret Sanger, although she wanted birth control in female hands, repudiated the notion of keeping male doctors out of the movement. Yet, unfairly, the image of a feminist as a man-hater grew and with it the belief that men and men alone were at the root of all women's troubles.

Although all the women in this book recognized the drift of this appealing argument it was only Emma Goldman who saw the real damage being done. She prophesied in 1910 that, if feminism continued as it was doing, very soon there would be no man worthy of modern woman. Women, she said, were making themselves unliveable with. They were suppressing and even forgetting one half of their natures, the half that wanted to love and be loved, the half that was "feminine" in a way they were being taught to despise as feeble. Women were becoming terrified of acknowledging their own desires. Working in a New York beauty parlour, Emma Goldman pitied the new "emancipated" woman. She thought her life was awful. Instead of being a drudge at home she was a drudge at work *and* home. She was so proud of her "independence" that she had sacrificed her happiness. Women, Emma Goldman decided, needed to be emancipated from emancipation. Certainly they must attack institutions like marriage which made women slaves in the form in which it existed but they should not attack love itself. She even dared to suggest that women might need love more than men and in a different degree from men. Love seemed to complicate a woman's life so much more than a man's, almost as though its very presence produced a chemical change. Love challenged ambition in women, but the answer was not to abolish it but to come to terms with it. This did not mean agreeing with the mid-nineteenth-century medical experts who had confidently asserted women were biologically inferior to men, but it did mean agreeing that love affected women differently and allowing for the difference in any plans for her future. Nor was Emma Goldman thinking only of sexual love. She thought mother love even more insidious. Once a woman had a child she changed in a way a man did not. Children, in her opinion, undermined a woman's confident progress through life even more than a lover did, which was one of the reasons she never tried to have any herself. She thought any understanding of what actually happened strictly limited and wanted more attention paid to it rather than less. What she did *not* want was true femininity either denied or ignored. There was no place within feminism for any doctrine that dispensed with the need women had for men.

Modern feminism, alarmingly, has found a place for that doctrine, but it is as yet a very small place. There are other more important problems to grapple with. But, although this is a history stopping considerably short of even the beginnings of contemporary feminism, it is the attitude to men which provides the link with it. From the early active feminists onwards women have worried about what they want their relationships with men to be based upon. This in turn has made them grapple with their own natures. Those who have been most honest have even felt, like Emma Goldman, that there is indeed something craven in them that wants to "give in" to a man. To say that this is because their role has been conditioned by society has not satisfied them. It is the easy but not the whole answer. Much more difficult is for women to look inwards and try to analyse why it appears to be so hard to be a feminist. All the women in this book found it a problem. None of them sprang from their mother's womb feminist in thought, word and deed. They all betrayed their own ideals over and over again, sometimes without realizing it, because the conflict between being feminine and feminist seemed unavoidable and feminism could not always win without asking them to pay a price they thought too high. Being true to themselves meant hurting others and so they gave way, in anguish, and subdued their own instincts. Elizabeth Cady Stanton said that being a wife and a mother should not be put before being a person, but that was thought feminist idealism gone mad. The three could not be separated and this "person" inevitably was submerged. She herself would have liked to be a full-time journalist on *Tribune* but with seven children she knew she was only dreaming: even if the person in her would have approved, the mother, if not the wife, would never have sanctioned it. Women, especially feminists, had to be realists too. The history of feminism shows women making the same bargains with themselves over and over again with monotonous regularity. The most ambitious of them have always wanted everything – career, husband (or lover) and children.

Some of them naturally managed it with more success than others. When they did, it was invariably due to a man's feminism. Josephine Butler was the only one of the eight in this book who was very happily married with children and followed an exacting campaign of work which corresponded to a career. She only managed to do so because her husband George backed her in everything she did. While Josephine travelled round Europe lecturing and investigating he held the fort at home, encouraging her to believe her work was not just *as* important as his but more so. He simply pitied those who thought the only place for all women was in the home. Elizabeth Cady Stanton was not quite as fortunate. Her husband, Henry, backed her almost all the way but unfortunately stopped short of encouraging her in what interested her most, which was full political rights for women. They argued, often in public, and as time went on their closeness was threatened.

Elizabeth Cady Stanton was never as happily married as Josephine Butler partly because Henry was not as thorough a feminist as George.

Caroline Norton was not, of course, happily married at all. All her troubles and the start of her feminism began with her marriage to a violently anti-feminist man. Caroline was obliged to live the majority of her life in a totally unsuccessful struggle to find the sort of relationship with men she wanted. So too a century later was Margaret Sanger, disowning as she did a husband who was an avowed feminist. Bill Sanger's feminism only unmanned him in her eyes and she found she could not do what she wanted without relegating both husband and children to second place. Nor could Emma Goldman, whose two marriages were both unconsummated and both made, in different ways, for practical reasons. Florence Nightingale denied herself the man she said she adored and Elizabeth Blackwell not only rejected suitors but tried to starve her body into having no sexual desires. Only Emily Davies seems to have had no conflict. She simply never met a man in whom she was interested, or who was interested in her. Her maternal instincts found an outlet in her great affection for and involvement with her Llewelyn-Davies nephews and niece. But none of these women thought the particular compromises she made satisfactory. The point was, and still is, that they were necessary not just because the way society was arranged made them so but because the women themselves felt them to be so.

Another conflict they faced was between the desire to be feminine in appearance while decrying what this entailed. Two of these women were outstandingly beautiful and utterly feminine in the accepted sense. Caroline Norton was a striking figure who was not only breathtakingly lovely but dressed in style and graced any gathering she attended. She never for one moment considered not making the best of herself and saw no reason to hide her love of clothes and jewellery. But all the same she was irritated by the assumptions made because of her appearance. She knew people believed stories about her because of her looks and she knew they suspected the worst because it could be easily imagined. If she had been plain and dowdy and had dressed like her sister-in-law Augusta in a bloomer-type costume then she would have had more of a chance with the gossips of London. To be so obviously feminine was to be thought frivolous and empty headed and, in her case, more than possibly wicked. Josephine Butler, also extremely beautiful and immensely elegant, was never thought wicked but she too found her femininity caused problems. She encountered surprise and in some cases opposition just because she was so attractive. People, especially people in authority, would not take her seriously because of her looks. She did not look earnest in her gorgeous silk dresses therefore how could she be earnest? Her attractiveness was both a weapon (which she certainly used) and a hindrance.

Yet neither Caroline Norton nor Josephine Butler thought for one moment of donning any kind of feminist version of sackcloth-and-ashes. They saw no point in denying the side of their natures which adored finery. Margaret Sanger, much later on, decided at one point to wear "mannish suits" to make her look more impressive but she soon gave up. The suits made her feel ugly and unnatural and inhibited her. The sneering at attention to and love of clothes and make-up which became fashionable in feminist circles during the nineteenth century was emphatically disapproved of by all these women. If becoming anti-man was the biggest wrong turn feminism took, becoming anti-adornment was the next. Emma Goldman, no beauty herself, raged against it. She almost never dressed up (most of the time she resembled a caricature of what a feminist was supposed to look like) but she hotly defended the right to do so. On rare occasions when she wore glamorous clothes she admitted she felt marvellous, refused to be ashamed of that feeling or to agree that all dressing-up was only to please men. It pleased *her* and that was enough. Elizabeth Blackwell too was pleased if she felt she looked pretty and only laughed when somebody reprimanded her, the first lady doctor in the world, for wearing flowers in her hair and dancing. Emily Davies thought no less of herself for buying smart new shoes with a present of money or for pinning on a new bonnet to attend a soirée; and Florence Nightingale had a passion for the beauty of real lace. Not a single one of these significant figures in feminist history saw any point at all in suggesting that women should stop beautifying themselves if doing so made them feel happier. They insisted this was a desire *existing in its own right* and having nothing to do with answering an image created by men.

They did not deny, of course, that there was, all the same, an image that must be attacked. This was the image which said women should be passive and inactive except in matters concerning the home. All the women in this book savagely tore that image to pieces. Some of them had to start as soon as they were born because they had fathers who subscribed to it. Judge Cady, although he educated his daughter Elizabeth far beyond the contemporary level, made her childhood a

misery by sighing she ought to have been a boy. Her feminism began
when she rebelled against his notion of what being a girl meant. So too
did Emma Goldman's. She had a father who told her all a girl needed
to do was learn to cook and give a man children. Florence Nightingale
bowed for years to her father's wish that she should be a conventional
lady and only wrote secretly of her burning hatred of his philosophy.
Gathering courage to break out of the mould he saw her cast in was far
harder than serving in the Crimea. But some of these women were
fortunate. They had fathers who actually encouraged them to break
the image and helped them to do so. Elizabeth Blackwell's father,
Samuel, made no distinction in upbringing between his boys and his
girls and neither did Josephine Butler's in all respects that mattered
most. Margaret Sanger's father ordered her always to think for herself
and speak out even if he resisted her ambition on many other levels and
she was grateful to him. In most cases fathers were a much more
formative influence, both good and bad, than mothers.

Many of these women adored their mothers and respected and
cherished them but none was inspired by them except, as it were, by
default. Only Margaret Sanger raged against her mother's lot in
retrospect, and mourned her unnecessary death, and was in some
measure pushed on by memories of her. Caroline Norton's mother
took her in at the height of the scandal surrounding her and heroically
supported her and Emily Davies's mother loyally wrote letters and
acted as unpaid secretary at one stage of the Girton campaign, but
neither of them fuelled any inner fires in the way that some of the
fathers did. No mother seems to have said "Do not become what I
have become – do not be like me". Whereas at least some of the fathers
urged their daughters to defy convention and make the most of
themselves. On a tiny sample of eight this is hardly representative but
it still indicates that not all men saw themselves as outside the struggle
their daughters were experiencing in their fight to become feminists.

★   ★   ★

A history ought to be objective and not prejudiced by the historian
intruding. But in this particular case it seems to me not only justifiable
but also relevant that I should state where I stand. (Researching the
material for this book has in fact radically altered where I *do* stand.)

In many ways, I myself am the product of everything the eight
women in this book fought for – much more so than the average

woman. If I had been born in 1838 instead of 1938 my lot in life would have been truly appalling. As it was, I benefited directly and enormously from every feminist gain and I am immensely grateful that I did. There is not a day goes by without my experiencing the joy of acknowledging that I have the best of both worlds even if I am also bound to admit this happy state is not maintained without effort. My husband and my children are precious to me but then so is my work. I could not continue to be happy if either were taken away from me. As I have grown older, the work has become more and more important, so much so that I have to restrain myself from the dangerous thought that women without a career are to be pitied. It would only be *myself* without a career that would need to be pitied. If life is about attempting to achieve total fulfilment then I am simply one of those women for whom being a wife and mother does not amount to that fulfilment. Perhaps, in that case, I am the one to be pitied though I do not of course think so. But without feminism not only would I have merited more pity than anyone could give me but I would have wallowed in my self-pity which is far worse. I always wanted to be everything – wife, mother, housekeeper, writer. More significant, *there was no role I disliked.* The problem was not choosing but taking all of them on at the same time and surviving.

I have survived, but I do not approve of how I managed it. I think the cost, to myself, has been great. True emancipation may have begun in my childhood soul but it did not flower as it should have done – not quite. I have been a feeble feminist. I have gradually come round to understanding that there is still a trap. It isn't marriage itself; it isn't motherhood alone; it is some subtle force which is not yet either fully understood or controlled. There is something in women which prevents them striking out as men do. Is it centuries of conditioning? Is it biological? Whatever it is, it intrigues me. It also intrigued the women in this book. The astonishing thing is that my life should touch theirs at so many points in spite of the vast changes which have taken place since their respective times and my own, and that I should be more struck by the similarities of our lot than impressed by the disparities in reading their thoughts. This sense of identification is what the study of feminist history needs to bring to women. Women, as Caroline Norton said so long ago, believe themselves to be isolated. It is up to feminist history to prove to them that they are not. There *is* a joint purpose and this brings not just comfort but hope.

★   ★   ★

This history is divided into categories, or, to use the Victorian term, spheres. I have chosen to examine eight different spheres in a woman's life in which vital changes were made. With one exception all the spheres are quite clearly defined. In each sphere there was one woman who was an instigator, whose significance is undisputed, and so I have chosen to trace biographically the history of what happened to begin the process of change. But in addition these women are significant for another reason: with each one, feminism itself changed too. There are therefore three strands running together at the same time; one following the life-stories of the women; one following the process of change; and one following the development of the ideology behind feminism. Emma Goldman is in a special category. There is no single change instigated by Emma Goldman. She is there because she is a bridge between the old nineteenth-century feminism and the new late twentieth-century feminism. Although this is a history, it is an unfinished history and I felt the need to attempt to point towards what happened next. Emma Goldman does the pointing admirably. What she points to, and what I hope this book demonstrates, is that in spite of all the ups and downs, the victories and disillusionments, the spurts of strenuous activity and the doldrum years, there is among all this apparent confusion a strong sense of direction which has achieved, and continues to achieve, a better balance between the sexes in our society. That, fundamentally, is what feminism is about and a feminist is no shrieking harridan obsessed with destruction but a man or a woman who strives to secure a society in which neither sex finds gender alone a handicap to their progress.

LAW

Caroline Norton
(BBC Hulton Picture Library)

Caroline Norton
1808–1877

Caroline Norton, the beautiful, witty, talented granddaughter of Sheridan the playwright, had a very clear idea of her own significance. "I believe," she wrote (in 1855 in her "Letter to the Queen") "in my obscurer position, that I am permitted to be the example on which a particular law shall be reformed. Does that create a smile? History teaches that 'in all cases of great injustice among men there comes a culminating point after which that injustice *is not borne*.' "[1] That point had been reached twice in her own life. Once when she was separated from her husband, after his brutality towards her, and discovered he had the right to keep their three young sons from her; and once again when she discovered that she had not the right to keep her own earnings or inheritance even when she was supporting herself. On both occasions the discovery of what the laws of England were on the subject of the rights of married women produced in her such a passionate disgust and rage that she was able to begin a process of change that went on for a century and has still not ended. It was Caroline Norton who first decided enough was enough. It was time, she said, "that the gentlemen of England should cease to answer with a mocking sneer the attempts made by women to plead their own cause."[2] By the time she had finished, nobody dared any longer to sneer. The threat to the status quo was too real.

And yet Caroline Norton has never been given her due in what passes for feminist history. She was despised by contemporary feminists who alleged, as though it were a crime, that she only thought of herself and had only started to take an interest in the wrong done to women by the law when she herself was wronged. This contempt, expressed most forcibly by Harriet Martineau, did not worry Caroline. She was quite relieved to be disowned by the feminists because she was terrified of being thought one of them. "I never pretended to the wild and ridiculous doctrine of equality"[3] she protested. All she wanted, she said, was that women should be put in the position of other inferiors and offered the same protection. She "only" wanted justice, not equal rights. "The natural position of woman is inferiority to man. Amen! . . . I believe it sincerely as part of my religion: and I accept it as a matter proved to my reason."[4] The feminists of her day chose to believe this statement at its face value but even before she had written it Caroline herself had realized the deeper implications of so called "justice". Her particular brand of feminism began as naïve and romantic but ended as something much more daring and closer to the ideas of those "strong minded women" she so abhorred. Like many women, both then and now, she began by genuinely believing men were superior to women and that the most women could claim, without flying in the face of both God and Nature, was protection. All she thought she wanted to change was men being legally empowered to be brutes. But once she started to examine married woman's bondage she came to a truth she found too startling to acknowledge publicly: protection was not enough, men were not always and automatically superior to women and a measure of equality was absolutely vital if wrongs were to be righted.

This was a shock to her. She found it hard to believe that the law said what it said. The facts she was obliged to learn about marriage for a woman were simple and cruel. Marriage was in fact a civil bond for men and an indissoluble sacrament for women. A married woman had no legal existence; she had no legal rights of property ownership; everything she owned, earned or inherited belonged to her husband; she could not determine where her children lived or how they were to be educated; she had no divorce opportunities; she had no rights either to keep or have access to her children in the event of being divorced by him or separated from him: the father's right was absolute and paramount. It was this last injustice which inflamed Caroline most. "Is this abuse to exist forever?" she thundered in one of her pamphlets "because it was not at first perceived? Or are we waiting for some frightful catastrophe . . . It is a strange and crying shame that the only despotic right an Englishman possesses is to wrong the mother of his children!"[5]

The "frightful catastrophe" she felt had befallen her, when her children were dragged screaming from her, brought her to feminism. What began as a fight for herself became a fight for all women. She once wrote in a letter ". . . if it should please God today to give me back my little children my interest . . . would still continue."[6] She saw no need to join any movement, believing as she did that women could not be made to band together because ". . . their experience [is] narrow. Each thinks the hardship of her own case more specially calculated to move compassion . . . They have a sort of unreasoning instinct that aggregate resistance will not serve them."[7] She was in fact to be proved wrong but there was nevertheless a basic truth underlying her opinion, especially with regard to the law. One woman had to be prepared to incur personal opprobrium before the law would move. Caroline Norton was that woman and to say she was not a feminist is to misunderstand, with her, the nature of feminism.

★　　★　　★

Caroline Elizabeth Sarah Norton was born on March 22nd, 1808, the third child of Thomas Sheridan, son of the playwright, and Henrietta Callander of Craigforth in Scotland. When she was five years old her father, whose health had begun to fail, was offered a colonial secretaryship at the Cape of Good Hope which he was urged to take as the only chance of recovery. His wife and eldest daughter Helen went with him but Caroline and her younger sister Georgiana were left in the care of two aunts in Scotland. Unfortunately, Tom Sheridan died at the Cape in 1816 of TB. Henrietta returned as a widow with Helen and two more children Frank and Charles, born at the Cape. She was lucky enough to be provided with a grace and favour residence at Hampton Court in 1817. There, Caroline, Georgiana and their elder brother Richard Brinsley joined the rest of the family.

Life at Hampton Court was happy. The Sheridan family were protected from the realities of their relative poverty by their excellent connections and the affection and respect felt for their mother. She taught them herself and was delighted to discover in Caroline evidence of the family literary talent. Caroline read and wrote early and by the age of eleven burned with literary ambition. She used to watch her uncle Charles Sheridan working in his study (over a collection of Romaic songs) and wrote that "I invariably left his study with an enthusiastic determination to write a long poem of my own."[8] She tried her literary wings with a pastiche of a famous contemporary series which she called *The Dandies' Rout* and with a collection of little poems bound into a book with some of her sisters' efforts.

But Caroline was far from being the studious girl this implies. On the contrary, she and her two sisters were thought of as being rather uncontrollable and certainly far too high spirited. They were extremely boisterous in company and adored shocking their elders. "The Sheridans are much admired," said Lady Cowper (Lord Melbourne's sister), "but are strange girls, swear and say all sorts of things that make men laugh."[9] Caroline was the strangest and made men laugh the most. She even looked strange when she was young, with huge dark eyes and a great mass of wild black hair. Her habit of lowering her head and looking at people through her thick black eyelashes was thought of as furtive (later it was considered "flirtatious and indecent"). People were not comfortable with her nor she with them. In spite of her quick tongue she was actually quite shy – not in the accepted sense of the word but more in that she felt "different from others". It was, she wrote to Mary Shelley years later, what she called "*sauvagerie*", or "a feeling of not being able to amalgamate with other and new associates because of something in one's mind different from and superior to the common nature."[10] She was only really herself with her family to whom she was devoted. The Sheridans had a distinct clan feeling which outsiders recognized and envied. The three sisters, all of them beautiful, were a very close and formidable trio but it was thought that their mother, who was herself quiet and dignified, let them run riot a bit too much.

To some extent Henrietta Sheridan must have agreed because she chose to send Caroline away to school. Why Caroline was selected and not the other two girls is not clear but Caroline herself gave a clue when she confessed to Lord Melbourne, "When I was whipped in days of yore I always defied consequences, bit the fingers of the whipper, and rushed to repeat my crime . . ."[11] Presumably Mrs Sheridan grew tired of bitten fingers. She despatched Caroline, aged fifteen, to a small school in Surrey, for her own good. This school, merely a house presided over by a governess without any training and offering a curriculum no better than Mrs Sheridan could offer herself, was near Wonersh Park, the home of Lord Grantley. Fletcher Norton, the third Lord Grantley (the peerage was very recent) was an unpleasant gentleman who also owned family estates in Yorkshire. He was married but had no children. His heir was his younger brother George whom he had put to the law, and over whom he exerted great influence. But one thing he could not influence was George Norton's infatuation for Caroline Sheridan who was brought, with other pupils, on a visit by her governess, the sister of Lord Grantley's agent. With George, aged twenty-five at the time, it was a case of love at first sight. He was instantly captivated by the young Caroline. She, on the other hand, barely noticed him. He was slow and heavy where she was quick and light, a country bumpkin figure whereas she was already a town sophisticate. He stood dull and speechless in the background while she sparkled and performed in the foreground. His sister Augusta, an eccentric lady with decidedly masculine habits, was also captivated by Caroline. George hung about admiring the young visitor while Augusta praised her singing and poetry reading extravagantly. The only one not bowled over was Lord Grantley himself. His plans for George did not include marriage to an impoverished Sheridan.

But George, though normally in great awe of his brother, was for once adamant. He wished to marry Caroline. An offer for her hand was made which Mrs Sheridan did not emphatically decline. She said George Norton must wait three years until Caroline had "come out" and then his proposal would be considered. Caroline, who maintained she had not exchanged six sentences with her suitor, was "astonished", but it was quite a pleasant astonishment. The offer was, she hoped, the first of many. She knew she was beautiful and her beauty gave her expectations ("perhaps I should say what I *expected* when I first began to look in the glass with satisfaction"[12] she once wrote to Lord Melbourne). There seemed no reason to be falsely modest. If she could catch George Norton without even trying what might she not achieve in the marriage stakes if she set her mind to it? In the season of 1826, when she came out with her elder sister Helen, she had her first try. She was chosen to be one of the twelve prettiest debutantes who took part in the Dance of the Months at Almack's (she was August) and attracted great admiration. But the admiration led nowhere. Helen, on the other hand, received an offer from Lord Dufferin's heir and accepted him. The season ended with Caroline, although only eighteen, feeling distinctly let down. She had not had quite the solid success Helen had had and next season there would be Georgiana at her heels. At that point, plodding old George Norton repeated his offer.

In another letter to Lord Melbourne years later Caroline tried to analyse her own attitude at that time. "The only misfortune I ever particularly dreaded," she confessed "was living and dying a lonely old maid . . . An old maid is never anyone's first object therefore I object to that situation."[13] She saw everywhere that married women had status, a definite sphere, a protector. Unmarried women did not. They were despised and pitied, especially by other women. To get married was the pinnacle of every girl's ambition and the sooner it was reached the better. Caroline was impatient and self-willed, always leaping before she looked, entirely impervious to restraint or "advice". She knew perfectly well that she did not love George Norton but then how much did love matter? Nothing that she saw led her to believe it mattered at all. Even her sister Helen, who had not loved her husband when she accepted him, now wrote from Italy that she adored him, that love had grown instantly after their marriage. Why should she not learn to love George Norton in the same way? The more she considered him the better he seemed. He had been called to the Bar since he met her and had also been elected Member of Parliament for Guildford. He was the childless Lord Grantley's heir. He had been constant and patient for three years. So, for all the wrong but easily understandable reasons, Caroline married George Norton on July 30th, 1827 and spent the rest of her life regretting it. As she said of one of her characters (in her novel *Stuart of Dunleath*) "She had married a man she did not love; whom she did not profess to love; for certain advantages – to avoid certain pressing miseries." The misery, in her case, was the ludicrous belief that her beauty had failed her and that she must snatch her one offer in case no other ever materialized and she died of mortification.

The Norton marriage from the very beginning was a disaster. Everything was wrong with it, except perhaps a degree of sexual attraction which hardly survived the honeymoon. Far from quickly learning to love her husband, as her sister Helen had done, Caroline just as quickly learned to hate hers. She had thought that at least he was quiet, sober, dependable and patient if rather dull but discovered before her honeymoon was over that none of these characteristics was his. On the contrary, he was frequently drunk, had an appalling temper and his patience had only been to get his hands on her. Once she was his, all pretence was over. He did not care what she thought of him and had no intention of being reformed. He was going to do exactly as he pleased and she, his wife, was bound to let him. But of course Caroline was an equally strong character. She did not react by turning pale at his excesses or sitting silently weeping or by accepting her lot and putting a brave face on it. Instead, she attacked him with her tongue and used her greatly superior brain to think of ways to outwit him. Nor did she try to conceal her dissatisfaction but exposed him at every opportunity to her family and friends as a brute. It is hard to decide whether George was a brute because Caroline goaded him beyond endurance or whether Caroline was driven to goading him as her only defence against his brutality. But whatever the interpretation the result was the same: George beat Caroline savagely.

This kind of physical violence was difficult to conceal even if Caroline had wanted to conceal it, which she did not. The moment the couple returned from their honeymoon to George's bachelor chambers in the Temple an old woman who was a servant there saw the young husband fling "an inkstand and most of his law books" with unerring aim at his terrified young wife. She excused it on the grounds that Mr Norton was drunk. The Sheridan family were the next to realize what was going on. George and Caroline went to stay occasionally with her various brothers and sisters all of whom reported to each other their horror at hearing Caroline's screams in the night and the roars and thuddings of George hitting her. Naturally, they rushed to protect her and to remonstrate with George but he soon learned to lock his bedroom door in any Sheridan household. Mrs Sheridan, appalled and distressed, was also even angrier than her children because she believed herself duped. She would never, she said, have given her consent to the marriage if she had not been assured Caroline was going to be well provided for but she now found that not only could George not provide for her adequately, he was actually looking to her to provide for him. If his violence made nonsense of his marriage vows as a sacred undertaking, his failure to provide made nonsense of them as a contract.

But there was nothing Caroline could do. She had made a mistake and had to live with it. This she set about doing with admirable determination. Firstly, she got the two of them out of George's chambers and into a small house in Storeys Gate overlooking Birdcage Walk. This home she made into a pretty, bowery sort of place in which George was ill-at-ease and not quite so confident and dominant. To it she invited her family and friends, none of whom were to her husband's boorish tastes. She also began to invite the literati of London soon after the publication (anonymously) of her 200 verse poem *The Sorrows of Rosalie* eighteen months after her marriage. Because she was beautiful and a Sheridan and tremendously amusing the literary set came, some famous figures among them. Bulwer

Lytton, Samuel Rogers, Abraham Hayward, even the young Disraeli all came and stayed and came again. George was damned if he was going to be turned out of his own home so he was there among the glittering company too. Caroline was not at all put out. She made a feature of George's awfulness and did not spare her mockery or hold her guests back from it. The biggest joke of all was that George actually thought he was being complimented when he was being subtly despised – he had not the wit to recognize an insult when it was offered. On one occasion when Disraeli politely said the wine was excellent, George boasted that he had "stuff twenty times better" in his cellar to which Disraeli smoothly murmured, "My dear fellow, this is *quite* good enough for such canaille as you have got here today."[14] George was perfectly satisfied with this answer and failed to appreciate the mirth of Caroline and her guests.

But it was a dangerous game Caroline played and she reaped the consequences in full. George used his strength to get his revenge and his beatings left her weak and miserable for days. The only thing they were united in was love for their children. George loved animals and children and was loved by them. The birth of Fletcher in 1829 and of Brinsley in 1831 gave him as much pleasure as they gave Caroline. He doted on his sons and Caroline, recognizing this, felt he could not be all bad. In fact, for the three years following Fletcher's birth they were as happy together as they were ever to be. She was presented at Court, had a play put on at Covent Garden (Fanny Kemble said it was atrocious) and published another long poem, *The Undying One*, under her own name to considerable praise. George was pleased with her because she earned money. He was even more pleased when, through her new friendship with Lord Melbourne, Caroline also secured for him a lucrative and undemanding post as a judge in the Lambeth division of the Metropolitan Police Courts at a salary of £1,000 a year. It did not worry him a bit that he was accepting this sinecure from a Whig when he was a Tory, but then points of principle never disturbed George Norton. In fact, getting him that post had not only been vital to stabilize the Norton economy but also to stave off a fate Caroline regarded as worse than death: moving to the country. In the election of 1830 George had lost his seat at Guildford ("he assures me," Caroline wrote contemptuously to her sister, "that although thrown out *he* was the popular candidate . . . that all those who voted against him did it with tears").[15] His brother, Lord Grantley, said he had lost it because he had not been around enough for the voters to see him and proposed that George should move to a little cottage on his estate. George didn't see why not but Caroline was panic-stricken ("Norton assures me . . . that I shall easily change my delight in society for pride and pleasure in my dairy! . . .").[16] she redoubled her efforts to find a plum job for George and was immensely relieved when he accepted the judgeship. Between them, they were now earning enough to stay in London in comfort and if George needed to go down to Guildford often to placate Grantley, then so much the better.

The house in Storeys Gate was refurbished and extended and Caroline went off to Margate for a holiday with her children. From there, she wrote a revealing letter to George. "Dearest George," she wrote, "I dreamed last night that you were dying and two old maids told stories of me and then persuaded you that you would not see me; but I rushed into your room and found it was a lie and that you were dying for my company; and then I thought, as I was sitting by you and explaining, I saw you grow quite unconscious and die wherefore I woke up with a flood of tears . . ."[17] In another fond note she wrote, "I cannot bear sleeping alone: 'hem!"[18] and in yet another later in the year when he had gone to Scotland, "Come back darling I am wishing for you."[19] Perhaps these endearments are merely rare, fleeting instances of Caroline forgetting how much she hated George but they at least show that, at that juncture, all was not lost between them, that there was some slim hope of avoiding a real breakdown of their marriage. But it is also true that Caroline, who had a warm and demonstrative nature, may not have attached the same weight to her tender words as others, including George, did. She was often inconsistent and saw nothing strange in that. She could write affectionately to her husband and yet at the same time write to Georgiana, "I have walked up and down the new walk by the seaside but the only visible effect is elephantiasis in my left leg and the gout in my right. I have stood looking at the sunset on the sea with Clarence Pigeon at my side but the results are merely a red nose and a hatred of my companion (together with some shame at being seen with him because he wears a tail-coat of a morning)."[20] George, in public, made her squirm. He was gauche and a philistine and *loud*. But in private, as well as the quarrels, there were undeniably some happier times.

By this time (1831) Caroline was quite famous in London and being famous made her happy. Everyone who saw her commented on her vitality and beauty. The Boston jurist, Charles Sumner, described how she combined "the grace and ease of a woman with a strength and skill of which any man might be proud."[21] The dark wildness of her younger days had matured into exotic good looks which made her stand out in any crowd. In her twenties the wildness had been replaced by a confidence and control observers found remarkable. The truth was, Caroline was unusual and original. She did not fit into the contemporary pattern of beauty or behaviour. She was bold in her opinions and brilliant in her arguments and never held back from either. Then there was her talent. She was a lady authoress *par excellence* and people found her acknowledged ability exciting. Wherever she went (and, like Thackeray, she went everywhere, adoring social life) she was admired and talked about. But she was also watched with envy and suspicion. She herself was acutely aware of what a splendid target she made. "A young bride," she wrote, excited "hard, unindulgent speculation."[22] She knew she invited that speculation by her unconventional attitudes. She went alone to a great many parties because George found them boring or was away, and she entertained when he was out. Naïvely, she assumed that since she was innocent of anything but enjoying herself she could come to no harm and need fear no idle gossip. She was in her element and refused to withdraw from it.

This might have continued to be the pattern of the Norton marriage, with Caroline using her married status to enable her to move freely in society, enduring occasional violence from George, and carving out a separate existence for herself as far as possible. It was a bargain many women then made because there was no alternative. Divorce for a woman was impossible and a separated wife had no status, innocent or guilty. Socially, she might as well be dead. But in 1832 certain events precipitated a crisis in the Norton marriage which smashed the whole precarious arrangement upon which it rested. The crisis partly arose out of Caroline becoming *too* successful. She became editor that year of one of the very lucrative society magazines of the time – *La Belle Assemblée and Court Magazine* for which she herself wrote satirical essays with provocative titles like *The Invisibility of London Husbands*. This took up a great deal of time and put her under great pressure just as she became pregnant for the third time. George, instead of being sympathetic or appreciative of how she was supporting their household, resented not only the time her writing and editing took but also what he thought was the self-importance of his wife. The quarrels which had rocked the marriage from the beginning began to get worse. As ever, they started over something trivial and rapidly escalated, always ending with George attacking Caroline. Once, it was over a letter she was writing to her mother: George said he could tell by the expression on her face that she was complaining about him and when she refused either to show him the letter or stop writing it he set fire to her writing materials with his cigar. Another time it was over whether she was deliberately sitting in a chair he said was his favourite and they then fought, in a room filled with chairs, over the possession of that particular one. Augusta Norton, George's sister who had originally been so infatuated with Caroline, chose this time to come on a long visit. Caroline loathed her. She was ugly and mannish and simply embarrassing to have about. She also interfered in the running of the household and encouraged George to believe that Caroline was not being "a proper wife" to him. This caused more quarrels until in the summer of 1833 the Nortons had their most spectacular yet.

It began, as usual, over very little. Caroline, who had been writing late into the night the day before, went into the dining-room after dinner the next day to begin writing yet again. George followed. She asked him to leave. He refused. Up Caroline got and swept out of the room in a fury, locking the door behind her with George pointlessly holding his ground inside. She settled herself in the drawing-room, with her maid, and locked that door too. George meanwhile had climbed out of the window and re-entered his own house by the front door. He tore up the staircase roaring that he was damned if he would be locked out of any room in his own house, and began kicking and hammering on the drawing-room door. The terrified servants clustered at the bottom of the stairs not knowing what to do. Inside the drawing-room Caroline calmed her own maid and refused to open the door. Enraged beyond endurance George hurled himself at the door like a battering ram until it not only caved in but the whole framework of the door came away from the wall. Then he went for Caroline. Although she was pregnant, he manhandled her down the stairs, punching and slapping her, all the time releasing a string of oaths, until the servants overcame their fear at the sight of the beating Caroline was taking and rushed forward to restrain him forcibly. This time Caroline escaped to the nursery, where she spent the night. Her family, summoned to her aid, arrived to find her a pitiable sight. They urged her to leave George at once: the limit had been not just reached but passed and they could not bear her to spend another night under his roof. But somehow, the quarrel was patched up. Even George was shocked at the sight of his bruised and battered pregnant wife. She was ill and listless all summer and not in a position to provoke or goad anyone. It was easy for George to leave her alone, which he did. In August, when their third son William was born, they were once more fleetingly reconciled and enjoyed a little temporary happiness.

But the balance in the marriage, never very safe, had gone. Nobody, least of all Caroline and George, knew how to proceed any longer. The Sheridans alone were adamant: they were finished with George. They would not try to like him any more. They invited Caroline to accompany them on a European tour in the following spring and wanted her to come alone. But she knew George would not allow it. Her only hope of the family holiday she so desperately wanted was to persuade George to come and her family to accept him. Reluctantly, both sides agreed and off they all went in the spring of 1834. Almost at once things went wrong. George felt ill and since he prided himself on being unable to speak a single word of any foreign language he could not be left to recover on his own. Miserably, Caroline watched her family depart and turned to nursing George, which she did devotedly. Instead of having fun with her sisters she "sat at a window and yawned and caught flies"[23] while from his bed George moaned and complained.

When he was well again they proceeded to Frankfurt where the Sheridans had agreed to wait. Unfortunately, Caroline arrived half-strangled. On the way, she had felt sick and asked George either to stop smoking his hookah pipe or to let her open a window. He refused to do either. Suddenly, Caroline snatched his pipe from him, slammed down the window and hurled it out. George jumped out of the moving carriage, recovered his precious pipe, got back into the carriage and then, placing his hands round her neck, told her what he would do if she ever did that again. She greeted her family in tears with the marks of George's strong fingers on her throat for all to see. The Sheridans found it difficult to tolerate George at all and ostracized him. They took Caroline off into the countryside and she wrote "we scrambled about the hills and laughed our hearts out."[24] By the time they all returned to London she felt quite restored but in fact her good health was an illusion. She had an illness from which she was very slow to recover. George, as usual, did nothing but abuse her for their financial difficulties which he appeared to think were her fault. The rest of the year passed in a haze of work and worry, with the sick

Caroline trying to write a novel that might at one blow solve her pecuniary problems. If it had not been for the support, both emotional and financial, of her beloved family she did not know how she could have survived. The £300 she received for her two prose tales (*The Wife, and Woman's Reward*) did not, after all, make her fortune (nor did her three novels – her poems and journalism earned her much more).

There is no doubt that neither Caroline nor George was looking for a complete break. In fact, when they were apart from each other both their rages quickly subsided. George became remorseful and wrote begging Caroline to forgive him and she always replied acknowledging her part in any quarrel they had had. After the hookah pipe incident, for example, when her family had whisked her away from George, he wrote saying he was repentant and she replied that he was "a good, kind husband in the long run and don't believe me when I say harsh things to you . . ."[25] This was the way of things between them: their incompatibility led to violent scenes and then partings during which both regretted what had happened. If George had been a really strong, cruel, domineering tyrant Caroline would have nerved herself for a final break however much she dreaded the social consequences. But he was not. Mostly, because she was cleverer, she could *manage* George. If other people had not interfered she could certainly have gone on managing him to her own advantage with only the occasional fight.

But other people did interfere. First there was Augusta, George's sister, and then a much more sinister figure, a Miss Margaret Vaughan who caused trouble between the Nortons throughout 1835. Miss Vaughan was a cousin of George's from whom he was likely to inherit land and money. She came to stay near Storeys Gate early in 1835 just as Caroline was recovering from a miscarriage, and was one of the causes of another bitter quarrel between them. Then in 1836, the quarrel over but not forgotten by the Sheridans, Caroline and her boys were invited to spend Easter at Frampton Court, the home of Georgiana, who was now Lady Seymour. George had not been invited. No Sheridan wanted him under their roof again (which was of course interference of another kind). George, who heartily loathed the Sheridans and detested their house parties, did not give a damn. He much preferred going to Scotland to hunt or shoot. But Miss Vaughan told him he was being insulted. She said no gentleman ought to stand for such treatment and that he should not allow his family to go where he was not invited. She said she could not respect him if he allowed it. So George, who was oblivious to insults but desperate to keep in with his wealthy cousin, suddenly told Caroline she could not go to Frampton. He absolutely forbade it. Caroline retorted that he was being excessively stupid and certainly she was going. Furthermore, she told him she knew who was behind this sudden ridiculous command: Miss Vaughan. She said she would never have her in the house again. The stage was set for another grand row but they were both going out to dinner and so had to control themselves. On the way home George said that whatever Caroline did he was not having his sons leaving his house. He rushed into the house the minute they got home and told the servants that the boys were not to go out with their mother. Caroline managed to keep quiet.

Next morning, she crept out of the house and went round to her sister's London house to confer with her. While she was there, one of her servants arrived in a great state to say that the children had been bundled into a carriage and taken to a secret destination. Caroline, knowing at once that it would be Miss Vaughan's nearby house, went there immediately. She was admitted but denied access to her children – "I could hear their little feet running merrily overhead while I sat sobbing below – only the ceiling between us and I not able to get at them . . . if they keep my boys from me I shall go mad."[26] Miss Vaughan, after abusing her at length, ordered her out of her house and threatened to call the police if she did not leave at once. Meanwhile, back at Storeys Gate, George had ordered the door to be barred to her. She was now a cast-off wife, deprived of her children.

The horror of what had happened stunned Caroline for several weeks. It was the first time her children had been brought into a quarrel and she found this development changed everything. She was so distressed and upset about their welfare that all other considerations were swept from her mind. She wanted to be re-united with them and nothing else mattered. She was willing to humiliate herself, to beg George's forgiveness even though she had done nothing wrong, to admit she had been harsh or unreasonable – anything. But to her astonishment George was implacable. She could not see the children. He had taken them down to his brother's house at Wonersh Park where they would remain behind high walls and locked gates. Then came the most unexpected and dramatic development of all: he was going to sue her for divorce on the grounds of the alienation of her affections by Lord Melbourne unless she agreed to a separation in

which the children would live with him, she would claim no allowance from him, and she agreed to live with her brother. They were
monstrous terms which Caroline could not possibly have agreed to
and for which there was no incentive since she was not even to share
the children. She rejected them outright. George immediately filed his
divorce suit.

It was the sensation of the year implicating as it did the Prime
Minister. Caroline, when the news was brought to her, could not
quite take it in. It was too ridiculous. Lord Melbourne was only a
friend, as George, who had been present at most of their few meetings
at Storeys Gate and had accompanied her to Melbourne's residence,
perfectly well knew. Obviously, there had been more interference.
This time it was from Lord Grantley and his Tory cronies who had
realized the splendid capital they could make out of George and
Caroline's domestic squabble. The newspapers of the day enjoyed
themselves hugely printing scurrilous paragraphs about the beautiful
Mrs Norton and the powerful Lord Melbourne. The *Age* and the
Satirist, two of the most scandalous sheets, included not only Caroline
but her sisters in all the innuendo and speculated openly about their
reputations, mentioning in the process every gentleman who had ever
been seen with them.

Caroline realized finally that she was trapped. The children had been
taken from her which gave George the ace card in all their negotiations. Whatever happened next, whether his absurd divorce suit
succeeded or not, he would still have the children. This, she was told,
was the law. She refused to believe it. What had she done? She was
innocent – she had not even left George much less committed adultery
and she could prove it – so how could the law give George the
children? What meaning did the word "innocent" have if the law did
not protect her? She consulted all the eminent lawyers of her acquaintance and looked up law books herself. The result was the same. She
learned, "piecemeal" as she put it, what the law regarding married
women said. She found she could not even apply to any court in the
land for a hearing because a married woman had no legal existence.
Fear began to dominate her actions. She was so terribly afraid that at
first she could see only two alternatives: either she must abase herself
and placate George somehow or she must abduct the children, take
them abroad, and spend the rest of her life as an outlaw. But, however
hard she tried, George would not be placated. "My hope," she wrote,
"was to come peaceably to an arrangement; I will not say to outwit

him but to secure the boys . . ."[27] Nor did she succeed in her
abduction though she went down to Wonersh Park and tried. "I
failed," she wrote dismally. "I saw them all; carried Brin to the gate,
could not open it, was afraid they would tear him to pieces they caught
him so fiercely. And the elder one was so frightened he did not follow
. . . If a strong arm had been with me I should have done it."[28]

What hurt her most and eventually brought her to a third alternative
was the reaction of those nearest to her. All her family and Lord
Melbourne and every friend of her acquaintance counselled caution
and best behaviour. They agreed it was unfair and that she was
greatly wronged but insisted that the best thing to do was lie
low and not inflame George any more. If she was very, very careful
and very, very good he might relent sufficiently to let her at least see
the children. She must not do anything to draw further attention to
herself. Melbourne in particular urged docility. He told her that since
they were innocent they should not make a fuss. It would perhaps be
better if they did not meet for a while. George, he said, was "a gnome"
and "quite frightful" but perhaps she ought to beg him to take her
back. Caroline lashed him for his cowardice ("all I say is *worse* women
have been better *stood* by").[29] Her mortification when she saw the
expression on Melbourne's face as she told him about the divorce
action was dreadful. She never forgot "the shrinking from me and my
burdensome and embarrassing distress."[30] In spite of his written
instructions not to visit him she did go to his house in South Street –
and was turned away by the servants on his order. The flowers he sent
round afterwards were useless to ease her bitterness ("I could not put
them in vases without sitting down to cry").[31] He made her feel vulgar
and disgusting – "It is the vanity of woman . . ." she wrote to him
"which has misled me into a painful struggle of hope and fear instead
of quietly taking my place in the past with your wife Mrs Lamb and
Lady Brandon . . ."[32]

Slowly, and very painfully indeed, Caroline began to see why she
was being so unfairly made a victim: because she was a woman.
Everything worked against her. It was not just the hard legal facts she
was up against but that amorphous thing called public opinion. Even
before any trial, whatever its outcome, she was being judged and
pilloried because she was a woman, and had behaved in a way women
were not supposed to behave. She saw how it had all begun with her
success in society. She realized how her beauty and her vivacity were
great misfortunes because they had made people cast her in a role she

had not in fact been playing. "Why, *I* am handsome," she wrote to her nephew ". . . but you may depend upon it it is the last thing a woman need wish to be and I do nothing but curse my regular eyebrows and straight profile and wish myself different, yea even if it were to be ugly – but to be *tolerable* were a thing to thank heaven for in one's prayers."[33]

Even more disastrous had been her general manner in company which laid her open to misunderstanding. She had complained of the unfairness of it to Melbourne himself in a spirited letter she wrote while at a house party in Scotland. After a jolly evening, during which Caroline (who was without George) had entertained the guests and been at her merriest, the eldest son of the Earl of Tankerville had come into her bedroom at two in the morning expecting to sleep with her. She related exactly what happened to show Melbourne how two and two were added up to make five in her case: " 'Don't be angry,' says he. 'Well' says I . . . 'I did not think you had been so wicked!' 'It is not so *very* wrong' says he. 'Pshaw,' said I coolly 'are you come here to teach me right or wrong? I really wonder at you – first for being so much worse than I thought you, secondly for being such a fool as to suppose any woman would give herself to you after four days merely because there was no other in the house for you to make love to, thirdly for being ass enough to come in here when you know (—) can hear every step or tone in the room if he is not sleeping.' 'I'm sure you're enough to chill anyone,' responded my offended visitor, 'but I don't care. I came here and I shan't go.' "[34] It took her a good half-hour to talk him out of the room (he finally burst into tears, buttoned his shirt up, and left) and afterwards she locked her bedroom door. But it was incidents like that which revealed to her how misjudged she was. She had incurred a reputation and now that she was being sued for divorce this reputation, so monstrously unjust, would count against her. She was beautiful, witty, extrovert, flirtatious, daring *and therefore she must be guilty*. A man with a similar reputation was merely thought manly. Even if his guilt was proven this only enhanced his status in people's eyes. But, found guilty or innocent, Caroline was going to lose.

It was this realization which made her decide to fight, to take the law into her own hands and change it. But first there was the ordeal of the trial in June 1836. It was traumatic for her. Since she had no legal existence, she therefore could offer no defence and have no representation. She had to sit at her mother's home in Hampton Court only able to send notes objecting to particularly vicious bits of "evidence" as they came up. She had been prepared for lies but what appalled her was "the loathesome coarseness and *invention* of circumstances which . . . made me a shameless wretch."[35] She wept when she heard a maid testify that she had been "painting her face and sinning with various gentlemen" at the precise moment when she had just been delivered of her third baby. It was this coarseness which she said "drove me quite wild." She struggled to endure the ordeal cheerfully – "I wished to seem in as good spirits as I could to the poor worn Mother"[36] – but could not stop herself crying half the night. Every afternoon she rode in Richmond Park, feeling sick and ill with worry, returning in the early evening fearful of hearing some new piece of vile slander had been produced in Westminster Hall. It was midsummer and the nights were long, especially since she could not sleep. She wanted to hear about the trial and yet she did not want to hear. She knew that there did not exist any incriminating evidence but cringed when it was reported how everyone had laughed as the supposed damning letters from Melbourne were read out ("I will call for you at half-past-four. Yours M.") Being made a laughing stock was almost as unendurable as being branded an adultress.

At last, and really very quickly, the end came. Without calling any of the witnesses who would have proved Caroline's innocence the jury threw the case out. "I was in Westminster Hall," wrote Lord Seymour, Caroline's brother-in-law, "with Bentinck just in time to hear the cheers with which the verdict was received." Caroline sobbed with relief as soon as she heard. "**It's given against him** – *against Norton*! And my children CAN'T grow up *believing* in their mother's shame – oh, I have spent such a long, long day and half a night waiting – but it *is* over."[37] Next day, *The Times* rejoiced with her and described her as "a calumniated lady." The entire Sheridan family celebrated the news with her and Caroline wrote to her brother that she had finally managed to stop crying and had "put on my cork jacket and become more buoyant."[38]

It was a short-lived buoyancy. George might not have expected really to win damages from Melbourne but, once the plot failed, his rage knew no bounds. Caroline wrote that she had heard "he has been giving drunken dinner-parties every evening and swearing he will *bring me to his feet* – he is gone quite mad – he wants someone to shew him he can be *proved* a beast."[39] Meanwhile, she still had no access to her children who were at Wonersh Park. In July she went down there, greatly daring, on a day when she had heard Lord Grantley would be out and managed to snatch a short interview with the boys until Lord Grantley returned unexpectedly and "behaved with his usual cold-blooded brutality."[40] She had no idea what was going to happen next. "As to what I shall do," she wrote, "I don't know. I hope I may not live long enough to do anything. I have spit blood twice, for 2 or 3 days at a time this last fortnight and am so weak I can hardly stand."[41] Her hopes were raised by George allowing her half-an-hour with her children, in front of his witnesses, at her brother's house but then she heard a rumour that this was a prelude to whisking them off to Scotland. Before they disappeared, she managed a secret meeting in St James's Park, thanks to a servant, but found it agonizing. "My eldest . . . gave me a little crumpled letter he had had in his pocket a fortnight directed to me . . . He was so dear and intelligent."[42]

Once the children had been sent to Loch Rannoch, the home of George's elder sister Grace and her husband, Caroline was for a while so stunned that she could do nothing. The feverish impatience with which she had attempted to negotiate a settlement disappeared. On all sides, she was still urged to be "good", to remain calm, to accept the inevitable. Her mother, who did not only upset herself but worried about Caroline's health, urged her to keep quiet and let George and his lawyers alone for a while. She must realize she could do nothing on her own. But sitting at Hampton Court pining for her children was torture to Caroline. She grew sick of all the sensible advice. All the relief she could find lay in *fighting*, in doing something however apparently useless. "The anger of an individual against a *set* always sounds ridiculous," she wrote to her nephew, "but some private wrong has generally been the cause of the important events of this world of changes."[43] She vowed vengeance on the Nortons and announced that her Austerlitz had scotched but not killed her. As she rode in Richmond Park and turned to gardening as a consolation she was all the time rebelling and arguing with herself in her own head. The law had given George their children but why should it not do more? Why did the law not allow a mother rights, too, rights that need not necessarily displace the father's but exist alongside his? Excitedly, she talked to her friends about her thoughts. They all sympathized but gently tried to show her what a mighty colossus she would be taking on if she tried to change the law – it simply could not be done as she envisaged doing it. But, after several meetings with Caroline, her friend the lawyer Abraham Hayward realized that her passionate outpourings to him deserved more serious attention. He knew she would not listen to advice – he had given her masses and been ignored – and so, as a kind of merciful therapy, he introduced her to Serjeant-at-law Talfourd, the young Whig barrister who had specialized in infant custody cases and was known to be advocating changes in the law.

This was exactly what Caroline needed. At once, the tone of her letters changed. She now had a sense of direction, a sense of solidarity with like minds. Instead of thrashing about helplessly she used her energies to compile a pamphlet setting down in an orderly fashion all the thoughts which had filled her head since the day George stole her children. It was a relief to be required to impose discipline upon herself, a relief to have work to do familiarizing herself not only with all the statutes she wished to see revoked but with all the cases she could cite as evidence of change being needed. Talfourd was invaluable because he had acted in so many famous cases in recent years. Through him, Caroline became familiar with the case of Mrs Greenhill, a young wife of irreproachable virtue who had discovered her husband was living with a mistress, also known as Mrs Greenhill, while away on business. She had left him, taking her three daughters all under the age of six, and had attempted to sue for separation and alimony. Talfourd had acted for her but in spite of the judge's sympathy the court had upheld Mr Greenhill's right to have the children. The judge deplored Greenhill's conduct but ruled that "however bad and immoral" the court had "no authority to interfere." Talfourd tried to appeal but discovered there was no court in the land, either civil or ecclesiastical, that would find for the mother. (Mrs Greenhill subsequently fled abroad with her girls.)

Caroline, under Talfourd's tuition, became an expert on case law. It astounded her to find that not only was she not the only mother legally robbed of her children but that hers was nowhere near the worst case. The knowledge steadied her. There was no more wild talk and extravagant vows of revenge: she got her head down and put in several hours every day of serious study. Nor was she as ill-equipped for it as she had supposed. On the contrary, she grasped points of law quickly and assimilated facts without difficulty. She also had a talent for spotting holes in arguments which stood her in good stead, and discovered within a very short time that not all lawyers were pillars of virtue. The law, in short, was after all nothing to be frightened of or intimidated by. Her so-called "weaker" feminine brain was more than capable of matching strong masculine ones. The more she learned the less respect she had, writing that it would have been preferable "to have followed a marching regiment than to see the seamy side of this intellectual trade."[44] Her confidence grew until she felt ready to write her pamphlet stating her point of view. It was the best piece of work she ever produced and she was rightly proud of it, so much so that she was prepared to have it privately printed, published and distributed. Her prose style, which had always been clear and direct, adapted itself well to polemic and gave the pamphlet a drive and vigour which demanded attention.

It was entitled *The Separation of Mother and Child by the Law of Custody of Infants Considered*, an unwieldy heading chosen from a short list of five. Caroline said she had bitten the top off her pen trying to select the most accurate and comprehensive title and could not help it if it was awkward – it said what had to be said. The pamphlet began by making plain what the iniquitous law was and then attacked it systematically from every side. It explained that the mother of a *legitimate* child was excluded from all rights over the child from the very moment of its birth: the father had custody and there were no mitigating circumstances whatsoever. But this precious custody was itself a fraud. The father could give the child to a perfect stranger if he so wished because his much lauded custody was only nominal. Even a new-born baby sucking at its mother's breast could be torn away and handed to anyone of the father's choosing (as happened to a Mrs de Manneville in 1804). This was cruel. Everyone agreed it was cruel, but it was said it was only cruel in a few extraordinary cases and that the law could not bother itself with individual, untypical instances of misuse. Wrong, said the pamphlet. On the contrary, it was precisely with extraordinary individual cases that the law was concerned and did interfere. In any case, what was this "principle of natural justice" upon which the father's sole rights of custody were founded? What was "natural" about it when in fact no father could look after a baby on his own but a mother could? The only "natural" thing was that a baby should stay with its mother who had given birth to it and was, on her own, equipped to feed and sustain it. Motherhood, said the pamphlet, was much vaunted. No thought was given to how the law harmed this ideal. "What degree of bodily agony or fear can compare with the inch-by-inch torture of this *unnatural* separation?" The mother suffered, the children suffered and the female character, "bred to think of motherhood as the highest fulfilment" suffered to the detriment of society as a whole. So let the law drop all talk about claims of nature.

The rest of the pamphlet was concerned with attacking objections to access if the law had to stand. The argument ran that if mothers knew they might get custody of their children this would encourage them to leave their husbands. This was contemptuously dismissed as specious. "It is monstrous to represent that as a *temptation* which can at best be but a slight *mitigation of misery*." No woman ever wished to leave her husband because if she did she committed social suicide and was only pushed to it in extremity. It was *men* who might be influenced by thoughts of having or not having custody – a man might be "restrained from indulgence of a vicious inclination" if he thought leaving his wife might lose him his children. The real crux of the matter was whether the rights of the father had to amount to the exclusion of the mother. The father's right to control his children's education was conceded; his right to retain them under his own roof was arguable, but the right to deprive a mother totally was unacceptable.

The pamphlet appeared early in 1837. Just before its publication and the distribution of 500 copies to MPs and other influential figures, Caroline wrote to Mary Shelley (the poet's widow who had written asking how to get a pension for her father, the philosopher William Godwin, and had become a friend). "I think there is too much fear of publicity by women; it is reckoned to be such a crime to be accused and such a disgrace . . . that they wish nothing better than to hide themselves and say no more about it."[45] But she did not wish to hide. She wished to stand up and claim attention, however great the cost. And it was great. Going out to a party after the court case was agony for Caroline. Her first appearance was at Lady Minto's where she was "cut" while talking to the kindly Lady Stanley. "I said to myself this is *their* world, this is *their* morality"[46] and she proudly lifted her head and consoled herself with thoughts of her own worth compared to such miserable wretches. It was not a form of consolation which worked very effectively. Every time she suffered from what she called "the privy nip" Caroline hated it. She had to force herself on, repeating to herself that she did not care. Braving grand establishments like Lansdowne House, home of the Earl of Shelburne and one of the great social centres of the era, took courage. On her first outing there she wrote, "People were very civil indeed to me which was lucky for I was dreadfully nervous."[47] The men were more civil than the women, a fact noted by the women and resented by them so much that their own incivility increased in proportion. Nothing, said Caroline, exceeded women's cruelty to women. But she would *not* be sent to a nunnery real or figurative. She would *not* act as though she were a bereaved person. So she dressed with even greater care than usual and sparkled even more than usual and only at home, at night, did she weep with misery at the hardness of her lot. "No man, perhaps no woman . . . knows what it is to bear undeserved disgrace (as I do)."[48]

All the time Caroline was working on her pamphlet she was thinking of and worrying about the welfare of her children. They were in Scotland but the servants who looked after them were friendly to Caroline, who had often stayed in Lady Grace and Sir Neil Menzies' household. Through them, bits of news drifted down to her. They were not reassuring bulletins. She knew Grace was a hard woman who considered whipping a cure for all childish misdemeanours, but stories of Brinsley being stripped and tied to a bedpost and whipped for defending his mother were extreme even for that "haughty and intemperate" woman. Brin, she was told, had said Mama wouldn't let him be punished but Mama was five hundred miles away and incapable of defending him. She knew that George himself loved his children and would never harm them but George was hardly with them and, when he was, imposed a discipline that Caroline had always feared too harsh. Little things hurt most. George did not beat his children but he made his authority clear in silly ways. "He has ordered the youngest child to go by the name of *Charles* – he was christened William Charles Chapple – the affectation and insincerity of the whole thing makes my heart burn."[49] But poor little Willy (aged two) having his name altered just as he had learned to say it was as nothing compared to what happened to Fletcher, the eldest (seven) but the most frail. "All the petty things he could do to spite me he has done. We used to dispute about a dentist being allowed to gold wire his (Fletcher's) jaw (he is underjawed). I had a horror of this . . . he took him yesterday – had it done – and merely remarked 'I can do what I please now with you, my boy.' "[50] This was typical of George. The suffering of children was never real to him as it was to Caroline who saw how all three would be deeply affected according to their different temperaments. She thought Willy, although youngest, would survive best. He was physically the strongest and most like George whereas Brinsley (five) was most like her. He was imaginative and daring and aroused hostility. Fletcher was the most sensitive. She knew that "a continual battle" would go on in his mind "between what he knows and what he comprehends." The thought of what all three were going through made her wish at her lowest moments that she had never had children at all. "I wish," she wrote, "I had never had any children – pain and agony for the first moments of their life – dread and anxiety for their uncertain future . . ."[51]

The pain, instead of lessening with time, grew worse, particularly when Caroline heard any of her boys was ill. Early in 1837, just as Talfourd introduced his bill to reform Infant Custody into the first session that year, she heard that William had been ill. She wrote begging George to return him to London and let her nurse him. She was now living with her favourite Uncle Charles at 16 Green Street in Mayfair and did not see why that should not be approved by George as a suitable place. George, meanwhile, was feeling more kindly towards her and towards the world in general because Miss Vaughan had finally died and left him £2,000 plus an estate in Yorkshire. He was also missing Caroline and was tired of his domineering brother who had dared to cheat him out of a foal he claimed was his. So he wrote back saying he would return the children to London although not to his wife's house – they would stay at his own town house and be looked after by Augusta. But Caroline could see them every day. Caroline was ecstatic, although the ecstasy was replaced by anguish when she first saw her sons. Their unkempt, neglected air distressed her deeply. William in particular had changed, ". . . this sharp, talkative little being does not seem to me my fat fair baby. They grow up in such a moment."[52] And she had missed so many of those vital moments. The daily visits she made did not seem enough to make them up – she wanted her children at home with her, doing ordinary everyday things, filling the silent house with noise and chatter. Most of all she wanted them to herself, not to share with either George or more often Augusta there. Each day she grew more restless and each day leaving became harder. Brinsley in particular was hard to part from. Every time she was forced to go he clung to her and she had to remove his arms from around her neck on Augusta's orders. Then suddenly, without warning, just as everything seemed to be going well, Caroline received a message saying the boys had been sent to Wonersh, to Lord Grantley's. She could not understand it and pleaded for an explanation but none was forthcoming. Obviously, George was once more under Grantley's influence. Meanwhile, as soon as the boys arrived at Wonersh, they got measles. Caroline heard they were very sick, especially Brinsley. She went down to Wonersh, forced her way in and saw the children just long enough to see how ill and pale and "pining" they were before Grantley returned and had Brinsley torn out of her arms. Shaking and hurt (she said she felt as if a cartwheel had gone over her by the time she had been forcibly ejected) Caroline returned to London to find a further communication awaiting her. George was making a final offer: either she gave up her struggle to get her children and accepted an annual allowance of £300 or George would publicly repudiate her debts and all financial responsibility for her in the newspapers.

At this juncture Caroline broke down. She was ill and exhausted. She asked Talfourd not to press his bill for the moment while she attempted a reconciliation through a new mediator, Sir John Bayley, who was one of George's lawyers. "I am in such pain with my wretched head that I can hardly write," she wrote to her brother. "It is so bad when I am, or have been, agitated and I am in a fever."[53] If this mediation failed, she added, she might as well drown herself. As she had no money, she thought it might be the best solution. "I am scrambling about with sixpences about *butter*," she went on, ". . . it is very uncomfortable for I have no ready money at all now and I have borrowed off Charlie."[54] She was reduced to sending out for a pennyworth of potatoes because she could not find "either a chandler or a grocer who would trust me" although she had "a willing butcher, milkman and coal merchant." It was a case of trying to live well on nothing a year but "as I have not a farthing . . . all shopping must soon cease."[55] Yet when it came to negotiations with Sir John he was surprised at how little Caroline cared about money. He had started by believing her reputation and thinking she must be "a vain and frivolous woman" but after three meetings discovered she had been "greatly wronged". All his client's abused wife cared for was the welfare of her children and Sir John publicly stated that he "blushed for human nature" when he realized how she was being treated. With his concern Caroline's confidence grew. "I really believe *at last* I am to settle and be comfortable," she wrote to her brother. "God grant it."[56] But nothing was granted. Unless she signed away her children and accepted a pittance George would not grant a legal separation. Negotiations broke down. The children were returned to Scotland. Caroline turned with renewed vigour to lobbying for Talfourd's reintroduced bill.

The bill reforming Infant Custody was passed in the Commons, while Melbourne was still Prime Minister, in May 1838 by ninety-one to seventeen votes (a very small attendance in a house of 656 members).

But in August the Lords threw it out, again with a very small number present. Caroline remarked bitterly, "You cannot get Peers to sit up to three in the morning listening to the wrongs of separated wives."[57] The *British and Foreign Review* chose this moment to publish a vicious attack on Caroline as the instigator of the bill to which she replied (although everyone begged her not to), under the name Pearce Stevenson, in another pamphlet *A Plain Letter to the Lord Chancellor on the Infants Custody Bill.* It was over emotional and long-winded, not nearly as impressive as her first pamphlet, but it helped to get the bill passed. There was a further debate, which incensed Caroline because the general assumption was made that *all* women at variance with their husbands must be unchaste, and then the bill went through both houses in 1839. Children under seven were now allowed to reside with their mother *if* the Lord Chancellor agreed to it and *if* the mother was of good character. The irony for poor Caroline was that as her sons were again in Scotland they were outside the jurisdiction of the Lord Chancellor. But nevertheless she now had hope and began assembling her case to present to the Lord Chancellor. George, at the same time, began having her house watched in the hope that he could thwart any good character references by proving men visited her while she was alone.

Caroline still did not have her children but she had come out of her slough of despair and was also solvent, at least temporarily, once she was paid for her new book of poems (*The Dream and Other Poems*) which earned her the title "Byron of modern poetesses." In 1840 she was received at court for the first time since the trial of 1836. Everyone, including Queen Victoria, saw how terribly pale and nervous she was. It seemed for a moment that she might faint but she managed to retain her dignity even when she trembled as she made her curtsey. She was, at thirty-two, if anything more beautiful than she had ever been. She wore Isle of Wight lace over white satin and had a train of palest lilac. Suffering had given her beauty a poignancy it had never had, calming down the flamboyancy of her style. Admiration for her was open, but Caroline drew no comfort from this. It no longer excited her to be praised. "Oh, depend upon it, there is no treadmill like the life of a woman of the world and you see it on the expression of the face,"[58] she wrote to a friend. Nothing mattered beside the fact that she did not have her children and they were growing up fast. Her heart leapt not at compliments but at the news that her sons had been moved to Yorkshire to George's estate and were therefore now technically accessible to her. "Do not drive me to seek (justice)" she wrote to George "but let me owe it to you at last."[59] He replied offering her portraits of the boys. She refused the offer disdainfully. She wanted no further reminders of what she was deprived of. Every night she had a fire lit in the room that would be her sons' if and when they returned but she wrote to her sister that she feared they never would as children. Even if she fought a case in the Lord Chancellor's court it would take forever, resisted at every step by George, and her children were already twelve, ten and eight. The most she was ever going to be allowed was to have them in their school holidays, which she did for one week at Christmas in 1841.

It was the last time she ever had them together. In July 1842 William, aged eight, fell off his pony while riding, alone, round his father's estate in Yorkshire. He contracted blood-poisoning and became seriously ill. Caroline was sent for but was told upon her arrival that her son was dead. "It is not in the strength of human nature," she wrote to her sister, "not to think this might not have happened had I watched over them!"[60] Nobody, in fact, had watched over them. All three roamed the estate doing exactly what they pleased. "Half of what is now so lavishly expended in ceremony and 'decoration of the coffin' would have paid some steady manservant to be in constant attendance."[61] But there were no ugly recriminations. Caroline knew that George was as distraught as she and that to his burden was added guilt. He was in "a state of bitter distress" and she had only kind words for him even though, she wrote to her mother, "*horror* is the main feeling with me – horror and bitterness – and in my quieter moments I feel *stunned*."[62] Hardest of all to bear was the attitude of her husband when the first shock was over. "Yesterday," she wrote to her mother before the funeral, "it was my wish that we should all read prayers *together* . . . Norton first said that he could not because he had so many people in the house – I said 'perhaps you could in the afternoon' – This was settled but in the morning he came late and hurried and said he had agreed to go to Grantley . . ."[63] And so it went on. George's grief, although real, did not produce the state of mind Caroline looked for. He could still think of other things, make other plans. She could not. She was haunted not just by memories of her dead child but by the realization of how bleak the last five years of his short life had been. That law which had given him to his father's care had robbed him of the real meaning of the word: care was exactly what had been missing. All three boys were neglected both physically and emotionally. "They have none of them learnt a new prayer, or said a prayer to anyone, since they left me,"[64] wrote Caroline to her mother. They were like little orphans, provided with food by the servants and not much else.

When the funeral was over and Brinsley had recovered (he had an attack of "hysterical fits" when he saw William in his coffin), George at last conceded that the two remaining boys could go home with their mother. Caroline, who had hardly dared to breathe when she sensed what was afoot, was so relieved she wept for hours – she had been so terrified that George might demand *she* came to live with them in Yorkshire. Hurriedly, she packed their few possessions and returned to her uncle's house, now in Bolton Street. Naturally, there were conditions. She was to have the boys half the year (they were at Eton) but George could order them elsewhere if he so wished (as he proceeded to do very often). Nothing at all was done to make her own position either clear or satisfactory. "I am in fear and trembling," she wrote, "standing firm for their actual residence under my own roof . . . I am so afraid that . . . I shall be cheated."[65] This fear meant she did not dare mention her own position or her desire for a proper settlement. She had to carry on "married", as she put it "to a man's name but never to know the protection of this nominal husband . . . never to feel or show preference for any friend not of (my) own sex."[66] It depressed her to think of the effect this had upon her boys. "I have often felt very downhearted," she wrote to her brother after they had come to live with her, "as to my human responsibilities for them – and cried over the fire when they have been gone to bed."[67] She worried about the effect on them of seeing "the playgoings and pleasurings in my house and the fireside boozings and snoozings at their father's."[68] However hard she tried to make up for the lost years (Brinsley's birthday was celebrated with a whole roast pig to make up for no celebrations at all on the five birthdays before) she felt the want of security and stability in both her sons' characters. They were not growing up the men they might have been and she felt inadequate to direct them. Mrs Coleridge recommended a curate friend to be a companion-tutor to them in the holidays but Caroline did not deceive herself. Fletcher and Brinsley, although good and kind boys, lacked the standards of a happy homelife in a proper family. No woman on her own could provide them.

After 1843, Caroline was on her own in every sense. Her beloved Uncle Charles, who had been of such use, died and his house was sold. She moved to Number 3 Chesterfield Street, to a house only fourteen-years-old, and resolved to remain without either a relative or a chaperone living with her. She *was* alone therefore she would be seen to be alone and hang the consequences. By then, she well knew the consequences: people talked. No gentleman caller's reputation was safe if he visited Mrs Norton alone at any hour of the day. Even if a gentleman brought a posse of ladies with him she was thought to be suspect. But she did not care so much about tittle-tattle as about her economic state. "I have no furniture in my new house," she wrote. "I must sit on the floor with a plate in my hand . . ."[69] It was an absurd situation. "It is a hard thing," she wrote to her brother, "to feel *legally* so helpless and dependent while *in fact* I am able to support myself as an intelligent man working in a modest profession."[70] Her poems and magazine work earned her good money but she had no right to it: a married woman could not keep her own earnings. She was obliged to resort to all kinds of subterfuges to keep her money from George who was legally entitled to it. The fact that he was also legally obliged to support her did her no good at all.

Yet Caroline never complained or was aggrieved in company. On the contrary, she held her head high and insisted on leading the life she wanted without a man at her side. She had friendships, close friendships, with many men but no love affairs. Men were "in love" with her but never her lovers. Scandalmongers ignored her innocence. Even when there was no proof of a liaison they invented plenty and were believed. Their theory ran "Mrs Norton is beautiful and lives alone and has many gentlemen friends – do you imagine she is any better than she seems?" Tennyson, who was placed next to her at a dinner-party was terrified and "shuddered" at her proximity. Jane Carlyle, although saying she was "a beautiful, witty, graceful woman" had to spoil the compliment by adding darkly, "Whatever *else*." The priggish Rev. William Brookfield, friend of Thackeray (himself an admirer of Caroline's) could find nothing wrong with her but thought her all the same not "suitable" for his wife as a friend. The Duchess of Sutherland, Queen Victoria's Mistress of the Robes, whose friendship towards Caroline restored her to good society, put what people felt in her charmingly muddled way. "She is *so* nice," she wrote of Caroline. "What a pity she is not *quite* nice: for if she were quite nice she would be so *very* nice."[71]

Caroline was well aware of how she stood. She had sinned against convention and that was a crime. Not only had she dared to live on her own but worst of all she had dared to enjoy it, she had refused absolutely to go into retirement. She was not guilty, nor ashamed, and she would not act as if she were. Nor would she conceal how much pride she took in her work. Her writing was no hobby. She was as determined as any of the contemporary male authors to earn good money and to be seen to be serious about her writing as a profession. Throughout all her troubles, it was her writing which kept her sane and gave her satisfaction when nothing else did. "The power of writing has always been to me a source of intense pleasure," she once wrote. "It has been my best solace in hours of gloom; and the name I have earned as an author in my native land is the only happy boast of my life."[72] She never lacked confidence in her own ability and sometimes over-estimated that "name" of which she was so proud. In March 1843 when Southey died she wrote an extraordinarily arrogant letter to Peel almost *demanding* the Poet Laureateship not only as her right but as just compensation for the wrongs she had suffered. "I do not know if there be any precedent for appointing a female poet laureate even in a Queen's reign," she wrote and then went on to hint that the Queen was a fan of hers and ". . . this seems an easy thing to grant if there be indeed any disposition to befriend me and would be of very great service."[73] Peel, in spite of the harangue that followed about how Caroline had earned more in a month than most husbands in a year, was unimpressed. He replied that he had no power to appoint the Poet Laureate and that the Lord Chancellor, who did, had offered it to Wordsworth. Caroline, whose letter for once had lacked the tact, charm and subtlety, as well as the wit, which usually characterized them, was disappointed and even aggrieved. Women, she was beginning to see, lacked more than standing in the eyes of the law: they lacked it in the eyes of the world.

Her opportunity to correct this, at least partially, began in 1848 and involved her in another sensational court case. George Norton was, as usual, short of money and wished to have access to a Trust Fund made for Caroline and her sons many years before. He asked Caroline, through Fletcher who was then nineteen, to agree to let him touch it. She quickly saw she had a rare advantage and agreed, on condition he sign an actual deed of separation giving her an income of £600 a year. What was odd about this bargain was that Caroline appeared to have forgotten that, as the law stood, a married woman could not make any kind of contract. George, however slow and stupid, was at least lawyer enough to know this very well. So they both signed a contract which had no validity and George got his money. Caroline, mean-

while, had had a piece of good fortune. Lord Melbourne died, leaving
a solemn deathbed declaration that Caroline had always been innocent, and it was found he had left instructions to his relatives to make
financial provision for his wronged friend. George was not told this.
He paid up the first instalment of Caroline's agreed allowance (which
she used to go to Lisbon to nurse Fletcher who fell ill as soon as he
arrived to take up a post there in the diplomatic service). Then, in
1851, Mrs Sheridan also died leaving Caroline £480 a year, secured to
her alone. George found out about this and also, rather late, about the
Melbourne money and instantly announced that the deed of separation
was invalid and the £600 a year allowance would stop. Caroline was
furious. Both legacies were made to help her *in addition* to any other
sources of income – neither her mother nor her old friend had intended
their money to be a substitute for her husband's allowance to which
she was entitled. She retaliated by referring all creditors to George.
These were many since the minute she had any money at all Caroline's
expenditure always got out of hand. Although she denied she was
extravagant she admitted to Mary Shelley that she was indeed "reckless (when I am out of spirits or want to be amused or excited) in what I
spend for the moment."[74] George was inundated with her debts and
instantly began issuing subpoenas to everyone in sight. He took
Caroline to court in August 1853. This time, even though it was
unusual, Caroline was called as a witness and was therefore present.

The case opened on August 18th at Westminster Court where there
was not even standing-room only. The actual test case was over a bill
for repairs to a carriage, a mere matter of £47. Thrupps, the carriage-
makers, sued George Norton as liable for the debts of his wife who had
defaulted. Caroline had to face George in open court. Her courage
sank, she wrote later, and . . . "I felt giddy – the faces of the people
grew indistinct – my sentences became confused . . ."[75] Her throat
felt "full of dust" when she was asked to speak and she faltered in her
replies. "What does the witness say?" roared George, coming very
close to her and pushing his red, angry face in front of her, "I cannot
hear. Let her speak up." He maintained she was acting, but as Caroline
acidly remarked afterwards all emotion was acting to George. Under
cross-questioning she managed to revive and began to defend herself.
The case hinged, of course, on the 1848 deed of separation. George
maintained he had only offered £600 a year on condition Caroline had
no money from other sources such as Lord Melbourne. Caroline easily
exposed this as a lie. The court burst into cheers and applause when

Caroline, finding her voice in her indignation, called out, "I do not ask for my rights. I have no rights; I have only wrongs."[76] But the court decided in George's favour. As the law stood, married women could not make contracts. When Caroline was again cheered George clenched his fist at her and pandemonium broke out before the court was cleared.

The newspapers were full of it. What added to the interest of the court report was Caroline's own letter to *The Times* pointing out more flaws in George's case. Her friends begged her to desist but she was adamant -- she *wanted* to be in the full glare of publicity, she *wanted* every sordid detail gone into. She had completely done with any kind of reticence – let the world know everything and see the injustice of it. George replied of course in *eight columns*, telling stories going back some twenty years and including little vignettes of his wife "having Lord Melbourne by the neck". Unfortunately for George his own solicitor, appalled by some of the lies that reflected on him, also wrote in disassociating himself from half of what his client said. Then, to Caroline's immense satisfaction, Sir John Bayley wrote, too, delivering a telling rebuke to George for his greed and dishonesty. George replied that Sir John was infatuated with his wife. And so it went on. Caroline was more triumphant as each day went on and the correspondence grew, but her family and friends were distressed. It was an unedifying sight, they thought, to see Caroline's private life spread every day across the newspapers. When they found she was also writing another pamphlet they were even more upset – could she not now leave well alone? No, Caroline said, she could not. Women had ended up where they were through leaving things alone.

All her energies were concentrated on preparing *English Laws for Women in the 19th Century* which appeared the following year. She took as her text a quotation from *Bleak House*. "It won't do to have TRUTH and JUSTICE on our side; we must have LAWS and LAWYERS." She began by refuting the idea that law was fixed and unchangeable and said that this view was held only by those who did not like "the duckweed on the still pond" of society ruffled. The time had come to disturb it. To show why, she reviewed her own case, with examples of the physical violence she had endured, and from which she had no legal escape. She made fun of the law for saying that an ill-treated wife should not "condone" that ill-treatment. How, asked Caroline, could she not condone it? By suffering blows without protest? By ignoring letters begging forgiveness? All wives wished to save their marriage, yet the minute they tried to they were accused of "condoning". Where was the sense in that? It was England's archaic divorce laws which made a wife who had fled from a brutal husband forced to "condone".

But by then Caroline was no longer alone in demanding changes. Intrigued by the Norton case another woman of quite a different type had also been prompted to collect and examine the laws regarding married women. Barbara Leigh-Smith (later Bodichon) was the eldest daughter of a rich, well-known political family with a Bohemian outlook. Unlike Caroline, whom she does not appear to have met, Barbara certainly believed in equal rights and was not afraid to say so. She had gone through life demanding them. With Mr Matthew Davenport Hill QC, the Recorder of Birmingham, she drew up a comprehensive pamphlet concerning *all* women (*A Brief Summary of the Laws of England concerning Women*). But, even more important, she did something which Caroline had not only not done but of which she actively disapproved: she called together a committee of women to collect petitions for a proposed Married Women's Property Bill. The headquarters was her sitting room at 5 Blandford Square. Here there developed among the women who gathered there (a nucleus of about twelve regulars) a spirit of what can only be called "sisterhood" totally foreign to the likes of Caroline Norton. Within a short time 24,000 signatures had been collected. It was obvious that a deep vein of resentment among the women in England had been successfully tapped. In June 1854, Lord Chancellor Cranworth took heed of it. He proposed the reform of the marriage laws – but afterwards withdrew the proposal. In March 1855 the Solicitor General announced that a Bill was "nearly prepared" but nothing was done. Again, Caroline took up her pen. She wrote *A Letter to the Queen*,[77] going over all the arguments again and tearing to shreds the idea that reforming the marriage laws was "too difficult". There was no difficulty except the laziness of men terrified to reform laws they admitted were barbarous, because it might open the floodgates to women deserting their husbands in droves. Her *Letter* was, said Lord Brougham "as clever a thing as ever was written . . . I feel certain that the law of divorce will be amended and she has greatly contributed to it."[78]

A month later a bill was introduced on The Reform of the Marriage and Divorce Laws. There was a debate during which Caroline Norton's words were quoted. In 1857 the Bill finally became law, with her influence directly seen in four clauses: clause 21, which said a wife deserted by her husband could keep her earnings; clause 24 which empowered a court to direct payment of separate maintenance to a wife; clause 25 stipulating a wife might inherit and bequeath property; clause 26 saying a separated wife could sue, and be sued, and make contracts. It amounted to a relatively small reform but a more comprehensive bill was introduced in 1867 and passed in 1870 once Lord Westbury's objection (that if wives could freely dispose of their property they would sell it and spend the money on "diamonds, racehorses and lovers") was overcome. In 1882 the Married Woman's Property Act at last enshrined the sought-after principle: married women should have the same rights as unmarried women. It had only taken twenty-five years to bring about the start of the greatest re-allocation of property in English history since the dissolution of the monasteries in Tudor times.

This came, of course, too late for Caroline Norton who died in 1877, but her last two decades were made happier by the knowledge of her contribution to the changes now definitely in view. She knew that in the process of helping to change the law she had made herself notorious and rather resented her image. She was seen, she wrote, as a cross "between a barn actress and a Mary Wollstonecraft." What she wanted to be seen as was a writer. Her beauty and reputation as a hostess did not matter. The historian Morley reported when she was over fifty that "it would have required a very powerful telescope to discover she had passed thirty" and that her teeth alone would have made the fortune of an ordinary face. The compliments she still received in late middle-age were nothing to Caroline. "I remember the day," she wrote, "when I was an intelligent being – but very vaguely. Also when I was cheerful and good company – but all *is* evaporated. I am fierce, sullen – and rather vulgar. I hunch my shoulders and say 'What?' when I am spoken to if I do not immediately catch what was said from sulky abstraction of mind."[79] But neither her family nor her friends ever found her sullen – she was always entertaining even when disconsolate. The death of Fletcher in 1859 laid her low for a long time but she found some consolation in caring for her grandchildren, Richard and Carlotta. Brinsley had married an Italian girl who, when he then fell ill, could not support her two babies, born in 1855 and 1856. Grandmother Caroline took charge of them and relished fulfilling the role denied her for so long twenty years earlier. They were very much the comfort of her later years. She allowed Grandfather George to visit them whenever he wished which was surprisingly often. George died in 1875, his brother a few months later. Caroline, released at last, married Sir William Stirling, an old friend, a few months before her own death in June 1877. She would have, she hoped, "an existence separate from the writs and shall be remembered and dreamed of when the gossiping women of my day have ceased to talk and are but a handful of dust."[80]

★　　　★　　　★

Caroline Norton represented in her day a minority of women. Most married women did not have recourse to the law. They married and stayed married. They had children and never realized these could be taken from them if a husband so wished. Therefore it could be argued that changes in the law hardly affected the vast majority of women and were not as significant as changes in other spheres. But in fact changes in the law, both then and now, are vitally important for feminism. They provide the framework without which there can be no progress worth having, no security worth winning. They put the firm stamp of authority on what are recognized as *needs*. The gap between those needs being felt and being responded to is often long. Protest has to be first registered, then organized, then approved by public opinion, then advocated by some strong person or persons. Where changes in the laws concerning marriage were at a disadvantage was in lacking for so long a champion who would feel strongly enough to call attention to the situation by exposing, in the full glare of the courtroom, what was being suffered. Caroline Norton was that champion even if the cause was thrust upon her.

What Caroline Norton discovered was that women within the last century had become chattels, things to be disposed of as men willed once a marriage had taken place. The only time a woman had any power was at the moment of marriage when she could agree or not agree. A girl of fifteen or sixteen, as Caroline pointed out, was thought capable of making this tremendously important contract but thereafter her opinion on anything else within the marriage became mysteriously valueless – "in the matter of maternal right she is no more considered than stock or stone."[81] Why women had gone on putting up with this iniquity was because "the boundaries of duty, religion and social necessity are walls round a woman's heart and light fences round a man's."[82] Her four novels are full of the bitterness of married women, tricked and cajoled into what was little better than a pleasant

servitude if they were lucky and a hideous form of slavery if they were
not. But Caroline did not blame either men or the laws alone: she
blamed women themselves. Her insight into how women contributed
to their own condition was more truly feminist than any of the openly
feminist tracts of her day. She had such contempt for *feebleness*, for the
supine, docile role she saw women playing everywhere – "feeble
natures respecting even exaggerated energies; the contrast strikes
them as a superiority."[83] How could her sex be so stupid, she asked, as
to equate physical strength and a domineering character with superiority? But they did. Even worse, women were proud of inspiring
blind adoration – "There are women," wrote Caroline, "who think it
sublime to be loved with this sort of passion"[84] and were horrified
when, the passion assuaged, the men lost interest. Women made
themselves into pathetic creatures and reaped the consequences. They
were afraid it was unfeminine to voice opinions or show independence. Caroline knew how she was despised for doing both. She herself
was proud of being able to hold her own in any conversation and of
being brave enough to go about alone and unchaperoned. She was
proud too of her earning power – the ability to earn made her feel
triumphant and she saw nothing sordid about it. Nor did she see why
earning money should in any way make her either less feminine or less
of a good wife.

In a letter to Gladstone (with whom she had had an interview the
day before, on March 26th, 1854) Caroline said she was not interested
in "greater facility of divorce". Those who thought she was had
misunderstood her. "To me," she wrote, "the ceremony of marriage
in our church seems utterly indissoluble and though in earlier life I
might at one time have *wished* my marriage dissolved according to the
laws of men it would have been with a strict conviction that no law
could really annul it or make me the wife of any other man."[85] Her
argument was that men who were brutal to their wives were making
nonsense of the marriage contract and must be brought to respect it. It
was only gradually that Caroline realized her faith in coercing men to
protect their wives properly was not enough. Half the fury with which
she fought for protection was inspired by shame at going into a
partnership where, because of what the law said, she needed it. She
knew perfectly well that even if George had protected her it would not
have prevented her feeling a fool for falling into the trap marriage
represented. She, like other women, had married because marriage
was an essential part of womanhood, an essential passport in their

world to its rewards. Like it or not, Caroline Norton was asking for marriage to be re-shaped as an institution. This became one of the most important feminist goals. Marriage had to become based on something more realistic than protection, something less materialistic than property of one sort or another. Unless it did, women would be forever mercilessly exposed to exploitation.

After 1839 child custody, always the most heartrending area of any marital breakdown, was still difficult for a wife to gain. The Lord Chancellor could grant custody *only* if the children were under seven and *only* if the wife was indisputably innocent. It was quite easy for an unscrupulous husband to throw doubts successfully on his wife's innocence. In 1873 things improved slightly when the age of the child under dispute went up to sixteen but it was not until 1886 that the actual *welfare* of the child was considered, which made a big difference. Yet the father was still, in law, the sole guardian of the child whoever had custody. This state of affairs, with a few minor alterations, continued until the Guardianship Act of 1973 when the mother was given exactly the same legal authority over a child as the father. She was also made as responsible as the father for supporting the child which has opened up a whole new set of complications in which women are again at a disadvantage. But in historic terms progress has been dramatically quick and complete. Caroline Norton would have been more than satisfied.

She would also have hailed as a total victory the changes in divorce laws and property rights. In her day it was almost impossible for men to divorce their wives and absolutely impossible for women to divorce their husbands. An Act of 1857 created a single new matrimonial court, instead of the cumbersome system of ecclesiastical courts plus Parliament, which was an enormous step in the right direction even if it was not until 1923 that women could obtain divorce on the same grounds as men. As for married women's property rights, these were finally secured in 1882. So the position now is incomparably better than when Caroline Norton began her battle. If her pamphlets and Barbara Leigh-Smith's are contrasted with a similar résumé today the difference is staggering. The incessant pressure which began in the 1830s has been magnificently productive. The fact that it does not satisfy many contemporary feminists cannot obscure this fact. But progress in this sphere is always towards a target which recedes: laws which would have given Caroline Norton more than she asked for do not content disaffected wives today because they are a different species. Women have changed, marriage has changed, society has changed and laws must go on changing to keep pace with the enlarging feminist experience. New Caroline Nortons, in fact, are necessary all the time to be that "example on which a particular law shall be reformed." Unless they are forthcoming, unless individual women are prepared to stand up to be counted as bravely as she did, feminism will lack the drive it must have to maintain hard-won gains.

THE PROFESSIONS

Elizabeth Blackwell
(*Courtesy of the Library of Congress*)

Elizabeth Blackwell
1821–1910

Caroline Norton fought for rights, basic legal rights, for women. Elizabeth Blackwell fought for options. She was the world's first trained, registered woman doctor and her entry into the professional sphere monopolized by men, through obtaining exactly the same qualifications as the men in exactly the way they had to obtain them, was of enormous significance for feminism. When Elizabeth Blackwell graduated in January 1849 the news spread with amazing speed throughout the entire western world. There was a sense of excitement about the future of women, about their new role in society, which had never been felt before. Yet Elizabeth Blackwell was part of no movement. What she did, she did on her own. Nor did she herself see her achievement as part of any general movement. On the contrary, she saw herself as special, as being peculiarly suited to following a career which she decidedly did *not* want all women to try to follow. Most women were meant to be mothers in her opinion. Motherhood, not any other career, was woman's highest calling, and women should apply themselves to it with diligence. The embryo Woman's Rights movement of her day found little support with her. She wrote refusing to speak at a Woman's Rights convention because "I believe that the chief source of the false position of women is *the inefficiency of women themselves* – the deplorable fact that they are so often careless mothers, weak wives, poor housekeepers, ignorant nurses and frivolous human beings. If they would perform with strength and wisdom the duties which lie immediately around them every sphere of life would soon be open to them . . ."[1]

This was both arrogant and patronizing of her and those who had

invited her were deeply hurt. They were also astonished. How *could* a
woman who had broken a monopoly, who had cleared the way for
other women to claim some other sphere apart from the domestic,
now turn round and say women should stay at home and be good little
wives and mothers? It did not make sense. Did Elizabeth Blackwell
want to be the only woman doctor in the world? Was she saying only
she was allowed to enter the professional world? There was consternation and anger in the new movement at her attitude as well as deep
disappointment. Men had tried to keep women in the home: if those
fortunate women who had managed to leave it were also going to try
to keep them there what hope could feminism have? It began to look as
though a far worse enemy of feminist progress than man was the
pioneer woman herself.

But in fact Elizabeth Blackwell's feminism was, like Caroline
Norton's, the product of her own confusion. She wrote to one of her
sisters: "I cannot sympathise fully with an anti-man movement. I have
had too much kindness, aid and just recognition from men to make
such attitudes of women otherwise than painful; and I think the true
end of freedom may be gained in another way."[2] What frightened her
into apparent opposition was this anti-man basis to the Woman's
Rights movement. She felt "perplexed" at the need for it. "My head is
full of the idea of organisation but not organisation of women in
opposition to men"[3] she wrote. That way, she saw only disaster.
What she most passionately wanted – every bit as passionately as any
Women's Rights supporter – was change for women but only through
society changing too. She disliked intensely the existing state of
relationships between men and women. Why could they not be
friends without society's strictures on morals and sex colouring the
friendship? Why was there not a healthier attitude towards male/
female relationships? Her dream, she wrote, was not of gaining
"rights" for women – these would only be "the foolish application of
plasters" – but of "radical action" which would "redeem the rising
generation."[4] This was why motherhood was so important. Far from
being reactionary she saw herself as being progressive. Women had
this power to mould and influence the next generation in a way they
had never appreciated and that was why motherhood was the highest
and most demanding of callings, far more so than being doctors or any
other professional calling.

What was even more significant was her opinion that those women
like herself who were not actual mothers were only a different kind of

mother, that they simply carried their mother instincts into medicine or whichever profession they entered. She gave many addresses to female students in which she told them categorically that far from trying to be like men they must strive *not* to be like men. They were both female and feminine and their true value to their profession lay in that combination. "The true physician," she told her audience at the opening of the winter session of the London School of Medicine for Women in 1889, "must possess the essential qualities of maternity." She believed firmly that woman had "inherited tendencies" of gentleness, sympathy and sensitivity which ought to be fully used and she dreaded above all else any suggestion that women were *not* different from men or that they ought to make themselves the same. It was in this that Elizabeth Blackwell separated herself from the Woman's Rights movement. She told women to treasure their female nature, to believe it existed, to make more and not less of it, to realize that "rights" in themselves were nothing.

But nevertheless Elizabeth Blackwell *was* a feminist. No one believed more than she did in gender not being an obstacle to achievement. The only thing which branded her as not quite feminist enough was her belief that choice was implicit in a woman's life, that she had to *choose* between being a wife and mother and having a career. It was a choice she wished to be available, which is what made her a feminist, but self-sacrifice would always in her opinion be necessary. The way was long and hard if a woman wished to take on a man's role, or what until her own breakthrough had been commonly held to be a man's role. Dedication and unremitting toil were part of the choice – there were no shortcuts, no exemptions. And for the majority of women she believed it was a way they would simply find too hard, which was, she thought, not something they should feel guilty about. No woman should feel a failure because she stuck instead to the time-honoured role of wife and mother: it was just as praiseworthy and potentially fulfilling as being a doctor or anything else. This was not what the feminists of her day, led by Elizabeth Cady Stanton and Susan B. Anthony, wished to hear, of course. They were busy trying to rouse women to get out of the home and did not want anyone telling them they were just as well-off there. So Elizabeth Blackwell was not popular even though she was regarded as a heroine. Her philosophy was too contradictory. She wanted *some* women to follow her into medicine but refused to urge *all* women to do so or to have equivalent careers. Her limit was set at the existence of the *choice* to have a career which is what she had spent her long life achieving. But expecting this choice to be made was unfair and often impossible. It was a verdict much too sophisticated for her kind of feminist to make but it should not be allowed to invalidate her contribution to feminist history.

★   ★   ★

Elizabeth Blackwell had an extraordinarily perfect feminist upbringing, unusual (although by no means unique) for a nineteenth-century girl. She was born on February 3rd, 1821 in Bristol, England, third daughter in an eventual family of nine children. Her father, Samuel Blackwell, was in the sugar-refining business. He believed fiercely in equality of every sort – for the workers, for slaves and for women. His own father had been a tyrant who had treated women as serfs but Samuel had rebelled against this very early. His own wife, Hannah, was treated with respect and deference and his daughters – Anna, Marian, Elizabeth, Emily and Ellen – were given the same opportunities as their brothers – Samuel, Henry, Howard and George – to develop their individual personalities. There were also four maiden aunts who lived with the family and enjoyed Samuel Blackwell's generous patronage and tried his patience to its full extent.

From her earliest days Elizabeth remembered being drawn with her father into agitation for the abolition of slavery and being far more interested in debating this issue than in following any of the traditional girlish pursuits. The maiden aunts disapproved of their nieces' preoccupations with what they thought of as "unfeminine" affairs. They complained that the girls had no interest in sewing or housekeeping, and they also complained about how they were dressed in practical, unadorned clothes. (So, as a matter of fact, did the girls themselves – Anna hated "the ugly and often shabby things we were made to wear from a mistaken notion that dressing us badly would keep us free from vanity".)[5] But Samuel had his own ideas about the upbringing of his daughters and he stuck to them. As far as he was concerned, girls were as much part of the community as boys and their voices ought to be heard equally.

In 1832 the Blackwell family emigrated to America. The reasons were to do partly with anxiety over the state of the sugar business and partly with letters from a friend who had already gone to America and was urging Samuel to join him. Elizabeth, aged eleven, remembered later the excitement of the voyage over on the *Cosmo* but her sister

Anna remembered the horror of it "so hideous were those horrid, stinking, filthy holes . . . what a dreadful experience was our 7 weeks and four days of misery in that floating hell!"[6] Once in America, the entire Blackwell family (which included not just the aunts but other assorted relatives) settled in New York City, and Samuel hired a sugar house. Elizabeth was sent to what she described afterwards as "an excellent school". Naturally, now that they were in America, the Blackwell family interest in the abolition of slavery became even more pronounced. Their house became one of those in which escaped slaves sheltered on their way to Canada and freedom, and Samuel even wrote a book on anti-slavery rhymes which was published. Elizabeth joined the Abolitionist Vigilance Committee, the Anti-Slavery Working Society, the Ladies Anti-Slavery Society and the New York Anti-Slavery Society. The highlight of her adolescence was attending a convention with her father and staying behind to shake the great abolitionist Lloyd Garrison by the hand. She felt she was living in "exciting times" and all that dimmed the excitement, at that stage, was faint worries about her father's prosperity. At first, Samuel seemed to be successful but then the great New York fire of 1835 destroyed his sugar house. It had been insured but the insurance company could not meet its debt and so, after he had sunk his remaining capital in a new sugar house, Samuel Blackwell was obliged to sit up every night guarding it against fire. Elizabeth sensed catastrophe, and in March 1837 she commented, "Papa condescended to inform Mamma yesterday that he had sold his . . . sugar house . . . What his plans for the future are we do not know, I suppose something about beets."[7] The house was suddenly full of masons working away but although "Papa is very busy with masons in the cellar . . . what he is doing or what his plans are for the future nous ne savons pas."[8]

But they were otherwise happy, at least on the surface. It was not the present that concerned Elizabeth, aged sixteen, but the future. The future was a prospect she found rather unbearable whatever happened to her father's business. She recorded in her diary that an uncle had offered her a hundred dollars a year to help look after his children but that she had turned him down.[9] To her consternation her mother thought she ought to accept the offer, "Papa being so poor" but in spite of adoring and wanting to help her father she stoutly refused to. She loathed looking after children and resented the assumption that because she was female she must automatically like it. She also hated another common assumption – that all girls should be ladylike and behave in a docile, modest, demure fashion. She had not been brought up to it, nor had her sisters, but to her fury when men criticized her manner her sisters rebuked her. "Marianne seemed *particularly* displeased with me and said I behaved in the same manner to every gentleman . . . to all this I could only say that I wished they would point out the faults of which I was guilty and until then I should most certainly behave in the same manner as I considered it perfectly proper."[10] This manner was to be bold, outspoken, casual and off-hand. It meant, as Marian well knew, that Elizabeth would gain no suitors and if she had not suitors she would not marry and if she did not marry – what?

It was the common dilemma of the age and Elizabeth was not oblivious to it. Another day of taking her uncle's children out moved her to write in her diary "I wish I could devise some good way of maintaining myself but the restrictions which confine my dear sex render all aspirations useless."[11] Her father's business declined and the one servant the family had was dismissed. The girls agreed to take turns, week about, doing her work. "This is my day for seeing to the meals . . ." wrote Elizabeth on June 7th, 1837. "I really do hate the employment and look with real dread to my week for work . . ."[12] What she dreaded even more was that kind of existence going on forever with no prospect of change. When her father announced they were all moving to Ohio, where he thought he had a good business opening, she at first welcomed the news as being at least some kind of activity to break up the "dearth of incident". The move to Cincinnati, down the Ohio river, was made in May 1838. The family, with two of the four aunts, travelled in a canal boat which Elizabeth described as "stuffed full of Irish women with whole trains of squalling dirty children."[13] Once in Cincinnati, the excitement she had felt rapidly evaporated. Nothing, after all, had changed. The daily régime was still the same, except she now gave music lessons, and her father was still worried. He was also ill. At the beginning of August he had an attack of fever which with alarming speed developed into real delirium. "We all stood round his bed that night," wrote Elizabeth on August 6th, "with the most intense anxiety . . . he was seized with a fit of excessive restlessness . . . Oh twas distressing to behold."[14] On the 7th, he died.

Elizabeth was stunned. She wrote in her diary "never till my dying day shall I forget the dreadful feeling . . . what a feeling of hopeless despondency came over me . . . I felt as if all hope and joy had gone and nought was left but to die also . . ."[15] But as well as the agony of real grief there was horror at how the family would be able to live. On the 10th, after the funeral, Elizabeth wrote that they had twenty dollars left. The only thing to do was open a school, which they did on the 27th, at nine o'clock in the morning. They also had "a grand shift round" of bedrooms to make way for boarders. The little school was quite successful but Elizabeth was glad to get thirty dollars from an old-clothes man she had asked to call. She could hardly bear the thought of the family income being dependent forever on running a school and was always on the lookout for other ways of earning money. But none appeared. By October, after a bare six weeks of teaching, she was writing, "Oh for a lodge in some vast wilderness far away from children."[16] She found the girls she taught sullen and impertinent and ungrateful. In December "we had the girls down to dance thinking it would please them but they came down in the most sulky temper and Anna had to force them to stand up. Oh, the delights of a boarding school."[17]

The next few years were bitter ones. Elizabeth missed her father dreadfully and, although she and Anna and Marian took pride in supporting the family, she hated teaching, confessing she thought herself "rather a deficient teacher". In 1839 she was eighteen and even more restless than she had been in New York. To her annoyance, her mother "seriously advised" her to "set my wig at Mr S.G." She and Anna had "a talk on matrimony. She fully intends *courting* somebody if a better does not turn up. I really could not help crying upstairs when I thought of my situation. I know it is very wrong to be so ungrateful and I try very hard to be thankful but when I think of the long, dreary years ahead I cannot always help it."[18] The thought of marriage was obnoxious but again and again she and Anna discussed it because "we are so sick of schoolkeeping." In March she wrote she was "sick and impatient of my scholastic duties" and by the time school was over each day she was "almost distracted". Surely *anything* was better, even if that anything was marriage. But when she took a drive with a Mr Smith, whom she seems to have liked, she got "some insight into his character. He has evidently always associated with low people . . . so many little instances betray his commonness of mind which convince me he would not suit me."[19] The disappointment contributed to "a terrible fit of crying in church". In desperation, Elizabeth tried to develop new interests. She began to learn how to make wax flowers but although she managed a rose she never progressed to a carnation.

Anna, meanwhile, had had a brilliant idea: why should not one of them go to England as governess with some friends they knew who were about to set sail? The thought of England made Elizabeth's heart beat faster – "I could fancy myself already on the ocean with the foam and the blue waves dashing around us."[20] But she did not go. Instead, she turned to religion, joining the Episcopal church (the Blackwells had always belonged to a Congregationalist sect rather like the Quakers). For a while, her sense of frustrated ambition seemed to wane a little. If she was not content she was at least not so ragingly discontented.

The time had come, in any case, for a change. Three of the Blackwell boys were by 1842 old enough to take over from their three elder sisters as breadwinners. They went into the milling business and earned enough to support the family. The school, which had not been doing well, was closed. In 1844 Anna went off to a teaching job in New York and Elizabeth, though regretting the necessity of sticking to her last, departed for Henderson, in Kentucky, in the same capacity. She was to teach in a small girls' district school for four hundred dollars a year. The experience was disastrous. She hated Henderson, which she wrote consisted of "three dirty old frame buildings and a steep bank covered with mud."[21] The people were dreary beyond belief and her sense of justice was continually outraged by the daily evidence of how the negroes lived and were treated. She felt she had come from civilization to a savage place. She was an object of great curiosity to the inhabitants and reported that inquisitive gapers even peered into her face and commented, "Well, I do declare she's got a clean mouth, hasn't she!"[22] Above all else, she resented the lack of privacy – "I, who so love a hermit life for a good part of the day, find myself living in public and almost losing my identity."[23] Before she lost it entirely she gave up and went home.

Here, she again faced the problem of her own boredom. She had plenty of interesting people to talk to once more and plenty of societies to belong to but her feelings of isolation and despair were as strong as they had been in Henderson. What she wanted was some "real work", some "hard challenge". There was no need for her to rebel, no cause to sigh for understanding from her family. They understood, unlike so many nineteenth-century families, but what they could not do was provide an answer. What she wished to do was hidden even from herself. She was suffering, as she left adolescence behind, from that common feminist dilemma: she could see what her life was *meant* to be like but not what it *might* be like. Her one strength was that, unlike Caroline Norton and so many others, she was not duped by the promise of marriage changing her life. She viewed marriage with a cold, clear eye, managing to separate the attractions of the flesh from the reality of the marital condition. Far from not being susceptible to men she maintained she was always falling in and out of love but that she saw "What a life association might mean and I shrank from the prospect, disappointed or repelled."[24] Her "bodily urges", about which she was remarkably frank, disturbed her. She felt they might prove "a fatal susceptibility" and tried to starve herself into losing them. It never occurred to her, of course, to go ahead and satisfy them outside marriage, nor did she reason that because she felt them she had an obligation to "nature" to see they were fulfilled. But by the time she was twenty-three, in 1845, she was feeling "the want of a more engrossing pursuit than the study of music, German and metaphysics and the ordinary interests that social life presented."

One day, Elizabeth went to visit a friend of hers who was ill. Visiting friends who were ill was in fact one of the main afternoon occupations of ladies of her time and she counted herself fortunate to be extremely healthy. If she even had a headache this was so surprising that it would feature in her diary and be remarked upon as extraordinary. But the majority of her contemporaries and their mothers were ill almost continually with one sort of minor ailment or another, half of them unmentionable. A huge number of these illnesses fitted into a category labelled "uterine disorders". The most common of these disorders was "uterine catarrh" which, according to one medical expert of the time, kept a quarter of the female population in bed for half their lives. Elizabeth's friend, whose name she did not record, had an uterine disorder of a grave nature. She was in great pain and knew she was dying. She told Elizabeth that if only she had had a woman as a doctor her sufferings might not have been so great because she might have been able to report symptoms early on that she had simply been too embarrassed to mention. "You are fond of study," Elizabeth reports her as saying, "you have health and leisure; why not study medicine?"[25] The very thought appalled Elizabeth and she said so. Then, soon after, the friend died and Elizabeth found herself haunted by the suggestion made so sadly and wistfully. Half the attraction was the sheer originality of the idea and the other half the obvious usefulness. Hadn't she wanted "real work" and some "hard challenge"? Slowly, slowly the notion of taking up medicine grew no matter how often she reminded herself of her natural repugnance towards disease and all it entailed. Hadn't she always hated biology, hadn't the sight of "a bullock's eye on its cushion of fat" disgusted her? Wasn't she unfit to study medicine? Almost in an attempt to close the matter Elizabeth wrote off to several well-known doctors asking for their opinion of a woman trying to qualify as a doctor. Their opinion was unanimous: quite impossible but a very good idea, because there was undoubtedly a great need for women doctors.

This verdict reflected the general concern with women's health felt at the time. Throughout America female invalidism seemed endemic. Catherine Beecher, who carried out a survey in 1835, was not unduly astonished to discover that very few women seemed to think they enjoyed good health. This was hardly surprising as so few of them led healthy lives. The middle-class woman was encouraged to think indolence desirable and the working-class woman was worked brutally hard. All of them wore clothes ruinous to activity. The average woman had a dress with fifteen to twenty pounds of material hanging from a severely constricted waist under which were the notorious whalebone corsets. It was hard to do anything but walk sedately, but then to be sedate was part of being feminine and feebleness was another. With physical activity curtailed or disapproved of and mental stimulation thought harmful the middle-class woman was often driven, through sheer boredom and inactivity, into "hysterics", so called because this was put down to the behaviour of the uterus. A Dr Robert Barnes declared that "all nervous disorders are caused by ovario-uterine disorders"[26] and he was overwhelmingly supported. The remedy was even more of that rest and quiet which had produced the condition in the first place. Either that, or surgery.

Gynaecological surgery was literally murderous. In 1835 a Dr Sims, who was a pioneer in modern gynaecological surgery said that when he began practising "doctors were killing their patients." The ways in which they killed them were various but one of the commonest was to follow surgery by the application *internally* of leeches. The doctor was instructed to count the leeches in case they crept into the uterus itself and stayed there, sucking away. One doctor remarked, "I have scarcely ever seen more acute pain than that experienced by several of my patients under such circumstances." Then there was cauterizing the vagina with all manner of poisonous solutions and perhaps worst of all clitoridectomy, performed as a cure for masturbation. It was hardly surprising that women preferred to suffer in silence, or rely on home remedies, nor was it surprising that they came to regard the female parts of their body with fear. The tragedy was that few women knew how their own bodies functioned since they were rarely taught the true facts of menstruation and pregnancy (and these facts in any case were not then properly established). When a book entitled *Female Physiology* was published in 1854 as an attempt to provide a handbook for young ladies the reviewer in the British *Lancet* was outraged – "What? Is it to be tolerated that a medical practitioner, a man above all others who should be imbued with modesty . . . shall unblushingly give to the ladies . . . drawings of the vagina, uterus, spermatozoa, various stages of labour etc . . . I was nauseated by the task of perusing this offensive volume." So women were kept in ignorance and learned about themselves only by experience. Modesty and delicacy kept them prisoners of this ignorance even when they had gained some experience – anything out of the ordinary, anything differing from what their experiences had taught them to expect, was worried about and whispered about with their friends but very rarely discussed with a doctor, until, as in the case of Elizabeth's friend, the pain or the bleeding or the swelling grew too great to be hidden. And by that time it was usually impossible even to alleviate suffering, never mind preserve life.

Elizabeth Blackwell had no statistics to show her how much woman doctors were needed, nor had she herself ever needed one, but gradually she became aware that she had accidentally uncovered an enormous area for improvement. Her sense of mission grew the more she learned. She was not "called" to medicine but called to applying her energy where it seemed to be needed. The precise nature of that need was irrelevant. "The idea of winning a doctor's degree," she wrote, "gradually assumed the aspect of a great moral struggle, and the moral fight possessed immense attraction for me." Medicine itself possessed none at all. Nor, at first, did any feminist considerations enter her head. The idea of being the first woman doctor was not something that attracted her in itself, not until the barriers blocking her progress were encountered. If being a woman was an essential part of her mission, because it was her femaleness which was going to help other women, then she was glad she was a woman but in no sense, in those crucial early days, did she see herself as a champion of a woman's right to be a doctor. She saw women doctors as filling a gap. The fact that it was a deliberately manufactured gap does not seem to have occurred to her. She seems, naïvely, to have imagined that nobody had noticed before what a good thing it would be if there were women doctors and that if they had they would have gone ahead and become them.

The true nature of her mission was slow to reveal itself and meanwhile her own resolution was by no means unwavering. When all this was happening, in 1845, she was for what seems to be the first time "experiencing an unusually strong struggle" against her attraction for an unnamed gentleman. It quite frightened her to be so attracted, especially when, in this case, no commonness of mind disqualified her suitor as it had the unfortunate Mr Smith. On the contrary, this mysterious man was "highly educated" and satisfied all her requirements. But finally, she rejected him. She wrote in her diary that her mind was "fully made up . . . I have not the slightest hesitation now."[27] She did up her beau's last bunch of flowers in a packet and labelled it "Young Love's Last Dream" and put it in a drawer. Romance was over. She had definitely decided on a medical career and intended to marry her work. She found, to her chagrin, that medicine was an unwilling bridegroom. There began a long, depressing period of writing for advice as to how to set about studying medicine. Nobody could suggest anywhere she might be accepted, except possibly in Paris. She also discovered the cost of studying medicine should she find anywhere to do it. She was informed that three thousand dollars was a realistic figure and she saw that she would have to get yet another teaching job in order to accumulate that kind of money. It seemed to her sensible to start earning this money while at the same time continuing to explore the studying possibilities, so she took a job teaching music at an academy in North Carolina. Her brothers Sam and Howard drove her there in a horse and wagon in June 1845.

The head of the academy, with whom Elizabeth boarded, had been a doctor himself. John Dickson allowed her to use his medical books to begin preparing herself for her chosen career and guided her through various useful periodicals. She was amused to discover during her stay in the Dickson household that she could mesmerize away headaches and wrote home jokingly that she was already called Dr Blackwell. She was not, however, nearly so good at an essential part of medical study, the dissecting of insects and animals. This she was most reluctant to do but forced herself to practise, using diagrams in Dr Dickson's books spread out before her. Meanwhile, she was doing all she could to secure her entry into some formal medical training. Anna, now in New York, scouted around for her and said she had found a practising doctor who was willing to take Elizabeth as a student but this was not what she was after. She was as well-off where she was if all she could obtain was another kind of home-study. It was her intention to stay with the Dicksons until she could get onto a recognized course somewhere but unfortunately, at the end of 1845, John Dickson closed his school and she was obliged to move. The next year was spent in another teaching job, in more private study, in more endless enquiries. It could, Elizabeth felt, go on forever. Suddenly, she had had enough. Against all advice, and without any prospects, she left her job and went to Philadelphia.

Philadelphia had some of the best medical colleges in the country and Elizabeth had decided that she ought to go personally to the leading Professors there and plead her case. She had had a letter, in reply to many of the sort she had written, from a Dr Warrington of the Philadelphia Medical School who had cautiously said that, although he thought women more suited to be nurses, she was welcome to call on him if she ever came to Philadelphia. This she now did. He suggested that her best hope was to disguise herself as a man and go to Paris. This idea Elizabeth rejected furiously – Paris, perhaps, but disguise emphatically no. The embarrassed Dr Warrington said that in that case he did not know what to advise. There was no point in applying to his college, although Elizabeth was welcome to visit his patients with him and use his library, because the authorities would reject her application outright. Elizabeth decided to go ahead all the same and while she waited for the verdict she took anatomy lessons privately. These quite changed her mind about dissecting. Her first lesson was on the wrist and "the beauty of the tendons and exquisite arrangements of this part of the body struck my artistic sense."[28] She now passionately wanted to have all the secrets of the human body and its organs revealed to her. It was a great relief to find her sense of mission re-inforced by some genuine enthusiasm.

But the outlook remained bleak. All the colleges she wrote to refused her, as had been predicted, with varying expressions of regret. None of them was very clear about why being a woman barred her from study but she had by this time divined the reason: she was a threat, part of all the new fangled "cures" and quack methods flooding the medical world at the time. The admission of women into medicine was simply seen as another crazy idea. Faced with this situation Elizabeth showed some degree of cunning. Looking at her letters of rejection she noted the carefulness with which these eminent institutions had turned her down and it struck her that she could turn their words, however hypocritically meant, to her advantage. The next batch of applications she sent out in October 1847 was to twelve country medical schools. In each letter she cleverly included the names of those who had turned her down, together with their excuses, and without needing to falsify anything made it sound as though these same influential gentlemen would be pleased if someone else *did* accept her. Her letter to Castleton Medical College read:

"Will you allow me to make an application . . . to the Faculty of the Castleton Medical College for permission to attend the lectures of the institution?

". . . Dr Jackson of the University of Philadelphia and Dr Mitchell of Jefferson Medical College expressed regret that the size and character of their classes would prevent my becoming a member of them but declared their hearty approval of my endeavour and both advised me to seek aid from your institution.

"I desire earnestly to obtain the education I need in America . . ."[29]

This letter, sent on October 20th, was answered on November 15th. It accepted Elizabeth Blackwell as the first female medical student ever admitted to a formal medical institution. But it came too late. Before it came, Elizabeth had been accepted elsewhere and had already left for Geneva Medical College in the state of New York where the term had already begun two weeks before.

Her admission was a fluke. The dean and faculty of the college, not wishing to offend either Elizabeth, who was as qualified technically as any man, or the doctors she quoted in her support, had put the matter to a student vote with the understanding that even one vote against admission would see it turned down. But the students, in a boisterous mood, all voted in favour. On November 6th, 1847, at eleven o'clock in the evening, an extremely excited and nervous Miss Elizabeth Blackwell arrived in Geneva to begin the studies she had decided on three years before. She did not know what to expect but she hardly cared – the first momentous step had now been taken. In fact, Geneva was luckier to get her than she was to get Geneva. As a medical college it was of doubtful reputation. It was barely ten-years-old, under-equipped, under-staffed and it did not draw its students (150 of them) from a very select band. None of this was at first apparent to Elizabeth who was much more bothered about finding somewhere to live. No landlady wished to take her in. When one kindly soul was prevailed upon she agreed only on condition she was not held responsible for the behaviour of her other lodgers whom she knew would be scandalized. Nor were Elizabeth's fellow-students any more welcoming. The joke being over, they were rude and sarcastic, but once Elizabeth appeared in their midst the transformation began almost at once. Half of them fell in love with her and the other half were either intimidated by her seriousness or alarmed by her competence. It was absolutely clear, right from the beginning, that no. 130, the first lady student, was in this particular class going to lead the field.

At the end of the first term Elizabeth passed her exams with ease. The work was no problem. What was a problem was loneliness. Even when her fellow-boarders, the students and the townspeople had all grown used to her she was lonely. It was the beginning of an experience which, as the years went on, she recognized as the price of her success. Women like her, who entered spheres where there were no other women, suffered a peculiar kind of deprivation hard to appreciate. What they wanted were *friends*, people with whom they could discuss absolutely everything, people with whom they could relax and be at ease. They did not find them. Elizabeth found she had colleagues but not real friends. Men were either suspicious and therefore at the best stiff and at the worst hostile in their attitude towards her, or else frankly admiring and amorous. It depressed her to discover how isolated she was, even though she was encouraged by her progress. Her professor of anatomy, Dr Webster (whom she described as "a fat little fairy") left her in no doubt that she had a great future. He was wholeheartedly delighted at her arrival and went out of his way to be helpful and encourage her. He also tested her. Soon after she arrived he sent for her to his consulting rooms where he was examining a poor woman of the town. He asked Elizabeth to examine her. Whatever it was Elizabeth saw appalled her. "My delicacy was certainly shocked . . . t'was a horrible exposure"[30] she wrote in her diary. But Dr Webster had no need to make his point: *this* was why she was becoming a doctor.

She had the same reminder in her first vacation, in 1848, when she went to work in the Blockley Almshouse in Philadelphia. There, she worked in the Women's Syphilitic Ward, a truly horrible place. Writing many years later she confessed that at the time she had absolutely no idea how these women got to be in the state they were in. She knew nothing of their world nor of the sort of women they were. All she knew was that they suffered terribly and that these sufferings were somehow connected with being women and that therefore they were of particular concern to her. She saw that they were treated with indifference. Attention was paid to their disease and that was all. There was none of the caring she had expected to find – caring was a luxury for which no doctor had time. The brutality and roughness with which the women were examined made her think that there must exist a feminine sympathy which would make women even more valuable as doctors than she had suspected. She began to have a vision of what women doctors could do which far transcended anything she had thought of before. Women doctors would care, they would know the value of kind words and gentleness, would realize that fear as well as disease must be treated, they would appreciate a patient's hunger for touch and sympathy. She tried to put into operation her beliefs but this roused the open enmity of her Blockley colleagues. Not only did they not help her but they now tried to obstruct her, resorting to mean little tricks of sabotage and petty destruction. "I must work by myself all life long,"[31] she wrote sadly. She wondered if the fault lay in herself. Was she failing to communicate properly? "I would I were not so exclusively a doer," she wrote. "Speech seems essential . . . but mine is at present a very stammering, childish utterance."[32] No one, in any case, listened to her. A new bitterness crept into her diary and letters and with it a dangerous notion gained ground. She began to believe that what was needed was female solidarity. She, who hated anything "anti-man", was nevertheless beginning to entertain the idea that women were *better* than men, that gender did have something to do with this superiority.

In January 1849 Elizabeth graduated from Geneva medical school, the acknowledged leader of the class. The *Geneva Gazette* reported "She is good-looking – a face that wins favourably on you; affable in her manner she pleases you; intelligent and witty she amuses you; amiable and confiding she wins upon you." Much has been made of her refusal to walk through the town in a procession with the other students but this had more to do with distaste at the nature of the procession, which was led by "a well-instructed brass band composed entirely of native Indians", than any desire to be ladylike. In any case, she was more interested in the fate of the thesis on Ship Fever which she had written in Blockley and which was published at the time of her graduation in the *Buffalo Medical Journal*. The pleasure its favourable reception gave her far outweighed applause from any crowd. But, in spite of this success and in spite of the solid qualification she had gained, Elizabeth appreciated only too well that she had yet another beginning to make. The problem now was to gain hospital experience, to become a practically qualified doctor as well as a theoretically qualified one.

Immediately after graduation she returned to Philadelphia. The same charade was gone through again with the same result: no entry into the hospitals. But she had been prepared for this and did not in fact let it worry her because she had already decided that Paris was her destination. Everyone told her Paris was the medical centre of the world so there she would go and somehow obtain experience. After that, no American institution would dare keep her out. Besides, she wished very much to travel a little after her gruelling course of study. She said goodbye to her family, wrote to Anna, who was in Europe already, that she was coming and then set sail in April 1849, shortly after receiving her American naturalization papers. She docked in Liverpool, then went on to London where to her amazement and delight she was warmly received. The medical profession showered her with invitations and although not used to socializing she found she greatly enjoyed being fêted (and developed a taste for iced champagne which she pronounced "really good"). But in Paris, where she arrived at the end of May, her reception was rather different. There were no dinners or other invitations and she was lucky to have her sister Anna with whom to share a flat. Her French was poor, she had little money and her introductions to medical people were few. Her fame had not preceded her and she had instead some difficulty establishing her identity. Nobody seemed the slightest bit impressed by her degree. She was rapidly forced to face the fact that a degree, said to be vital before it was won, suddenly became, in the case of women, of no importance once it was. The question changed to one of experience and it looked as though the chance to gain that was not to be given to her.

But Elizabeth had come a long way and had no intention of returning empty-handed. Luckily, she had learned to be thick-skinned and to persevere. To all suggestions that she should just be content and perhaps start a *women's* medical career she turned a deaf ear. She was not going to be caught on that one. Women had to become qualified in exactly the same way as men or they would always be inferior. So she went on seeking out medical men who might help her and finally hit on one – a man called Pierre Louis who advised her to enter La Maternité, the major lying-in hospital in France, and said he would back her application. Elizabeth promptly took his advice and accepted his help even though she was not immediately attracted to La Maternité, a grim old convent of little appeal. Nor was she attracted by the conditions of admission when they were presented to her. No concessions were to be made to her doctor's degree. She would enter with the same status as all the other young girls who came to train as midwives, would live communally with them and be subjected, as they were, to the same schoolgirl discipline. She accepted because she had no alternative. On June 30, 1849, aged twenty-eight, she entered La Maternité, but privately hoped only to use it as a stepping stone to greater things – she intended only to stay three months and then use her experience there to gain entry to another more general hospital.

It was a strange experience for her. She slept in a huge dormitory, took a bath with six others, was served poor food and had not a moment to herself. Most of the girls were around eighteen and naturally behaved quite differently from Elizabeth who felt ancient beside them. They came from all over France so there was every variety of accent for her to learn. The day was extremely long – fourteen hours at a stretch was common – and the work hard. La Maternité delivered 3,000 babies a year and the students were present for all "interesting" cases which happened at the most inconvenient times. But Elizabeth, in spite of what she always called her "hermit-like tendencies", settled in well. She felt more camaraderie among those young girls than among her colleagues in either Geneva or Blockley and enjoyed helping and mothering them. And she came to have enormous respect for some of the staff who were efficient and as hardworking as the students. She learned so much in her first three months that she realized she would be stupid to leave and ought instead to complete the course. So she decided to stay on. What also influenced her was the attitude of some of the staff who were helpful and interested in her (she was disgusted by the immorality of others) and encouraged her to believe she would make a good obstetric surgeon. One in particular, Hippolyte Blot, a young resident physician, went out of his way to assist her. Elizabeth described him in a letter home – "He colours, or passes his hand through his hair, and looks intently at the baby – in a very unfrenchmanlike manner – I think he must be very *young*, or much in awe of me, for he never ventures to give me a direct look and seems so troubled when I address him that I very rarely disturb his life that way."[33] But Blot asked her to give him English lessons; she agreed and they became quite close. He helped her study outside the prescribed curriculum and drew her attention to any interesting papers.

By November Elizabeth was being given more responsibility. On November 4th she got up early, after snatching a few hours' sleep at the end of a particularly exhausting day, and made her way along the cold corridors to the ward where she was to syringe a baby who had purulent ophthalmia. The light was poor, she was still sleepy, and as she injected warm water into the baby's tiny eye she was aware of her own clumsiness. What she thought was some of the water she was using spurted up into her own eyes as she bent over the baby. She dashed it out and went on with the job. By the afternoon she was uneasily admitting to herself that she had a prickling sensation in her right eye. By the evening there was no pretending – both eyes were visibly swollen and closed and even before she went to be examined she had no doubt that she had contracted the dreaded disease for which she had been treating the baby. Every possible treatment was instantly resorted to. Her eyelids were cauterized, leeches applied to her temples, her eyes syringed every hour with scrupulous care. M. Blot supervised her treatment himself, sitting at her side and every two hours, with fine pincers, peeling off the false membranes constantly forming over the globe of the eye. She lay for weeks in bed with both eyes closed, in an agony of apprehension, remembering the words of Dr Webster in Geneva – "Your fingers are useless without your eyes." After three weeks her left eye finally opened. She had a split second's clarity and then total blackness. She was blind in one eye and her vision was impaired in the other.

On November 26th she left La Maternité and went to convalesce in Anna's flat. In December, to her relief, her right eye was good enough to enable her to read and write. Her brother Sam wrote in his diary back home "Poor Elizabeth writes for the first time with her one eye. The physicians have no hope of saving the vision of the other. Elizabeth hopes we all still hope. She can distinguish the flame of a lamp as through thick mist and can discern something when the hand is passed across the eye. Her sense of the greatness of the loss is unspeakable . . ."[34]

The next six months were a nightmare. Pity, Elizabeth discovered, was destructive. Everyone pitied her. The cruelty of her affliction, for a brilliant young doctor who hoped to become a great surgeon, aroused an appalled pity in everyone who knew her. No one, not even the devoted M. Blot, knew what to say or how to console her. Worst of all, although she struggled against it, Elizabeth pitied herself. She did not mind the disfigurement ("I never had much beauty to boast of"[35] she wrote) but she could not bear to think her future as a surgeon was over. Pathetically, she toured Europe in the first months of 1850, trying to believe against all evidence that somewhere there was someone who could restore her sight. She tried cures, she tried exercises, she tried medicines, but eventually she had to face facts. She would never, ever see with one eye (which was finally removed) and would have impaired vision with the other. The oculist Desmarres had done as much as he could but was quite adamant that even her one remaining eye could never be perfect again. She could not be a surgeon. The realization that this had to be admitted brought her as near to collapse as she was ever to be. What had all her struggles been for if she was now forced to abandon medicine? She simply could not bear it and out of her misery and rage at the gross unfairness of it came a new determination. There was more to medicine than surgery. Why should she not turn now to general doctoring?

This is what she did. With superhuman courage she once more began seeking out people who would help her to complete a practical training as a doctor. Not only did she have her sex against her but she also had her disablement. A one-eyed woman was not exactly going to be a prime candidate for an arduous hospital training. But thanks to the endeavours of a cousin and the genuine sympathy her accident had awakened St Bartholomew's Hospital in London agreed to let her enter as a student. In October 1850 she returned to England to become a student for the third time. She took rooms at 28 Thavies Inn and walked every day to Bart's where she found her class of sixty "very gentlemany". James Paget's wife wrote of her "Well, we have our 'Lady Doctor' here at last and she has actually attended two of James' lectures, taking her seat with perfect composure . . . Her manners are quiet and it is evident her motives for the pursuit of so strange a vocation are pure and good."[36] Elizabeth was not only composed but happy. To her great pleasure she had at last discovered real friends – not at Bart's (although she was well-treated there) but among that small group of ladies who were at that time leading the embryo Woman's Rights movement in England. Barbara Leigh-Smith and Bessie Rayner Parkes both came to make themselves known to her and she was delighted to become part of a group. In many ways, it was the niche she had been looking for all her life and she was so comfortable in it that she thought seriously of staying in England and beginning work there. Unfortunately, she had no money and thought establishing a private practice in London, where there was much more prejudice against women than in America, would be beyond her means. Back home she had the support of her family and the comfort of knowing that already other women had been enrolled in medical colleges (although not in any of the leading ones). It would be wiser to return home, establish herself, make some money and then quickly return.

But there was no prospect of a speedy return. Elizabeth arrived in New York in August 1851 to discover she was not even allowed to put a plate up outside her door in spite of being so indisputably a hospital- as well as a college-trained doctor. Not only was the profession determined to keep her out but society itself seemed equally determined to join it. In her first year she had hardly any patients and her sister Emily wrote "her pecuniary poverty and dearth of patients weighed very heavily with her." Nobody trusted her, least of all the very sex she had trained to help. It was reported to her that ladies said to each other "Oh! It is too horrid! I'm sure I never could touch her hand! Only to think that those long fingers of hers had been cutting up dead people!"[37] Every day, as she went about the little business she had, she had to suffer this kind of ridiculous hostility. She was harassed in the streets if she went out on a case at night and had to put up with open jeering. She never thought of pretending not to care because she did care. "I am a woman as well as a physician,"[38] she wrote, and as a woman she was shocked and distressed by the slights and insults heaped upon her. "Poor E." wrote Emily, "I cannot bear to think of her lonely poverty stricken winter." But then, in the spring of 1852, Elizabeth's luck slowly began to turn thanks to her own efforts. She gave a series of lectures on what she called the *Laws of Life, with Special Reference to the Physical Education of Girls.* These were attended by some Quaker families who were so impressed by the good sense contained in them that they began to come to Elizabeth as patients. The lectures were in fact such a success that they were then collected and published and became Elizabeth's first major work available to the general public.

From a feminist point of view the *Laws of Life* was a curious publication. As far as Elizabeth was concerned the whole development of the female child was towards one goal: motherhood. Her message was that the reason why girls must take care of their bodies was to make them perfect vessels for motherhood. They must not treat them "Like the poor over-driven hacks in our omnibuses." In particular, girls must look after themselves at the onset of puberty, even delaying it if they could. She explained (erroneously) that "the physical education of the body, its perfectly healthy development, delays the period of puberty." Once puberty arrived and a girl became a woman and a potential mother there were four laws she ought to follow: she should exercise regularly, live in an orderly fashion, try to blend "the life of the soul and the body", and always put her body to proper use. "By the age of 16 or 17, under proper training, she will have acquired a strong, graceful and perfectly obedient body." The "proper use" of her body was now child-bearing. During pregnancy she should follow a régime of "regular habits, early hours, periodic exercise, cold bathing, plain wholesome food and loose comfortable clothing." Then followed a description of childbirth so romantic that it would call into serious doubt Elizabeth Blackwell's actual experience if this were not so well authenticated. "The mother," she wrote, "forgetful of weariness and suffering lifts her pale face from the pillow and listens with her whole soul . . . the mother's face lights up with ineffable joy as she sinks back exhausted and the sentiment of sympathy, of reverence, thrills through the physician's heart." This idea of the holiness of motherhood was expanded into something even more far-fetched in a letter she wrote at the time to Lady Noël Byron. "Women have hitherto been the mothers of men," she wrote, "but Woman must become the Mother of Man . . . collective womanhood must be acknowledged in every sphere of life."[39] It was almost as though, because she had deviated from the norm, Elizabeth Blackwell was determined to discourage others from doing so – as though she was afraid the norm was threatened and she herself was part of the threat therefore she must try to balance the harm she had done by idolizing this view of a woman's role.

But her philosophy proved acceptable to the Quakers and the turning point was reached. Early in 1853 Elizabeth was solvent and confident enough to open a small dispensary near Tompkins Square. She also borrowed money and bought a house on East 15th Street – a very good district in New York. Partly she wanted an address befitting her status but most of all she wanted to gather as many of her family as possible under one roof with her. Gradually, over the next three years, she made welcome her sisters Ellen and Marian; her brother Henry and his new wife Lucy Stone; her brother Sam and his new wife Antoinette Brown; and Maria Zakrzewska, a German woman who qualified as a doctor in America and came as a partner, and her sister. The last to arrive were Emily Blackwell, who had been following in Elizabeth's footsteps by gaining experience in Britain after qualifying in America, and little Kitty Barry, the orphan Elizabeth adopted in 1856.

The adoption of Kitty, aged seven, was Elizabeth Blackwell's indulgence to herself. She was thirty-five years old and had long ago renounced all thoughts of marriage. To this she was quite reconciled. But what she found hard to reconcile was being childless as well as husbandless. Her carnal desires, while acknowledging their existence, she could control and sublimate but her maternal ones were not so readily dealt with. She felt she must have somebody who was hers to love and be loved by. Her family were not enough. And so she began going down to Randall's Island, where four hundred orphans were housed, and looking for a child to be hers. She finally settled on Kitty Barry, whom everyone thought plain and stupid. Kitty described years later how a "very pleasant voiced lady" with gentle hands came up to her and asked her if she would like to be her little girl and come home with her. Kitty said yes but would the lady please wait until she had finished watching the sunset. Elizabeth waited, convinced she had made an excellent choice and that this very pale-faced, black-haired child was not "stupid". As soon as they reached East 15th Street, she told Kitty about her eye and explained about her artificial eye which she called her "toilet". "She never said 'Don't speak of it'" remembered Kitty, "but I never in all my life mentioned it to anyone . . ."[40]

Elizabeth's life took on a new dimension. Although she wrote that she was intending to train Kitty up to be "a valuable domestic" there was no doubt that she very quickly realized she was going to become something much more precious. "I feel full of hope and strength for the future," she wrote soon after the adoption. "Kitty plays beside me with her doll . . . Who will ever guess the restorative support which that poor little orphan has been to me?"[41] She sent Kitty to school – what Kitty referred to as "the crack school of the day" – and carried her there herself through the snow to keep her feet dry. Out of school they went on picnics together – "Aunt Elizabeth sat somewhere on a rock and read while I experimented with paddling among the rocks"[42] – and joined a gymnastic class together.

Kitty openly adored her benefactor and felt none of the unease the rest of the Blackwell family did about their relationship. The family did not deny it was a success, but they felt Elizabeth was too possessive and was not prepared to allow Kitty to develop independently. Kitty was all too clearly meant to fulfil two functions only – to be of practical assistance (she was put very early to doing the household bills) and to be a love-object. Any real existence of her own was ruled out. Elizabeth kept her to herself and did not help her to make friends of her own age. Apart from the family, there were others who saw the adoption as a confession of failure. Women were meant to be mothers, it was a perversion of nature to deny it, and this craving for a child proved it. Elizabeth, however, dared to suggest it proved something quite different – that society was wrong to expect self-realization in one sphere to go automatically with self-denial in another. By adopting Kitty, by agreeing her maternal instincts were thwarted, she was rejecting the theory of self-abnegation. She was saying that although self-sacrifice was necessary if a woman wished to have a career there was no need for it to be total. When it came to Kitty's turn to wish she had been a mother, Elizabeth promptly fostered a baby for her to look after. She took in an eight-month-old boy and kept him for five years because "I knew it would give you so much pleasure."[43] It was this attitude which helped to steer feminism away from the dangerous shoals of martyrdom on which, at that time, it could well have been wrecked. Never try to suppress your maternal instincts, Elizabeth Blackwell said, and provided a valuable example.

Meanwhile, Elizabeth's life was taking on a better (and a more feminist) shape in other ways. If she was happier in her domestic life now that she had Kitty she was also much happier professionally because she had been able to enlarge and open up her dispensary to a wider and more needy public. She moved her premises to a much poorer area, south of 14th Street along the East River, where her dispensary became the New York Dispensary for Sick Women and Children (although her home remained in East 15th Street as did her private consulting rooms). It was her intention that it should be a kind of hospital run for women by women but she was obliged for the time being to make use of the services of friendly male doctors. Her friends and family thought she was mad. They thought she ought to go on with private practice but Elizabeth scorned anything so tame. Private practice was deeply unsatisfactory and did not answer her need to retain that sense of mission with which she had begun. Every time a case became interesting in private practice she always had to end up calling in a male doctor to perform whatever complicated operation or treatment was needed and she was tired of it. Unless women ran a hospital and gained hospital experience they would always be looked on as inferior. "We must be able," she wrote, "to command all the exceptional and difficult cases."[44]

The work was hard but at least the patients came in droves and she found herself treating those very illnesses she had wanted to reach – menstrual disorders, pregnancy complications, sexual diseases, mammary tumours and abscesses, and prolapses of the uterus. She experimented with all kinds of treatments and began to amass a useful bank of knowledge on female problems. In May 1857, after a giant fund-raising campaign, she was able to move on to the next and most significant stage of expansion: the dispensary officially became an Infirmary. At 64 Bleecker Street the New York Infirmary for Indigent Women and Children was opened. Women served on the board of trustees, women were on the executive committee and the attending three physicians were all women – Elizabeth, Emily and Maria Zakrzewska. It was a moment of great triumph, followed at once by months of gruelling work. In the first six months 866 cases were treated, 48 as in-patients. In the next six months the numbers doubled and Elizabeth had to take on five new members of staff, all girls straight out of medical college. Emily, as the surgeon among them, was the star and Elizabeth had nothing but praise for her. But as the Infirmary consolidated its success she began to feel less indispensable and to plan a trip to England to raise more funds for even greater things. Part of the truth was also that she still missed the circle of friends she had made there. She never found equivalents for Bessie Rayner Parkes, Lady Noël Byron and Barbara Leigh-Smith. Barbara Leigh-Smith, now married to Edward Bodichon, came to see her in 1858 and together they discussed Elizabeth's return. One justification for it appealed to Elizabeth strongly: she could rally the women of England to enter medicine like the women of America.

On August 18th, 1858, Elizabeth once more set sail for England, accompanied this time by the excited Kitty. She was worried about taking Kitty but was even more worried that if she left her behind she might be unhappy. They had a very stormy passage and Kitty was "ignominiously seasick"; Elizabeth got her nose sunburned towards the end of the trip. At first, Kitty was no problem. She toured parts of England and Wales with Elizabeth and was thrilled by all she saw, but then Elizabeth had to go on to Paris to start trying to raise money in earnest and it was really not convenient to tag along a nine-year-old. So poor Kitty was sent to a boarding school in Surrey, vouched for by Barbara Bodichon. But even with this recommendation Elizabeth cared enough about Kitty, and was understanding enough of her position, to give her secretly three stamped addressed envelopes which, if there was anything wrong, Kitty could use to write to her. She told Kitty that if she had something confidential to say she should drop the envelopes into the village post-box, not the school's. This was what a miserable Kitty was eventually obliged to do after suffering several punishments for nothing. Elizabeth immediately had her removed and sent on to her in Paris where she placed Kitty in "a class of young Americans . . . supposed to be a kind of kindergarten".

Once she had secured a definite promise of money for use in America she returned with Kitty to England. Here, she had discussions with Florence Nightingale and also had her name put on the new British Medical Register. She lectured, too, on the principles of health, disease prevention and the advantages of opening the medical profession to women. The young Elizabeth Garrett attended one lecture. Afterwards Elizabeth Blackwell wrote to her sister Emily, "I saw a young lady who is quietly forming her determination . . . to study medicine . . . she consulted about the preliminary studies and will give this year to classics and chemistry."

The return to America, in August 1859, was something of an anticlimax. In England, Elizabeth Blackwell felt at the centre of things, she felt permanently excited by the possibilities in front of her, but in America she was restless and impatient. This was odd because she had achieved so much there. What seemed to be the trouble was that she was no longer in harmony with Emily, Maria and their small circle whereas she felt she was with her friends in England. Towards Emily in particular she had ambivalent feelings, admiring her skill as a surgeon but quite naturally feeling envious because she had been unable to realize her own ambition. Emily, in fact, was thinking of giving up medicine which placed the future of the Infirmary in jeopardy. However much she wanted to go and settle in England, Elizabeth could not in all conscience do it. She wrote to Barbara Bodichon explaining she felt she had to stay another three years in order to see the work she had started thoroughly completed, which it would not be until a Medical School for women was established as part of the Infirmary. "The fact is," she wrote, "that until women have a very large experience their consciousness will stand in their way and they will either be less reliable or more reliable physicians than men – for when the conscientiousness is properly supported by thorough culture and a very wide practical experience then they will become the better physicians – they will never I think stand on the same level. Now, it is our problem how to reach this higher level for let us once reach it and it will not be conquered only for ourselves."[45] The Infirmary was "indispensable" for this purpose. She explained what she meant to Barbara by describing most graphically a case that had happened the week before which normally, as still relatively inexperienced women, she and Emily would not have dealt with. ". . . We had a case of convulsions, high application of the forceps and perforation of the cranium – one of the most formidable complications of obstetric surgery. Now, in private practice, the case would have been instantly taken out of our hands but here our kind consulting surgeon stood by and I supported Emily with all my power and she had a grand experience accomplishing it all herself – and the woman is getting well."[46] Even if the patient had died Elizabeth thought one life worth the experience – "If we kill a few it does not matter," she maintained, "the authorities receive our certificates without question . . . and then we are really not as bad in the killing line as the male hospitals."[47] But the hospital was by no means established enough and she felt she simply could not leave while that obliging male surgeon was still necessary to supervise Emily and while others were not being trained on the premises to join her. "We have resolved," she wrote, "to make this a test winter." If the test was passed and the 50,000 dollars raised to start a training school in the hospital then she was going to urge "Miss Garrett or some other English girl" to come over.

By the spring of the following year, 1860, the "test winter" was safely over. A subscription list had been officially begun to endow a medical school, a house at 126 Second Avenue had been bought for use as a hospital and dispensary, and several student doctors had begun studying at the hospital as well as acting as assistants. In addition, a nurses' training programme had been established. The outbreak of the Civil War then diverted Elizabeth's plans. She naturally was anxious that women doctors should now show what they were made of and, of course, all her life-long sympathies were with the side of emancipation. A meeting was held at the Infirmary and Elizabeth became chairman of a Registration Committee responsible for all matters to do with training and despatching nurses to the war fronts. She was furious to discover that the United States Army was hostile to female nurses and doctors and wrote to Barbara Bodichon that "we soon found that jealousies were too intense for us to assume our true place."

Her contribution was not as great as she would have liked it to be but now, more than ever, she felt she could not abandon America, so she contented herself during the next seven years with only one quick trip to Europe. It took until 1868 before the Infirmary Medical School was opened and she felt free to leave it and to go home to England possibly for good. But she did not see her departure as in any way severing her connection with pioneer work. "I am coming," she wrote, "with one strong purpose in my mind of assisting in the establishing or opening of a thorough medical education for women in England."[48]

Elizabeth arrived in July 1869, determined to get properly settled before sending for Kitty. Unfortunately, she found it impossible to do any settling at all without Kitty. "You can help me so much," she wrote, "by taking charge of my things and telling me where they are; and reading and occasionally stitching for me and doing errands and keeping my rooms in first rate order and above all loving me very much."[49] Kitty arrived in August 1870 apparently flattered and not daunted by what was demanded of her. In fact, she did not like England very much. As well as trouble with her eyes (which had begun when she was ten) she had also grown increasingly deaf which prevented her making new friends with ease. She was shy and reserved by nature and used to taking a back seat so this deafness doubled her social handicap. Elizabeth did nothing to help her overcome it although she was always solicitous about Kitty's health and did her best to improve it. But she treated Kitty as a man would his wife. Kitty's role was to love, honour and obey without complaining – and Kitty never complained. Patiently she put up with all the moving about as Elizabeth searched for her ideal home. No sooner did she organize their household in Upper Norwood than they were back in Central London and then very soon in Swanage with trips to Europe in-between further to complicate domesticity. These trips were to benefit Elizabeth's health which, in her forties, showed signs of cracking. She began to suffer from continuous chills and fevers and alarming attacks of colic. Kitty wrote home to an American friend that she preferred being in France or Switzerland because London had little appeal. "I can't go to parties but that's no great loss . . . very often Aunt Bessie is out in the evening . . . in which case I am left alone . . . the evening is soon over and I go to bed . . . As I don't know anyone to visit in London I can't send you an account of anything very likely."[50] Luckily, Elizabeth had decided London was not for her anyway and began househunting on the south coast. It took her a long time to find what she wanted but in 1879 she and Kitty (and Marian) became "settled" at Rock House in the old section of Hastings. This became their home for the rest of Elizabeth's life.

But they were rarely in it for long. Elizabeth's career had taken a new direction which meant she was always rushing off to committees and meetings in a wide variety of places. Although she had worked hard at it she had not quite managed to achieve that position she desired as unchallenged leader of the movement to open up the medical profession for women in England. She was looked up to, of course, and consulted and involved in most plans and projects on the subject but she did not become an absolute authority. She did not practise medicine herself and was not at the centre of the agitation. Nor, slightly to her distress, did she find she occupied the social position she had anticipated. Barbara Bodichon and her circle were still her friends but they could not automatically give her the standing she sought. But with good sense she began enlarging her interests and embarked on a social reform programme which kept her as active and lively as she had always been. The power of women to do good still obsessed her and she decided that she ought to set down all her ideas on the subject in a book. This became *Counsel to Parents on the Moral Education of their Children* which finally appeared in 1879. She wrote it, with some excitement at her own daring, during one of the continental tours she made for her health with Kitty. Kitty was, for once, indignant that she was not allowed to read what Auntie was writing because she was unmarried.

In fact, *Counsel to Parents*, in spite of Elizabeth's claims, was not exactly thought explosive even at the time, although she went on maintaining it was. True, several London publishers declined to print it on the grounds (according to Elizabeth) that it was too outrageous but sister Emily when she read it could not see what all the fuss had been about. Emily thought it a bit dull and certainly tame enough to read aloud in mixed company. She commented tellingly, "It is simply a plea for purity in life in both sexes." It was slightly more than that. According to *Counsel to Parents* sexual activity began at too early an age and this damaged moral development. "This life of sensation will . . . obtain a complete mastery . . . if Reason does not exist and grow into a controlling force." So it must be curbed. But remembering her own "life of sensation" Elizabeth wrote emphatically that girls as well as boys had "a natural passion" and that there must be a single standard of sexual morality for both. She scorned the prevailing doctrine that ladies did not experience sexual sensations and stressed that mothers should develop and not try to halt the sexual instinct in their offspring. Sex, she emphasized, was noble and should be venerated, not turned away from in disgust. But in spite of striking this blow for feminism *Counsel to Parents* was extremely vague and unhelpful as to how mothers were meant to carry out the author's instructions. Elizabeth seemed to imagine that she had fulfilled a promise to Lady Byron that, where sex was concerned, "mothers' . . . attention should be firmly grasped and facts laid before them which could not be forgotten."[51] She was delighted when it was favourably reviewed and felt that her ideas would now permeate throughout society as she had always wanted them to.

She had begun to further her aims in another way too. Realizing that unless the very grassroots of society were reached social reform through the action of mothers would never happen she had begun, in 1871, a National Health Society. This focused on her passion for hygiene and sanitary care which she wanted to spread throughout the land. A phrase was coined – "Prevention is Better than Cure" – which it was hoped would help to combat bad living-conditions in poorer homes. Always ambitious, its founder saw the society opening branches all over the country and officers of the society visiting them to lecture mothers on how to keep a clean home. Eventually, though this target was not reached, Elizabeth had the satisfaction of seeing the society inhabit headquarters in Berners Street and functioning without the need of her personal energies. These were greatly stretched in the next decade. Kitty became quite concerned at the amount of work Auntie took upon herself with such zeal. "She has been elected on the Council of the National Vigilance and also on its Parliamentary sub-committee . . . she also has the Branch of the National Vigilance here to look after. Just now the question of Poor Law Guardians is up – they want Auntie to stand . . ."[52] It seemed that the single-mindedness of Elizabeth's early days had gone – she jumped from one topic to another so that Kitty was dizzy trying to keep up. And yet, throughout all this feverish activity, there was a certain consistency of outlook. Elizabeth's views on society hardly changed at all. She was still emphatic that a woman's influence was pure, that her role was maternal. Over and over again, in different guises, she stressed that those qualities most natural to women were "tenderness, sympathy, guardianship." And yet, at the same time, she rejected woman's subservience to the male. Women were much more important than men and potentially much more powerful. It was a potential she wished them to fulfil.

The remaining decades of Elizabeth's long life were filled with an extraordinary mixture of causes, all taken up and applied to with tremendous enthusiasm. Christian Science, spiritualism, anti-vivisectionism, rabies treatment and psychology all at one time or another dominated her thoughts. She also took a strong interest in local Hastings politics and in co-operative farming, not to mention agriculture as a career for women. Continental travel took up a lot of her time, very pleasantly, and so did supervising Anna who continued to live outside Paris and became increasingly eccentric. Anna had become convinced she knew where the lost treasure of King James II of England was buried and was always trying to dig it up (she also thought the startled Kitty was the reincarnation of Captain Kidd). But in spite of all this hectic activity Elizabeth began at last to have intimations of mortality in her eightieth year. She found, to her annoyance, that walking to the top of the hill on which Rock House was situated exhausted her. In 1907, aged eighty-six, she had a fall which confined her to bed, and in 1910 a stroke. Kitty, aged sixty-two struggled to make her comfortable but Elizabeth was paralysed and unable to speak. On May 31st, six days after the stroke, Elizabeth Blackwell died. She was buried at Kilmun in Scotland, a place she and Kitty had visited on holiday and to which she had been greatly attracted. Kitty returned to America in 1920 and died in 1936. Very near the end Kitty quoted Tennyson's lines –

> "O that 'twere possible
> After long grief and pain
> To find the arms of my true love
> Round me once again."

And she explained that by her true love she meant Dr Elizabeth.[53] Her ashes were sent to Kilmun and placed in the same grave with Elizabeth Blackwell.

★   ★   ★

The diaries and letters of the late eighteenth and of the nineteenth century are filled to capacity with the frustration the female sex felt at their lack of options. There seemed so little choice and what choice there was seemed so narrow. The woman who was satisfied with her lot was fortunate and exceedingly rare. Even if allowance is made for the fact that discontent finds its way quicker to the page than contentment, the evidence is still overwhelming: women felt confined and trapped by their destiny. The happy wives and mothers whose self-fulfilment lay in domesticity anyway were lucky, but even then luck was not always with them. They too experienced *ennui* and exhaustion faced with the unrelenting nature of their daily timetable, which is why so many of them turned to "good works" to give some other meaning to their lives. But for a great mass of women "good works" did not provide an answer. Doing good to the poor only emphasized their own uselessness. What they wanted, as Elizabeth Blackwell wanted, was "something hard", some "hard challenge", something structured and disciplined to which they could apply themselves. This is what entry into the professions gave them.

The important point for feminism about this entry was how it was done. There was nothing, before Elizabeth Blackwell, to stop any woman from practising as an unqualified doctor. Harriot K. Hunt started practising medicine at the age of thirty in Boston in 1835 after trying repeatedly to get into Harvard Medical School. She studied on her own and gained some experience from accompanying friendly male doctors and then she set herself up in practice in spite of her lack of formal training. She was remarkably successful and built up a good practice of female patients and their children but the fact that, even as late as 1847, she was still re-applying to Harvard showed that she was under no illusions about her status. She was one of a few isolated examples who would always be regarded as freaks however successful they were. They were the exceptions who served simply to keep the rules rigid. The point about Elizabeth Blackwell's career was that it proved there was no justification for regarding women doctors as freaks. Clearly, after her, it could no longer be argued that no woman could survive a medical training or pass through examinations and practical tests. The minute she had breached the wall of prejudice there were scores, literally, of others who were ready to follow her and the infuriating thing was that these others all seemed to possess Miss Blackwell's own determination and ability. From the beginning, the women did spectacularly well and more than kept up with their male counterparts. Any girl entering on a medical career was (and still is) a choice candidate but even so the authorities were genuinely startled at the way they swept the board in examination after examination. It was this sort of outrageous success which made the male medical profession so hostile. The women dared to lack humility, that was the trouble. And this in turn presented feminism with a new problem.

In England, the problem was particularly acute. Although Elizabeth Blackwell herself had registered with the General Council of Medical Education and Registration in 1858 no other British woman could do so because from 1860 the rules were changed: now no one without an *English* medical degree could register and this was impossible because the English universities still excluded women from admission. Elizabeth Garrett, whom Elizabeth Blackwell had inspired, only obtained a licence to practice (in 1865) by qualifying for the diploma of the Apothecaries Society and then had to obtain her degree in Paris. The battle had to be fought and won, by Sophia Jex-Blake, all over again. It was not until 1876, after the parliamentary bill permitted universities to grant women degrees that the teaching hospitals were persuaded to accept women students. The unpleasant truth was that the male sex as a body had been proved to be unscrupulous. They did not hesitate to change their arguments as soon as they were convincingly demolished, and this became a problem for all feminists. Cunning was shown to be vital if women were to be admitted to every profession – it was simply naïve to imagine that once the male authorities saw women *could* follow the men successfully then they would concede they had been wrong to bar them. On the contrary, they would not admit it proved anything of the sort and instantly sought other ways to keep women out. What women learned in this first battle of the professions was that success could be fatal. It was better to proceed softly, softly, than to aim a knockout blow.

This took some doing. Women of the calibre and with the temperament of Elizabeth Blackwell were not good at such a technique. It was humiliating. There were many women who argued that this should not have to be put up with, that men should not be allowed to humiliate them – why bother with their exams and tests and degrees, why not set up their own branches of the professions? But Elizabeth Blackwell knew this would be disastrous. Women wanted to be doctors not something different called a woman doctor. What kind of species would that be? No one would know, nor would the vast majority wish to find out. It was not just pride which made her want to follow the same medical course as men but that visionary sense with which all the early feminists were touched. She thought all the time of the future, and of this future for the whole of society. Nothing was done for herself alone, to remedy her own dissatisfaction. What she did she did because she felt there was something out of joint in society and she wished to put it right, and in particular put it right through women entering medicine.

She only partially succeeded in her wider aim. In 1889, in a lecture,[54] she said that in recognizing "the failure of so many panaceas for the intolerable evils that afflict society" she, like everyone else, longed for "the untried force – the action and co-operation of good women." Women, she maintained, were waking up to this truth in ever-increasing numbers – "women are . . . rising above the errors of the past and blind acceptance of imperfect authority." They were entering medicine in great numbers (3,000 registered doctors in America, 73 in Britain when she spoke) and would soon be capable of revolutionizing society through the practice of medicine. She directed their attention to midwifery, to preventive medicine, to chronic illness and to the treatment of the poor – all areas where their influence was not only most needed but could be most powerful. She reminded them that Love, Intelligence and Will were as important as knowledge. "It will be a real service that we, as medical women, may render to the profession if we search out – calmly, patiently but resolutely – why what revolts our enlightened sense of right and wrong is not true." Aware that this might sound vague and high-minded, she then gave some specific advice which irritated some of her audience. She announced that the true future of women must be as family physicians and *not* as specialists. She did not want to see them "rushing to exciting operations" but studying the common diseases where they began. She thought it their "special duty" to "thoroughly master measles" and worried that they were not valuing obstetrics enough because in that field they could gain a mother's confidence for the future. Women were not, in short, to become doctors to satisfy any cravings of their own but to do good, to fight in a moral crusade.

This undoubtedly carried feminism forward but at a price. It was an improvement on Caroline Norton's initial brand of feminism, on the claim that all that women wanted was the protection of men, safeguarded and enshrined in law. But the moral obligations of Elizabeth Blackwell's feminism, although more attractive initially, were just as perilous for the future, as women soon found out. Many of them did not wish to be crusaders any more than men did. This was reflected in medicine itself. Elizabeth Blackwell got her wish about women mainly becoming family physicians but they did not follow her directions as to what those who specialized should specialize in. Today, almost one hundred years after she gave this order, the biggest specialist area in which women have gone to the top and become consultants is anaesthetics followed by radiology with obstetrics well down the list. Women, in fact, have not been attracted to those areas which Elizabeth Blackwell thought cried out for them: they are outnumbered 8 to 1 in gynaecology and obstetrics by men. (Ironic, when it is remembered why women were moved to enter medicine in the first place.) Nor have they entered medicine in the droves she so confidently envisaged. In 1980–1 the number of women admitted to the medical curriculum throughout Britain was 1,580, the number of men 2,328. In the same year, the percentage of women consultants was 11.4 of the total.[55] Clearly, although progress has been steady, it has not followed the path she predicted nor soared to the heights she expected.

The answer to the question of why women have not taken over the medical profession and used it to embark on a moral crusade is of great interest to feminist historians. It is twofold. On the one hand it seems to be true that medicine requires a degree of commitment incompatible with other demands upon women. The training is long, arduous and at some stages barbarous. Women in their twenties find it unacceptable to shut themselves off from child-bearing and this is effectively what anyone ambitious in medicine has to be prepared to do – either that or proceed in a series of disruptive bursts almost impossible to organize. It can, of course, be done but never easily, not if the final aim is a consultancy (nor is it easy for men but the additional handicaps for women must at least be acknowledged). The single woman may still do it but most women are not single and spinsterhood ought not to be a prerequisite for becoming a consultant.

On the other hand, it is also true that women appear to have rejected the "moral crusade" notion. There are no measurable signs that the entry of women into the medical profession has significantly humanized it. No broad changes exist for the better which are the result of female medical action. Once women become doctors they become as one with the men, as a body, whatever individual capacities they retain for different action. This is, of course, desirable. Elizabeth Blackwell, after all, wanted women to become doctors not women doctors. But at the same time it would have been curiously disappointing to her, she would have seen it as some sort of failure, and in feminist history that is what it has come to be.

Yet the entry of women into the medical profession signposted a wonderful new direction for all women to take if they wished hard enough. "Attractive industry," wrote Elizabeth Blackwell to Lady Noël Byron, " . . . can alone render every individual happy . . . I know that a Life of *Duty* is not a life of happiness."[56] For all those to whom sewing and housekeeping and child-rearing was not attractive, to whom dabbling in painting and piano playing and learning conversational French was not industry, Elizabeth Blackwell provided an alternative. Women, her own life said, can be *anything* and not lose their femininity in the process. That great fear – that trying to enter man's spheres might either be beyond woman's scope or else make her masculine in the process – was laid to rest.

EMPLOYMENT

Florence Nightingale
(BBC Hulton Picture Library)

Florence Nightingale
1820–1910

The most important point about the opening up of medicine as a profession for women was that it gave them high aspirations as well as emphasizing their equal right to such a career. But nobody, least of all the pioneer women doctors themselves, ever imagined that the entire female sex, or even very large numbers of that sex, would actually avail themselves of the opportunities now before them. It was recognized that there would not be an overwhelming majority of women who would in the first place be clever enough and in the second dedicated enough. Nor was this necessarily regretted. Elizabeth Blackwell, with her passionate convictions about motherhood as a woman's highest calling, was echoed by countless others. It was absurd to pretend that the so-called "choice" was a real one for all but a minority of fortunate women. What, then, of the rest? There were millions who felt just as frustrated with their lot as Elizabeth Blackwell had done but who could not begin to contemplate becoming doctors. Their desire to work might be just as consuming as hers but it was unthinkable for them to follow a path like that taken by Miss Blackwell. They might be, apart from any other considerations, simply lacking in her massive energy and single-mindedness. What was needed was some other "profession" which would not only be less academically difficult but also more accessible. Nursing was the first of the mass-market professions for women to answer these requirements, and it was Florence Nightingale who established it as such.

Florence Nightingale was Elizabeth Blackwell's exact contemporary and she began, so far as feminism is considered, from a remarkably similar standpoint. But there was, from the beginning of her work, a crucial difference. Florence Nightingale rejected absolutely any suggestion that women should enter men's spheres and compete to be as good as they were. What she wanted was for women to make a new sphere for themselves and to keep it for themselves. Therefore she was not interested in women becoming doctors and would do nothing to help them along. Although she was at first friendly towards Elizabeth Blackwell she nevertheless sneered at her in private and said she had "only tried to be a man," which was of course grossly untrue. (She also accused the world's first woman doctor of rating little higher than "a third rate apothecary of thirty years ago.") It irritated her profoundly that women like Elizabeth Blackwell were breaking into new territory when she herself saw so much to be done in the old. This greed to break into a man's world was, she thought, plain stupid. It filled her with disgust to see so much written about "woman's work" – "the enormous Jaw, the infinite ink which England pours forth . . ."[1] There was no "want of a field" for women in her opinion – the field was right there under women's feet and they could not even see it. What they ought to be doing was getting down to the existing work all around them for the asking instead of complaining men would not let them do *their* work. "The more chattering and noise there is about Woman's Mission," she wrote furiously, "the less efficient women we can find. It makes me mad to hear people talk about unemployed women. If they are unemployed it is because they won't work. The highest salaries given to women at all we can secure to women trained by us. But we can't find the women. They won't come."[2]

It sounded like contempt for her own sex and a definite anti-feminist approach, which is how it has been interpreted ever since. The famous statement "I am brutally indifferent to the wrongs or the rights of my sex"[3] appears quite straightforward and indisputable and so does Florence Nightingale's equally famous refusal to become a member of the first Committee of the London National Society for Women's Suffrage when asked by John Stuart Mill. But these comments have been removed from their context. They amounted to flashes of anger on Florence Nightingale's part and masked a feminism far more real and deeper than that of many of the Woman's Rights supporters. In fact she explained fully to John Stuart Mill exactly what she *did* mean in her letter declining to join the committee. "I can't tell you," she wrote to him on August 11th, 1867, "how much pleased I was nor how grateful I feel that you should take the trouble to write to me . . . That woman should have the suffrage I think no one can be more deeply convinced than I. It is so important for a woman to be a '*person*' as you say. And I think I see this most strongly in married life. If the woman is not a person it does almost infinite harm even to her husband. And the harm is greatest when the man is a very clever man and the woman a very clever woman."[4] What held her back from lending her name, then, was not any anti-feminist belief " . . . It will be years before you obtain the suffrage for women," she went on, "and in the meantime there are evils which press so much more hardly on women than the want of the suffrage." She was worried that fighting for the vote would actually "retard still further the legislation which is necessary" to give women other rights which the existing legislature might otherwise be willing to grant them. She said she suggested this "humbly" and was "afraid you will laugh at me". Far from being "brutally indifferent" to her sex she wrote that, as a matron, she was horribly aware of how hard poor married women in particular were pressed upon. "Till a married woman can be in possession of her own property there can be no love or justice,"[5] she wrote and in case there should be the slightest misunderstanding as to her position she emphasized "woman's political power should be direct and open not indirect."[6] Her refusal, therefore, was based on practical considerations and not on any essential difference in principle. And both John Stuart Mill and the zealous Harriet Martineau were at pains to reply that they fully understood her point of view – far from being anti-feminist it was (in its day) perfectly tenable.

What Florence Nightingale thought she had done was spotted a trap. "I would earnestly ask my sisters," she wrote "to keep clear of both jargons now currently everywhere (for they *are* equally jargons); of the jargon, namely, of the 'rights' of women, which urges women to do all that men do, including the medical and other professions, merely because men do it and without regard to whether this *is* the best women can do; and of the jargon that urges women to do nothing that men do, merely because they are women, and 'should be recalled to their sense of duty as woman' and because 'this is women's work' and 'this is men's' and 'these are things women should not do' which is an assertion and nothing more. Surely woman should bring the best she has *whatever* it is to the work of God's world without attending to either of these cries . . . You do not want the effect of your good things to be 'How wonderful for a woman!' nor would you be deterred from good things by hearing it said 'Yes but she ought not to have done this because it is not suitable for a woman.' "[7] Any woman who held back from doing work she was equipped to do because she thought it might not be ladylike ought to be "burnt alive".

This was a very peculiar feminist stance but it had tremendous appeal and was far more attractive, to men as well as women, because it seemed less revolutionary. Once Florence Nightingale had made nursing respectable, and made payment for it just as respectable, it seemed the ideal solution for all those legions of unemployed women. If anything, it reinforced the Victorian idea of femininity. A Nightingale nurse, in her starched and spotless uniform, working in one of the new hospitals in an atmosphere of order and discipline, really did appear an angel. If letting women out of the home to work for money meant *this*, where was the harm? None. The harm lay in the demand for martyrs. What Florence Nightingale wanted was for women to give up the "soft option" of motherhood and marriage. She wanted them to choose work instead. She wanted them to realize that work could be even more fulfilling than a husband and children. When they refused to do so in the numbers she had imagined she was disappointed and furious. "My doctrines have taken no hold among women," she wrote bitterly. "Not one of my Crimean following learnt anything from me . . . or gave herself for one moment after she came home to carry out the lesson of that war."[8] She despised her sex for being obsessed with romantic love. "Women crave *for being loved* . . . they scream at you for sympathy all day long, they are incapable of doing anything in return . . . People say to me 'you don't know what a wife and mother feels.' No, I say, I don't and I am very glad I don't. And *they* don't know what *I* feel . . . I am sick with indignation at what wives and mothers will do of the most egregious selfishness. And people call it all maternal or conjugal affection and think it pretty to say so."[9] She did not think it pretty. She thought it cowardly, and through nursing she presented women with what she wanted them to see as a much more fulfilling life. The way in which she did this makes her, ironically, a feminist extremist, far more radical than Elizabeth Blackwell and far more significant in feminist history.

★ ★ ★

Florence Nightingale spent thirty-two years trying to conform to the feminine stereotype of her day. She was born on May 12th, in Florence (hence the name), to Frances and William Nightingale who were still on their two-year protracted honeymoon. (Their first daughter, Parthenope, had been born the previous year in Naples.) Shortly after Florence's birth the couple returned home to Lea Hurst, their country-home in Derbyshire and took up the threads of their extremely comfortable existence. William Nightingale, although not out-rageously rich, had inherited his estate while still a minor and when a lead mine was discovered on it the income from this was wisely invested for him. He could afford to be lazy, which he was, and to indulge his taste in good books, which he did. His wife Fanny, six years his senior, had "never thought of anything all day long" but her own pleasure. She intended to continue doing so. When the Nighting-ale house at Lea Hurst proved not as pleasurable to live and entertain in as she wished, she persuaded her husband to buy Embley Park, near Romsey in Hampshire, which was in a much more attractive area where Fanny's two married sisters lived. So the pattern of Florence's childhood was set: summer in Derbyshire, the rest of the year in Hampshire, and two annual visits to London.

There were no more children which both Fanny and William regretted, not just because the estate needed a son to secure the inheritance, but because they loved children. But with so many relatives near them (Florence had twenty-seven cousins before she was fourteen) the house never felt empty. Neither Florence nor Parthe could ever have felt lonely. They appeared to lead an enviable exist-ence in a beautiful home with loving parents, surrounded with every kind of comfort and pleasure. Yet by the age of six, Florence recorded, she had decided her way of life was "distasteful". She feared she was a monster, not like other children and unable to act as they did. She hated being sociable which made things difficult in her mother's extremely sociable house. Florence hid and moped and irritated Fanny by being "unreasonable". Parthe, on the other hand, was the daughter Fanny wanted except that she was not as pretty as Florence nor as intelligent. It was Florence, in fact, who had it within her to be the credit to the family that Fanny wished for. It was Florence who could undoubtedly shine in society should she choose to do so. But she did not choose to do so. She was awkward and attached herself to her father instead of her mother. To her mother's horror, she began to show a marked preference for the library rather than the drawing-room. William Nightingale was delighted by this. He may have turned himself after his Cambridge days into a model country gentleman but he was still well-read and passionately interested in all the topics of the day. It gave him such pleasure to talk with both his daughters, but particularly with Florence, that he decided in 1832 when they were thirteen and twelve to continue their education himself. A governess was engaged for accomplishments – music and drawing – but he himself took on the real work. And it was "real work". The syllabus included Greek, Latin, German, French and Italian as well as history and philosophy. Every day the girls and their papa proceeded to the library to work to a strict timetable, leaving Fanny to her entertaining, and every day the work became more exacting. Very few girls indeed were ever privileged enough to obtain quite such a complete education. Florence appreciated it but Parthe quickly found it unbearably hard and began to trail behind. Fanny defended her against such a monstrous *unfeminine* régime and very soon Parthe was dropping lessons to help her mother do vital jobs like put new flowers in the vases.

Florence, left alone more and more with her father, was in her element. For four years she was utterly content to learn what her father taught her and revelled in becoming his intellectual companion. But of course her father, no more than her mother, had never for one moment intended that this fine education Florence was receiving should actually lead anywhere. Indeed, where could it lead? The whole object was simply to make her cultured without in the least planning anything else. It was an end in itself. This was laudable but, as far as Florence was concerned, also cruel. Unlike her father she was not lazy. She had inherited his intelligence but her sense of purpose and will-power were her own. At sixteen what she most wanted was to put her education to some use, the very thing denied to her. Instead, the whole family set off on a European Tour when Florence was seventeen (in 1837). This seemed at first the perfect solution to her growing restlessness and she even pleased her mother by developing a passion for dancing. She was the belle of balls in Genoa, Pisa, Florence and Geneva. She was admired for her looks and vivacity wherever she went and recorded in one of her "private notes" to herself that she enjoyed the admiration and must subdue this base desire to shine in society. The only kind of society she wished genuinely to shine in was the intellectual variety and her chance came when the family stopped off in Paris on the way home. Here Florence met Mary Clarke, the friend (and later wife) of Julius Mohl, a distinguished Oriental scholar. Mary had many such friends and Florence was entranced by her company. She was unconventional and yet accepted by the best society and she lived a kind of life quite different from anything Florence had come across. She gave the young, impressionable Florence a glimpse of what life might be like among stimulating companions who appeared to make no distinction between a man and a woman in all matters that were important. Women, in Mary Clarke's circle, seemed equal, so far as Florence could see.

But once back home Florence realized that for her Mary Clarke's life was a mirage. Her own life could not come near it. In April 1839, just before she was nineteen, Florence was presented at court and began her first London season. Once more she was dancing at balls, once more excelling in this worthless way. The whole summer was spent cavorting and then came autumn and the day of reckoning. For the first time it was forced upon Florence that her whole future was decided for her. Her education was over, her "duties" had commenced – "faddling twaddling and the endless tweedling of nosegays in jugs" as Mary Clarke put it to her. She was filled with a raging discontent all the harder to bear because so far as she could see no other woman seemed to feel it. "Look at the poor lives we lead," she wrote years later when she had had even more experience of life at home for an unmarried woman. "It is a wonder that we are so good as we are, not that we are so bad."[10] And yet no one seemed to agree. She looked around her and was bound to conclude that if other women felt what she felt they hid it very well. They even seemed to connive at their own imprisonment. She hated the way women told each other to "come in any morning you please" as though nothing could possibly be more important than a tête-à-tête. This, in fact, was the real puzzle: women did nothing at all of importance and yet they were always busy. She found that her own "duties" left her with no time at all to herself and yet what did these inescapable duties amount to? Sorting out the china cupboard, picking and arranging flowers, sewing useless ornamental articles, going on visits and worst of all talking, talking, talking but never ever *saying* anything. "Why is it more ridiculous," she asked, "for a man than for a woman to do worsted work and drive out every day in a carriage? Why should we laugh if we were to see a parcel of men sitting around a drawing-room table in the morning and think it all right if they were women?"[11] But nobody else seemed to agree with her (except Mary Clarke who was a long way away). "I like riding about this beautiful place, why don't you?" her contemporaries in Hampshire said to her. "I like walking about the garden, why don't you?"[12] *Why* didn't she? She herself did not know. She tried desperately to conform but could not still the raging frustration inside. Gradually, she grew tired of trying. If she was discontented, so be it – better to acknowledge the discontent, better perhaps to start regarding it as a privilege, as meaning she was clear-sighted when others were not. It occurred to her that Jesus Christ, if he had been a woman "might have been nothing but a great complainer."[13]

Faced with this truth which she had divined – that her problem was that she was a woman – Florence tried hard to come to terms with it. It was her misfortune to belong to a highly conventional family and her further misfortune to love them too much to hurt them by outright rebellion. There was never much hope that she would be able to convert either her mother or her sister to her point of view but she continued to try to engage her father's sympathies. He, at least, did not think her peculiar for not wanting to fritter her time away, but on the other hand he did not see why she could not be content with private study – why was anything else necessary? Florence tried to explain her feelings of claustrophobia and uselessness but her father, encouraged by her mother, persisted in misunderstanding her. He thought her restlessness only a phase which would pass, especially when she married. But the thought of marriage made Florence despair even more. Marriage was worse than spinsterhood. Upon marriage, a woman took on a man's way of life and was even more securely trapped. The idea of marriage bringing self-fulfilment made her laugh – "The intercourse of man and woman – how frivolous" she wrote, "how unworthy it is! Can we call *that* the true vocation of woman, her high career?"[14] Marriage, on the contrary, was something to be strongly resisted.

But if she ruled out marriage there had to be some other alternative to her stifling existence. At first Florence thought satisfaction might come through a different kind of study. She went to stay with her Aunt Mai, her father's younger sister, and from her house wrote asking permission to study mathematics because this was a disciplined, hard subject. She had begun on her own but quickly discovered she could not get far without lessons and for those she needed a teacher and for that she needed permission. It was refused. Her father was a little troubled at this refusal but her mother had no doubts – it was quite absurd for a girl to devote herself to mathematics. Florence was resigned. The idea of pursuing a proper course of study was abandoned. Instead, she turned to the only other "work" available –

charitable work. There was a ban on a studious daughter but none on a philanthropic one. That was quite in order, gratifyingly charming in fact. She began leaving the big houses where she lived or stayed with relatives and visiting the cottages on the estates. She became conscious, in her early twenties, of the awful sufferings outside her own privileged sphere and the knowledge appalled her. What she saw on her charitable visits was harrowing – "my mind is absorbed with the idea of the sufferings of man"[15] – but far from putting her off it only increased her interest. From visiting she made tentative steps towards helping. She not only took food on her visits but stopped to perform small, obvious acts of the most basic nursing. This pleased her. She felt involved, not totally an observer. It began to occur to her that here was "work" and at the same time that if it was work it had to be learned properly to be done properly. Yet she had no idea how to go about learning to nurse. She knew no nurses. They hardly existed outside convents and those store houses for the sick called hospitals which no woman of her rank ever entered. She asked the advice of an American philanthropist visiting the family – "Do you think it would be unsuitable and unbecoming for a young English girl to devote herself to works of charity in hospitals and elsewhere as Catholic sisters do?" He said he thought not, which encouraged her and gave her hope. "I dug after my little plan in silence,"[16] she recorded.

But however hard she dug she always had grave misgivings. She knew perfectly well that charitable visits were one thing but training another. Training would introduce a stigma. And so she began to employ a certain degree of conscious cunning. Realizing that the emotive words were "training", "nursing", "hospitals" Florence avoided them. She began to make a speciality of volunteering to look after sick relatives and in the process both escaped from home and gained a sort of training through experience. This pleased her mother – how kind of dear Flo to go and look after her ill granny or aunt – and was acceptable to her father although he missed her company. For a while it even satisfied Florence herself, although never completely, but inevitably she reached the stage when she saw she was simply learning the same things over and over again and that all the time the skill needed to alleviate suffering efficiently was not hers. She needed to know more than how to soothe a fevered brow – she needed to know how to treat the fever itself.

In 1844, when she was twenty-four, she resolved to ask permission to go for three months into Salisbury Infirmary to study nursing and become as trained as it was then possible to be. The resulting scenes were even worse than she had thought they would be. Her mother and sister became hysterical and even her father called her "spoiled" and "ungrateful". The mere thought of Salisbury Infirmary gave Fanny Nightingale convulsions. Florence could only want to go there, she said, because she must have "an attachment with some low, vulgar surgeon." Her request was not just a personal insult but socially quite offensive. Nurses were drawn from the domestic-servant class and the taint of that class could not be overlooked. Faced with this vehement hostility, Florence at once gave in. She never once thought of defying her family and going ahead with her plan. If they could not be persuaded she must give in and carry on as before, hoping that one day she would convert them.

The strain of doing this was tremendous and led her to a nervous breakdown. Instead of seeing that it was having her ambitions thwarted which had precipitated ill-health her parents believed it was having such ambitions at all. Until Flo got them out of her head, they concluded, she would never be well and "normal". Hoping that a change would help to distract her, they let her go to Rome with some relatives to convalesce. Unfortunately for them, Florence met Sidney Herbert (then Secretary to the Admiralty) in Rome and was immediately drawn into an intellectual companionship with him which made her more determined than ever to do something with her life. Once back home, she made other friends through Sidney Herbert all of whom were interested, as she was, in the conditions of the poor and in hospital reform. Since these friends were all impeccably well-connected the Nightingales had no idea how Florence's ambitions were being stimulated. Nor had they any idea that she was getting up before dawn to study Blue Books, those Government reports on social conditions which formed the basis for all reforms. It was her way of preparing herself, of making sure that she was well-informed about this subject which so troubled her. She could only manage to get through the monotonous days being the perfect dutiful daughter if meanwhile she could occupy her mind with something more demanding.

The Blue Books were certainly demanding. One of the first Florence obtained was the 1840 report from the Select Committee on the Health of Towns and it is a good example of exactly what she taught herself to grapple with. It consisted of twenty pages of summary followed by two hundred and twenty-two pages containing the three thousand five hundred and twenty-two questions (with answers) asked by the inspectors. Florence read the statistics on population returns, on mortality rates, on fever rates. She absorbed details on the condition of Liverpool, where, she read, 7,800 cellars were inhabited by 39,000 people. "These melancholy details . . . can scarcely be read without shuddering . . ." said the report but Florence wanted to read them because she wanted to be in possession of the facts. She did not flinch from reading how "excrementitious matter" was mixed with water and poured straight into the gutters; how "the putrid effluvia" arising from dead bodies made grave-diggers ill; how the people of Bethnal Green lived "perfectly in the condition of the wigwams of the vilest savages." She studied maps of back-to-back houses and of the position of privies. She read how children were killed through lack of proper sewerage provisions. Nothing was spared in this report. She read that one child died in Drury Lane of gangrene of the mouth contracted from the disgusting filth in his home. The gangrene "successively destroyed the whole of the roof of the mouth, perforating the palate bones and eventually opening a communication between the mouth and the nose by the mortification of all the intervening parts. The nose was next attacked and removed; the upper lip, detached from its adhesion to the jaw fell down . . ." It was the kind of thing no lady was supposed to know about, the kind of hideous detail guaranteed to produce a faint. But Florence did not faint. She read on and on, challenging as she did so the whole concept of what a lady should or should not be told. Then when she had finished she got dressed, went downstairs in her silk dress, breakfasted with her family in the beautiful Embley morning room and began her day of "duties" without once betraying the turmoil in her mind.

By the time she entered her thirtieth year, in 1849, Florence had become an expert on Government Social Statistics. Her opinion was sought by Sidney Herbert and his friends and she was pleased to give it. Such meetings with like-minded people were the only occasions upon which she felt truly in control. Otherwise, she felt she was going mad. Far from gradually winning her family over to agreeing to let her nurse she had antagonized them by clinging to the idea. Her father called her "theatrical" and her mother, who longed to have her married, called her "wilful". What was even harder to bear was the knowledge that marriage, which would make them all happy, now actually tempted her.

She had met a man, Richard Monckton-Milnes, who attracted her.

She met him originally in the summer of 1842 at a dinner-party given by the Palmerstons. He was an only son and heir to a wealthy Yorkshire estate. Thackeray said of him that he always put people in a good humour with his gentle wit and everyone liked him. He was popular, sociable and had many different sides to his character. The side that particularly attracted Florence, apart from the physical attraction she felt, was his love of children and his philanthropic efforts on their behalf. In 1849, after they had met many times over this long period since the first dinner party, Richard proposed. Florence wrote he was "the man I adored",[17] but she turned him down. Every night, she confided in her "private notes" to herself, she dreamed of him and the pencilled writing trembles on the page as she records her reasons for refusing him. "I have an intellectual nature which requires satisfaction and that would find it in him. I have a passional nature which requires satisfaction and that would find it in him. I have a moral, an active, nature which requires satisfaction and that would not find it in his life. Sometimes I think I will satisfy my passional nature at all events because that will at least secure me from the evil of dreaming. But would it? I could be satisfied to spend a life with him in combining our different powers in some great object. I could not satisfy this nature by spending a life with him in making society and arranging domestic things."[18] It all sounds very rational, very cool, but later Florence wrote (and here the pencil stops wavering and digs into the paper) "I do not understand it . . . I am ashamed to understand it . . . I know that if I were to see him again . . . the very thought of doing so quite overcomes me. I know that since I refused him not one day has passed without my thinking of him, that life is desolate without his sympathy."[19] Still she had not done with agonizing. Finally, she came to the conclusion that although it hurt she had made the right decision. "I know that I could not bear his life, that to be nailed to a continuation, an exaggeration of my present life without hope of another would be intolerable to me – that voluntarily to put it out of my power ever to be able to seize the chance of forming for myself a true and rich life would seem to me like suicide."[20]

Suicide, in spite of her strong religious faith, was very much on her mind. She felt little desire to live with so little prospect ahead of any real change. Richard Monckton-Milnes seems to have made no attempt to try to present to her a different view of marriage or to persuade her that it could be a beginning and not an end. He took himself off and never bothered her again. (What he took himself off to, according to Thackeray, was a secret life of debauchery and an interest in the works of the Marquis de Sade as well as other more worthy pursuits, so perhaps Florence had a lucky escape.)

Her parents were exasperated and thought their daughter was deliberately making herself ill again. They sent her on a cruise to Greece to try to get her over her depression and on the way home she visited the Institution of Deaconesses at Kaiserworth in Germany. Kaiserworth, near Düsseldorf, had been founded in 1833 by Pastor Theodore Fliedner as a home for discharged female convicts and had grown to include a hospital, a lunatic asylum, an orphanage and two schools. It did not train nurses ("The nursing was nil and the hygiene horrible,"[21] commented Florence) but it did care for the sick in a way not unlike the modern hospice. Florence was not, of course, by any means the first English woman to visit it but she was the first to be inspired by it. When she reached home she could talk of nothing else. Her one aim was to return.

She was now thirty and yet still she asked and waited for permission. When it went on not being granted the extraordinary thing was the *lack* of hate this aroused. She continued to love her parents so much that if she could not have their co-operation she could not go ahead. Even when she was staying with a relative she asked permission to extend her stay – "Perhaps you will decide what you wish me to do and tell me your decision",[22] she would write. She would apologize constantly for her absence – "I am very sorry to leave home just when you are going to be alone" . . . "I am very sorry to be so long away from home" . . . "I remain at your disposal."[23] Her anxiety to please was painful but it was genuine. So was the concern felt for her welfare by her parents. If they appear now to be cruel and domineering in their resolute refusal to allow Florence to become a nurse they did not seem so then, even to her. They were doing what they thought best for a daughter whose happiness was their main, if not only, objective. When Florence announced that she intended to return to Kaiserworth for a longer visit, the Nightingales were not pleased but they did not absolutely forbid her to go. Even Fanny had begun to realize how serious Florence's depression was and she was becoming a little frightened. If going to Kaiserworth made her happy it was perhaps worth going along with.

Florence arrived at Kaiserworth for the second time in July 1851 and was instantly transformed. She began each day at five o'clock and from then on she was in constant demand in a way she found most satisfying. But she had by no means cut the umbilical cord. A letter from Fanny was received rapturously – "It was the greatest possible relief to hear from you"[24] – and brought an immediate response. "I am afraid my accounts of what I do would be very uninteresting to you,"[25] she wrote but then followed a description of her working day which was far from uninteresting. She spent a lot of time helping with sick children and taking the convalescent ones for long walks along the Rhine. "The world here fills my life with interest and strengthens the mind and body,"[26] she wrote. She only had ten minutes for each of the four daily meals and had no time to send her clothes to the wash. She went wherever she was sent to do whatever was needed in the hospital or the school and the variety as well as the obvious usefulness of her days made them happy. Thoughts of suicide were forgotten – "I should be sorry now to leave life – I know you would be glad to hear, dearest mother, this – God has indeed made life rich in interests."[27] By the end of August "I am as happy as the day is long,"[28] she wrote. But what she still wanted, and did not have, was her parents' total blessing. "I cannot bear to grieve you – life and everything in it that charms you you would sacrifice for me . . ."[29] This was the crux of Florence's problem: duty alone would never have kept her from following what she felt was a vocation. It was her own love, her deep love, for her parents and even more her realization of their love for her that prevented her acting. It would be foolish to represent the Nightingale parents as ogres, interested only in repressing their daughter. On the contrary, it was because they truly believed that nursing would repress her that they resisted it. How could their beautiful Florence find happiness and fulfilment *as a woman* if she buried herself in one of those disgusting hospitals? They were, they thought, saving her from a terrible fate, and Florence appreciated that this was what they believed. What she found herself incapable of altering was their concept of womanhood and what it meant.

She returned from Kaiserworth after three months, determined to convince them that her only chance of happiness lay in returning there, or somewhere similar, as soon as possible, but as soon as she got home her father contracted an eye infection and she immediately became his nurse. Thoughts of leaving were out of the question until her adored father was better. But as soon as he was recovered her sister Parthe fell ill. Florence turned from nursing her father to nursing Parthe (who said later "she was a shocking nurse"). She by no means adored Parthe, who had always irritated her, but the sense of commitment was the same. It was as though she had never been away. Kaiserworth receded as a vision and was replaced by the more accessible Convent of the Sisters of Charity in Paris. As soon as Parthe was better, she swore she would go to Paris and enter the convent to gain nursing experience. But Parthe did not get better, she got worse. Florence's only bit of luck was that their doctor decided it was Florence who was making Parthe ill and that they ought to be separated. On Februrary 4th, 1853 Florence obeyed with alacrity. She arrived in Paris ready to begin nursing. Unfortunately, she was pursued by a telegram announcing her grandmother was now gravely ill and she had to go back, all arrangements once more cancelled. "There is nothing," she once wrote "like the tyranny of a good English family."[30] Such families, like hers, bred daughters to reciprocate the love lavished on them and to answer the call of that love whenever it was made. Self must not be thought of. Daughters had an identity only within the framework of this family love whereas sons were given their wings to fly away as soon as they left childhood.

It took two actions outside her control to release Florence from the never-ending confines of family responsibility. The first was the offer of an actual job which forced her to make a clear decision. Up to 1863 she had always had to do the pushing herself – nobody pushed for her. But now she was asked to be the Superintendent of the Institute for Sick Gentlewomen in Distressed Circumstances. She could, of course, have turned it down on the same grounds as those which had always kept her at home but she knew that if she did so there really would be no hope left. For the first time a hand was being extended, a solid means of extricating herself from the morass of "duties". If she spurned it, she was lost. So she accepted. And then a wonderful thing happened. Her father decided to make her an allowance of £500 a year. She could be truly independent. This gesture of faith made at such a vital moment gave Florence the courage to face the inevitable appalling scenes with her mother and Parthe. On August 12th, 1853, aged thirty-three she finally left home and took up residence in the Institute's premises at No. 1 Harley Street. "It is," she wrote triumphantly, "a fait accompli."[31]

Within a very short time Florence was rather regretting those words. "I am now in the hey-day of my power," she wrote to her father, adding, "Praise and blame are alike indifferent to me."[32] But she quickly saw that her new position was far from being satisfactory. Being Superintendent of the Gentlewomen's Institute certainly did not train her as a nurse. It was primarily an administrative post and, though an excellent outlet for her formidable powers of organization, it taught her little about nursing. Once the run-down home she had inherited had been streamlined she was restless again. By January 1854 she was speaking contemptuously of "this little molehill". She found herself trapped into endless negotiations to get things done and wrote, "I do all my business by intrigue." It was not at all what she wanted to do and brought her only slightly nearer her real objectives which were to train as a nurse, make nursing a profession, and reform hospitals. She began to look around for another post, preferably in a real hospital. She began bombarding Sidney Herbert and lobbying Dr Bowman, one of the best-known surgeons of the day, to get herself made Superintendent of Nurses in the newly re-organized Kings Cross Hospital. Then, she could really show what she was made of.

But fate gave her a better chance. In the summer of 1854 a cholera epidemic broke out in London and Florence went to the Middlesex Hospital as a volunteer "to superintend the nursing of cholera patients". There, she set a superb standard of care for others to follow. It was "sanitary" nursing at its best and, though she did not know it, a dress-rehearsal for the Crimea. Florence was then formally invited by the Government to go out to Scutari in command of a party of nurses to try to alleviate the terrible sufferings which were currently being exposed by *The Times* correspondent, William Russell. She accepted, but made quite sure that her authority was clearly defined. She had already had a little experience of being a woman working in a male-controlled world and knew that she must have unequivocal power in her particular sphere right from the start. So she had Sidney Herbert, Secretary at War since December 1852, put in black and white that "everything relating to the distribution of nurses, their hours of attendance, their allotment to particular duties is placed in your hands."

Her official appointment by a Government minister was the first of its kind. Her family were stunned, caught between pride and terror, and even her influential friends were awestruck. "I hear you are going to the East," wrote Richard Monckton-Milnes. ". . . you can undertake that when you could not undertake me." Florence very nearly decided that she would have to undertake it on her own because she could find no other nurses of sufficient calibre to accompany her. Using the Herbert's house as her headquarters she interviewed all the applicants herself and was disgusted by them. "All London was scoured for them," wrote Mary Stanley who helped her. ". . . We felt ashamed to have in the house such women as came." If Florence had needed any proof that nursing needed to be reformed this was it. The candidates she saw made her despise her own sex and produced more of those violently anti-feminist sounding statements which were in fact a mask for her passionate belief that women ought to get up and change their unsatisfactory lives themselves. She could not find, in that crisis, good women to be nurses, good women to sacrifice themselves for the greater good and yet everywhere women screamed they could find no employment. She had the means to give them employment so why did they not take it?

In the end, Florence left England in October with thirty-eight nurses who passed muster – but only just. (Twenty-four were nuns and she thought little better of them than of the others.) But she sailed in good heart, excited that at last she had a real, indisputable mission and enormously relieved finally to have gained her mother's as well as her father's blessing. The journey was long, the conditions bad and the arrival at the Barrack Hospital in Scutari horrifying. The filth, the mud, the wretchedly inadequate facilities, the hordes of wounded all added up to a vision of hell. It was much worse than anything Florence had imagined but her self-control remained rigid. She realized at once that nursing was the least of her problems. "I am," she wrote home, "a kind of General Dealer . . . A whole army having been ordered to abandon its kit . . . I am now clothing the British Army . . . I am really cook, housekeeper, scavenger . . . washerwoman, general dealer, storekeeper."[33] She became as obsessed with cabbage soup and scrubbing-brushes as with dressing wounds and assisting at operations. But she had correctly realized that not only did these menial jobs have to be part of nursing in those circumstances but that they provided a way to gain the power she needed to achieve what she wished to achieve.

Upon her arrival the army authorities had resented her presence and so had the doctors. She had had the foresight to appreciate that, the system being what it was, there was nothing to be gained by challenging these men or setting herself up as a rival. She had to convert them to seeing she could help and was no faint-hearted lady sent to get in their way. So, although she loathed them, she set herself to work through these men with meticulous attention to the existing system. The Army operated through written chits. Very well, she would wait for instructions through written chits even though all around men were dying for want of simple care. She stopped her nurses rushing in and made them wait for orders. It was exactly the same tactics other women had to resort to in order to break down male hostility but nobody else was ever obliged to play this game in quite such earnest. Hurting male self-esteem was fatal. Her sole concern was to prove the value of women as nurses and to do so she was prepared to appear to be humble before the male authorities.

At last, her approach worked. After the battle of Balaclava all pretence that Miss Nightingale was not in charge of nursing (and much else) was over. "On Thursday last," she wrote on November 14th, 1854, "we had 1,715 sick and wounded in this hospital (among whom 120 cholera patients) and 650 severely wounded . . . when a message came to me to prepare for 510 wounded . . . arriving from the dreadful affair of Balaclava . . . We had but half an hour's notice before they began landing the wounded. Between one and nine o'clock we had the mattresses stuffed, sewn up, laid down – alas! only on matting on the floor – the men washed and put to bed and all their wounds dressed . . . The operations are all performed in the ward – no time to move them."[34] It was a scene of continual horror with Florence always at the centre trying to keep her vow that no man should die alone. The vision of her in white floating around with a lamp in her hand softly uttering kind words is not entirely a myth but it distorts the much more impressive truth. She never reached that end-of-the-day ritual without unremitting, backbreaking toil during which she came to hate almost all the men she had to deal with. "Alas, among the men here," she wrote to Sidney Herbert, "is there one really anxious for the good of these hospitals? One who is not an insincere animal at the bottom, who is not thinking of going in with the winning side whichever that is?"[35] She never said, "Women would not act like this," but it was implicit in all her searing criticisms. She herself put the welfare of the men first and was furious if any of her party did not also do so. It was beyond her comprehension that any woman could actually come to her and complain that her cap didn't suit her (as one did) or think of consorting with some of the less ill men in the wards (which became something of a problem). Women, so far as Florence was concerned, were on trial, they had something to prove, they had to be (as she herself was) *beyond reproach*.

After two years, when Florence Nightingale at last returned home, her sense of mission had shifted its centre. To reform hospitals and establish nursing as a profession were no longer her main objectives. Instead, she saw she had much more important work to do. It was her intention to see that never again would the British Army be in the mess it had brought upon itself in the Crimea. The whole organization of the health of the Army must be reformed and she must do it or have on her conscience forever the memories of all those thousands of soldiers who had died unnecessarily. Besides that, work for nursing was puny. Ill and exhausted as she was, she side-stepped the adulation that was hers, shut herself away (from 1857 onwards she spent long periods in bed or on a couch immured in her room) and at once began preparing a scheme to reform the health of the British Army. All her depleted energies went into writing to Ministers, powerful friends, even the Queen herself in order to get agreement that there should be a massive inquiry. She organized the Royal Commission and wrote a Confidential Report herself.

But meanwhile other people had not forgotten her old ambition even if she appeared to have done so. During the Crimean War a Nightingale Fund had been launched to enable Florence Nightingale, when she returned, "to establish and control an institute for the training, sustenance and protection of nurses paid and unpaid." That fund now stood at £45,000 and was waiting for the attention she was not prepared to give it. A committee was approved by her to administer the fund and a secretary appointed but the work of setting up any kind of training-school for nurses hung fire while everyone waited for Miss Nightingale herself to tell them what exactly she wanted done. There was no doubt that the climate was right – the popular image of the nurse had been changed overnight, as it were – and the money was available, but no movement was made. Nobody knew how to proceed, how nurses should be trained and for exactly what and they waited in expectation of a Nightingale blueprint. What nobody realized was how difficult it was at that particular time to provide such a thing, even for Miss Nightingale.

Nursing, together with medicine, was at that time changing dramatically because of the scientific advances of the mid-nineteenth century. By 1846 anaesthetics were in use all over the western world and therefore the horizons of surgery were suddenly enormously expanded. There was so much more the surgeon could now do without fear of the patient dying of shock and therefore there was also so much more for the nurse to do. As well as "sanitary" nursing there now existed technical nursing in which the nurse had to become – or had the chance to become – the partner of the doctor. She could stop being primarily a handmaiden and become a colleague with her own skills.

But what, in that case, should she be taught? Should a nurse follow much the same course as a medical student and if so where did that leave the medical students? Medical training itself was in a state of flux and was becoming a severely structured standardized business geared to tests and examinations and culminating (after 1858) in attaining registered status. At the other end of the scale was the question of what sort of menial tasks a nurse should be expected to perform. If she was to be a skilled colleague of the doctor should she, any more than he, be down on her knees scrubbing the ward floor? Nobody quite knew where nurses stood or what exactly they were and yet it was a matter of some urgency to decide. The number of girls and women wanting to become nurses after the Crimea was naturally large and with a conservative estimate of a million and a half spinsters and widows needing employment the establishment of nursing as a proper profession looked like the answer to a great many prayers. Suddenly, there *was* work, paid work, that a lady could contemplate other than governessing. Miss Nightingale was a nurse: the stamp of impeccable respectability had been put on a hitherto socially despised job.

The first meeting of the Council of nine men Florence Nightingale had appointed to take charge of the public money collected was in December 1859. At this meeting the Council was formally entrusted with setting up an "Institution for the Training, Sustenance and Protection of Nurses and Hospital Attendants." To guide them its members had only *Notes on Nursing: What it is and What it is not*, a short book published in the same month (price 5s) by Miss Nightingale. This was not intended to be a nursing manual or in any sense a text-book but merely a guideline to show which way nursing should go. Florence herself said she only wanted to make people "think how to nurse." Practically every line struck a blow for the feminism she was meant to decry. "It has been said and written scores of times that every woman makes a good nurse," she wrote. "I believe, on the contrary, that the very elements of nursing are all but unknown." It was, she went on, quite ludicrous for example to imagine that to be a nurse all you had to be was female, as if the female sex automatically carried within it recuperative powers. It was equally silly to argue that making sick people better "ought to be left to the doctors". That was only an excuse for ignorance. "Did Nature intend mothers to be always accompanied by doctors?" she asked sharply. "Or is it better to learn the piano forte than to learn the laws which subserve the preservation of offspring?" Nor was it any good bleating as mothers were prone to do, "But the circumstances which govern our children's health are beyond our control." What nonsense. *All* circumstances could be to some extent controlled: nobody could stop a cold east wind blowing but learning how to cope with the ill-effects of that wind was possible. This was what nursing was about: being practical and sensible and also imaginative. She had no time for anyone who saw themselves delicately dabbing a fevered brow. The image of a woman as frail, modest and gentle, a creature whose sensibilities must not be offended, was a curse on nursing. To be a nurse you had to be tough and unsqueamish and if that meant losing your femininity in the eyes of the world then lose it you must. Being a nurse had nothing to do with being "nice". A straightforward discussion on chamberpots made her point forcibly. All chamberpots should be emptied and washed daily *by the nurse*. "If a nurse declines to do these kind of things for her patient," she wrote, "because it is 'not her business' I should say that nursing was not her calling." She thought, in fact, that it was a waste of manpower for nurses to do it and she had no wish to see nurses as drudges, but, if they had to do it, then they must and "women who wait for the housemaid to do this or for the charwoman to do that when their patients are suffering have not the *making* of a nurse in them."

This attack on the contemporary image of women continued in the description of how a nurse should behave. Dress, for example, should be simple. Any woman dressing fashionably for nursing was ridiculed . . . "the dress of women is daily more and more unfitting them for any 'mission' or usefulness at all . . . A man is now a more handy and far less objectionable being in a sickroom than a woman. Compelled by her dress every woman either shuffles or waddles . . . What is become of a woman's light step?" Nor was the notion that nurses did specific jobs very useful – nurses must concern themselves with the whole environment of the patient and seek as far as possible to control it. Hurry and bustle was painful to the sick, gossiping in corners agony, irresolution of any kind harmful. Visitors must be carefully watched by the nurse so that their confounded "chattering hopes" did not prove upsetting.

A nurse was an observer above all else and her observations might be vital. There was "a physiognomy of disease" they must learn which would help them to know which observations to report. "Apprehension, uncertainty, waiting, expectation, fear of surprise, do a patient more harm than any exertion. Remember, he is face to face with his enemy all the time internally wrestling with him, having long imaginary conversations with him. RID HIM OF HIS ADVERSARY QUICKLY." The way to do this was to be decisive and always to let a patient know what was going to happen. But if this implied sticking to a rigid timetable it was wrong. Convenience must never be put first. If, for example, a patient had a dry mouth and could not masticate properly then a nurse must be prepared to sit with a teaspoon feeding him little by little. Nor should "fancies" be rejected, within reason. These should be indulged whereas any love of frippery in a sickroom should not. All carpets and wallpapers were an "abomination" because cleanliness was vital and all surfaces should be washable. It was a nurse's job to see that they were.

These *Notes* made quite a stir and were applauded by the majority of medical people who read them but they were not actually much use to the Council of the Nightingale Fund. They said nothing about procedure, nor did they prescribe an exact course of study. Doubtless Miss Nightingale had ideas on those too, which the secretary and committee of the Fund would have been glad to learn, but she was too busy with the British Army to contribute them. Meanwhile, it was being argued that there was nothing wrong with nursing as it was and there was no need to have any training other than formalizing what already existed – that is, nurses simply going on the wards and learning by experience (which was all Florence herself had done). Mr J. F. South, Senior Consulting Surgeon of St Thomas's, the very hospital under whose roof the Fund intended to establish their school, also published a little book at this time entitled *Facts relating to Hospital Nurses Also Observations on Training Establishments for Hospitals*. In it he made cutting remarks about nurses being "in the position of housemaids" who only needed simple instructions on the spot (he implied they were incapable of understanding any others). There was, Mr South wrote, nothing wrong with this – all doctors in fact needed were efficient housemaids. The idea of "training" nurses, of instructing them in medical theory, was ridiculous and merely a ruse to snatch power from where it rightly belonged: in the hands of the doctors. The purpose of training nurses was, he said, to place the whole nursing establishment "in the hands of persons who will never be content till *they* become the executive of the hospitals and, as they have in the military hospitals, a constant source of annoyance to the medical and surgical officers."

Faced with this kind of internal hostility the committee had to step carefully. A memorandum from Miss Nightingale told them that she wanted the training school to be near enough to a big hospital to give the nurses practical experience. In fact, it was eventually located *in* St Thomas's for the sake of economy and because in Mrs Wardroper, the Matron of St Thomas's, Florence Nightingale thought she had an ideal head. She accepted the second job as superintendent of the Nightingale Fund School. In May 1860 applications were invited to train at the new Nightingale School but to everyone's disappointment the response was discouraging. It seemed women were now daunted by what was required to become a probationer at the Nightingale School. They were asked to be paragons. A nurse was to be a nurse first and a woman afterwards. The fifteen finally enrolled for one year's training were brave indeed. They took up residence in the "Home" – an upper floor of a wing in St Thomas's – put on their brown uniforms and began trying to match up to Florence Nightingale's standards. Their board, uniform and lodging were provided for out of the Fund and they received in addition £10 a year pocket-money. There was a formal record book in which each probationer's character was detailed and criticized. Otherwise, the training rested in the hands of the Matron and 'was not categorically laid down by Miss Nightingale.

What Mrs Wardroper gave the probationers was a thorough grounding in the handicraft of nursing which was straightforward and traditional: how to apply dressings and leeches, how to give enemas, make beds and so forth. But, in addition, there were supposed to be lectures and it was over these lectures – the academic part of training which Miss Nightingale so desired – that there was trouble. Partly no one quite knew what these lectures should contain nor what was their precise object but partly the trouble was also that the standard of education of most of the probationers was very low. Classes on reading and writing and not lectures on anatomy were obviously more necessary. The authorities muddled on, learning by trial and error and constantly changing the regulations and training specifications, but as far as the public was concerned Nightingale Nurses were a visible success. Without stopping to inquire precisely what they had been trained in and for, hospitals throughout the land clamoured for them. When a Nightingale Nurse became a Matron she took with her Nightingale notions of organization and discipline, not to mention dedication, which in many cases made her seem much more impressive than she actually was.

Florence Nightingale herself was far from satisfied by the product her school turned out. Until 1868 she was far too absorbed in other more important work to take any real part in the affairs of the school but after that, when the accession of Gladstone put an end to her influence, she began to apply herself to its problems and was shocked by them. To start with, the fall-out rate was so high. This, she thought, must be due to faulty selection but when she began helping with that selecting she was driven to the further and much less attractive explanation that women found the life of a probationer too hard. They rebelled against the régime. They did not take kindly to being closely supervised, to only being allowed out in pairs, to not being able to raise their eyes in male company without being accused of flirting, to not being allowed to "chatter", to having even their off-duty time and clothes scrutinized. Women, in short, were letting her down. Even the best of the nurses her school turned out were not good enough (with the honourable exception of perhaps half a dozen.) It made her furious to find Nightingale Nurses resigning from, or refusing to take, important jobs because *they were going to get married*.

There was, for example, the case of Miss Torrance, selected as Mrs Wardroper's assistant and the organizer of the Highgate Workhouse Infirmary. When, in 1872, Florence Nightingale's eyes were opened to Mrs Wardroper's shortcomings she wrote of Miss Torrance, "*She* has been the most successful woman we ever had."[36] She was so pleased with Miss Torrance she invited her to stay at Lea Hurst. But then came the betrayal: Miss Torrance became engaged to Dr Thomas Dowse, the Medical Officer at Highgate. "She has poured out the whole of her story with that wretched little Dowse . . . in a moment of weakness she has engaged herself to him."[37] In spite of her engagement, Miss Torrance became first assistant Matron and head of the probationers' home and did excellent work. Florence breathed easier and hoped the "weakness" over. But in January 1873 Miss Torrance left for good to get married. "The greatest shock one ever had in one's life (not excepting Agnes Jones' death) in this work"[38] commented the heartbroken Florence. Women, even the best women, were not measuring up to her expectations. Where were others like herself, willing to sacrifice everything to their work?

She tried, in her annual addresses to the nurses in the Nightingale School, to raise standards. These addresses, often read for her, almost always had a text – either "Conceit and Nursing cannot exist in the same person" or "There is no real nursing without self-denial" or some such warning. In them, she forbade gossiping and noisy laughter. "This night," she once advised, "if we are inclined to make a noise on the stairs or to linger in each other's rooms, shall we go to bed alone with God?"[39] Those who were not attracted by this idea had no place in nursing. But the addresses always emphasized sisterly solidarity. Nurses must support each other and she certainly did not intend her homilies about noise to be interpreted as meaning she was in favour of isolation. On the contrary "there is something not quite right in a woman who shuts up her heart from other women"[40] – it was just that there was no place for levity. The fact was "a nurse *is* like a traveller . . . soldiers are sent everywhere and leave home and country for years; *they* think nothing of it because they go 'on duty'. Shall *we* have less self-denial? . . ."[41] She felt, as the years passed, that the answer, sadly, was "yes". Women did not want to deny "self", nor could they bury "self" in the way she could and find similar satisfaction. She had given them a choice and they were not making the right one but clinging, as ever, to marriage and motherhood.

Parthe thought it absurd of Florence to expect so much. She told her she was more like a man than a woman. This was intended as a criticism but Florence chose to interpret it as a compliment. If being like a man meant she was strong, decisive, hard-working, disciplined and aware of a wider world than the domestic then she was glad she was like a man. If being womanly was synonymous with being meek, subservient, self-effacing and utterly absorbed in the home then she was glad she was not thought womanly. But Florence knew Parthe was talking nonsense. She did not feel in the least de-sexed by her sister's accusation because she had confidence that her femininity resided in other aspects of her nature – it was merely society which equated womanliness with the virtues she herself despised. It was society which had to think again, not she. She felt she saw in her friend Hilary Bonham-Carter the perfect example of what striving to be feminine according to the dictates of society meant. Hilary died young in 1865 of cancer. She had been a fine artist but had never allowed herself to develop her talent. She was, wrote Florence, "unworked gold" and so great was the waste of her life, striving (as Florence had once striven) to behave as a girl should that it filled her with murderous rage. She was even glad Hilary died when she did rather than have to endure another thirty years subscribing to the norm. Until women stopped being terrified that they would be thought "like a man" their lives would go on being wasted and like Hilary they would live "a caricature of a life".

But there were times, as she grew older, when Florence saw the snags in her own kind of life. For twenty years her work more than fulfilled her – it overwhelmed her and those empty, useless days before she went to her first job almost became an attractive memory in contrast. But then, in her fifties, circumstances changed. She had felt, until 1872, that she was actually a Secretary of State running an office but when, as the result of political changes – the death one by one of the men in power she had used and directed behind the scenes – her influence came to an end, she discovered what it was like to be out of office and growing old. Facts and figures about Indian affairs, which had become her main preoccupation after the British Army's health in general, were no longer sent to her. The new Governor General of India, Lord Northbrook, did not consult her. If she requested reports on India she was told that they were private. Her reaction verged on the panic-stricken. "1872. This year I go out of office," she wrote. What was she to do without that feverish hard *important* work? What else was there in her life? At an age when women were enjoying the fruits after the labours of family life she had none. There was, of course, the Nightingale School and hospital reform but work for both lacked that sense of urgency which had always galvanized her into action. Adapting to anything less important than vital was difficult. There were suddenly yards of slack to take up. Then, just as she was beginning to make the necessary adjustment, both her parents and her sister (who had married at forty to Sir Harry Verney) fell ill. She fell victim to another of society's little maxims: unmarried daughters in middle age had nothing else to do so could look after ailing parents. She was back where she had started, fulfilling "duties", without the excuse of husband or children or what anyone would call "real" work. In 1873 she spent eight months immured in Embley caring for her father until he died in January 1874. The years after his death were, she wrote, the most miserable in her entire life. She took Fanny to Lea Hurst and looked after her until her death in 1880. At last, all those morally inescapable "duties" were over. She was free.

She was also sixty years of age and very aware of her own vulnerability. Florence's personality was such that she always seemed to observers entirely self-contained and self-sufficient. It would have seemed ridiculous to worry about her being on her own. And yet, after her mother's death, Florence did begin to feel alone in a way she had never done before. *She* certainly was not going to cry out to be loved as she accused the female sex in general of doing but all the same the need for affection and companionship grew. All her closest friends were dead, including Sidney Herbert with whom she had had an intellectual relationship that meant so much to her. It may be true that she helped to hound him to his death through overwork but her grief after he died is pitiful to read. She wrote to her mother on March 7th, 1862 . . . "I have lost all. All the others have children . . . to live for. While I have lost husband and children and all . . . If Paget could amputate my *left forequarter* I am sure I would have sent for him in half an hour."[42] Twenty years later her feelings remained much the same. Nobody had taken Sidney Herbert's place. In this situation Florence behaved with the same courage that characterized her whole life. She analyzed her position and vowed not to become an ogre in her old age, not to exact devotion from friends or family who had cause to be grateful to her or who felt a sense of duty. She saw that as a woman on her own she must make visiting her an attractive proposition and not a dreaded chore. She determined not to whine or try to arouse pity, not to go in for emotional blackmail. "Should there be anything in which I can be the least use, here I am" was a common ending to her letters to the young. She made herself interested in what she knew interested her visitors. She looked after their individual needs and gave as well as took. She was enthusiastic and entertaining and built a place for herself in the large Nightingale circle of younger people – nephews, nieces, cousins and the children of all of them. She became a trusted confidante and succeeded so well in her desire to be understanding and supportive that Margaret Verney (daughter-in-law of Parthe's husband (Harry) could write in 1895, when Florence was seventy-five, "We are crazy with joy that you give us so blessed a hope of seeing you in November."

Florence's old age was happy – happier by far than her tormented youth, happier even than her fulfilled middle age when she was driven mad by memories of the Crimean tragedy and by the incompetence of those who were in a position to make sure it did not happen again. People, for the first time, were more important than work or the desire to work. This was because she discovered that personal relationships need no longer *clash* with anything. At the height of her powers, and even before, love, affection or duty had always presented her with an unpleasant choice about how close she was to become to people. She never forgot that it was love for her parents that had kept her confined at home so long and ever after she took care to side-step love. This made her appear ruthless, as it made all feminists appear ruthless at that stage of feminism. Love of any personal sort was the great, cunning, insidious enemy. Fall in love with man or child and you were done for, sucked into that whirlpool of conjugal bliss in which you would swirl dizzily around for the rest of your life. But after her sixtieth year Florence discovered that love was no longer going to ensnare her. On the contrary, personal, loving relationships could actually become her work. There was no need any longer to fear social intercourse, to dread those personal intimacies which always inevitably brought with them time-consuming responsibilities. Her bitterness about how other people, particularly women, always let her down faded.

Many people recorded what a pleasure it was to visit Miss Nightingale. Both her home and her hospitality were attractive in the then accepted sense of being "feminine". Her passion for work never made her oblivious to her surroundings and she was always contemptuous of those who used work as an excuse for slovenliness. She was a superb housekeeper and an excellent hostess. She always had fresh flowers around her – even at the height of her powers when she was buried in correspondence she would find time to write to her mother detailing exactly which flowers she wished to be sent to her from Embley. She liked any room she was in to be neat and pretty and above all *light*, which, in the Victorian era of plush and velvet, of clutter and heavy drapes, was quite unusual. She had told her nurses not to forget that "the sun is a sculptor" and a painter and she never forgot it herself. Her windows were always open and, most revolutionary of all, uncurtained, except for "side curtains" of plain blue serge, which made more than one visitor feel naked and exposed. She showed the same marked taste for simplicity and style in her own clothing, refusing to wear fussy things, but loving lace and paying meticulous attention even to her nightgowns all those years she stayed in bed. When her mother sent her some new ones in 1863 she wrote that although they were very nice she would have liked them two inches longer and "a little sloped round the throat in front i.e. cut down in the neck."[43] Looks in everything were extremely important to her. Her dinners, her father wrote, were "perfect". They looked appetizing and the quality of the food as well as the standard of cooking was superb. To the butcher she was as explicit as to any Minister at War ("a forequarter of your best small mutton . . . I prefer *four* year old mutton")[44] and to her cook equally exact ("Brisket of beef must be cooked with herbs, onions, carrots, celery in a light broth on the hot plates from 10 am to 9 pm").[45] Any idea that work was an excuse for letting the housework be the concern of the servants entirely was misplaced. Florence's scorn for "bad mistresses" was deep. She was an overseer of her maids all the time – nothing escaped her vigilant eye. She wrote in March 1862, when she was overwhelmed with work, "I am going to try for a housemaid who will clean not dirty my house . . . You see I have three maids who know how to do literally nothing . . . Anne Clarke who was during her three months under me at Harley Street the brightest, cleanest girl I ever had is come back to me a dirty half witted slattern. So much for the mistresses of the present day. Anne Clarke will still do things excellently under my eye."[46]

All these facets to Florence Nightingale's character make her as intensely "feminine" as her sister Parthe would have wished and there was also another quality she possessed in abundance which is little written about. She was a very tender-hearted person, with a deep compassion for suffering of any kind. Many of her more famous sayings sound brutal and cruel but they do her an injustice. She detested any doctor who was impervious to a patient's agony and she stood at the side of many such men. Like Elizabeth Blackwell, she looked to women to be different, to have time to be sympathetic and realize what patients were going through, and above all not to be afraid to become involved if it would help. Parthe, who thought of herself as the epitome of tender-heartedness, was actually taken aback by evidence of Florence's kindness and the lengths she would go to. On August 4th, 1856 she wrote with some distaste to Mrs Gaskell that "Some of Florence's spoils of war have arrived – a one legged sailor boy who was 10 months in her hospitals, a little Russian prisoner who came into Hospital for a scald . . . a big Crimean puppy given her by the soldiers (who) was found in a hole in the rocks near Balaclava . . ."[47] Florence had had them all brought back to England, received them in London herself and then when they were rested enough had them taken to Embley where she gave orders that they were to be looked after. Her nurses, too, were well aware of how real her kindness was. She was immensely concerned about any nurse who was ill and always offered her home for convalescence. She would send fruit and flowers to sick nurses and no Nightingale Nurse ever went to a new post without finding flowers there to welcome her.

Nor was this anxiety for other people's welfare confined to those she knew – she was equally concerned about the legions of "sick poor" and well aware of the conditions in which they were obliged to live. It distressed her that her own emphasis on personal cleanliness was not much good to the majority of the population – "it is impossible to many poor women – many can never have a bath in their lives,"[48] she wrote and she was a great supporter of the scheme to initiate "penny baths" in public bathhouses. She loathed people who smiled and shrugged their shoulders philosophically and spoke about "fate" and "the wheel of fortune" in reference to the plight of the poor. "I own myself to be completely at a loss when people use such expressions . . . If *I* believed in indiscriminate fate I should go at once and hang myself."[49] She detested socialism, which she thought stopped people helping themselves (and it was the government's duty to teach them how to do this) but she would not go along with any ideas about the sufferings of the poor being either "fate" or nobody else's business. She was, she said, an advocate of Savonarola because he made everything that happened in a state or country the business of everyone in it. "I cry educate them to do better," she wrote of the poor in 1850 to her father and added, "I think the Poor Law has been the ruin of England."[50] When she came to writing a pamphlet on training nurses for the sick poor she stressed that she wanted to foster "the spirit of work (not relief) in the district nurse and for her to foster the same in the sick poor." If the district nurse began by giving relief then she would end up doing nothing but that and this was not the idea. "Philanthropy is the biggest humbug I know," she wrote in 1867. "Philanthropy is to the love of Mankind what property is to Christianity – all parade."[51]

On August 5th, 1887, when she was sixty-seven years old, Florence wrote to her beloved Aunt Mai, "In this month 34 years ago you lodged me in Harley Street and in this month 31 years ago you returned me to England from Scutari. And in this month 30 years ago the first Royal Commission was finished . . . In this month 26 years ago Sidney Herbert died . . . And in this month 24 years ago the work of the second Royal Commission (India) was finished. And in this month, this year, my powers seem all to have failed and old age set in."[52] But not quite. There was one more battle she was to be engaged in which revived her flagging powers. In 1886 a proposal had been made that the trained nurse should, like the trained doctor, be registered. A committee of the Hospitals' Association proposed that an examination, or series of examinations, should be taken by nurses and marked by an independent body of examiners and then, if passed, a nurse would be entitled to have her name placed on a state register. A standard of nursing would thus be established which would enhance the status of the whole profession. Florence Nightingale instantly sprang to the alert. She was not against registration itself but against the possibility of operating such a scheme. A register of nurses, she wrote, could be of two kinds: either a mere directory, or "a list published by authority". The second was the only kind worth having but "the only way in which such a register can be usefully compiled is by the appointment of a number of officially qualified persons who shall have the time and the will to go minutely into the career of every applicant for registration . . ."[53] What she wanted above all else was to avoid registration ever being automatic – "registration is not a matter of right but of selection." Nurses were not engineers and nursing was not *just* a profession but a vocation too. She had not "raised nursing from the sink" to have it plunged back into it. But other people thought differently and, although they dreaded opposing Miss Nightingale, were prepared to do so.

Mrs Bedford-Fenwick was one of them. She herself had been a Nightingale Nurse, progressing with great speed to become Matron of St Bartholomew's at the age of twenty-four in 1878. She founded the British Nurses Association in the drawing room of her house after she had resigned as Matron because of her marriage. In addition, she edited the *Nursing Record* (from 1893) and was powerfully placed to speed the registration scheme she wholeheartedly advocated. She believed her idol Miss Nightingale had been wrong to try to make nursing into a religion and wanted it to be stripped of such mystical overtones. It was a profession like any other and ought to be organized accordingly without delay. In May 1893, after tremendous efforts by both sides, a special committee of the Privy Council announced its judgement: a Royal Charter was granted to Mrs Bedford-Fenwick's association but the use of the word "register" was forbidden. The Charter allowed them only the right to have the "maintenance of a list of persons who may have applied to have their names entered thereon as nurses." It looked like a victory for Miss Nightingale – and in fact the voluntary listing of nurses was indeed a failure – but Mrs Bedford-Fenwick only had to bide her time. She concentrated her efforts on Parliament and finally, in 1919, a bill was passed. Mrs Bedford-Fenwick herself became State Registered Nurse No. 1 on the new official register.

But of course by then Florence Nightingale had been dead nine years. After 1896 she never left her house in South Street and was again immured in her bedroom for many years just as she had been once before. What was interesting about her extreme old age was that she never fell victim to wallowing in nostalgia. She continued to look to the future even when her own future was so clearly limited. She herself was intrigued by this outlook which she knew to be untypical. She had nursed many old people and she had observed their total lack of interest in anything or anyone new but she was always "eager to see successors" she wrote. Even more amazing was her rejection of flattery in any form and her instant recognition of sycophancy. She detested both. When she grew very old, in her late eighties, she saw how carefully people handled her and it irritated her. "Believe me dear Papa," she had once written, "what success in life I have had is due to my not seeing double with my eyes as so many do."[54] She never saw double, nor put on rose-coloured spectacles. She was disgusted by the fuss made over the relics of the Crimean War which she had been persuaded to lend for the Victorian Era Exhibition to celebrate the Queen's Diamond Jubilee in 1897. When the exhibition closed she wrote to her great-nephew, "Now I must ask you about my bust (Here I stop to utter a great many bad words not fit to put on paper. I also utter a pious wish that the bust may be smashed.) I should not have remembered it but that I am told somebody came every day to bedeck it with fresh flowers. I utter a pious wish that the person may be —— saved . . ."[55]

In 1901 she became almost blind which was a great blow, and began to lose her memory. The bestowal of the Order of Merit in 1907 (the first time it was given to a woman) and of the Freedom of the City of London the following year came too late for her to relish (or to utter any caustic comments). On August 13th, 1910, after six months during which she could not even speak, she finally died, leaving orders that her body should be used for dissection (which was not done). But another wish of hers – that there should be no national funeral or burial in Westminster Abbey – was deferred to. She was buried in the Nightingale family grave.

*   *   *

Florence Nightingale's feminism was the most contorted variety available in the nineteenth century. It solved no problems for other women and created many new ones. Worst of all, it presented women with a whole new area of guilt to bear when they were already quite burdened enough. And yet, for all that, Florence Nightingale's contribution to feminist history was of overriding importance.

The corner-stone of Florence Nightingale's feminism was her refusal to admit that women were discriminated against, that all that was wrong was women themselves. Should they choose to they could rise up everywhere at any time and fulfil themselves. She herself, she said, had never found her sex an obstacle – all that had ever got in her way was stupidity. This was a gigantic lie. It only needs the most cursory glance at the Nightingale Papers to see that it was her sex which made her life difficult from the very beginning and kept her from her work for so long. Once she was at work, her sex debarred her from a position of power in which she could act without having endlessly to work through the men who were in those positions. She should herself have served on the Royal Commissions not merely given advice to them. *She* should have been the Secretary, the Minister, the person responsible for decisions. Because she was so adept at pulling the strings behind the scenes, because she enjoyed that particular kind of power, she allowed herself to think that her sex had robbed her of nothing. Success blinded her to realities of the situation even though she was so proud of her clear-sightedness.

There was also the point that she was an upper-class woman. She was listened to not only because of what she had proved she could do but because of who she was – friend of Sidney Herbert, friend of Palmerston, on dining-out terms with half the cabinet and related to some of the most influential families in England. She had received an extremely rare education which put her on a level with the most educated men. Long before her rise to fame, when she was in her twenties, she had sat next to Sir Henry de la Beche at one of her father's dinner-parties and terrified him with her scholarship. "She began by drawing Sir Henry out on geology and charmed him with the boldness and breadth of her views which were not common then. She accidentally proceeded into regions of Latin and Greek . . ."[56] Then she turned to her other neighbour at the table and discussed with him his speciality, Egyptian Inscriptions, quoting Lepsius to him in the original. It was hardly surprising that she never found men patronized her or spoke over her head.

But her argument was never that all women could be like her. She was not so sheltered from the realities of the world that she could think that. It was that each woman had it within her grasp to alter her own particular world according to where she stood. What angered her was that those who would have found it easiest to do so were the least inclined. It was women of her own class who earned her greatest scorn. There are a hundred searing pages on this subject in *Suggestions for Thought to the Searchers after Religious Truth among the Artizans of England*. It was women like her mother and sister who enraged her in spite of her great love for them. They were typical of the kind of "femininity" which she thought did so much harm. While she herself worked so hard after the Crimean War "the whole occupation of Parthe and Mama was to lie on two sofas and tell each other not to get tired by putting flowers into water . . . I cannot describe the impression it made on me . . . It is a scene worthy of Molière where two people in tolerable health lie on the sofa all day doing absolutely nothing and persuade themselves and others that they are victims of their self-devotion for another who is dying of overwork."[57]

What stirred her to even greater contempt was the way women like Parthe actually dared to imagine they knew anything at all. Without studying a document or analysing a report they made themselves utterly foolish by offering opinions upon matters totally beyond their comprehension. "When Mrs Herbert was setting forth to me her views upon hospital nursing," Florence once wrote to her father, "I exclaimed quite involuntarily what can *you* know about it? . . . Does Parthe know more about my work than Mrs Herbert about hospitals? Where should I have been now in any part of my life's work had I followed any part of her life's advice?"[58] It was *these* women who, she thought, needed no other privileges or rights. They had all of them under their own noses. All they had to do was examine their own lives and then *put them right*.

Florence Nightingale found what she thought the truth unpalatable: too many women liked their "poor lives". They revelled in them, they wanted no change. So she damned them. They were not worth helping. John Stuart Mill or anyone else was wasting his or her time in trying to get such women the vote. What she would not accept was that she, and others who were clear-sighted, had a duty to awaken women to the indignities of their sex even if they did not recognize them. She was prepared to cast them off and declare they were not worth bothering about if they could not help themselves. What she refused to admit was that it was not the fault of women like her mother and sister if they lived how they lived – it *was* their fault in her opinion and therefore she could only blame them and not the system. But underlying her scorn there was also a good deal of unacknowledged blame for the system. "Our female schools are a disgrace to us," she wrote to Cardinal Manning. ". . . the stupidity of our education is marvellous . . . It is the ignorance of our women which gets them into mischief – but what do our *educated* women *know* who profess to teach them? Nothing but music and French and a kind of literature which they had better not know . . ."[59] That was blame for the system even if she would not allow it as an adequate excuse for Parthe at any rate (because she had been offered something else).

At the beginning of her career Florence Nightingale had thought that once employment of a dignified and satisfying nature was offered to women they would take it enthusiastically. All that needed to be done was to open the floodgates and women would thankfully stream through them. She was sure there must be hordes and hordes like her just waiting for the opportunity. By the end of her active life she was bitterly disappointed. There were no hordes. Even worse, the calibre of those who came to nurse was not high. There were honourable exceptions but the rank and file did not impress her. They were soft, indolent, too interested in money and not dedicated enough to obliterate all memory of pleasure outside work. She could not understand it. *Why* could women not "marry" a career as she had done? Why did they continue to find marriage to a man and the bearing of children more tempting? The wastage in nursing appalled her especially after she had discovered it was not due to faulty selection. In the first ten years of the Nightingale School the fall-out rate was 30 to 40% and even after selection procedure was overhauled it remained as high as 20%. Nor were the numbers for those who gained their certificates astronomically high. Between 1860 and 1903 a total of 1,907 nurses got one-year certificates from the Nightingale School. Nursing, even after it had been made respectable and had become a properly structured career had not after all been the answer to the problem of what to do with all those surplus spinsters, especially the well-born ones.

But, if the army of nurses was nothing like as vast as Florence Nightingale had envisaged it would be, it was an influential force. In a letter written in 1867 she had said, "The whole reform of nursing both at home and abroad has consisted of this; to take all power over the nursing out of the hands of the men and put it into the hands of *one female trained* head and make her responsible for everything . . ."[60] This is, to a large extent, what happened. Nightingale-trained Matrons sought and gained positions of great power in hospitals where previously men had ruled supreme. They became greatly respected, even feared, by men who until their advent had attracted all respect for themselves as doctors. And, since the spread and reform of hospitals was greatly accelerated in the last quarter of the nineteenth century, this bid for power on the part of women came at exactly the right time. Because of Florence Nightingale's strategy women claimed nursing for their own, as soon as it started to become professional. "There comes a crisis in the lives of all social movements," she wrote in 1892. "This has come in the case of nursing in about 30 years. For nursing was born but about 30 years ago. Before, it did not exist, tho' sickness is as old as the world."[61] In that crisis, women triumphed, for good or bad. It became as odd to think of a man as a nurse as it had once been to think of a woman as a doctor.[62]

To grab a profession for women and claim it for them was no mean achievement particularly in the context of the struggle for emancipation then going on. But Florence Nightingale did more than that: she made *paid* employment a thing to be desired. She herself was rich but she understood the significance of money for services rendered. Women as nurses must not be exploited. Her anxiety was intense when she discovered that because of the nature of the agreement signed, St Thomas's Hospital was actually using trainee nurses as an underpaid workforce. Women had put up with this too long. Greatly as she admired the work of Elizabeth Fry and all the various sisters of Charity she did not want nursing to be founded on notions of voluntary contribution. Certainly she saw nursing as a vocation, certainly she thought no nurse should think of the money first, but at the same time she wanted wages for nurses and did not in the least think that money changing hands would taint the calling. If nurses were not paid, which was part of nursing being professional as opposed to amateur, then they would go on being regarded as a superior kind of maid or companion. They would not, in short, be valued for what she wanted them to be: skilled people. If she was adamant that nursing was a vocation she was equally adamant that it was a skill. Nothing roused her formidable anger so much as any misunderstanding on this point. "I am always asked," she wrote, "to send a nurse because the friends of the patients are 'worn out' with 'sitting up' – or to save the servants 'running up and down stairs'. I am never asked to send a nurse that the patient be *better* nursed. I do believe this is the root of it all."[63]

Inevitably, her success at making nursing a skilled profession had its own pitfalls – people came to believe only a professional nurse could nurse at all which had never exactly been her intention. By the end of the century a letter from one indignant lady appeared in the nursing press saying, "Will you allow me to protest against the modern ridiculous fad for calling in a professional Nurse on the very smallest provocation? A few years ago we were considered quite capable of nursing those nearest and dearest to us and excepting in cases of acute delirium etc where great muscular strength is required I maintain that we are so still."[64]

By the turn of the century there were 64,000 nurses and midwives of whom 10,000, the élite of the profession, were fully trained. Nursing had become one of the great professions for women, far more accessible than doctoring. And yet this was not as satisfactory for feminism as it appeared. Florence Nightingale had laid down too firmly the need for self-abnegation. It was a curse called down on feminism which took half a century to lift. Florence Nightingale saw nothing wrong with "choice" – she only regretted which side most women came down upon. She herself loved babies – her correspondence is littered with instructions to "kiss any babies for me" – but she could manage without having any of her own. The cruelty of it does not seem to have distressed her. She never challenged the necessity of having to deny this side of her nature – it simply seemed to her obvious that a woman could not be everything. She accepted (if reluctantly) that some women could not resist the temptations of domesticity with all it implied and also accepted that therefore they must give up their careers. Matrons resigned upon marriage. How could they avoid doing so? Work was for *unmarried* ladies in the main (or for widows). It was for women who had chosen to deny half their natures because there was no other way. It became the greatest quest in feminist history to find that other way.

EDUCATION

Emily Davies
(The Mistress and Fellows of Girton College; photo by John Edward Leigh, Cambridge)

Emily Davies
1830–1921

There was one topic upon which both feminists and anti-feminists were in perfect agreement in the nineteenth century and that was the education of girls. It was a disgrace and must be reformed. As early as 1730 Mary Anstell had pointed out that if there *was* a difference in intellect between men and women (a point by no means conceded) a great deal of it must be due to training. If girls were given the same education as boys it might then, and only then, be possible to discover if there was any innate difference between them in mental abilities. This argument was repeated over and over again for the next hundred years and meanwhile the state of girls' schools in Britain grew worse and worse until, by 1830, Frances Power Cobbe judged that they had reached a new nadir. Schools in her grandmother's day had, she swore, been much better. The harm had been done, in her opinion, by the rising passion for "accomplishments". However bad the schools for boys (and no one denied that they too were in urgent need of reform) they were not bedevilled by these dreadful accomplishments.

Frances Power Cobbe herself went to school in Brighton where by 1836 there were a hundred establishments calling themselves girls' schools. They were all outrageously expensive. Frances went to a school at 32 Brunswick Terrace, where her parents paid £1,000 for two years' doubtful education (including board). "The din of our large double schoolroom was something frightful," she wrote. ". . . four pianos might be heard going at once in rooms above and around us while at numerous tables scattered round the rooms there were girls reading aloud to governesses and reciting lessons in English, French, German and Italian. This hideous clatter continued the entire day."[1]

Yet this was one of the better schools. At the other end of the scale were the shocking places like the School for Clergymen's Daughters at Casterton in Yorkshire, upon which Charlotte Brontë based Lowood Hall. In between were hundreds of establishments many of them with under forty pupils and all of them staffed by totally untrained teachers. These teachers were mostly impoverished gentlewomen who had been driven into these schools as an alternative to private governessing. There was, in any case, no training available except for the Home and Colonial Training Scheme where teachers for the National schools were trained, and no gentlewoman expected to put herself through that nor did the sort of establishment she taught in regard it as a qualification. No woman could possess a University education which, even if not a training to teach in itself, was regarded as such by boys' schools.

It was ironic that a working-class girl was much better off in this one respect. Since 1830 girls as well as boys came under the care of the two great voluntary societies, the National and the British and Foreign, which set up schools for the working classes all over England, aided by a government grant. These were staffed by certificated teachers and were infinitely superior to the great mass of middle-class girls' schools that sprang up everywhere as part of the answer to genteel poverty. This state of affairs was on the one hand well-known and on the other a great secret. The true nature of middle-class girls' education was not exposed for the sham it was until the Taunton Commission made its report in 1868. This proved to be the greatest indictment of girls' education there could possibly have been and was invaluable to those who wished to see it reformed. And yet the Commissioners had the greatest difficulty finding out anything at all because ". . . the advances of the Commission were received with unrelenting hostility." One self-styled headmistress sent back the inspector's eight sheets of questions with a note saying "I am sincerely sorry to find that ministers have nothing better to do than to pry into the ménage of private families, as I consider my establishment, which has been in existence 30 years and always held the highest position."[2] Another replied "I think, sir, you have entirely mistaken the character of my establishment which is not so much a school as a *home* for young ladies."[3]

That was precisely the trouble: the emphasis everywhere was on domestic virtues plus accomplishments. Mr Giffard, inspector for Surrey and Sussex, reported to the Commission that although piano playing was *the* accomplishment "it was not thought worthwhile to tune practising pianos or those which are used by junior girls who usually get the broken down . . . It would be an act of mercy to a child with a musical ear to take out the wires."[4] Needlework, another vital accomplishment, concerned itself with the decorative rather than the useful. Inspectors expressed contempt at the bits of embroidery brandished as proof of skill while straight seam sewing and the ability to cut out a garment were unknown. But, if piano playing and needlework were inadequate in spite of the prominence given to them, academic subjects hardly existed. "I never expected," wrote Mr Fearon of the Metropolitan district, "to find young ladies of 16 and 18 whose parents were paying £100 to £150 a year for their education ignorant of the inflections of the most common irregular verbs . . . and unable to turn simple sentences into French without blunders."[5] He, with other inspectors, was distressed and surprised to find the premises of girls' schools so very much worse than the worst of the boys'. "A classroom is supplied," he reported, "with nothing but a bench round the wall on which the pupils sit while the teacher occupies a chair in the middle and if the pupils write at all they do so on little scraps of paper held in the hands . . ."[6] Mr Stanton, reporting on Devon and Somerset, echoed his concern. "I remember," he wrote, "entering a country school room ill ventilated and redolent of hair oil and apples where great girls . . . were diligently learning the mysteries of 'tatting' who had no idea of writing a simple piece of English." But their English was brilliant compared with their arithmetic. That subject was hardly taught at all. One report commented "A young lady of 20 years of age . . . was perfectly startled when I pointed out to her that three halfpence are 1½d . . . she could not with any degree of fluency count by twos, such as 1, 3, 5 etc – 2, 4, 6 she did better. And yet the same young lady was an expert on the piano . . ."[7]

The report concluded that "the general deficiency of girls' education can be stated with absolute confidence." Those who had been saying this for years were gratified but they waited suspiciously to see what would now be done. About that, there was no agreement. On the one hand were those who said that, now girls' education has been shown to be appalling, let us reform it to make it as good as *but different from* boys; and on the other were those who said let us reform it so that it is as good as boys and *the same in all essentials*. Between these two fiercely opposing points of view there was a great gulf. In addition, the issue was complicated by feminists dividing on *both* sides so that there was

not even solidarity in the feminist ranks. This division was particularly
acute over the prospect of Higher education for girls – those who
wanted girls to have exactly the same education as boys particularly
wanted to secure for them colleges and degrees on a par with them. In
their opinion, "different" could only mean "inferior". The person
who believed this most fervently of all and who fought hardest of all to
make sure "different" was not allowed to become "inferior" by
refusing to accept it was Emily Davies, the founder of Girton College,
Cambridge. She believed that there was no sex in intellect and that
there should be none therefore in the training of the intellect. She
wanted an end to the outrageous assumption that girls were "by
nature" intellectually inferior to men. She wanted an end to any role
being pre-supposed by virtue of the training available for it: education
and employment were in her opinion inextricably linked. Girls could
do so little in life because they were educated to do so little. Change
their education and their prospects were immediately changed, their
horizons automatically widened. Take them, educationally, to the top
and you would take them to the top eventually in all walks of life. So
she took them to what was commonly held to be the top: to the oldest
universities where they studied with the men. When Emily Davies
was born there were four universities in England, none open to
women; when she died there were twelve, all open to women. Within
her lifetime she spanned the greatest upheaval in girls' expectations
there had ever been.

★   ★   ★

Sarah Emily Davies was herself no scholar, nor were her interests
primarily scholarly. Her own education was strictly in accordance
with what was usual for a clergyman's daughter . . . "Do they go to
school? No. Do they have governesses? No. They have lessons and get
on as well as they can."[8] In her own case this was nothing like as well as
she desired, but then she was singularly unfortunate in being excluded
from the teaching her father could have given her if he had wished and
in having an out of London upbringing. London, when Emily Davies
was of school age, was the centre of exciting educational develop-
ments in girls' education and she was three hundred miles away.

She was born in Southampton on April 22nd, 1830, the fourth child
and second daughter of the Rev. John Davies and his wife Mary. Her
father was a clever, highly-strung man who was out of place as the

headmaster of a small boys' boarding-school. He was almost made a professor of moral and political philosophy at London University just before Emily was born but withdrew his candidature when he found the stipend of £300 a year was not guaranteed. There was no doubt that in this post he would have been a much happier man. His wife would also have been a much happier woman. She desperately wanted to move to London and reprimanded herself for her "carnal heart" in wanting it. By the autumn of 1832 John Davies' health was deteriorating rapidly so the whole family, by then enlarged to five children, went to Normandy for a year. Then they returned, this time to another boys' school at Chichester. For three years John Davies struggled to do his job but in 1836 he again approached complete collapse and had to retire once more. This time the family went to the Isle of Wight. There, they rented an extremely small cottage. John Davies liked the isolated cottage very much but the children were less pleased. They longed for the social intercourse their father dreaded and for some of the hustle and bustle of a town which was so bad for him. Mary Davies too was unhappy. She had "shooting pains" in her teeth and found it burdensome to be solely responsible for the entertainment of five small children. She was not sorry when her husband's convalescence came to an end and they once more returned to Chichester.

But they were not there long. In 1840 John Davies was offered, and accepted, a living in Gateshead. Emily remembered vividly the excitement of the arduous journey from Chichester to Gateshead, by a devious route to make the most of the new railways. In Gateshead, a town then of some 15,000 people, they moved into a large, rambling, slightly depressing rectory which Mary Davies knew at a glance was going to be hard to run. She had brought a maid-of-all-work with her and found she had inherited a gardener, who also obligingly cleaned shoes, but that left a great deal for herself and her two young daughters to do. On the other hand, the Rev. John Davies was much better suited. There were three churches to look after but he had two curates to help and did not find the work anything like as gruelling as teaching. One of the curates, a Mr Bennett, also ran a small Foundation school called the Anchorage which took girls as well as boys. Emily recorded years later, relishing the irony, that one of her father's first actions was to restrict the school to boys "under the belief girls lowered the status."[9]

Emily was ten when she arrived in Gateshead and had reached the stage of finding what her mother could offer her in the way of education insufficient. She was particularly attracted to languages, especially Italian, and science. Mary Davies knew no science and was weak on languages. Just before Emily left Chichester she had begun attending a small girls' day-school but once in Gateshead she was back again to having lessons with her older sister Jane from an increasingly hard-pressed mother. The only help offered by John Davies was the supervision of a weekly composition for which he set a theme. These became the highlights of Emily's existence. She put her heart into the "themes" and competed eagerly with her brother William for her father's praise. William was two years older than she and her favourite companion. Together they began writing a newspaper, all laboriously copied out in narrow columns to imitate exactly *The Times*. Emily put in an advertisement for a governess for herself, warning applicants that they must possess "firmness and determination as the young lady who is to be the object of . . . care is rather self-willed. Phrenologically speaking she has the organ of self-esteem rather largely developed."[10]

Until her brothers left home Emily survived on the intellectual stimulus with which they provided her, but once all three had gone off (two to Repton and one to Rugby) she began to suffer from acute boredom. She became increasingly restless as she did the ironing in the basement with Jane and tried to interest herself, after the household chores were done, in private study. But there was no spur, no incentive and she felt herself falling into a stupor from sheer lack of intellectual companionship. The only breaks in the monotony of her existence were visits to friends – the kind of lengthy visits girls were allowed to make because they had no education to be interrupted. Emily made one such visit when she was sixteen to Torquay and stayed six months. The only bit of luck she had came rather late in her early life – an interesting family moved to Gateshead in 1848 with four congenial daughters of just the right age. This was the Crow family and in Jane Crow, who was exactly her age, Emily found a stimulating companion. Jane had been to school at Blackheath and knew all kinds of lively girls with many of whom she kept in touch and to whom she introduced Emily. (One of them was Elizabeth Garrett whom Emily first met in 1854.) Yet in spite of this valuable new friendship Emily felt there was little real change in her prospects. A visit to Geneva with her parents and sister in 1851 only seemed to emphasize how narrow her life was compared to her brothers'. She felt this particularly when

William went to Cambridge where Llewelyn, the eldest son, was President of the Union. She and William had been, once upon a time, equal scholars. Now William was allowed a University education while hers had come to a full stop unless she counted her own pathetic attempts to instruct herself. What had made this all the harder to bear was what William had proceeded to do with his privileged education. In 1849 he went sadly astray – he drank, fell in with cardsharpers and inevitably into debt. When he found himself in the hands of a moneylender he had to throw himself on his father's mercy. He was extricated from this disgrace but it made a deep impression on Emily. The waste of William's chances not only distressed but angered her. Young men like William threw away what she would have given anything to have and it was monstrously unfair.[11]

By the time William had been packed off to China as a naval chaplain Emily had come of age. She was not frivolous, she had no yearning for balls and parties, but she craved interesting companionship and it was hard to come by. Those who knew her well (few in number) were aware that behind the rather stiff façade there was a great sense of humour but others thought her reserved and cold. She was never immediately popular or attractive and because of this apparent gravity she tended to be overlooked in company even though she had decided opinions to offer. It was not that she was shy but that she weighed people carefully and they did not always like it. She was, in fact, exactly the kind of young lady who in Victorian times was particularly trapped by her very common situation. She had neither the means nor the opportunity nor the daring to break out of the mould into which her circumstances were pushing her. She was the dutiful daughter upon whom Fortune had not smiled in the way of beauty or wealth, destined to stay at home and serve. And that home itself was not the home of a Florence Nightingale with all that this implied – it was a remote North Country rectory inhabited by an anti-social reclusive father. The days were long and dreary, the treats tame and sparse.

Then real misfortune hit Emily. In 1857, her sister Jane developed lung symptoms. Emily was sent to the south coast with her but Jane died the following year. Henry, the youngest of the family, meanwhile fell ill in Algiers. As soon as Jane was buried Emily set out to nurse Henry, accompanied by her friend Jane Crow and chaperoned by Llewelyn on the journey. She nursed her brother devotedly and brought him home but he too died. To complete the agony, news arrived from China that William was also dead. There were only Emily and Llewelyn, the eldest, left. Since Llewelyn was by then a curate in Limehouse it was obvious that Emily must take charge of her heartbroken parents in Gateshead.

Life for her was suddenly twice as grim as she had ever thought it. The enormous rectory was the very worst place to be stuck with sorrowing parents and there seemed nothing Emily could do to alleviate not just their grief but her own. What was even more cruel was that she had met in Algiers, in the intervals between nursing Henry, an extraordinary woman who had changed her life. This was Barbara Bodichon (née Leigh-Smith), the woman who seems ubiquitous in the histories of so many active feminists in the nineteenth century. Barbara and her sister Annie, who was Emily's original contact, were the first people, she wrote "who sympathised with my feelings of resentment at the subjection of women."[12] Before meeting them, she had never even heard of Mary Wollstonecraft (with whose books they immediately supplied her); she had thought her outlook entirely her own. Occasionally, she had met other women, like her friend Elizabeth Garrett, who she felt shared her general sympathies, but even Elizabeth was a pale shadow compared to Barbara who said things Emily had never expected to hear uttered. Moreover, Barbara had been amused at the idea that Emily thought her unique. On the contrary, she assured her little North Country friend, there were *lots* of other women who shared her views and spoke openly of wishing to change the lot of women in all sorts of ways, there was an actual body of opinion existing and a real movement beginning. The excitement Emily had felt was painful. Although she was not at all the sort of person who adored anyone, adoration being quite foreign to her critical nature, she quickly came to adore Barbara. She even approved of how she dressed, in loose flowing clothes with her long blonde hair flowing down her back. She was, in every sense, a revelation.

Back in Gateshead, the revelation dimmed. Emily wrote to Barbara, who replied, and she drew courage from the correspondence but she felt very remote and isolated again. "On my return to Gateshead," she wrote, "I went back to parish work but tried to combine it with some effort in another direction."[13] But "other directions" were limited in Gateshead. Everything that was revolutionary happened in London. Emily began a reading class, did a little teaching of arithmetic and became increasingly and miserably aware that not only was there not much else she could do, there was not much else she was equipped to do. Her own inadequacies pressed heavily upon her. She began to wonder which came first, the lack of opportunities or the lack of any training to take them. "It is no wonder," she wrote, "that people who have not learned to do anything cannot find anything to do."[14]

Up in London that "body of opinion" of which Barbara and Annie Leigh-Smith had spoken agreed with her. Her sole surviving brother, Llewelyn, had himself become interested in the subject. When Emily went to visit him in the spring of 1859 he discussed with her the subject of girls' education and their possible employment and then Emily went to tea with Elizabeth Garrett at the Leigh-Smith family home in Blandford Square, where Barbara still spent half the year. Here she met, among others, Barbara's great friend Bessie Parkes, another member of what was becoming known as the Langham Place set because 19 Langham Place was where the newly-formed Society for Promoting the Employment of Women met. It was also the head-quarters of the *Englishwoman's Journal* which had begun the year before. Emily went to Langham Place and felt she had come home. But of course she had not. Home was the rectory in Gateshead. Home was a monotonous routine far removed from this hive of activity. Back she was obliged to go, but she was determined to take with her some of the enterprise and enthusiasm which characterized the Langham Place set who now counted her as an honorary, if absent, member.

As soon as she got home, Emily started a Northumberland and Durham Branch of the Society for Promoting the Employment of Women, with herself as treasurer. She also formed a committee of prominent local people which opened a Register for Governesses and began making enquiries about conditions of working for women in the local factories. As well as giving Emily the kind of activity she needed it also brought her a new and valuable friend – Anna Richardson, a highly intelligent well-read woman, who agreed to teach Emily Greek and to attend with her a course of lectures on Physiology in Newcastle. "Though I did not care for the subject," Emily confessed, "I very much enjoyed being associated with others in learning *anything*."[15] She also discovered that she enjoyed committee work. The detail and organization which others found dreary and irritating she actually found stimulating. She was a natural committee woman, rejoicing in the meticulous preparation of agenda and circulars, of reports and resolutions. To her surprise she found that not only did committee work bring gratification but it also brought power. She controlled the work of the committee to such an extent that through her familiarity with its workings she exercised great influence. How to use that influence for the best began to interest her. The main problem, she decided, was enlarging the scope of the committee's work – many more people needed to be informed and stimulated into helping.

So, in 1860, a year after the committee had been launched, Emily wrote a series of letters to the Newcastle daily paper on the subject of women's employment. In them, she painted a graphic picture of the typical life of a young middle-class woman: a few years at a so-called "school", followed by days of "laborious trifling" helping mother. If she did not marry what were the options of such a lady? She could be a governess, keep a school, or do "good works". Yet in Mr Ward's Trades' Directory for Newcastle there were listed 320 different trades and professions open to men. Why was a large proportion of them not also open to women? There was surely no natural incapacity which prevented women administering estates or managing businesses. "It is certainly not easy," wrote Emily, "to see why it should be unfeminine for a girl to sit in her father's office under his immediate eye." As for keeping a shop, surely women were *much* more suited, so how had men come to monopolize that trade? What was masculine about shop-keeping? Even more extraordinary, how had they come to be hairdressers? "It is scarcely credible though I am afraid true that at this moment," Emily wrote, "it would be useless to ask a respectable hairdresser to take a female apprentice." She then tried to examine the objections to widening female employment. They divided, she thought, into two main groups: moral and economic. The first line of argument was hardly worth bothering with. Women *were* already in public life and suffering no ill-effects. They appeared at bazaars and all sorts of public functions involving commercial transactions. It was only false notions of propriety which confined their appearances to this category and she appealed to readers to break these down. As for the economic worry, she argued that, far from robbing men of jobs, women would only fill existing gaps and would by working relieve their families of a burden. "No man in his senses," Emily pointed out, "would keep two or three sons doing nothing." Yet all over England large numbers of able-bodied girls were kept at home because of the assumption that indolence was "feminine and refined".

The letters were well-received and Emily was pleased to have contributed something solid to the general debate. When she visited Llewelyn again and once more went almost daily to Langham Place she felt she could hold her head up at last. She was pleased to be asked to help edit the *Englishwoman's Journal* and even more pleased to become actively involved in helping her old friend Elizabeth Garrett gain a medical education. She accompanied Elizabeth on her depressing rounds of colleges and doctors seeking assistance and "cut up her style" in her written applications. But then, as ever, it was back to Gateshead and that familiar, sickening feeling that whatever she did in Gateshead, whatever miracles she performed there, it was all basically trivial. She was thirty-years-old and the pattern seemed irrevocably set.

But then another family tragedy brought an unexpected change. John Davies had an attack of bronchitis while on holiday at Ilkley in the summer of 1860 and died very suddenly. Within six months Emily and her mother had moved to 17 Cunningham Place in St Johns Wood, London. At once, a new life opened up. Emily, who already had more than a foot in the door was now at the very centre of all that happened in Langham Place. All it had needed was accessibility to make her indispensable in twenty different ways. Nor was her new life all work – her social life blossomed. Every day she helped in Langham Place, every evening she went to soirées and parties, enjoying them almost more than she dared to admit. "The love of dissipation grows on me as I get more at home in society," she wrote. London was spoiling her. "I feel quite injured now," she wrote home to poor Jane Crow still stuck in Gateshead, "if I don't see everything that's going the moment it comes out."[16] She saw Garibaldi, met Trollope, Holman Hunt, Robert Browning ("nice and genial") and heard Jenny Lind sing. It was all quite intoxicating and revealed to Emily more than she had ever guessed about herself. She discovered that quiet and serious though she might be she could more than hold her own in discussion, quite losing her habitual reserve in the cut-and-thrust of intellectual debate. She also, for the first time, was able to indulge her passion for people. She had always loved to stare, to speculate, to analyse people's appearances and now she was provided with wonderful material to satisfy her urgent curiosity. It was an unexpected side to her which amused her friends. Take Emily to a concert and afterwards she would describe the audience, not the music. Take her to an art exhibition and she would record not the paintings but the people looking at the paintings. For such a committee woman it was out of character to find her in love with human beings and not the statistics she was so adept at mastering.

And yet, for all the pleasure of this new way of life, Emily felt even more anxious about her future. What was she going to do? If she received any marriage proposals or entertained any notions on matrimony as a prospect there is not a whisper of them surviving among her own papers nor do any contemporaries record anyone having designs upon her. In fact, rather the reverse. Most men were afraid, even repelled, by her – not because of her appearance, which was quite pretty when she was young and certainly diminutively feminine in the best Victorian tradition, but because of her sharp tongue and steely eye. Men felt nervous in her presence (James Stuart said later he found it hard to concentrate on lecturing with her formidable person in the room). They had to get to know her very well indeed through working with her before they warmed to her lighter side and at that stage in her life few had done so. At thirty, then, Emily had no marriage prospects and she began to think "what to do for the future in the changed circumstances". She came to the conclusion that the best thing to do would be "to follow Elizabeth Garrett" and try to become a doctor. But as soon as she tried to do so Emily discovered she was unsuited. It was not just that she was not basically attracted to medicine (neither was Elizabeth Blackwell) but that her heart was not in it. She, who was so determined, lacked true determination in this one respect. She pretended to herself that the real stumbling block was the impossibility of leaving her mother during the training which would require her to leave London but more honestly she also mentioned[17] that her diaries for the time reveal a certain listlessness about lessons and that there were unaccountable gaps between them. It was at this crucial point that Emily heard through the Langham Place grapevine that the University of London was about to apply for a new charter. It was her idea to seize the chance this presented and ask for the new charter to include women as eligible students for degrees.

It was a daring, and in many ways an absurd idea, for where would such women come from? Where were the women educated enough to be able to go on to study for degrees? There were in fact only a handful of girls' schools worthy of the name turning out girls capable of further study. Emily knew this but since her contact with the Langham Place set she had grown to admire the products of these schools and to wish both that there could be more of them and that they could go further. Her own brother Llewelyn had become involved with one of these schools, Queens' College, because it had been opened in 1848 by his friend F. D. Maurice, the Christian Socialist lecturer of King's College. Maurice had begun by giving lectures to oblige the Governesses Benevolent Institution and had felt that the instruction he gave could well do with starting further down the line. The "college" establishment had classes open to girls over twelve, preparatory classes for younger girls and also evening classes for girls already governessing (to which Frances Mary Buss walked each night from Camden). The following year Bedford College had opened on much the same lines.[18] Both schools quickly drew to themselves all the intelligent, middle-class girls in London whose thwarted ambition to learn was recognized and approved by liberal parents. Emily envied them in retrospect but her envy did not hold her back either from wishing many more to enjoy what she had not enjoyed or from wanting to raise the sights even higher for those already receiving this privileged kind of girls' education. She resolved to organize a memorial to all university members and other prominent people. She roped in her mother to help (several surviving letters are in Mary Davies' handwriting) and wrote to each person individually. "It was thought best," she wrote later, "not to give my christian name in full Mary Llewelyn Davies [her sister in law] remarking that they'd think it was some horrid woman in spectacles and in consequence I receive many letters addressed to S. E. Davies esq."[19] But in spite of prodigious efforts the application failed.

Emily, however, was stimulated rather than disheartened by the experience. It seemed to her that there had been a real and impressive response to her letters and that the application had certainly not failed through lack of support. She began to think that possibly she had begun too high – perhaps it would be better to attempt something that appeared more reasonable to the reactionary authorities who would always stand in the way. The new Local Examinations seemed the perfect test case. These were a recent invention, only started in 1858 to provide some external measure of achievement for all the many middle-class schools not covered by HM Inspectors who kept the National Schools up to the mark. Emily saw them as a halfway house to getting entry to degree examinations. There was also the point that the Locals were administered by Oxford and Cambridge Universities and so access to them would influence the other universities.

She set about forming a committee, which was constituted in October 1862 with the avowed object of obtaining the admission of women to University examinations, starting with the Locals. One by one the centres where the Local Examination were held were tried, and the two older Universities canvassed for support. Emily's true work had now begun in earnest. She wrote that it was "hateful work" but that "incessant and un-remitting talking and pushing is the *only* way of gaining our ends."[20] Within a remarkably short time this pushing had achieved results. Oxford turned the idea down but the Cambridge examiners said they had no objection to copies of the boys' papers being provided at the next examination *as an experiment*. The secretary in charge of the London centre, H. R. Tomkinson, said he was willing to allow the girls to be examined in his centre so that was no problem. The only snag was that permission was granted by Cambridge in the October of 1863 and the next examination was in December. It would have been feeble to turn down the sought-after opportunity on the grounds of not being ready so Emily began frantically scouring London for candidates. She wrote to every head-mistress she could think of but then was disturbed by some of the replies she received. Some were illegible, some ungrammatical, some both: what hope of the pupils if this was how the teachers performed?

Finally, however, a respectable tally was secured. Eighty-three candidates submitted themselves for the first public examination to which girls had ever been admitted. Twenty-five were from the North London Collegiate (where Miss Buss reigned) another twenty from Queens' and a further twenty from schools like Octavia Hill's. The rest were from untried establishments, some out of London (Cheltenham Ladies' College would have been invaluable but Miss Beale at that time was against competition.) Great care was taken to see that the whole exercise was conducted in a dignified way and that supervision was above reproach. The papers duly arrived, the girls did them, the examiners (paid out of a subscription fund) marked them. The results were encouraging, except for Arithmetic. In that subject eight out of the forty-five juniors failed and only six of the thirty-eight seniors got more than 25%. But in English the girls did very well and in every other subject held their own. The examiners' Report was debated the following April at a special meeting of the Social Science Association, an influential society which had concerned itself closely with girls' education.

To Emily's fury the main thing that came out of this meeting was a feeling that Arithmetic should be "lightened" in any examinations for girls in the future. She would have none of that, seeing the assumption behind such a suggestion as dangerous for the whole future of girls' education. She was always to be adamant that Arithmetic and every other subject should stay *exactly* as they were for the boys and that what should be changed was the *teaching* of them in girls' schools. To those who suggested that this way lay "brain fever" for overpressed female intellects she once responded, "Why should simple equations brighten their intellects and quadratic equations drive them into a lunatic asylum?"[21] Surely people could see that the whole failure in Arithmetic was due to the absence of proper instruction? When it appeared they could not, Emily felt obliged to convince them. She wrote a paper entitled *On Secondary Instruction as Relating to Girls* in which she described exactly what girls *were* taught and how they were taught it and by whom. It was read aloud for her at another Social Science meeting. Emily slightly cringed as she heard her own words coming back at her. "This is too strong," she murmured to her companion but the meeting was impressed by her arguments. If she was right, girls' education was, with a few honourable exceptions, in a pitiful state.

It was at this point that Emily Davies heard that the Taunton Commission which had just been appointed to enquire into the condition of middle-class schools might not also look at girls' unless specifically asked to do so. She wrote off immediately to Lord Lyttelton who was the chief commissioner. "We are very desirous, therefore, that the instructions should be framed as expressly to include girls and we should be greatly obliged if you would have the goodness to bring the matter before Lord Granville."[22] She also wrote to the other commissioners and then prepared a memorial to the entire Schools Commission Board urging that "the education of girls and the means of improving it are within the scope of your enquiry." If she had not been so perceptive and zealous in doing this it is more than probable that the already over-loaded commissioners would have failed to have girls' schools inspected and the whole rotten edifice of what was laughably termed "girls' education" would never have been brought crashing down. But Emily proved a good watchdog and sounded the alarm in time. Not only did the commissioners include girls' schools but they themselves showed almost as much enthusiasm as Emily herself. Mr Roby, who was made secretary, kept Emily minutely informed. He was a member of the Social Science Association and had been Emily's ally in the Cambridge Local examinations. As a young don at St John's, Cambridge, he had published a paper, *Remarks on College Reform*, and had gone on to become interested in all kinds of educational reform.

This was heartening for Emily and the other feminist reformers who quickly discovered that in the Taunton Commissioners they had been extremely fortunate because everyone concerned seemed to "go in for" (as Emily put it) the girls. Emily was invited to propose witnesses "best able to speak and able to speak best" about girls' schools. The questionnaire to be sent out was discussed with her and when she was given the date for her own appearance before the Commission she was told "If you will draw up some list of heads under which your evidence could best fall it will contribute to the good order of the examination."[23] When, added to this favour, one of the assistant commissioners, Joshua Fitch, brought out a pamphlet urging the improvement of girls' education in which he plainly stated "Intellect is of no sex" it was hardly surprising that the *Quarterly Review* detected a feminist bias in the final report of the Taunton Commission.

This report (finally presented in 1868) was a vindication of everything Emily Davies had said and was something of a personal triumph for her. So, too, had been the decision to admit girls officially to the Cambridge Local Examinations taken in March 1865. "Never having counted on success even when things looked most promising," Emily wrote, ". . . now it is come I cannot half believe it . . ."[24] But the victory was solid and real. Girls had now been brought into touch with a national standard and all else, she felt, would flow from it. But it would not flow very fast. The growth of good girls' schools, now that the bad ones had been revealed for what they were, was bound to be slow – simply because the money to start them was not there. Section 12 of the Endowed Schools Act (which followed the Taunton Commission) left the position of girls open. It said they should share in the endowment of new schools "so far as conveniently may be." It was a hopelessly ambiguous phrase, leaving the way open for people to claim that while the boys needed new laboratories or playing fields it was not "convenient" to let girls have a share of whatever money was available. Money for girls' schools had to be clawed from the boys' giant share and with public sympathy still non-existent the clawing was timid. It was a measure of how much support there was for the feminists among the commissioners administering the Act that ninety schools for girls were in fact endowed in the next thirty years.

It was a debt Emily Davies was very ready to acknowledge. She, of all people, knew the help she had received in getting girls admitted to examinations and in getting their schools reformed. But it was a disappointment to her to find that this support was much more cautious when it came to the next step in her programme: the founding of an actual University College for women. If it seemed to her logical and inevitable this was not how her scheme was regarded by those who up to then had given her such magnificent support. She came up against a strong alternative they found more attractive. This was that women should found a university of their own and not try to join any existing institution. They should have a university education as well as men but it should be *different*. The argument behind this was that the universities needed reforming anyway so why should women try to gain entry to a syllabus and to an examination system which were in many ways anachronisms?

Emily Davies rejected this attitude scornfully. It was one she had recognized very early as dangerous. Women would never force their way into men's colleges but this did not mean they could not be part of their universities.[25] All through the battle for the Cambridge Locals there had been this threat of offering a "special" examination specifically designed for girls and she had had to stamp on it ruthlessly. London University, with its offer of a "special" examination at matriculation level was trying the same thing. "Special" colleges and "special" degrees would be fatal. Again and again Emily reiterated her belief that different would *always* mean inferior. It was absolutely vital to provide the *same* education at university level for women as for men. A friend who reproved her for her fierceness said ". . . you are so eager to be reckoned equal that you will not hear of different."[26] No, Emily replied, she would not. But support for the next stage had to come from a much less influential source – the schoolmistresses who knew, as she did, that, without a university education like men, women would always lack prestige and a sense of direction. In 1866 Emily Davies formed a Schoolmistresses Association at her house in an attempt to break down the isolation felt by teachers in girls' schools and so that she could form a nucleus of women as determined as she was to raise the sights of girls' education even higher. Many of the schoolmistresses who met there were achieving great things in their respective schools but all of them were overcome, like Frances Buss, "with a sort of sick despair" when they saw how much was still to be done. What in particular depressed them was the necessity of employing men in their Upper Schools. "I absolutely burn with indignation," wrote Frances Buss ". . . at the bare notion of *men* teachers in Upper girls' schools . . . it is degrading to women's education."[27] At the third meeting of the new association Emily Davies proposed that a new College for Women should be established to provide women with that higher education they so obviously lacked, and to put an end to "degradation".

From the beginning of this new and hardest campaign Emily Davies was sustained by a vision of the college in her head. Outwardly calm, quiet, serious, even cold and prosaic, she burned with an imaginative, highly-coloured, utterly extravagant vision of what her college would look like. "It is to be as beautiful as the Assize Courts at Manchester and with gardens and grounds and everything . . ."[28] She had begun to compose a college hymn within days ("For thee, O dear dear college/Mine eyes their vigils keep . . .") and could exactly visualize the rooms and the furnishings and the whole arrangement of the place. This touching dream of the future she was determined to bring about kept Emily going through those endless, mundane weeks of organization and hard work which followed. A programme was drafted, leaflets printed and a memorial organized to launch her audacious scheme. Entitled "Respecting the Need of a Place of Higher Education for Girls" the memorial was signed by 521 teachers and 175 others and was presented in 1867 to the Schools Committee. It had no discernible effect. Yet another committee was called for and Emily Davies, not daunted by the already long list of committees upon which she had served, set to once more and composed one. It met for the first time on December 5th, 1867, at 9 Conduit Street. At once, the opposition made itself felt.

Barbara Bodichon, the first to donate £1,000 to the founding of the college, was nervous about the antagonism she sensed in influential circles throughout London. There was, she thought, "a frightful coolness" and she hardly dared point this out to Emily. People thought the reform of girls' education had gone quite far enough. It was only right they should have better schools but to suggest sending them away from home to a college attached to a men's university was absurd. But Emily herself was sanguine. She had expected this reaction. What worried her far more, as she got down to collecting money and making concrete plans, was opposition of a different sort. A rival movement to her own had just begun in the North of England. This was to establish separate lectures just for women. "It is better," wrote Emily at the start of 1868, "frankly to acknowledge that at the present the lectures stand in the way of the college."[29] The full force of her anger was turned against those friends who ventured timidly to suggest that perhaps Emily ought to forget about the college idea and accept the lectures as an effective compromise. Compromise in Emily's opinion, however, was never effective. It was always out-rageous. It was also disgracefully easy, that soft and spineless option she so despised. "You see," she explained, "you must take into account that when you give the choice of the difficult best or the easy second best the latter is more likely to be taken."[30] She would not allow her committee in any way to signify approval of the lecture scheme and when in addition another scheme, to have a "special" examination for women at Cambridge, was mooted she drove her committee to oppose this formally. When Cambridge University approved it, Emily was furious. She said the university had "put its stamp on the principle that women's education is to be lower and narrower than that of men." Her distress was genuine. "It makes me very unhappy," she wrote, "to see the Ladies Lectures . . . spreading. It is an evil principle becoming organised and gaining the strength that comes from organisation."[31] The suggestion from her own committee that she might be wrong, that the lectures and special examination might pave the way for women's full entry into university life, was unaccept-able to her.

Meanwhile, Emily was doing the only thing she could do to meet the challenge – moving ahead with all the speed she could muster with the founding of a college. In August 1868 a constitution was drafted and discussions begun on the curriculum. At every step Emily found herself in opposition to her own committee and yet in virtually every instance her own unpopular view won the day. Her passion was not of the dramatic or showy variety. She made no magnificent speeches, no emotional appeals. What she did was go on and on and on, meeting every objection with a counter-objection and never for one instant appearing to flag. Nobody could match her intensity, nobody even approach the evangelical fervour of her outlook. Her greatest asset proved to be her stamina. There were battles royal over the location of the proposed college, over the curriculum, over the teaching. Emily won them all. It was she who wanted the existing classics course kept, she who wanted the college outside Cambridge, she who insisted the male lecturers could travel to the college. With a dreadful feeling that they were being foolishly shortsighted the members of the committee gave in. None of them was able to feel as sure that they were right as Emily Davies was. The "business of talking", she wrote, was arduous, but it had to be done and so did the visiting of influential people. "So much working of the jaws is a considerable effort,"[32] she commented, but so far as her listeners were concerned the exhaustion was not all her own. Barbara Bodichon wrote that she was "staggered" by Emily's daily toil and that she did not know what kept her going. The answer was inspiration.

Long before sufficient money had come in to finance the college, a house had been rented at Hitchin, in Hertfordshire, in which the venture could be started. Emily would rather have set up shop near Oxford, because she found the "kind, gushing way Oxford men have" preferable to "the cool Cambridge manner,"[33] but Cambridge as a university was more receptive. She had personally looked at houses in Baldock, Stevenage and even Mill Hill before settling on Hitchin as a location. The committee criticized her choice but as usual Emily was adamant. She wanted to get started because "in practical working, one finds that the way to kindle faith is to *show* it by running risks . . ."[34] It was important to have something tangible as soon as possible so that a college for women did not go on sounding like some ridiculous Tennysonian idea. With the house rented, a circular was printed and sent to all likely parents. By January 1869 only three names had been put forward but Emily was undaunted. She immediately fixed the fees at £105 a year and announced there would be an entrance exam in July. Eyebrows were raised: why selection with only three to select from? But the theory was sound behind what seemed a slightly ludicrous idea. From the beginning, a standard would be fixed and evidence that there *was* a fixed standard would in itself attract serious applicants. When July came eighteen entered and fifteen passed.

In October the first five students – Misses Gibson, Lloyd, Lumsden, Woodhead and Townshend – took up residence with Mrs Manning as Mistress. (Emily herself declined the honour saying she was neither old nor distinguished enough.) Miss Gibson, one of those first students, described arriving. Before she had time to knock or ring "the door was opened and on the threshold there stood the keen little lady to whose courage and energy the whole scheme of a college for women was due and who was now quivering with excitement thinly veiled under a businesslike manner in this moment when her cherished hopes were actually beginning to materialise."[35] But another student observed that "her dainty little figure and smiling face were most misleading. They concealed untiring energy, a will of iron, and a very clear and definite set of opinions."[36] What all five girls were quick to appreciate was that in the founder's opinion the College did *not* exist for them but they for the College. They were only part of a Grand Design and would never be allowed to forget it.

The position of the college when it opened was perilous. Far from signalling a triumphant arrival at a chosen destination it was only a first step in the right direction. The new college could too easily become just another variety of girls' school. No one was more aware of that than Emily Davies. She was terribly afraid of this fate and fear made her appear "narrow and intransigent". Every detail came under her possessive eye in her desire to make sure that the girls were treated like the men. Even the food had a hearty, masculine sound ("we have good plain food," wrote Emily with satisfaction, "milk, bread, beef and mutton and it disappears very fast").[37] The girls had good appetites because they were encouraged to go for long walks and to swim in the nearby open-air swimming-pool. Their chief pastime was "to rush out after dinner to the walk on the edge of the cliff and see the Edinburgh express slip its carriage."[38] Otherwise, recreation was limited. They were taught fives by one of their lecturers but Emily vetoed football. Often, they were reduced to more childish amusements like trying to walk on the heavy iron roller as it was pushed across the lawn. Seeing Emily Davies coming towards them the girls waited for the inevitable reproof but to their astonishment the founder merely said, "I believe I could do that. Will you hold my hand?"[39] But such moments were rare. A tradition as serious as the founder believed the men's to be had to be laid down. The college must impress. At Hitchin, the dining-room tables were from the start arranged on the collegiate plan so that one student was moved to comment, "we might have been 50 undergraduates instead of 5 harmless young women."[40]

Nor was it only the students who found the régime a little repressive. Emily kept a very close watch on the lecturers too, not because she feared any fraternizing but because she suspected they might deviate from the syllabus laid down for the men. And she was right. Two lecturers did indeed see the chance to throw out stuffy subjects and introduce new ones. Emily pounced immediately. One resigned, saying, "Just at the moment when education is taking a new shape I cannot take any pleasure in attending to the details of a college where the old and to me obsolete routine goes on . . ." Emily accepted his resignation not in the least concerned about what was alleged to be obsolete. When the men's colleges rejected the obsolete so would she but until then she saw any rejection as a trap. Women *had* to prove themselves capable of doing what the men did. This was especially true in examinations. Men took a preliminary examination in their first year, entitled the "Little Go", and she was determined the girls should do so too, as a necessary preparation for the Tripos. The fact that this Little Go was not part of the Tripos and more a test of what the men had been grounded in at school (unlike the girls) did not deter her. Different *always* would mean inferior and therefore could not be thought of. It made the girls unhappy and resentful but it could not be helped. "The student was a mere cog in the wheel of her [E.D.'s] great scheme," wrote Louisa Lumsden. "There was a fine element in this, a total indifference to popularity but . . . it was plain we counted for little or nothing except as we furthered her plans."[41]

This was not quite fair. Emily's joy in her students was unfeigned and touching. She loved their "bright faces" and was made happier than she had ever been by their "entire cordiality". Their excitement was her excitement and she was touchingly flattered that they seemed to want to talk to her so much. She recorded their "innocent spontaneous hilarity" and valued it. When she saw how thrilled they were to have a room each, prettily decorated, she was glad she had stuck out for privacy and relished it with them. But, unlike the students, Emily Davies carried the burden of moulding the future. Hitchin was temporary, the position and the building of a real college as yet unaccomplished. The first test was not just to get girls through the Little Go but to get them allowed to sit it in the first place. The Council of the Senate graciously indicated that they would have no objection to the girls sitting the examination papers *after* the men had received them, nor to private arrangements being made with willing examiners to mark them. But nobody was quite sure if the plan would work since it hinged on such favours. The relief felt when the papers actually arrived for the girls to do was tremendous. Emily Davies then supervised the examination herself, sitting in the corner and knitting ferociously like some Madame Defarge. Then there was the agony of waiting for the results. "Everything has gone quite smoothly," wrote Emily, "and the kindness shown on all sides has been exhilarating."[42] Even more exhilarating was the news that all five candidates had passed in classics and the two entered in addition for maths had also passed.

When the rejoicing was over, Emily got down to planning the building of the new college. It was, surely, an opportune moment. In any case, the lease on Benslow House at Hitchin had expired and it was no longer big enough to take the new students expected. The original target to reach before building could be started had been £30,000 but this was now dropped to a mere £7,000. It seemed an insignificant sum to raise when it was considered that the previous year Harrow school had raised £78,000 with no problem for a new building but, however hard she struggled, Emily found it seemed impossible to accumulate. "I go through a certain amount of hair shirt every day,"[43] she commented dismally, but still the money only trickled in. The only solution was to borrow since further delay would be fatal. A proper legal association was formed, the money borrowed on the strength of it, and building at last began on a site at Girton, three miles from Cambridge itself. Every detail obsessed the founder. She journeyed backwards and forwards, supervising the planting of trees and the choice of tiles, walking across the muddy fields with Mr Waterhouse, the Architect of her choice, and explaining to him *exactly* what must be done, while appearing to ask his advice. When it came to furnishing the inside she was indefatigible and relished all the bargains she managed to find (especially some cheap borders for the wallpaper which exactly matched the curtains and were only ½d a yard). Once, she came across some undergraduates who had come out to help lay bricks and she watched delightedly while they solemnly wrote their names on them first. It pleased her not just that the men were helping to build the women's college but that they had a sense of history, of the significance of what was happening.

In September 1873 Girton was opened, amid chaos, with building work still in progress both inside and out. Emily Davies had become Mistress of the college (while it was still at Hitchin) in 1872 because nobody else suitable could be found but she enjoyed it as little as she expected. She did not like positions of prominence, nor did she like any confusion of role. She was also beginning to feel exhausted. "I suppose I don't show illness much," she wrote, "for it seems impossible to make people understand how worn out I am. I have often felt I could bear it no longer . . ."[44] But she always did bear the strain because she saw her own contribution as vital. All the time new threats to the college loomed ahead and she felt she had to be eternally vigilant. The whole system of receiving examination papers and depending on sympathetic examiners to mark them was a continual worry and during her short time as Mistress it almost broke down. Emily was informed that it was to be discontinued and fought tenaciously to keep this crucially important concession. She only just managed it. Then the application to sit the Tripos examination was defeated so the same wearisome process had to be gone through with that examination too. She herself took the students into Cambridge where a room at the University Arms had been reserved for them to take the examination. Louisa Lumsden described the agony as the minutes ticked by and still no papers arrived. ". . . Miss Davies knitted away steadily by the fire – I can hear the click of the needles still! Minute after minute slipped away and still, until a whole hour had gone by, no paper came. Miss Davies said nothing . . ."[45] But the papers arrived, the girls steadied their shaking hands, and the ordeal was gone through. All three candidates passed. Emily wrote, "We have just heard that Miss Cook's translation of Aristotle was the best in the Tripos examination . . ."[46] She did not object to her students climbing onto the roof and ringing bells with such violence that the fire engine came racing out from Cambridge. It *was* a great day. The last hurdle had been taken and nobody could stand in any doubt that women could match men intellectually if given the chance.

Yet Emily Davies never relaxed. Any sign that standards need not now be so rigid and she pounced upon the offender. This led to a rebellion among her students which depressed her greatly. They said they did not want to continue taking the Little Go – the Tripos was quite enough of a strain. Emily was angry and upset. "I am afraid," she wrote, "that it is true that I feel very vindictive generally. It is the fierceness of fear. If I felt more confident I might perhaps be more amiable."[47] She could not understand how girls as intelligent as her students could fail to appreciate that the battle was far from won. Girls had come to college, been given the same lectures and teaching as men, passed the same Little Go, passed the same Tripos – all that was true, but it was also true that none of this had been officially acknowledged. Girls still had to be content with their own college certificates. They had no degrees, they were not even in the smallest way members of the university. If once they began to deviate from the course the men followed their enemies might seize the opportunity to say they were not equal to the men's course. The Little Go was tedious but it *must* be taken, the girls *must* conform. Emily won in the end but the resentment she incurred distressed her. "When I see such a spirit it makes me terribly out of heart with our work," she commented. It hurt her that anyone should think she had anything but the good of the college at heart. She was extremely relieved, in 1875, to become merely secretary again instead of Mistress, although there was no "merely" about it. The students called her "The Little Instigator" and their admiration for her was tinged with apprehension.

After she had ostensibly handed the reins of Girton over to Miss A. F. Bernard, Emily went back to London. On April 22nd, 1875 she wrote, "I am 45 today – a good age for retiring into private life."[48] Quite what this "private life" was going to be she did not know. It was the familiar story of a woman who had found self-fulfilment through working indefatigably for a cause arriving at a stage where she had succeeded so well that she was no longer needed in the same way. Girton College was established and the machinery had been set in motion which would eventually secure true participation in the University. Emily by no means dropped out of the action – she was rightly accused of "wire pulling at a distance" – but she was no longer at the centre. There was time for other things. At first, she found it satisfying just to be back in London but after the very first party she attended she wrote, "Do you know I was so tired . . . that it took me two days to get over it. Does that not show what a wretched weakling I am, and how unworthy of attending routs?"[49] It also showed something else. Playing, for her, was never going to be enough. Nor was being an aunt to her brother's six sons and one daughter. She took them out often and had great fun (even learning to skate and being told she was "getting on like anything") but her restlessness continued. She felt irritable and looking after her mother did not help. "If I felt more equal to work," she wrote, "I should wish not to take up public agitations but something that I could be paid for so that I could contribute more towards the household expenses . . ."[50] But in 1876 she fell ill, was confined to bed for a month and far from being equal to work had to resign as secretary of the Girton College Committee.

From then on, as Honorary Secretary only, her influence at Girton ceased to be paramount – and there were those who were glad. There had for some time been mutterings that, although the founder always stressed that what she wanted was a "real" college, she herself did not understand what that meant. She did not understand the position of research in a "real" college. Everything, in her opinion, ought to be geared to expansion, to extending what already existed to more students instead of improving things for those already there. It was Emily Davies who chose to build twenty new rooms with a legacy left to the college and not a library. In any conflict of interest numbers always won. She would not allow any research fellowships which might benefit two or three girls to be established if the money could be diverted so that ten more could be accommodated. Nor did she understand that keeping the Mistress off the Executive Committee of the College was robbing her of power she needed to have. Wonderful though she was, there were those who said all Miss Davies wanted was a superior kind of Training College, and they were glad when she resigned. The rest of the committee had watched anxiously as spending on building work seemed to grow more and more reckless and they were eager to curb it. With Miss Davies gone, they managed to do so and at last to get properly laid out lawns and a well equipped library.

Yet they still needed Emily Davies' determination in the following years. Though she was now on the sidelines she alone had the necessary drive to arouse support when again it was needed. In 1880, when a woman gained the position of 8th Wrangler in the Maths Tripos, and in 1887 when Agnata Ramsay stood alone in the first division of the first class of the Classics Tripos (above all the male candidates for that year) Emily formed a committee to press for the formal admission of women to degrees. Admission to examinations was formally granted in 1881, but admission to the university body continued to be refused. The University authorities went on making themselves look ridiculous as more and more women scored impressive successes but were kept out of the University. By 1921, the year Emily Davies died, women were allowed to wear caps and gowns and to call themselves BA but it was not until 1948 that they were fully admitted to the governing body of the University (whereas at Oxford they were fully admitted in 1919 and at London and the provincial universities considerably before that).

The withdrawal of Emily Davies from a position of power at Girton had not been the pathetic business it might have been. She was always well-balanced and sensible and accepted gracefully that her main contribution was over. The "wire pulling" gradually stopped although her annual visits continued. But after the death of her mother, in 1886, and when a long period of poor health was over, Emily began to look around for another way in which she could advance the cause of women. She had always been keenly for the suffrage, canvassing in her earlier days for John Stuart Mill and presenting the first petition to him with Elizabeth Garrett in 1865, but she had not wanted her educational work to be possibly prejudiced by agitating also for the much more controversial suffrage so she had dropped out of that movement. Now she returned.

In 1886 her name again appeared among the subscribers to the London National Society for Women's Suffrage and three years later she was back where she belonged – on the General Committee. At the age of sixty, she joined the Executive Committee and from then onwards began to appear in public at meetings and on deputations. It excited her, when the militant movement began, to recognize that there were young women who felt as passionately about an issue as she had felt about hers and though she disapproved of their methods she sympathized with their feelings. She was not afraid, as many of the older suffragists were, to take part in demonstrations. In 1908, when she was seventy-eight, she was among the 15,000 women who gathered in the Albert Hall after walking down the Embankment. She said she had never enjoyed herself so much. In 1918, when enfranchisement for women finally came, she walked triumphantly to the polls to record her vote (Tory). Within her lifetime yet another great work for women had been accomplished.

The last years of Emily's life were spent in Hampstead living with her brother and his daughter. In 1919 the jubilee of the foundation of Girton College was celebrated and an address signed by all the past and present students was sent to her which gave her great pleasure. Hers was a serene old age, in which she seems to have accepted the gradual loss of faculties very well. One faculty she never lost was her mind. To her death, on July 13, 1921, in her ninety-second year, she was "so rational and serene and kindly accommodating," wrote her niece, "and her good sayings and humour continued."[51]

★   ★   ★

Emily Davies was not an immediately attractive person, nor was she ever popular. Said to resemble Queen Victoria in later life she also shared that lady's obstinacy. Her family, of course, knew how much she laughed and smiled and how affectionate and kind she was but other people did not. They saw the set face, the pursed lips, heard the rather staccato speech and met the straight, piercing gaze with nervousness. She made people feel ill-at-ease and jumpy. They also felt reproved by her and this put them automatically on the defensive. Few outside the family circle got to know her very well, although she had some lifelong devoted friends. Barbara Bodichon, who of all people knew Emily best, was obliged to agree she had a formidable manner. "I think we all felt the want in Miss Davies of genial wisdom and influence . . . she, who has an immense love of justice for women, would die to give young women what she never had herself in early life, die to get it for them, though she might hate every individual."[52] Unfortunately, too many felt the presence of this capacity to hate. Emily Davies never shouted, never turned purple with anger or created scenes, but there was a grimness in her expression when she was displeased which was far more disturbing. Feminine wiles were quite unknown to her. She never used tears, never threatened to faint, never threw herself on anyone's mercy, never fluttered her eyelashes or seduced anyone with a caressing look. Her methods were those of the civil servant, and a civil servant not entirely lacking in bureaucratic arrogance. This attitude, this belief in the power of logic, made her seem harsh and unfeeling. Josephine Butler, whose sympathies were wholly with Emily Davies at the time she was trying to get Girton started, wrote, "I can feel for her and if it were not for the fear of a snub I would write and comfort her . . ." She added, "I believe that it is difficult for men to think gently of *women* like Miss Davies."[53]

It was a feminist problem. Women like Emily Davies were always suspected of being unfeminine. It was hurtful not just when the sneer came from men but particularly when, more often, it came from women. A good deal of Emily's hate was turned towards those women who *themselves* shrank with horror from the idea that they might have a brain and could be taught to use it. She hated women who were afraid to be thought clever, who were embarrassed by the idea of intellectual activity, who appeared to imagine that the female sex would lose something if it gave up its reputation for being feather-brained. She hated most of all those who insisted the female brain was different from and smaller than the male. "I should like," she wrote to Mr Roby when he was secretary to the Taunton Commission, "to have Huxley examined about the brain because that physiological argument is constantly used and people believe it."[54] They also believed, as she well knew, that not only the female brain but the entire female body might be overtaxed by intellectual activity. In 1874, when Dr Maudsley (a well-known mental health specialist) printed an article in the *Fortnightly Review* saying girls needed a special education adapted to their particular needs or they would be made ill, Emily Davies leapt to the defence of her own point of view. She was, she wrote to Madame Bodichon, "glad that this question has been raised and discussed."[55] Parents believed that, as Dr Maudsley said with such authority, studying made girls ill. There was a great deal of delicate talk about "girls' organisation" which meant menstruation. This was supposed to make it impossible for girls to study hard for weeks at a time. With great restraint, Emily chose not to reply herself. She got Elizabeth Garrett Anderson to answer, which she did more than adequately, taking the opportunity to review the whole treatment of health in girls' schools. There was no doubt, she said, that the cleverest girls appeared to be also the healthiest. Throughout all the best schools in England the health of the girls was of paramount importance and everywhere exercises and games, with visibly excellent results, were the order of the day. Miss Buss was thought eccentric when, in 1872, she marched her girls from the new Camden School to St Pancras Public Baths for swimming lessons but within the next decade it was considered normal and desirable.

But at least Emily Davies could understand these common fears. What she found it almost impossible to understand was why women could not see what higher education would *do* for them. It seemed so obvious to her. In 1866 she wrote a book entitled *The Higher Education of Women* in which there was a chapter called "Things as they Are". In it she wrote "There is no point on which schoolmistresses are more unanimous and emphatic than on the difficulty of knowing what to do with girls after leaving school." The point of higher education was that it gave an intellectual training which was needed for all worthwhile purposes in life, for all kinds of work – social, philanthropic as well as professional. It was, she wrote, "the best corrective of the tendency to take petty views of things and on this account is specially to be desired for women on whom it devolves to give the 'tone' to society." The effects of higher education would be immediate and dramatic and she was impatient with those who failed to appreciate this and with those who mistakenly thought she wanted women in some way to replace men. Quite the contrary. She explained in a letter once, "Probably they will never do as well as men. I mean to say that very likely there will always be some man in every field who will do better than every woman. But that does not seem to me a reason for hindering women from doing their best and choosing for themselves what they will try. It is not likely that they will ever want to be soldiers or sailors as hobbies. If they do attempt things for which they are unfit they will be taught their folly by failure . . ."[56] The great point was that, if higher education became a reality, women would actually have the opportunity to find out what in fact they *could* do. It was the intellectual equivalent of the franchise and in her opinion much more important. "The scoffers don't see how much is involved in improving education . . ."[57] she complained.

But the leading educationalists of the day were well-aware of how important Emily Davies was in setting the target in their movement. Some naturally found her a menace with her perfectionist attitude but they respected her and gave her credit for raising the sights of female education at a crucial time. Henry Sidgwick, who worked with Anne Jemima Clough to found the Lectures for Ladies in Cambridge and the residential home which later became Newnham College, was extremely irritated by Miss Davies who made him into an arch-enemy quite unnecessarily. She was for many years a thorn in his side and he grew to dread even the sight of a communication from her. But later, after Girton had been founded and Newnham also, he worked with her to get women formally admitted to degrees and he came to like her better. Her absolutely unshakeable faith in the ability of women to obtain *everything*, to have all doors opened, impressed him. What Barbara Bodichon called her "attacks of audacity" took his breath away and, as one of the first Girton students had remarked, "her pluck was contagious." When she announced she was "ready to go round a corner and garotte somebody"[58] if she could not get what she wanted everyone smiled but also trembled.

It became Sidgwick's job to make Emily Davies contain her admittedly fierce temper. When she sent Sidgwick her pamphlet "Women in the Universities of England and Scotland" before publication he told her "your tone seems to me dangerously aggressive and challenging" and she altered the wording accordingly. She knew herself how violent she could sound and was always anxious to restrain herself. "Men cannot stand indignation,"[59] she told Barbara Bodichon and she tried not to be publicly indignant. Not only did she approve of masking true anger but she also actually advocated disguise of every sort. "I think there must be truth . . . as to the peculiar fitness of women for fighting – I cannot help enjoying it,"[60] she wrote to Helen Taylor but at the same time she once told the young Elizabeth Garrett off for being "cheeky". She also packed the front rows of many a vital meeting with the most docile, pretty, demure looking women she could find so that men would not be scared of them. Anybody dressing in "masculine" clothes infuriated her. It was playing into the hands of the enemy who went about saying higher education would unsex women and make them battleaxes. The students at Hitchin and Girton were bullied constantly by her to be at all times *emphatically* ladylike in appearance and actions.

In that attitude, as in some others, Emily Davies was not feminist enough. There were strict demarcation lines within her progressive ideas. What she called "radical looking women" earned her scorn and she was as hard on them as the worst of male chauvinists. "It is a great relief to me to get away from uncongenial companionship," she wrote in her Family Chronicle (after attending a dinner party full of "radical women") "and to abandon the vain attempt to work with radicals. Heaven protect me from trying it again. The more I hear of them the worse they appear qua Radicals. No doubt some of them have the domestic virtues." She loathed "fast" and "masculine looking" women and resented any suggestion that highly educated women could be as objectionable. In an article in the *Victoria Magazine* she defended intellectual women saying ". . . the masculine women are not those who sit down to their books and devote themselves to an orderly course of study." But what was more serious was her rigid moral attitude. The *Victoria Magazine*, which she edited for a year in 1863, had as its slogan "Our watchword is Liberty and our motto Let every woman do that which is right in her own eyes." But only, it then transpired, if it was also right in Emily's. The proprietor of the magazine, Emily Faithful, was referred to in a divorce case and was obliged to withdraw from society. "I, and others, ceased to be associated with her,"[61] announced Emily Davies coldly.

Emily Davies was, after all, a victim in some respects of her own culture and it was that "fear of failure" which made her force conformity on her students. Feminism had come only so far by the time Girton was established – it was still anxious to embrace conventional outward notions of "femininity" because it was so busy attacking the much more important and injurious inward notions of it. Emily Davies was absolutely in step with this stage of feminist history in her overwhelming desire to reassure society that far from wanting to banish the differences between the sexes she wanted to maintain them *so long as doing so did not hinder woman's development as a person.* The suggestion that not being able to wear the clothes she wanted came under that heading would have been frivolous then. And the schoolteachers agreed with Emily Davies. From Girton (and Newnham, and Somerville and Lady Margaret Hall in Oxford, all founded at roughly the same time) the new generation of highly educated college women went out and ploughed back into the female educational field all they had been taught. Just as Emily Davies had hoped, they were inspired by the sense of mission which had created their colleges in the first place. They went to schools throughout the country where they set a new pace, a new standard, which in itself revolutionized girls' education. There were still, of course, not nearly enough good schools for middle-class girls (the educational pioneers at this stage did nothing about the working-class girls) and the reluctance of parents to educate girls as well as boys was still deeply ingrained. The Report of the Taunton Commission believed that this was "so deeply embedded in human nature" that it would never die out. It would just have to be acknowledged and allowed for.

What the Report did not also comment upon was the reluctance of girls themselves to take the opportunities before them and use them to the full. In the nineteenth century, this was hardly a problem. Middle-class girls were dependent on the permission and the wealth of parents to obtain the new education as well as on their own brains. However desperately they might want to go to college it was not an ambition they could realize, in the period when women's colleges opened, without parental co-operation. But from 1870, after Forster's Education Act, the sights of *all* girls, from whatever class, were at least theoretically raised and by the middle of this century, with the entry of working-class girls as well as boys into the grammar schools, the sky was the limit. Neither lack of money nor lack of opportunity could stop any girl who had the brains to go onto higher education. But then a "LOA" (Lack of Ambition) factor began to emerge. Girls appeared not to want to avail themselves of all the different forms of higher education. Many of those who were able chose not to continue their education beyond school. The fact that, nevertheless, thousands availed themselves of the system Emily Davies and her contemporaries inaugurated is no comfort to the feminists. There is the suspicion abroad that girls do not actually choose to forgo higher education, that they are discriminated against in all sorts of subtle ways during their scholastic careers. And the attitude the Taunton Commission noted is still prevalent: girls do not get encouraged to stay on and go further. Parents still suffer from LOA on their daughters' behalf.

But the tide may at last be turning. In 1982 statistics showed that for the first time in Britain more girls than boys sat for "A" level examinations.[62] Girls may at last be seeing higher education as Emily

Davies wished them to see it and, if this prompts them also to use it as she wished them to use it, then at long last there will be a basic and highly significant change in how women see themselves in relation to society.

SEXUAL MORALITY

Josephine Butler
(Josephine Butler Collection, Fawcett Library, at the City of London Polytechnic; photo by John Freeman & Co, London)

Josephine Butler
1828–1906

There was one kind of equality, one sort of liberation, about which nineteenth-century feminists found it embarrassing to speak. Higher education for women, better employment opportunities for women, protection at law for women – these were all good, clean, decent issues. Nobody was afraid to voice opinions upon them, nobody ashamed to sign their name on a petition. But the attack on that infamous "double-standard" which so bedevilled relationships between the sexes in Victorian times did not attract such eager support. Even the bravest of self-confessed feminists trembled at the implications of involving themselves in this particular fight. Signing the petition of the Moral Reform Union as late as 1884 was still thought of as a courageous thing to do in spite of the fact that what was demanded was couched in the most sober and discreet terms: "That having before them the fact that women are constantly annoyed and imperilled by the solicitation of profligate men in the streets and elsewhere, your Petitioners humbly pray that your Honourable House will, in justice, make the male offender in the matter of solicitation equally punishable with the female offender against whom laws now exist; and that in all future legislation the same principle of equality between the sexes shall be observed." At the time of this wistful request a great battle to establish "the same principle of equality" had just been won and yet there was no confidence among those who had won, nor among those for whom it had primarily been won, that the victory was anything but hollow.

The parliamentary battle in question saw the end (in 1883 during Gladstone's second ministry) of the twenty-year fight to get the

Contagious Diseases Acts repealed. These Acts had amounted to wholesale anti-feminist legislation, the very first of the kind in Britain. In other ways the law had worked against women negatively, by excluding them from privileges and denying them protection, but the CD Acts worked against the female sex in a much more dangerously positive way, specifically singling them out for punishment. There were three of these Acts, passed in 1864, 1866 and 1869, all under different Liberal ministries. They made it obligatory for any woman merely suspected of being a prostitute in the areas where the laws operated (ports and army towns) to have to report to the police station for a medical examination to inspect her for venereal disease. If diseased she was then obliged to enter a lock hospital until declared clean when she would be issued with a certificate guaranteeing this. All three Acts were thought of as part of a general cleaning-up operation, part of the wider reform of the British Army which would improve the health of soldiers. The campaign against them was led by Josephine Butler, a woman who had worked among prostitutes in the workhouses and prisons of Liverpool and who had come to see prostitution not only as a moral evil but as a form of male persecution. It seemed clear to her that *all* women were debased by these Acts, that the very notion of womanhood was viciously attacked. In them the buying and selling of the female body was sanctified by statute law and the whole position of women in society was degraded. Women were declared to exist for the gratification of male lust which was acknowledged to be a "natural" urge. Her campaign was, she declared, "one of the most vital movements of Christian times."[1] In the history of feminism it was crucial.

Yet Josephine Butler did not see her mission in purely feminist terms. Like all the best feminists she was concerned not just with the position of women in society but with the position of men in relation to them. She insisted that she fought for men as well as women. God's voice, she wrote, called upon her to "combat the double violation of principles . . . as a citizen of a free country first and a woman secondly I felt impelled to come forward."[2] She kicked the "double standard" in its most private parts and was hated and despised for doing so. She brought to feminism a strong concept of "womankind" which had barely existed before (and was not sustained afterwards) and her greatest triumph was to cross class barriers and make middle-class women identify themselves with a form of sex persecution from which they did not themselves suffer.

Under the CD Acts it was working-class women only who suffered. They were the ones going about the streets of poor areas in the proscribed districts who could be arrested by plain-clothes policemen and forced to submit to a shameful and brutal examination. Without an upper middle-class champion like Josephine Butler, one woman who was prepared to expose herself to unbelievable abuse, State Registered Vice might have become an accepted part of the social fabric and nobody, least of all respectable women, would have thought that it mattered that it was. The CD Acts seemed so obviously "good", an excellent hygienic measure, protecting men as they surely must from unclean women. It took Josephine Butler to point out that if the women were unclean they had not become unclean by themselves and yet those who had helped them become unclean got off scot-free. She said it would not do: men and women must be accused together – either both must be punished or neither. She maintained that all legislation on the subject was useless. Women as a class, she declared, were being denied their constitutional rights and the outlook for society as a whole was perilous if this continued. She said that sex was a subject women could no longer be officially supposed to know nothing about, that women, ladies, must acquaint themselves with unpleasant facts and wake up to how all women were being abused by what some had to suffer. She was quite right. The repeal of the Contagious Diseases Acts was as significant for feminism as any of its more respectable victories.

★　　　★　　　★

Josephine Elizabeth Butler's life was far removed from that of the working-class girl upon whose behalf she initially became involved in the campaign against the CD Acts. She was born on April 13th, 1828 in a remote part of Northumberland, the seventh of eight surviving children. Her father was John Grey, descendant of Border Barons and a cousin to Earl Grey of Reform Bill fame. Her mother was Hannah Annett, of Huguenot descent. The estate at Milfield which was Josephine's home until she was seven when the family moved to Dilston, also in Northumberland, was a model of its kind. John Grey's chief interest was in agricultural reform and when, in 1833, he was appointed to take charge of the Greenwich Hospital estates in the north he was able to put into practice on a grand scale all his own theories. He was in charge of 34,356 acres covering 290 tenancies stretching the length and breadth of Northumberland and Cumberland and he supervised them all himself. Riding about on his big, black horse he was known as "The Black Prince" because of his dark, handsome appearance and authoritative bearing. His whole life, wrote Josephine, "was a sustained effort for the good of others."[3] Every kind of liberal reform interested him and he would, said his daughter, have become an MP if his loathing of London had not been so great. But as it was he stayed in the north, managing the Greenwich estates with enlightened and successful methods.

The family home at Dilston over which he presided was spacious and beautiful. Josephine grew up, with her sisters and brothers, used to being allowed a great deal of freedom. John Grey taught all his children to ride when they were very young and Josephine developed a healthy respect for this form of exercise. "I can do with any amount of spirit," she once wrote, "but I like a businesslike horse who does not make a flourish and a splash and a curvette and coquette as park horses do."[4] She and her closest sister Hatty actually dreamed of a future as circus girls and practised for hours riding in circles standing on their bare-backed mounts. But there was another side to their upbringing. John Grey read the Bible to them every Sunday afternoon and in addition insisted that they become familiar with Coke and Blackstone as well as the Blue Books studied so secretly by Florence Nightingale. The six girls as well as the two boys were taught languages and grounded in the classics and history. They were expected to take part in an intelligent fashion in discussions with the many visitors on topics of the day. But they also had fun. "My father used to drive Aunt Hatty and me from Dilston to Milfield," Josephine once wrote to a nephew, "in a high, small, open gig . . . Alnwick we knew well of course. We used to go to the great annual County Ball there and always stayed at the Swan . . . Aunt Hatty and I were great *belles* in our snowy book muslin frocks and natural flowers wreathed in our heads and waists and skirts . . ."[5] They were both very beautiful and lively and when they were sent for two years to school in Newcastle took occasional advantage of the not very strict discipline. Yet by eighteen, her brief schooling over, Josephine had been troubled by very much the same kind of doubts about the future as her much less privileged contemporaries. Unlike Emily Davies she had had an excellent education; unlike Florence Nightingale she had had a great deal of freedom and parental encouragement; unlike Elizabeth Blackwell she had never had to work; unlike Caroline Norton she had not been trapped into early marriage; but, like all of them, she experienced feelings of terror when she looked ahead and thought about herself. Brought up by her parents to an awareness of the world she lived in, and to a feeling of social responsibility, she agonized over what she should do with her life and this drove her into a religious crisis: what did God *want* her to do?

By that time, fortunate though she was in her circumstances, Josephine had seen a little of that England described in those Blue Books her father made required reading. She knew enough to be aware that not all estates were run as her father ran his, that the beauty of the landscape hid terrible poverty and injustice. The certain knowledge that starvation existed and could be witnessed even near at hand made her wonder if there was a God at all. "I could not love God," she wrote "who appeared to my darkened and foolish heart to consent to so much which seemed to me cruel and unjust."[6] She felt she was going mad and said she used to shriek out loud for God to come and deliver her. Everywhere she looked she saw the stark contrast between her own life and that of others, between the principles upon which she had been reared and those which governed the world at large. She wrote years later that this made her into a Christian Socialist before she had ever heard the term and that from this period of late adolescence onwards she was no great respecter of "the church" as such.[7] She was looking for some other key to an understanding of life than those words spoken by parsons from pulpits which "did not even touch the fringe of my soul's deep discontent." Then, in 1850, when she was twenty-two and safely through her period of religious doubt, she met George Butler, aged thirty, a tutor at Durham University.

The historian J. A. Froude said of George Butler that he was "the most variously gifted man in body and mind that I ever knew," an opinion shared by all with whom he came into contact. The son of a headmaster of Harrow, George had sown his wild oats early. At Trinity College, Cambridge, he was renowned not just for the effortless brilliance of his Greek iambics but for smashing chimneypots with unerring aim. He was sent down after a year and spent three more years doing nothing much until he suddenly redeemed himself by winning a scholarship to Oxford where he took a First. By the time Josephine met him he had been on the straight and narrow path of duty and virtue for some time. His popularity at Durham was immense – the boys of University College burned with a poker the words "Butler is a brick" on the stout outer oak door of his room in

Castle – and his reputation unsullied. "I have a longing to be of use,"[8] he wrote to Josephine early in their courtship. So had she. When George said he disliked parsons and did not want to become one (although eventually he did take orders soon after his marriage) but wanted to devote himself to education she was happy to concur. Together, they envisaged a future in which they would both strive to secure educational reforms. They intended theirs to be a true partnership, and it was. From the moment they were married on January 8th, 1852, in the parish church at Dilston, Josephine and George Butler were that rare thing: a perfect union. As Josephine commented years later, George never had to be asked to consider her his equal because "the idea of justice to women, of equality between the sexes . . . seems to have been instinctive in him."[9]

After their wedding the Butlers went to live at 124 High Street in Oxford where George had been appointed an examiner of Schools (the final degree-examinations). Josephine's father had made her a present of a "fine, well bred chestnut" and she and George spent many happy hours riding about the woods and meadows of the Oxfordshire countryside. Their first son was born in November. Named George, also, he was from the beginning "very knowing and old fashioned," wrote Josephine and very like his father. "We find housekeeping hard work," she confessed, "with small means and prices so high. I pay 22 shillings for a ton of coal."[10] Nor was this worry over money the only thing that disturbed her even though in her personal life she was utterly content. The society of Oxford was alien to her and she missed home. "This pleasant life at Oxford has its shadow side," she wrote. "I had come from a large family circle and from free country life to a University town – a society of celibates."[11] The trouble was not that she did not like Oxford's academic celibates but that they did not know how to treat her. Most of them were embarrassed and uncomfortable in her presence and surprised George did not send her away when the conversation turned on subjects they thought unsuitable for her ears. But George had no intention of dismissing his wife from any discussion. There she was, presiding so gracefully over the teapot and "large stacks of buttered teacakes" and there she would stay. The celibates had to accept this but it did not prevent them from being patronizing and superior about women. Josephine, although perfectly polite, found this hard to take and did not always keep silent. She defended staunchly the woman's point of view on numerous occasions and complained to George of the prejudiced attitudes of his colleagues. George simply shrugged and said it made him feel sorry for them because they knew no better.

The young Mrs Butler's activities were not just confined to the teatable. The celibates were startled to see her in Duke Humphrey's library looking up certain manuscripts to help George prepare an edition of Chaucer's works based on fifteenth-century sources. It was not, the celibates thought, quite the thing for a woman. They were also uneasy about the trips Mrs Butler made to London to help George, who was Art critic for the *Morning Chronicle*, prepare a bibliography of Turner's works, and about her support at George's lectures for working men. But what really astounded the celibates was the stand George Butler allowed his wife to make on moral issues. When Josephine heard that a young girl was in Newgate after murdering her baby, which everyone knew had been fathered by a Balliol don who had then cast her off, she went straight to Jowett, the Master of Balliol, and asked him to confront the man in question with the iniquity of his behaviour. Jowett refused. Josephine promptly took in the girl when she had served her sentence. With George's approval, she came as a maid to the Butler household, a constant reproach to the man who had wronged her. "Mrs Butler takes an interest in a class of sinners whom she had better have left to themselves," commented the unrepentant Jowett.

But Josephine did not see this girl or those like her as sinners at all. She was beginning to suspect that such girls were victims, that the common view of them as wicked hussies was quite wrong. Their plight preyed on her mind and she found that during the times when George was away her thoughts kept turning to what she could do about it. Although she now had two children – her second son, Stanley, was born in 1854 – she had a sense of aimlessness still which troubled her. "George had to be in London for some days," she wrote soon after Stanley's birth. "On Monday evening, feeling lonely, I went in to St. John's Park and sat there until 9 p.m."[12] While she sat she pondered on what she could do to justify her own existence and became depressed at her uselessness. The fact that the Oxford climate, so damp in winter, did not agree with her pulled her down even more and George became worried about her health. Her lungs seemed affected and he insisted she should see a London specialist who alarmed him by saying his wife should never return to Oxford. Fortunately, soon after this verdict, George was offered the post of vice-principal of Cheltenham Boys' College. In the autumn of 1857 the Butlers moved to Cheltenham where their third son, Charles, was born.

At Cheltenham Josephine's health and spirits rapidly improved, to everyone's relief, but socially she found the place no more congenial than Oxford. She had simply swapped celibates for stuffy county Tories who were censorious of her liberal sympathies and no less critical of her feminist aspirations. As an intelligent wife sharing her husband's work she fitted in no better. But with four children instead of two – a much longed-for daughter, Eva, was born at the beginning of 1859 – she was more fulfilled in her family life and never again lonely. Then, in 1864, there occurred a tragic accident.

One evening George and Josephine went out to dinner and on their return Eva, who was in bed, rushed onto the landing outside her room to look down into the hall and greet them. The banisters gave way and she fell onto the tiled floor. George picked her up and cradled her in his arms. Her hair "which had grown very long lately and was of a deep chestnut brown which in the sun flashed out all golden"[13] hung bloodstained and tangled. They sent for a doctor and carried her to bed. She did not die for several hours but never regained consciousness. Arthur Butler, George's brother, who arrived first of the family early the next morning wrote "never did I see more crushing touching sorrow."[14] When she was an old lady Josephine finally managed to write to Stanley that Eva's cruel death had "a horrible sting in it. She was 5½, never had a day's illness – healthy, strong, beautiful, our only daughter – father and I just adored her, and in a moment she fell, *smashed*, her head broken and after hours of awful convulsions she died . . ."[15] For the next twenty-five years, she added, she had never woken from sleep without a vision of Eva's falling figure and without the sound of her head hitting the ground ringing sickeningly in her ears. Eva was buried in Leckhampton cemetery and Alexander Munro engaged to make a bust of her from some drawings.

The Butlers tried to pick up the threads of their life again but although they managed to be outwardly composed they were both inwardly shattered. Josephine dreamed constantly of Eva running laughing through the garden calling to her – "I dreamed I had my darling in my arms, dying; that she struggled to live for my sake, lived again a moment and died."[16] What made her pain worse was that for the first time in their lives the Butlers seemed divided. They grieved separately. Josephine admitted she ignored George's pain, that she was oblivious to his suffering and could not allow that it might equal hers.

She had a terrible physical hunger for her dead child that tortured her so much that she actually went out looking for a little girl who might resemble her dead daughter. When she found an orphan whose face was similar she "took her up" and had her fostered. The child, called Polly, was only three and soon outgrew her resemblance to Eva but twelve years later Josephine was still visiting "my dear child."[17] The fact that George might be experiencing the same torment never occurred to her until she accidentally found some thoughts he had written down on scraps of paper and hidden together with every pathetic gift Eva had ever made for him – clumsily worked bookmarks, pressed flowers, drawings all tenderly laid to rest. Before she left him to go to Italy on a recuperative visit to Hatty (who had married an Italian) they were emotionally reunited.

But the agony of Eva's death in Cheltenham made it imperative to leave the place and in 1866 George accepted the post of principal of the Liverpool College for Boys. He worked very hard there which was excellent therapy and the boys too were happy but Josephine found that she had "many hours every day, alone, empty handed and sorrowful."[18] Unlike George she could find no way to make her pain bearable. "Most people," she wrote, "who have gone through such an experience will understand me when I speak of the ebb and flow of sorrow."[19] Prayers helped, her sons helped, George's understanding helped but they did not help enough. She confessed her restlessness and distress to an old Quakeress who advised her to forget her own sorrows in other people's and directed her specifically to houses where she would find fallen girls who needed the pity and care she was lavishing on herself. Josephine went – "I became possessed with an irresistible desire to go forth and find some pain keener than my own."[20] She found it abundantly available. Beginning in the best philanthropic tradition, she began to visit the workhouse at Brownlow Hill where 4,000 prostitutes and destitute girls were housed, and very soon she had moved onto a far more inspiring crusade.

A great many ladies of Josephine Butler's type and class did what she did. Workhouses and prisons were quite used to visitors coming to read the Bible to their inmates, to give them small articles of food and clothing, to encourage them to pray for forgiveness. The authorities could never quite guarantee that these virtuous ladies would not be jeered at and spat on, ridiculed and derided, nor could they protect them from language and behaviour they had neither seen nor heard in their sheltered lives before. It was quite common for the visitors to burst into tears and run away horrified at such ingratitude in the face of their kindnesses. But Josephine Butler rode the storm well. Perhaps the reasons why she did so were not psychologically healthy – there was undoubtedly a masochistic element present at the beginning – but they protected her from panic or revulsion. The most interesting part of her attitude to the inmates of Brownlow House, especially to the prostitutes in the Bridewell (a gaol below ground level) was her ability to express her compassion through physical contact. The girls and women incarcerated there were not pretty specimens. They were dirty, dishevelled and very often diseased and yet Josephine Butler not only allowed herself to be touched but touched first. More than one prostitute remembered how amazed and even shocked she was when Mrs Butler took her in her arms and held her tenderly and kissed her kindly. It was enough to make even the most hardened melt, especially since Josephine was herself so beautifully and immaculately dressed and groomed. It unnerved these women to have such a figure sit down with them and try to pick oakum, as they had to, while she talked. Her talks were always religious, she wanted to lead them to God just as other visitors did, but she also asked them about their lives and how they came to be there and showed sympathy rather than self-righteousness. What seemed to fascinate her most was their resignation, their expressed belief that nothing could change. They might escape briefly from the gloomy, ill-ventilated cellar where she sat with them on the stone floor but they would be back there soon because all that waited for them outside was starvation and the same escape from it leading to the same result.

After a year of this visiting Josephine had learned a lot. She had confirmed her own suspicions that all prostitutes were not wicked, licentious women who preyed on innocent men who were only seeking to satisfy natural urges. She had become familiar with two distinct patterns in the prostitution trade. The first was found among domestic servants who found a situation, were seduced by a master or son of the house, then turned out without a reference when their pregnancy was discovered. It was then prostitution or starvation. The second pattern was found among dressmakers or shop girls whose meagre earnings had to be subsidized when they fell below a bare maintenance level. These turned to prostitution as a temporary expedient and got out of it when and if they could. In both patterns Josephine detected men as the real villains – men, and the economic conditions of the times. She went with prostitutes released from

Brownlow to the quaysides of Liverpool and saw the realities of their situation. She saw the gin shops, the alleys, the backyards where pitifully dressed emaciated girls hung about trying to sell themselves – the penny whores. It was a world as far away as it was possible to get from the popular image of the prostitute as an ease-loving, sex-loving vamp lolling back among the silks and satins of a boudoir bought with her body. But, when Josephine Butler turned to what she could do about it, none of the remedies seemed anything but piecemeal. What was the good of preaching reform if reform did not carry with it the prospect of real escape? What was the point of rehabilitating a few girls when a whole industry existed maintained by the ability of men to pay for the gratification of lust?

At first, Josephine contented herself with doing the obvious thing – providing a home for girls released from the Bridewell of Brownlow House. She had two spare rooms so she took two girls at a time but within weeks this was so well-known that she was overwhelmed by women "swarming up from the town." The next step was to persuade some Liverpool merchants to finance a house where girls could be cared for. "The House of Rest is a little hospital of my own I have set up," she wrote, "for dying Magdalenes . . . It will hold thirteen."[21] The family doctor, Dr Moore, said he would give his services free. He was so affected by his patients that Josephine found she had to keep wiping his eyes behind his spectacles to keep them clear enough from tears to see to examine them. George was a less emotional support. He would conduct each girl to her room as she arrived with grave courtesy and shared the nursing with his wife. With her, he witnessed some miraculous conversions and heard heartrending stories. He also saw the gratitude and admiration aroused by Josephine. Mary Lomax, a girl who died in her arms, tried to express it in a poem:

"What worthy offering can I make to one I love so well
My heart seems nigh to break when on her love I dwell
When I think of how she found me so wretched and so low
So torn with pain and sickness, so plunged in guilt and woe
How sweet she said she loved me, even me, the wicked one
And answered my despairing words with joyous hopeful tones."[22]

But in fact Josephine was far from feeling joyous. She was exhausted both mentally and physically. As well as her work among prostitutes she had also been drawn into the educational reform movement by Anne Jemima Clough and had accepted the position of President of the North of England Council for the Promotion of Higher Education for Girls in 1867. She wrote an introduction for "Women's Work and Women's Culture" in which she drew from her direct experience to argue, as Emily Davies had done, that without wider employment opportunities for women, and training to equip them to take these opportunities, there could be no hope of a different and better future for the great mass of the female population.[23] On top of her regular work looking after her Magdalenes this administrative and writing work took its toll. She was driving herself hard and already George was helping domestically in a way few Victorian husbands were called upon to do. When she was once away from home in 1867 he wrote, "The boys did justice to their provisions and had a good play in my lecture room afterwards. They seemed very happy."[24] He sent her "a triple bouquet of love" from her sons as well as from him.

But the strain was obvious as Josephine tried to balance her dual role. In February 1868 she wrote she had consulted nine doctors about her heart and none of them could help her. In May she was so ill that she wrote, "I am nearly blind with the pain behind my eyes."[25] She had terrible dreams about her reclaimed girls and in the night "I used to cry out for some way of escape for starving women and saw thousands of them being swept up with a broom and hidden like ashes under a huge grate by political economists and I kept saying O take care they are tenderer than you."[26] Dr Moore visited her four or five times a day throughout that period. She went away for a rest but while she was absent all the servants fell ill with diphtheria and George had to farm the boys out which made her feel guilty, and so back she came.

By the following year she was even worse. To her mother-in-law she wrote, "I try to hide from George as much as I possibly can what I suffer. I sleep alone now and his dressing room is a long way off so he cannot hear me cough at night and I am always down at half past seven every morning. I sleep very little . . . The other day he saw me very weak from loss of blood and not able to hold myself up . . . Life is short, and I dread separation prematurely . . ."[27] And yet at the same time she told old Mrs Butler that even though her breathing was so bad she was "the merriest person in the house" and "wonderfully tough". She worried more about her mental state than about her physical condition. She had, she wrote, been making "the most extraordinary mistakes" all the summer – misdirecting letters, forgetting names, becoming in general confused and erratic. The reason for this was the appalling struggle she was having with herself ever since she had heard of the passage of the second Contagious Diseases Act in 1866. "For three months I was very unhappy," she wrote later ". . . the toils and conflicts of the years that followed were light in comparison with that first plunge . . ."[28]

Josephine Butler was by no means the first to feel unease or to express alarm. She was not even the first woman. In 1862, when a committee was appointed to look into the state of disease in the Army and Navy and to report on the working of the Regulation of Prostitution abroad, Harriet Martineau had written four leading articles on the subject in the *Daily News*. When the committee reported in favour of regulation and the 1864 Act was passed, followed by the 1866 Act which widened its scope, she protested strongly. So did two Nottingham doctors and Mr Daniel Cooper, who was in charge of a large institution devoted to the rescue of young girls. He had realized what was going on and had managed to get a copy of the Acts. What he read so alarmed him that he called a conference in Bristol for all other Reformatory Associations to attend. They worked out a protest which was then sent to every single MP, with no result whatever. What they needed, they decided, was a wife and mother who would come forward to lead a repeal movement and mobilize outraged female opposition. The Third Act of 1869 made this need even more imperative because it signified that the government meant to add to the places where the Acts operated until the entire country was covered. Before she was ever asked Josephine Butler had a terrible sense of destiny. She had read the Hansard reports on the passage of the Acts, she had read the report of the Bristol conference, she knew her work for prostitutes was by then common knowledge among reformers and she waited for the inevitable.

But what finally made Josephine take the job on was anger. Anger, not pity or duty or moral fervour. She wrote in September 1869, "Nothing so wears me out body and soul as anger, fruitless anger; and this thing filled me with such anger, and even hatred, that I fear to face it. The thought of this atrocity kills charity and hinders my prayers."[29] The way in which these revolting Acts had been passed particularly disgusted her. "These Acts were passed in a Parliament of men," she wrote, "no woman knowing anything about them. At the very base of the Acts lies the false and poisonous idea that women (ie *ladies*) have 'nothing to do' with the question and ought not to hear of it much less meddle with it. Women have unfortunately accepted this dictum for generations back . . ."[30] But she had no illusions about her fate if she stepped forward to show her sex how it should act. It was not just courageous to contemplate leading a Ladies' Association against the CD Acts but almost insane. Not only her own reputation would be vilified but so would her husband's. His career would be ruined. Her three sons, aged seventeen, fifteen and twelve would be exposed to merciless abuse if their mother spoke out on the subject of prostitution. Her entire family, who were not as radical as she was (except for Hatty, and her parents who were by then both dead) would suffer by their connection. Could she do it to them all? Had she the right to do it? At this juncture George's advice and encouragement were crucial. He not only did not object he actively urged her on, fully aware of what it would mean. So, at the end of 1869, Josephine Butler, aged forty-one, accepted the urgent invitation of Daniel Cooper and friends to lead a Ladies' Association against the CD Acts. She knew, as did her family and friends that as one observer put it she was stepping "straight into the jaws of hell."

But the minute the deed was done Josephine felt a great surge of energy. On January 1st, 1870 her newly formed Ladies' Association issued an eight point protest against the CD Acts, which was published in the *Daily News*, signed by 2,000 women including Florence Nightingale and Harriet Martineau. This protest attacked the Acts on every possible count – that they had been passed furtively; that the offence women were accused of was not defined; that they did not punish men who were partners in the professed "crime"; that it made vice easier for young men (who believed themselves safe); that the object, to control venereal disease, could not be attained (the history of such regulation on the continent was cited); that the real evil, which was moral, was not touched. It was a splendid, hard-hitting, cool, intelligent, rational indictment. It had no effect whatsoever. The government greeted it with total silence. Josephine's letters to every MP and other notables received few replies. Her personal appeals did no better. Even the press, initially intrigued by the prospect of salacious copy, soon lost interest. If anything, this fuelled Josephine's anger. She decided that her tactics were much too genteel and predictable – something else was needed. She must go to the people affected most by the Acts, to the working people whose wives and daughters were at risk. The prospect of making speeches in public filled her with terror and the thought of travelling around doing so made her feel faint but she saw no other way. Leaving George at home in charge of the boys, and telling her mother-in-law only that she was going off on "a sort of preaching tour of a delicate nature" she went off to Crewe, Leeds, Newcastle, Sunderland and Darlington where she addressed large groups of working-class people. It was the beginning of three years "on the road" throughout England. In the first year alone Josephine attended ninety-nine meetings and travelled 3,700 miles.

At first, Josephine was hopeful that her meetings and the collection of petitions would be effective enough. She was not a good speaker but she was surprised herself at how well she was received wherever she went. Elizabeth Cady Stanton later in Josephine's career thought her mode of address "like a methodist minister's" and was unimpressed by her low voice but she admitted that she had a certain power growing out of her obvious "deeply religious enthusiasm."[31] This communicated itself to her listeners and made them so carefully attentive that Josephine had no need, as she had feared, to "speak down" to her audience. But when, in spite of the spate of petitions, still no action was taken by a complacent Liberal government it was obvious something more drastic must be tried. Interference in by-election campaigns was the next step and it was one which pushed Josephine Butler into a glaring and much more dangerous lime-light.

Until the Newark by-election (in May 1870) she had suffered discomfort and some distress. She had slept in cold trains on her many trips and experienced rowdyism (though not much) at first hand. But once she began interfering in by-elections the full weight of vicious attacks crashed down upon her. She was no longer speaking to respectful, respectable working people sitting quietly, by arrangement, in a hall to hear her speak on an issue to which they were already sympathetic. Instead, she was standing outside on street corners, whenever a hall was refused her, facing gangs of louts hired to silence her by any means they chose. The fact that she was a well-dressed middle-class lady simply made her better game. Now she had to speak against constant barracking, against vulgar abuse shouted out to coarse laughter, against dirt of every kind flung at her. Mobs filled the street outside every hotel in which she attempted to stay. Stones were thrown through windows and she had to have a bodyguard to get her to and from meetings. And back home George began to receive obscene drawings of his wife through the post.

But at last there was a glimpse of success. The government were

furious when their candidate, Henry Storks, a great supporter of the
CD Acts, was defeated. They began to sit up and take notice. A Royal
Commission was hurriedly appointed to look into the working of the
Acts in the hope that it would keep the ladies happy. It did not.
Josephine Butler was against commissions, committees, reports or
any other measures less than total, absolute, instant repeal. She herself
was called to give evidence and made a poor showing because she
could not control her fury that a body of men who did not know what
she knew could be appointed to sit in judgement. She hated the
impression she got, which was perfectly correct, that these men
thought she was making a fuss about nothing. Their questions she
interpreted as impertinences and she resented bitterly the way one of
her mistakes was jumped upon. She had wrongly accused the Secretary of State for War, Sir Edward Cardwell, of malpractice in a certain
case concerning a Mrs Heritage and the details of this were dragged
out apparently to illustrate how unreliable she was. Though she knew
that she had indeed been wrong Josephine also knew this one instance
was irrelevant compared to the many, many proven cases of innocent
women being seized and forcibly examined. It was anger at the sneer
implicit in the line of questioning which drove her to burst out that if
anyone doubted her she would expose the doings of half the upper-
class gentlemen in the country to prove what prostitution was really
about. The final report was as useless as she had known it would be
and satisfied nobody, containing as it did the statement "there is no
comparison to be drawn between prostitutes and men who consort
with them. With one sex the offence is committed as a matter of gain,
with the other it is an irregular indulgence of a natural impulse." The
Home Secretary, Henry Bruce, began to prepare a new Bill on the
basis of the report but meanwhile Josephine herself was preparing an
answer.

She published two pamphlets in the next two years. The first was
The Constitution Violated (1871). Its 170 pages argued from a historical
standpoint that although the moral and health aspects of the Acts had
been endlessly stressed nobody had yet pointed out that for the entire
female population they amounted to a virtual suspension of Habeas
Corpus, that cornerstone of freedom. Security from arbitrary imprisonment and spoliation was the foundation of Habeas Corpus and, by
allowing women merely *suspected* of being prostitutes to be arrested,
to be forcibly examined and to be imprisoned if they resisted, this
security was breached. It amounted to trial without jury. Nor was it any

excuse to say the offence came under the heading of minor cases for which trial by jury was not needed. A woman's honour was not a minor affair to be equated with petty thieving. "These Acts," wrote Josephine Butler, "virtually introduce a species of villeinage or slavery. I use the word not sentimentally but in the strictest legal sense." If the Acts were allowed to stand a momentous decision had been made against the freedom of the individual. It was a straight choice: "Shall we have liberty in lust or shall we have political freedom? We cannot retain both." But the most interesting aspect of *The Constitution Violated* was the attack Mrs Butler made on the concept of prostitution.

Parliament, she said, had acted as if there was no doubt – "the upper classes talk as if there was the same difference as between a negro and a white man." This was absurd. There was the widest possible variety of opinion as to who was a prostitute. The CD Acts could only have been respected if either they had defined a prostitute as any woman found associating with a man to whom she could not prove she was married or as any women who voluntarily assumed the name. What the Acts did was confuse the distinction between vice and virtue. Under them, there was now state-regulated and unregulated vice. The report on the operation of the Acts had mentioned "the women now look fresh and healthy" in the towns where the Acts operated. The implication was that if prostitutes were made pleasant creatures everything was all right. "Obedience to the Acts will be mistaken for moral rectitude," wrote Mrs Butler in disgust. She extended this disgust to all those who thought prostitutes should be treated as "foul sewers". Sewers, she reminded her readers, had neither souls nor rights. The CD Acts amounted to a corruption of the law and people were urged "to awe the legislature" by withholding their confidence. The mistake was to imagine Parliament was infallible.

The second pamphlet, *The New Era* (1872), was written specifically to deal with the medical problem. Again and again Josephine had heard the claim that the CD Acts were "medically necessary". It was the government's strongest card. People really had come to believe that only by enforced medical examinations of prostitutes could the floodgates against rampant venereal disease be closed. The pamphlet gave a detailed history of what had happened in Germany to show how regulation did *not* control disease. It cited the evidence of a Dr Simon, six years resident in Berlin, who had written a pamphlet himself proving statistically that VD increased under regulation of vice because it drove prostitution underground and in these conditions VD became uncontrolled and endemic. The trouble was that regulation applied to women only. It was time for a new era in which the voice of women would be heard and that voice would proclaim the injustice as well as the uselessness of legislating against women only. The medical board of New York had claimed "for 100 years the governments of Europe have tried in vain to dry up the sources of prostitution" but this was a gross lie, and so was the assertion that in the state regulation of vice there was no aggrieved person. On the contrary, "never has there existed on earth a class of wronged or injured persons whose silence was less voluntary and more enforced, or a class whose history presents more than this, the rebellion, the wretchedness and the agonised writhings of tortured humanity." But to attempt to legislate about prostitution in any way whatsoever was pointless. "I am deeply convinced," Josephine Butler wrote, "that the state cannot with profit to our moral well being in any way whatsoever deal with the question of prostitution. A parliament of men, if it deals penally, admitting no protective element whatsoever, will deal penally with woman only." She did not even want legislation on soliciting because it fostered "in the minds of men the unequal standard which is at the bottom of the whole mischief." England, she said, would no longer stand for it.

In fact, England was more than prepared to stand for it. Another by-election success for the abolitionists at Colchester (1872) only gave a false sense of triumph, although it amounted at the time to a decisive victory and Josephine mistakenly thought it ushered in the new era of her pamphlet in which complete repeal was imminent. At Colchester, Storks was again defeated amid "a saturnalia of rioting" during which Josephine's life as well as her honour were put at risk. Before one meeting in the town she was penned into her hotel by a mob whose "deep throated yells and oaths and the horrible words spoken by them sounded sadly in my ears."[32] She had to hide in an attic while the men of her party went out to see if the meeting could safely be held anywhere. They returned bruised and battered and in need of "a good deal of lint and bandages". When she did finally manage to get out herself and address a gathering she had to leave by a back way and was pursued by a gang of men. She sheltered in "a dark, unused warehouse filled with empty soda bottles and broken glass" until a poor forlorn "woman of the town" rescued her and took her to safety.

But the worst experience of any she ever had was at Pontefract, the same year, when another by-election gave her party the chance to interfere again. There she became trapped in a hayloft with some other women. A gang of men (hired by brothel keepers) set fire to some straw beneath to smoke her out and then "to our horror, looking down the room to the trap door entrance, we saw appearing head after head of men with countenances full of fury . . ."[33] There was no escape. She and her friends were "like a flock of sheep surrounded by wolves." She stood there, terrified, and just as "these men's hands were literally upon us" the men of her party arrived to rescue the ladies. Unfortunately, they were easily overpowered by the ruffians but it gave the ladies time to "make a rush for it." The people of Pontefract, she said, were "outraged". This comforted her, but she was disappointed to find that ultimately the outrage felt at Pontefract, or Colchester, or Newark always seemed to peter out. The CD Acts were still on the statute books in spite of the abolitionists stumping the country, in spite of two well-received pamphlets, in spite of hundreds of petitions. What more could be done?

The Ladies' Association had all this time been trying, with considerable success, to organize resistance to arrest among the women of the regulated towns themselves and now they redoubled their efforts. They knew that from 1869 onwards large crowds of furious women had daily gathered in the streets to watch alleged prostitutes being dragged off and they realized that if this fury could be harnessed the authorities would be greatly embarrassed. *The Shield*, the Association's own newspaper begun in 1869, urged women to resist and a support system to help them do so was organized. Paid agents were employed and flysheets distributed. ("Many ladies have taken great trouble, have been put to great expense to come and speak to you . . . Are you glad they are come? Are you grateful to them? Then Reform and Resist! Don't go willingly to the examination or to the Hospital but let them make you go.") Gradually, women began to take this advice. The Association provided legal aid for them when they were brought to trial and the trial proceedings in turn provided wonderful propaganda. The definition of what constituted a prostitute was forever under dispute just as Josephine Butler had known it would be. Some women were arrested because it was alleged they looked or dressed like prostitutes. Justice Liddell of Devonport pronounced that "gaily dressing" did not provide grounds for arrest "for it so happens nowadays that there was such peculiarities in dressing even by persons of good character that it would be difficult to draw the line." Then there was the even more important question of how VD was to be defined. In the case of Harriet Hicks the Association's lawyer made a fool of the resident medical officer who said Harriet was diseased because she had a vaginal ulcer. Pressed to define VD this officer offered "All genital diseases in men or women arising from excessive or impure sexual intercourse." "Excessive?" inquired the defence, incredulous. Harriet Hicks was discharged. Afterwards, a report of the trial was distributed as a flysheet. In the following months twenty-nine women summoned to attend for examination stoutly refused. Mary Jeffries, mother of a girl summoned for examination, called the police constable who came for her "a black looking bugger and a bloody sneak" and threw him out. That, said the Association, was the spirit.[34]

Yet the beginning of 1874 saw Josephine Butler at her lowest ebb. She was utterly exhausted. She felt unable to refuse any request to address a meeting, which imposed upon her endless travelling. "The middle of the day is my most weary time," she wrote to a friend organizing a meeting, ". . . if I might have a bit of food to go to my room to rest for an hour I shall be able to be all alive about 3 or half past."[35] She usually then began meetings at four pm, finished at six and if humanly possible travelled home. George was always at the station to meet her, or standing at the door at home. Once "I came home to find my dear husband ill in bed. I am nursing him today and trying to get through immense accumulations of letters. He is hardly ever ill. I felt a pang of fear when he failed, for the first time in his life, to meet me either at the station or at our own door."[36] She knew she was not being fair to George or to her children. "I want a bit of rest at Easter," she wrote in 1873 "When our boy George comes home. He only has a week and I don't see him so much now . . ."[37] George, as dutiful and serious as ever, was at Trinity, Cambridge, where "his chief motive, dear lad, is to get some money to make it easier for us . . ." She was thrilled when he won the Bell Scholarship. More worrying was Charles, the youngest, about whom she wrote "I am so sad – he is so delicate."[38] He did not seem to thrive in Liverpool and was sent, in 1874, to school at Clifton College near Bristol. If anything, Josephine fretted even more. "Don't think me weak," she wrote to the friends putting Charles up for his interview "if I ask you to send me the enclosed telegram as soon as Charlie arrives – you need not tell *him* . . . I am afraid of his cold making him sick as it generally attacks his stomach."[39] Those who accused her of being an uncaring mother never knew what a stupidly wrong conclusion they had drawn from her absences.

Thoughts of what was still happening under the operation of the CD Acts preyed on her mind endlessly. William Acton, doyen of medical writers, had written, "The inspection, for which the speculum is frequently used, is performed with all the delicacy consistent with accuracy and great despatch; the average time occupied being three minutes which includes filling up the papers." Josephine's growing experience was that what women suffered in that three minutes was "worthy of the Spanish Inquisition." She had heard, first-hand, of what awaited any women taken to the police station "on suspicion". She was put on a surgical couch, her legs parted by clamps, her ankles tied in leather stirrups, and then held down while surgical instruments, dipped in boiling water, were used to inspect her. If she struggled a strait jacket was always at hand for use. Sometimes, if a girl was not only not diseased but a virgin the inspection would rupture her hymen and produce a flood of blood. Then, she was usually told she was a good girl and given five shillings to buy herself a hot dinner. Sometimes a miscarriage was brought on, sometimes such internal injury was done that the woman had to be removed unconscious. Josephine had been told by hardened prostitutes that they had to make themselves drunk to go through with it. She would not accept that these examinations were mere formalities and the vast majority over, painlessly, in seconds. At their best they were degrading and at their worst brutalizing. They treated women's bodies as pieces of meat.

The effect that carrying out these inspections had on the men who were obliged to make them also concerned her – they too were brutalized. It made her furious to hear uninformed people talk as though the whole experience was no worse than going to the dentist and much less painful. As more and more reports came in from field workers on the spot in the affected towns she began to be haunted by the fear that this monstrous treatment could not be stopped. Every day, some innocent women suffered, every day womanhood was being insulted. Worrying about it made her ill and she felt she ought to redouble not decrease her own personal efforts for repeal.

But she was incapable of doing so. Worry about the victims of the Acts, worry about her sons, worry about her husband and her own ill-health made her increasingly depressed. She found it hard to put up with the stories which circulated about her marriage too. "A certain

class of our enemies," she wrote bitterly, "thought themselves happy
it seemed in inventing a dart which they believed would strike home in
our case; they sought diligently to spread an impression that some
tragic unhappiness in our married life was the impelling force which
had driven me from my home to this work; and coarse abuse was
varied by hypocritical expressions of pity and sympathy. But they
were the most unworthy of all – the 'lewd fellows of the baser sort'
naturally – by whom this kind of scourging was inflicted or
attempted."[40] What hurt most was that these "lewd fellows" were
often clergymen and members of the aristocracy who ought to have
known better. Not only did these people vilify her but they pilloried
George.

In 1872, when George had obtained leave to read a paper at the
annual church congress on the subject of "The Duty of the Church of
England in Moral Questions", he was howled down as soon as he
mentioned the CD Acts, and the Bishop of Lincoln, who was in the
chair, ordered him to abandon his lecture. The outlook for his career if
he went on supporting his wife's campaign was bleak. Often, George
was left to face hostility while Josephine was away and it placed a great
strain on him. They both found the constant partings almost unbearable. "I feel ridiculously much this parting," wrote Josephine
". . . about him I have the yearning of heart."[41] Wherever she went
she carried a special prayer George had composed for her – "to my
dear wife, to use when we are apart." She had had to use it far too
often. With George at Cambridge, Stanley about to go up to Oxford,
and Charlie at Clifton, her husband was all on his own in a home
which was suddenly desolate.

In October 1874, just in time to save her health and sanity, Josephine
thankfully relinquished the leadership of the campaign against the CD
Acts to Sir James Stansfield, MP for Halifax. Gladstone had that
spring been defeated, to be succeeded by Disraeli which depressed the
repealers, but this released many Liberal MPs from the parliamentary
restraints necessary to a party in power. In opposition, many more felt
free to support Josephine Butler, and the battle shifted from the
hustings to the floor of the Commons. But, instead of this releasing
Josephine to go home to George and stay with him, it drove her to
quite another course of action. In the winter of 1874/5, after a brief
holiday, she undertook a continental tour to seek international support.
How she found the strength to contemplate it, considering that only a
few months before she was complaining of feeling so giddy she could

hardly see and suffering from "congestion of the brain" which only total rest would cure, is difficult to understand. Her secretary had just replied to an invitation from the American suffragists saying Mrs Butler was "too frail" ever to be able to even think about an Atlantic voyage, yet, compared with what she then undertook, such a trip would have been a rest cure.

She began her tour in Paris, where she visited St Lazare – "an immense prison, hospital and general depot for all the unhappy women of Paris" – and had an interview with Lecours, the head of the Police des Moeurs, who made the mistake of trying to flirt with her. Afterwards she went on to Lyons, Naples, Rome and Geneva in one of the hardest winters of the century. Everywhere she went she visited prominent people trying to enlist their support, addressed meetings of working people and, wherever she was allowed, visited the prisons and workhouses where prostitutes were suffering under the law she hated. On her return, she formed an International Society against State Regulated Vice which held its first congress in Liverpool in 1875. Not surprisingly she was ill again. "Stronger lungs than mine might have been injured," she commented "if you consider how often I have spoken – long addresses in large rooms with a naturally weak voice, and how often I have had to come out of heat into bitter, cold winds or damp air – how often on long railway journies [sic] I have slept from sheer exhaustion and awoke shivering violently."[42] Once more, George nursed her back to health. For a while she rested and turned to writing but, with the return to power of the Liberals in 1880, she was once more back at the heart of the struggle. The CD Acts had stood for ten years: this time, they *must* be repealed.

The House of Commons was by then heartily sick of the subject. The idea of the CD Acts being extended to cover the whole country had long ago been abandoned and it seemed pointless to go on defending such a half-hearted operation. In addition, a Minority Report had been produced which revealed that disease among prostitutes was actually *worse* in the regulated areas. Another Select Committee was appointed, this time with members much more sympathetic to the repealers. Josephine again gave evidence, but on this occasion much more effectively. She described her work in Chatham clearly and unemotionally. "I spent one whole night in going into the brothels in the town," she said " . . . I was introduced to low, dancing saloons, drinking saloons and wretched theatres in connection with the brothels and with doors leading into them . . . I saw there evidence of

the degradation of the young soldiers who first join the army . . .
There were boys who appeared to be not more than thirteen . . . a
look of perfect innocence . . . I gathered them round me . . . it was as
solemn as hell itself . . . a business-like exhibition of superintended
vice." The committee was impressed and hopes ran high that success
was only a matter of waiting for the report. Josephine worked
frantically to rally support in the crucial debate which would follow
but she was held back from total commitment by the illness of Stanley.
"Tell the public that domestic troubles hold me back,"[43] she wrote
and then worried that she would be despised for putting her family
first for once. But in April, when the debate at last took place, she was
in the gallery of the House of Commons watching and listening. On
the afternoon of April 20th, a week after her fifty-fifth birthday, she
made her way there through thick fog to hear a Bill to repeal the CD
Acts read. At six, when it was clear the debate would go on all night,
she went to the Westminster Palace Hotel to hold a prayer meeting
with George. At midnight he stayed while she returned. As she
climbed the stairs to the Ladies' Gallery the steward whispered he
thought she was going to win. He was right. At 1.30 am when the
figures were called it was 182 to 110 in favour of immediate suspension. Josephine went out onto the terrace of the House. "The fog had
cleared away and it was very calm under the starlit sky. All the bustle
of the city was stilled and the only sound was that of dark water
lapping against the buttresses of the broad stone terrace . . . it almost
seemed like a dream."[44]

The Butlers celebrated by going on holiday to Switzerland. George
had resigned from Liverpool College in the autumn of 1882 and had
been appointed to a canonry at Winchester. It upset Josephine to
realize his work at Liverpool had never properly been appreciated. "He
rarely absented himself from his post at the college for even a short
hour,"[45] she wrote, but people acted as if he had subordinated his work
to hers. Yet she was relieved to leave Liverpool where she said there
were "too many calls on our purse" and too much constantly expected. Winchester would give both of them some peace in their
approaching old age. A period of calm was to be inaugurated for them
both, in which Josephine was determined to put George first whatever
others said – but she was highly sensitive to what they would say. In
the summer of 1885 when she went with her family to Scotland while
the actual repeal Bill for the CD Acts was going through Parliament
(and proving a more tedious process than anyone had suspected) she

wrote, "I dread so that some of our committee should accuse me of deserting them in a crisis . . ."[46] She resolutely kept her vow to stay with George in the precincts of Winchester Cathedral but this did not prevent her from embarking on another cause connected with her life-long work which shattered the peace she had promised him.

In 1876 the famous journalist W. H. Stead had written to Josephine saying that what her crusade needed, to make it catch the public imagination, was an Uncle Tom and would she provide it? Josephine declined, but kept in correspondence with Stead who was then editor of the *Northern Echo* in Darlington. He had been a firm supporter of her cause ever since his mother had gone round collecting signatures for a petition after hearing Josephine speak in 1870. In 1885 Stead, now editor of the *Pall Mall Gazette* in London, formed a Secret Commission to investigate West End prostitution. Josephine had of course been acquainted with the true facts of prostitution for a very long time. All her speeches and writings had constantly striven to inform people about the circumstances in which girls became prostitutes and to demonstrate that it had become an organized trade in which girls were victims. She had always been particularly concerned by the evidence of the existence of child prostitution. She knew there was an international traffic in young girls, in which they were enticed into the hands of unscrupulous women who sold them to both private customers and brothel keepers. Now Stead was willing to take on the job of exposing this trade if she would help. Josephine was more than willing and so was George. They left the holy atmosphere of Winchester Cathedral, assumed disguises and gained access to brothels and "private" houses. The three Butler sons all helped. The investigations, led by Stead, began on the Saturday before Whit and took six weeks to complete at the cost of £300. The results were printed in the *Pall Mall Gazette* in four issues throughout July entitled "The Maiden Tribute of Modern Babylon" with an introduction by Lord Shaftesbury. The disclosures were devastating – it was investigative reporting at its sensational best.

The revelations shocked the uninformed and excited the knowledgeable to come forward with more evidence of corruption. Josephine Butler said "a gentleman" offered to sell her "a photograph and other authentic proofs of Mr Gladstone's orgies in a brothel."[47] She declined them. Stead's report was sufficient, proving that "the violation of virgins" was systematic and "constantly perpetrated with absolute impunity." Stead asked for three virgins to be delivered to him and they duly were complete with promissory certificates ("I hereby agree to let you have me for a present of £3 or £4. I will come to any address if you give me two days notice"). The system of procuring was revealed with precise details as to how it operated – how women made friends with young girls in the park, asked them home to tea, chloroformed them and then held them down to be raped. The existence of houses where "used" virgins were "patched up" to be resold was described. Most pitifully of all, the extent of the girls' ignorance was established. Many of them were indeed willing to be seduced but what they thought of as seduction was the medical examination to prove they were virgins. When the examination was over they were very relieved, put their clothes on and asked for their money commenting they were glad it was done with. By that time they were literally trapped and the actual violation inescapable. They were kept in locked rooms without any but the scantiest clothing and, since they were almost always homeless girls who had left their families, without anyone trying to track them down. All Stead failed to prove was that it was also possible to buy a child of, or under, thirteen. He knew and Josephine knew that it could be done but he failed to secure one. This in itself was useful proof that raising the age of consent had been worthwhile and that if it was raised higher to sixteen as the Vigilance Committee, formed by Mrs Wolstenholme Elmy, wanted then legislation would be even more protective.

This was something Josephine was determined to achieve and she thought she saw a way of doing it. She had housed in a cottage in the precinct of Winchester Cathedral one Rebecca Jarrett, a reformed prostitute sent to her by Mrs Bramwell Booth. Rebecca ran a Mission for reclaimed prostitutes in the cottage, with Josephine's help and encouragement, and had shown herself to be a tireless and most successful worker. Now Josephine approached Rebecca, who had herself once run a brothel, and asked her if she would go back to her old haunts and help Stead buy a child so that the whole wicked system could be exposed. Afterwards, Josephine wrote a short history of the affair in which she emphatically denied she had put any pressure on Rebecca. "Rebecca had lived sufficiently long with me to have learned to share my conviction and wishes concerning the mass of criminal vice existing in London"[48] she wrote. Yet she herself also printed some notes of Rebecca's which made it plain that it was Josephine's personal wish that had made Rebecca agree. "In an exceptional enterprise we were forced to use exceptional means,"[49] claimed Josephine defensively – and guiltily. At any rate, Rebecca agreed to act as an intermediary.

A child of thirteen, Eliza Armstrong, was bought from her mother for five gold sovereigns, certified a virgin by a brothel keeper (one Madame Mourez, an old friend of Rebecca's) and given to Stead masquerading as a customer. The story was then printed and led directly to the raising of the age of consent to sixteen in the Criminal Law Amendment Act of 1885. The price was higher than Josephine had estimated. What Rebecca had not realized was that Eliza had a known father, "Basher" Armstrong, who was produced by Stead's enemies to claim Eliza had been abducted. Stead, and Bramwell Booth who had also been involved, went to prison for three months (which Stead greatly enjoyed) but the real scapegoat proved to be Rebecca Jarrett. Under cross-examination she was, wrote Josephine, "put in an exceptionally difficult position for a person of her poor education and miserable antecedents. Her head ached and her brain reeled . . ." Instead of refusing to answer irrelevant questions about her past life she was "very stupid – very blundering."[50] Seething with rage at how Rebecca was treated Josephine sat in court regretting her own "imprudence . . . in asking Rebecca to undertake this difficult work." Across the courtroom Rebecca "looked at me with an expression on her pale face which I shall never forget."[51] She was sent down for two years during which she suffered terribly but more from the thought of what she had done to poor Eliza than from the physical hardship. "I have been so tired and knocked about," she wrote from the dock to Josephine, still her idol. "I do feel I would like to be alone with God in the prison . . ."[52]

The royal assent was given to the Bill for the repeal of the Contagious Diseases Acts in April 1886. Josephine was in Italy and wrote, "I hardly felt as if I cared . . . Much of the joy of the triumph seems to have been lost in being deferred."[53] Everything in any case was overshadowed by George's serious illness. He had collapsed with rheumatic fever while Josephine was in London, visiting and supporting Rebecca Jarrett through the trial, and although she had taken him to Italy to recuperate he was still far from well. She was frightened and remorseful. She obtained the best medical advice but even though the fever seemed to be successfully treated she wrote, "his dear face bears traces of much suffering. He cannot use his hands; he can only look on while we do everything for him."[54] She would never leave him again. At last, she began consistently refusing all invitations. "My choice was deliberate," she wrote firmly. When George was stronger they returned to Winchester and Josephine stayed dutifully close, insisting on frequent holidays in the sun to conserve her dear husband's strength. In January 1889 she took him to Cannes, to the Hotel Continental, and "basked in the sun" with him. But it became obvious that George must retire and on August 25th, 1889 he was helped up the steps of the pulpit, his arm in a sling, to preach his last sermon. There was a last family party before the Butlers went abroad for another long holiday. In November, at Amalfi, George was laid low by influenza. Josephine was told there was not the slightest chance of recovery. George, who knew it, expressed a wish to die at home but did not quite make it, dying in London, with Josephine holding his hand, in March 1890.

The shock was appalling and Josephine suffered acutely. She was almost sixty-two and had been married for nearly forty years to a man she had adored. What was there left for her? "I am terribly lonely now," she wrote. "I feel as if I can hardly go on."[55] She and George had shared everything – thoughts, ideas, hopes and especially work. Few understood the nature of their union. Between them there had been a balance of uncanny delicacy which in any age is rare but in Victorian times was extraordinary. Their life had been fitted round Josephine's work – it was she who had travelled, George who had stayed at home – yet nobody had made the mistake of thinking George was a cipher. He was strong, not weak, a rock in the background not a shadow. When people expressed amazement that he should "allow" his wife such freedom he told the truth: he was as much part of the campaign she headed as she was. He held no contemporary notions of a wife's place, never expected her to be immured as the "angel in the house". He did not think it demeaning to be the one who for long stretches of time looked after his children – he regarded it as a privilege. When Josephine wired she was delayed and could not return as promised he told the boys "we must manage as best we can" and proceeded to do so. Nor did he hold it against her that after he was ordained she was rather less than the perfect Church of England wife. "I thought everyone knew I am *not* of the Church of England and never was," she wrote. "I go to the church once on Sunday out of a feeling of loyalty to my husband – that is all . . . I inherited from childhood the widest ideas of vital Christianity. I have not much sympathy with *the church*."[56] This George respected. Other people's opinions never worried him. When his old colleagues at Harrow pointedly rose and turned their backs on him, because of his wife, during a return visit to the school he was not hurt – it was Josephine who was cut to the quick on his behalf at such an insult.

For a long time Josephine was restless and wretched and her sons did not know how to console her. Charlie was in the Transvaal, a constant source of worry to her (and a drain on her purse) as he tried to make a career for himself in mining, but George and Stanley were attentive. George, who was a Civil Service commissioner, was the most like his father but Josephine, although she loved him dearly, did not find him nearly as congenial as Stanley. Once her husband had died Stanley became her chief support. "You are the dearest of my sons," she wrote to him. "Since Father died you are the only one of my family to whom I can turn in the *certainty* of your sympathy and of you understanding me."[57] She also liked Rhoda, the woman Stanley married in 1886, and doted on their two children, Josephine and Bobby. But she would not make her home with them in St Andrews (where Stanley was a lecturer at the University). She preferred to flit about from one lodging to another for ten years until in 1901 she returned to Cheltenham where she wrote to Stanley she had no friends any more – "no, not one, but I don't much care to make new friends now . . . I have a curious comforting feeling of companionship in being so near Eva's grave . . . "[58]

There had also been comfort in a return to work. After George's death she felt she never wanted to work again – she was weary, discouraged and entirely lacking in any kind of energy. But at the annual general meeting of the Ladies' Association in May 1891, an address was presented to her which was "like a resurrection". She felt the old sense of urgency returning and turned to helping with the production of *The Stormbell* and to involving herself with the outcry over the sale of women to soldiers in India. She was back in the movement again and within a very short time once more producing articles and pamphlets rousing others to action. Her family were delighted at the change in her. She became the centre of their own family activities and proved a wonderful grandmother. George's three children (he married in 1893), Charles' two (he married in 1897) and Stanley's children all worshipped her. She took them on outings, wrote them long letters, looked after them when they were ill and was a delightful and cheerful companion to them whenever they visited. As she grew older she felt a great wish to return home to Northumberland. She left Cheltenham to go back to Northumberland in 1903 where she settled at Woller, near Ewart Park, the home of her son

George whose wife had just died. Here, she kept up her interest in politics and world affairs writing, "I am not sorry *socialism* has got into parliament,"[59] and other comments on what was happening which revealed her sympathies. But she was "so tired" and wrote to Stanley in December 1906, "I think I may have to die. Don't mourn too much."[60] She died on December 29th, aged seventy-eight, quite reconciled to the idea of death, but with no delusions that she had achieved what she had set out to achieve. True, the Contagious Diseases Acts had been abolished, never to appear on the statute books again, but state-regulated vice still flourished elsewhere in the world and the double standard lived on.

★   ★   ★

But Josephine Butler had achieved for feminism more than she knew and much more than she has ever been given credit for. The campaign she so bravely led alerted people to the knowledge that sex legislation existed – legislation, that is, against one sex only. She made her audiences understand that the woman was made the victim and that this made the whole female sex into a commodity for men's use. Parliament, consisting entirely of men, had been compelled to see the truth of this and they had not liked it. Every man there had daily experiences of the "double standard" but had thought nothing of it: it was the way of the world, men were born with "natural urges" and these had to be satisfied. In order to satisfy them, which was not always possible within, never mind without, marriage, prostitutes must exist. If they existed they must be kept clean or men would become diseased. It was all quite simple. But then came Josephine Butler and her many helpers and suddenly it was not quite so simple. The idea that prostitutes might not wish to be prostitutes but were driven to it as an alternative to death by starvation was alarming; that clean prostitutes did not guarantee clean men even more alarming; and that there was no justification whatsoever for the existence of prostitution the most alarming of all. Slowly, by infinitely painful degrees, the double standard was shown up for what it was: a sham. Men and women so far as prostitution was concerned could not be judged separately. The prostitute was no more wicked, no more deserving of punishment, than the customer. Women had not been created for the gratification of male lust.

This was a startling line of thought and quite contrary to informed medical as well as to popular opinion. The idea that the prostitute is wicked and the customer exploited (because he is only satisfying "natural urges") still exists: the double standard survives. But Josephine Butler's contribution was to make sure it came out into the open. Before she spoke out it was hidden, never properly acknowledged for what it was, continually disguised by other names. Afterwards, society knew what it was dealing with – one rule for men, one for "good" women, and one for "bad" women. A very long time indeed had to elapse before these distinctions became blurred which they did through a change in sexual mores of which Josephine Butler would have emphatically disapproved. Never for one moment did she wish women to treat sex as simply an urge which they had the right to satisfy as men did. She did not want women to share men's sexual freedom because she did not see it as freedom. She wanted purity for both sexes. Sex and love, in her opinion, were inextricably connected and both could only find true expression within a Christian marriage. Yet she never saw the prostitute as wicked, was never interested in persecuting the species. Her principle was not to pursue them (prostitutes) with any outward punishment, nor drive them out of any place so long as they behaved decently, but to attack *organized* prostitution, "that is when a third party, actuated by a desire of making money, sets up a house in which women are sold to men, or keeps any place for his own gain which is a market of vice."[61] In short, what concerned her most was the exploitation of women by men.

Josephine Butler knew more about this subject than she was ever able to reveal. After visiting the prison of St Lazare in Paris she believed she had plumbed the depths of what men could do to women. She saw children of five and six, arrested as prostitutes, kept in cages like animals. She saw girls who she said were just "shells", bodies so wrecked by depravity that the minds in them had become completely vacant. After Stead's campaign she said she never again would wonder what hell was like because she had seen it here on earth. The contrast with her own experience made what she saw seem all the more terrible. She had enjoyed, in her marriage, the love of a man who had never treated her with anything but consideration and tenderness, for whom the words of the marriage service – "with my body I thee worship" – had literal meaning. The letters which passed between the Butlers never speak overtly of physical passion but their harmony is easily read between the lines in that, as in all other, spheres. They "longed for" and "yearned" to be "once more, alone, together"; they wrote of hardly being able to bear a longer separation; they reminded each other of "joyful" reunions; they missed each other's "tender ministrations". So Josephine Butler knew what the sex act could be. She was no prudish spinster but a married woman passionately in love with her husband. But she was also an extremely beautiful and attractive woman who knew her own sexual power. No other feminist leader ever aroused men in quite the way Josephine Butler did. The impact of this elegant, lovely, utterly virtuous, upper middle-class married lady earnestly talking about prostitution was devastating. Men she addressed individually on the subject of "natural urges" hardly knew where to put themselves. Men who jeered and leered at her in public meetings left her in no doubt of the thoughts she gave rise to – she could not for one moment forget the existence of sex. What disturbed and disgusted and ultimately terrified her was the element of torture in sex. She knew the facts and the reality of rape. What she tried so hard to convey to people was the horror implicit not just in the organized rape of virgins but in the surgical rape practised under the CD Acts.

The hardest step for Josephine Butler to take was to start calling a spade a spade. Euphemisms, in her day, were all. The sexual act, prostitution, venereal disease, all bodily functions were covered by endless euphemistic talk. When Josephine Butler first began her campaign she bowed to convention and conceded that she too protected the susceptibilities of women like her mother-in-law. But she soon grew tired of this. Her own sex could not go on being protected – it only did them harm, made them even more the dupes of men. So she began to speak plainly. Words like "prostitute", "rape", and "venereal disease" were in the end freely used by her. A kind of contempt for her own sex and particularly for her own class began to distinguish her speeches and writings. She despised women for playing into men's hands by pretending to be virtuously ignorant of the facts of life. Towards the end of her life she wrote, "Where are we? All these 'forward women' movements, political and other, seem not to have done much to correct certain men of their determination to enslave women to their lusts by law. I have some anxious feelings about our women. I see a tendency even among the best to knock under too much to *male* opinion."[62] It was a tendency which led her to believe that female suffrage was more important than she had ever thought. As early as 1873 she wrote, "I feel more and more anxious to get woman's suffrage . . . it is a more *urgent* matter than I once thought"[63] and "if I were not working for repeal I should throw my whole force into getting the suffrage."[64] By the 1880s and 1890s she was even more convinced that votes for women were essential and might achieve more than she had ever done.

Yet more important than votes, in her opinion, was a sense of identification with each other for all women. She breached the high walls of class prejudice fearlessly in this respect, making middle-class women see not just how their sisters suffered but how their own standing was attacked by these sufferings. There is an impression in everything written about Josephine Butler that she was guided in her work by some sort of mystical, religious fervour – that she was carried away on an emotional tide of religious ecstasy. Nothing could be further from the truth. She indignantly resented any suggestion that her religion was an emotional response. "I think there prevails among clever men," she once wrote, "who do not know intimately the hearts of many women an idea that women generally accept Christianity without a thought or difficulty; that they are in a measure instinctively pious and that religion is rather an indulgence of the feelings with them than anything else . . . for myself, I can say that to be guided by feeling would be simply dangerous . . . I sometimes gave whole nights to prayer . . . Do not imagine that on these occasions I worked myself into any excitement."[65] But people did. Religious excitement and a hysterical reaction to Eva's death are advanced as explanations for Josephine Butler's commitment. What is left out is her deeply *feminist* belief that women as a sex must all help each other. She had no time at all for emotional nonsense and could be extremely cutting about any attempt to base arguments on feelings. In 1883 she tore to shreds a draft manifesto because "I could not endorse the style. It was the wildest, massinian 'high fallooting' style – 'we solemnly declare by the sacred womb of maternity' – and half of it would not have been understood by the MPs and others to whom we wish it to go. My idea of a manifesto is that it should be dignified and somewhat formal in style while leaving no doubt whatever as to its meaning . . ."[66] She wished to tell people the facts of the case in language which needed to be all the more plain and sober because those facts were dramatic and shocking.

She succeeded. She made all women who heard her care about what happened to some women. She made most men who heard her ashamed of some of their sex. She made everybody examine the existing moral basis to society and, if she failed to make them totally reform it, she at least encouraged them to begin to think that they should do so. The way to do it was believed, by the last quarter of the nineteenth century, to be through obtaining female suffrage. Then, all else would follow.

POLITICS

Elizabeth Cady Stanton
(BBC Hulton Picture Library)

Elizabeth Cady Stanton
1815–1902

The decision to claim the vote changed the nature of feminism more than any other single factor. Right up to the middle of the nineteenth century the whole emphasis in feminism was on putting right existing wrongs within the accepted framework of society. None of the early feminist activists wished to overturn that society or to alter radically the framework. In fact, they were at pains to deny that any sort of revolution in the body politic was necessary. As the activists began to campaign for changes in the laws affecting women, in the education and employment and general treatment of women, they stressed again and again that all they wanted was "justice". Nobody wanted to take from men what they had, only to share it. The fears of social revolution ending in anarchy were as strong in the feminists as in their opponents. But gradually, as so many changes were resisted, the activists began to understand that until women shared equally in the ruling of their country and in the law-making process they would never succeed in gaining true justice at all. It became no longer sufficient to sit and wait for men to grant what would after all be concessions. What right did they have to this overwhelming power they possessed? Who had given it to them and why? Logically, the most fearless feminist thinkers were led to the conclusion that all their sufferings stemmed from men controlling government in all its forms. And so, in 1848 at Seneca Falls in the State of New York, the first collective public claim was made that women should "secure to themselves their sacred right to the elective franchise."

Once this daring claim had been made the suffrage cause was embraced with astonishing passion. Everything suddenly seemed to hinge on gaining the vote. The feminists themselves were breathless with excitement at the glorious vista which opened up before them: give women the vote and the whole world would change. Women's interests would automatically predominate, women's problems be recognized and solved, women's tender influence work miracles. The opponents of female suffrage believed all this would be true if anything more firmly than the feminists themselves. Certainly the world would change and they hated the thought of the consequences so much that they fought against it with absolute fury. Yet both parties were mistaken. One of the most extraordinary aspects of feminist history is how little gaining the vote mattered, even though trying to gain it mattered very much. The truth is that almost every reform that changed women's place in society had been made, or was well on the way to being made, before the vote was won. Furthermore, society did not change dramatically because of women sharing in government. Women did not act collectively at the polls. Women's issues did not come to the forefront of political debate. Women did not flock to enter parliaments or congresses throughout the western world. In country after country they proved unable or reluctant to enter the political arena at all. The "feminine influence" was hardly felt. Wars did not stop, the "bond of humanity between all peoples" spoken of was not recognized before all else. Paradise was not gained for feminists or anyone else.

Yet all the prodigious effort expended on giving women the vote was not wasted. The suffragists expected too much once their cause was won but they were correct all the same in thinking political status so important. The suffrage movement had immense practical benefits for feminism and even greater ideological implications. It bound women together in a clearly-defined way which no other issue had ever done. It made feminists, men as well as women, into a collective and carried them into the centre of the stage – no mean feat. But it also altered forever what feminism meant. All talk of merely wanting protection or pleading for merciful justice was finished. The idea that women should stay only within the domestic sphere was finally rejected and with it all notions of basic inferiority. By demanding political power feminists at last grew up. Their self-esteem was raised and with it their expectations. They were elated by their own courage but also frightened. "No matter how much women prefer to lean, to be protected and supported," they were warned by Elizabeth Cady Stanton, "nor how much men desire to have them do so, they must make the voyage of life alone and for safety in an emergency they must know something of the laws of navigation."[1] Learning those laws, learning to stand truly on their own feet, was what being involved in government was supposed to mean. Winning the vote, wherever it was won, removed the last constraints on women's potential self-fulfilment and for that reason alone it was a vital feminist victory not to be scorned simply because in the end its measurable gains seem few. Each time the vote was won the news travelled fast and wide and inspired feminists everywhere. The first women to win the vote on equal terms with men were those in the state of Wyoming in America in 1869. This was fitting for even if the whole feminist world did not look to little Wyoming for a lead it undoubtedly looked to America where the ladies of Seneca Falls had become the architects of the suffrage movement. What was surprising was that this movement had become necessary at all in this country – the one place where women had had the opportunity to arrange new terms for themselves when they arrived with their men as immigrants.

Women were a vital factor in stabilizing any colony when the new settlers came over in the seventeenth century and they were always in short supply. Of the twenty-nine who came over in the *Mayflower*, for example, only four were left by the end of the first year and yet they never used their position of strength to give themselves any kind of better deal in the New World. In fact, their position by the early nineteenth century had become every bit as subordinate as it had been back in England. The usual repressive laws and customs with regard to women had been transposed wholesale causing one early feminist writer to complain furiously, "the very phrases used with regard to us are abominable – 'dead in the law,' 'Femme couverte' – how I detest such language."[2] But nobody seems to have objected successfully to it being employed in the first place. Women were given the vote in some of the earlier colonies but appear not to have objected effectively when it was taken from them as new legislatures were formed after Independence. A few brave souls did indeed protest but there was no positive collective resistance. Yet many of the men themselves felt guilty. Tom Paine's *Pennsylvania Magazine* carried an article urging men to "feel for the tender sex" because "even in countries where they may be most happy (they are) constrained in their desires, in the disposal of their goods, robbed of freedom and will by the laws, the slaves of opinion which rules them with absolute sway . . . surrounded on all sides by judges who are at once tyrants and their seducers . . ." These noble sentiments achieved nothing, nor had the warning of Abigail Adams who wrote in 1776 to her husband, "Remember, all men would be tyrants if they could. If particular care and attention is not paid to the ladies we are determined to foment a rebellion and will not hold ourselves bound by any laws in which we have no voice or representation."

But no rebellion materialized. The ladies were after all docile for many more years until in the 1830s the formation of Anti-Slavery societies gave women the chance to challenge publicly the accepted status of women. Sarah and Angelina Grimké, daughters of a South Carolina slaveholding family, began to address large mixed public audiences, in itself an outrageously daring act, and in the course of their speeches on the rights of slaves they found themselves claiming rights for women, too. The two slaveries became linked: the negro and the woman were both in need of freedom from unjust and unnecessary servitude. Sarah Grimké wrote a series of articles on the Province of Women in which she said: "I ask no favors for my sex. I surrender not our claims to equality. All I ask of our brethren is that they will take their feet from off our necks and permit us to stand upright on the ground which God has designed us to occupy." She said that to her it was perfectly clear that "whatsoever it is morally right for a man to do it is morally right for a woman to do." It was not so clear to Congress. At that time Congress was considering depriving women of one of the few political rights they had in America – the right to petition. The numbers of petitions brought forward by the Anti-Slavery societies were so vast that in 1834 a measure was introduced in the House of Representatives forbidding the presentation of any more and it took ex-president John Quincy Adams to defend this right. "Why does it follow," he asked, "that women are fitted for nothing but the cares of domestic life? . . . The mere departure of women from the duties of the domestic circle far from being a reproach to her is a virtue of the highest order." Even more outspoken was his reply to the assertion that women had no right to petition because they had no right to vote. "Is it so clear," he asked, "that they have no such right as this last?"

It was exactly this vital question which a young woman called Elizabeth Cady was beginning to ask. It took her until 1848 to formulate properly her thoughts on this subject but when she did, when she and four others proposed Resolution number nine in a Declaration of Sentiments at the Seneca Falls Convention, she began a fight that was to last seventy-two years in America, until the final ratification of the 19th Amendment to the Constitution (giving women the vote on equal terms with men) was made in 1920.

★   ★   ★

Elizabeth Cady was born on November 12th, 1815 in the small, prosperous New York town of Johnstown. She was the fourth in a family of six surviving children, all of whom were girls except for one, Eleazor. Her father, Daniel Cady, was a judge, elected to Congress the year she was born. He was an awesome figure to his children while they were small, feared and respected rather than liked or loved. Her mother, Margaret, although also clever and strong, had a softer side which prevented Elizabeth's childhood from being altogether austere. She felt, all the same, that she had been denied the warmth she gave her own children later. Her parents, she recalled, "were as kind, indulgent and considerate as the Puritan ideas of those days permitted but fear, rather than love . . . predominated."[3] Nobody doubted Judge Cady's immense authority. Most of his work as a lawyer was done at home in the large white framed family house on the corner of Market and Main Streets and his children were used to seeing clients come and go. Their image of him was of a stern figure sitting in his office surrounded by law books dispensing wisdom. He had a large number of female clients and Elizabeth described in her autobiography that she noticed that not only did these women arrive at her father's office looking anxious and careworn but that they left it looking even more worried and often in tears. This aroused her curiosity (which was always intense). She sat near the door of the office and listened. She heard women tell her father that the farm they had brought to their marriage had been mortgaged by a drunken husband and they did not know what to do. She heard her father, to her astonishment and indignation, tell them that there was nothing they could do. Their farm, or their goods or whatever was under dispute, no longer belonged to them. They were married. What had been theirs was now their husband's. When the women could not believe this was true Judge Cady would get down one of his law books and show them the relevant passage. It was then that they left, weeping.

The solution seemed to Elizabeth quite simple – all she needed to do was cut out and destroy the offensive passages in the books. Discovered, aged seven, with scissors in her hand and the books before her she was gently put right by her father. Cutting laws out of books would do no good, he told her. He gave her a little lecture on the true nature of law and of the process by which it could be changed. He agreed that the laws affecting women' which she had seen him administer were cruel and unjust but emphasized that the law was the law even so. Elizabeth argued back with all the spirit of an intelligent and independent child but her very determination saddened her father. He was aware, even then, that she was the most remarkable of girls and it seemed to him a tragedy: if only she had been a boy what a delight he could have taken in her intellectual strength. As it was, her talents would be wasted. In 1826 his son Eleazor died, aged eighteen, and the waste seemed even more cruel. He shut himself up in his office and when Elizabeth, aged eleven, crept into the darkened room to try to comfort him he could only stroke her hair and wish aloud that she were a boy. Distressed, Elizabeth tried to analyse why boyhood was more desirable than girlhood. How could she become like a boy and console her distraught father? She decided that, essentially, boys were braver and cleverer. Very well, she would visibly demonstrate both courage and learning. She learned to ride a high-spirited horse previously only ridden by men and she learned Greek to a prize-winning standard. But although Judge Cady admired her achievements they seemed to depress him even more – what a wonderful boy Elizabeth would have made.

So his daughter gave up. She also began to query whether being a boy was so desirable anyway. Why should gender be so important? Why should it automatically dictate one's role in life? All sorts of incidents seemed to her to illustrate the absurdity of this situation and she began to resent it. As President of the local Girls' Club she helped to raise money to educate a young man for the priesthood and on his graduation sent him money to buy a suit, a hat and cane for the occasion of his first sermon. The young man, upon whom so much girlish effort had been expended, took as his text "But I suffer not a woman to teach nor to usurp authority over the man but to be in silence" (I. Tim. 2:12). Elizabeth promptly stood up and led her girls out of the church. She refused to stay and listen to such an insult. It proved harder to escape them at home where the students her father had working with him loved to tease her. Two, in particular, were adept at digging out the worst laws with regard to women and taunting her with them. Henry and Edward Bayard, who were living-in students of her father's, endlessly tormented her. Henry especially was fiendish. One Christmas morning when Elizabeth danced around thrilled with a new necklace Henry said she'd better enjoy it while she could because when she got married her husband was entitled to sell it to buy himself a decent cigar. Elizabeth's rage was all the worse because by then she knew he was right.

But at least she was not doomed to stay at home and sew, immured in the useless existence of so many of her contemporaries, simply waiting for marriage to release her into another kind of servitude. Instead, she was privileged to enjoy what amounted to the best education a girl could obtain at that time. Until she was fifteen she and her sisters, dressed in red flannel dresses and black alpaca aprons, went to Johnstown Academy with the boys of the town and then, when the boys went on to Union College where girls were not admitted Elizabeth was sent to the Troy Seminary. This progressive school had been established in 1821 by Emma Willard, an educational pioneer as original and daring as the English Misses Beale and Buss and with much the same attitudes. The Troy Seminary was no finishing school concerned with accomplishments. It provided a fairly rigorous course of study along enlightened lines. Geography, for example, involved drawing maps and did not consist of reciting names of capital cities. Both algebra and geometry had a place in the curriculum as well as arithmetic, and learning by rote was discouraged. The girls had to understand what they were doing. Elizabeth, although initially sulky at being sent there instead of to Union College with the boys, quickly understood better than most. She was exactly the kind of girl to profit from Miss Willard's theories and was afterwards grateful for her luck. But by the time she left Troy nothing had changed in the outside world. Girls went home when their education was finished no matter how progressive that education had been. Again, Elizabeth was luckier than most. The home she returned to provided a stimulating environment, especially as one of the students, Edward Bayard, had married her elder sister Tryphenia. There was plenty of lively conversation, plenty of intellectual nourishment. All it did for Elizabeth was accentuate her desire to escape.

The only place she did manage to escape to was her cousin's house in Peterboro, another New York State town not far away. This was the home of Gerrit Smith, a nephew of Elizabeth's mother and a man not really approved of by Judge Cady who thought him a dangerous radical and feared his influence on Elizabeth. He was right to do so. Elizabeth loved the Gerrit Smith household. It was much freer than the Cady establishment, much more relaxed and easy. The Gerrit Smiths were just as wealthy as the Cadys but it was an unobtrusive wealth. Everything was simpler there. Formality was absent, there was no wine or rich food, people came and went as they wished. The Gerrit Smiths were Quakers and their philosophy was God is Love. To Elizabeth, brought up in a Presbyterian house where God was Fear, this was deeply attractive. She responded to it and revelled in her opinions being sought and held in as much esteem by her cousins as any man's. She had a real friend there too, Libby, one of the daughters of the family who was exactly her age and every bit as independently inclined. Libby was involved, as were all the Gerrit Smiths, in the anti-slavery movement. A constant stream of young men came to the house on anti-slavery business and runaway slaves were hidden there *en route* for Canada. Elizabeth was inspired by the idealism and found it hard to go home after each visit. On one visit she met Henry Stanton, a passionate young orator who had dedicated his life to campaigning against slavery, and she found it more difficult than ever to leave.

The only attraction at home was her brother-in-law Edward. Without realizing what was happening Elizabeth had fallen in love with him and he with her. Living as they did in the same house the situation became quite unbearable and the strain of such a relationship was hard to tolerate. Elizabeth could hardly stop seeing Edward but on the other hand, although she was sure she did love him, she could not bring herself to do what he suggested and run away with him. It was not flouting convention which worried her – on the contrary, this appealed to her – but causing her sister and her whole family agonizing pain. Nothing could be worth that, she thought. Martyrdom and self-sacrifice were alien to her nature and repugnant to her but the personal suffering of those she would wrong meant more to her than her own happiness. The temptation was great but she resisted it. But then, after three years of this unhappy struggle with her conscience, Elizabeth met Henry Stanton, who very soon proposed to her. She was under no illusions: she did not love Henry as she loved Edward, yet she was attracted to him and the attraction was strong and confusing. Was physical attraction, in fact, the same as love? Years later, when Elizabeth read Walt Whitman's *Leaves of Grass* it annoyed her that the poet seemed unable to believe that a woman could experience sexual attraction in the same way as a man – "he speaks as if the female must be forced to the creative act apparently ignorant of the great natural fact that a healthy woman has as much passion as a man, that she needs nothing stronger than the law of attraction to draw her to the male."[4]

Henry Stanton was a strong, determined character who would not take no for an answer. He proved a fervent suitor, sweeping aside all Elizabeth's doubts with regular displays of that fine rhetoric and oratory she so admired. His conviction finally persuaded her and she said she would marry him. They became engaged in spite of Judge Cady's extreme displeasure. Henry Stanton was just the kind of fiery liberal he detested. Her brother-in-law Edward hurt Elizabeth by siding with her father, saying Stanton was unreliable, untrained in any profession even though he was thirty-three, and improvident. In vain Elizabeth produced the letters in which her fiancé spoke of his good financial habits and the 3,000 dollars he had saved. It was useless – her family set their face implacably against Henry Stanton. Depressed and miserable Elizabeth found the doubts she had suppressed rising to the surface again. She was not sure she had the strength to fight for a love to which she was by no means totally committed. So she broke off her engagement. She wrote a sad little letter to her cousin about it – "You have heard dear cousin I suppose that my engagement to S. is dissolved and I know you wonder and so do I. Had anyone told me at Peterboro that what has occurred would come I would not have believed it but much since has convinced me that I was too hasty. We are still friends and correspond as before. Perhaps when the storm blows over we may be dearer friends than ever."[5] Henry worked solidly towards that end. With great patience and understanding he accepted Elizabeth's scruples and did not allow his disappointment to make him angry or hasty. He went on telling her how much he loved her and said, teasingly, "nor do I believe you will drown yourself like Ophelia but live to bless me. And as to myself I can not only say with Hamlet 'I *did* love you, fair Ophelia' but can add, with all my soul 'I *do* love you.' "[6] He sensed that it was not feebleness but on the contrary the strength of her own honesty which he valued. He had to make himself an even more attractive proposition in her eyes so that her desire to marry him would override her genuine hesitations.

At the end of 1839 he wrote to her saying that in the following May he was being sent as a delegate to the anti-slavery convention in London. If she would marry him it could be their honeymoon trip. As he anticipated, the idea excited Elizabeth. It also gave her hope of resolving her family's opposition by conveniently removing herself. If she married Henry they would be away six months, quite long enough for everyone to adjust. She felt herself responding to Henry's confidence that everything would then be all right with equal confidence and his ardour stilled her own vacillation. They were married on May 10th, 1840 in a simple, private ceremony in which the word "obey" was not mentioned, although the bride then took the bridegroom's name, merely preserving her own in the middle. She was not entirely happy about this – "there is a great deal in a name. It often signifies much and may involve a great principle . . . Why are the slaves nameless unless they take that of their master?"[7] But she felt she had defied convention quite enough for the time being.

Once ocean-bound on the *Montreal*, one of the last great sailing ships, Elizabeth's feelings of guilt and nervousness vanished. So did her doubts about Henry. She decided she had loved him all along. She enjoyed the voyage and proved a splendid sailor, commented satirically years later that "I have always felt especially in a choppy sea that one of my claims as a woman's rights leader is based on immunity to sea sickness."[8] She was on deck all day every day alarming the other travellers by her daring. Up and down she marched whether it was blowing a gale or not and once she even had herself hoisted to the masthead in a basket so that she could see as far as possible. When the ship reached the English Channel there was not enough wind to take it into port so the Stantons opted for a longboat rather than waste time waiting. When the longboat could not get near enough to the beach to land because of the shallowness of the water they transferred to a rowing-boat and rowed happily into Torquay. From there they went by coach to London – "a journey into Fairyland" Elizabeth said. Cheapside, where they lodged in London, proved not quite so fairy-like but the young bride was still bubbling over with enthusiasm about everything she saw and heard. As well as feasting her eyes she listened intently to all the conversations that went on between the delegates who shared the lodging-house and began to understand that the convention they had all come to attend was not only about slavery but about all human rights. Religion as well as politics was involved and there were vested interests influencing both. The more she listened the more fascinated Elizabeth became. She heard many of her own resentments voiced, many of her own objections to the status quo stated.

On June 12th, a brilliantly sunny day, she went with Henry and the others to the Freemasons' Hall for the opening of the convention. When they reached the hall an announcement was made. Women delegates were to be banned from taking part in the debate. The indignation Elizabeth felt was, she commented in her autobiography, the beginning of her real feminism. All the talk at the Gerrit Smith household, all the arguments in her own home, all the discussion among the delegates on board ship and in the lodging-house had been a mere preparation for this lesson: women were to be treated as subservient just like the slaves they had come to fight for, and this must not be endured.

But in that instance, it was. The women delegates never did gain access to the debate but were compelled to listen from behind a screen where they were joined by Lloyd Garrison, the great anti-slavery leader, who chose to sit with them as a matter of principle. Each evening, back at the lodging-house, the women made up for lost time by haranguing their men on what they should have said and what they must go on to say. To Henry's irritation Elizabeth, who was not only not a delegate but much too young to be speaking out at all in such distinguished company, joined in. He kicked her under the table and frowned but she ignored him. She also ignored his uneasiness about her new friendship with one of the women delegates, Mrs Lucretia Mott, whom Henry had been told by his sponsor was "a very dangerous person . . . a disturber of the peace." Within hours of having met Lucretia Mott, Elizabeth was heavily under her formid-able influence. She walked everywhere with her, arm-in-arm, deep in animated talk. In the evening she read the books Lucretia gave her, including Mary Wollstonecraft's *Vindication of the Rights of Woman*. She found for the first time that others had already publicly expressed their belief that the sexes were born equal. As they sat in the entrance hall of the British Museum, oblivious to the treasures they had come to see, the two women, one middle-aged and calm, the other young and excitable, decided that they would "hold a convention as soon as we returned home and form a society to advocate the rights of women."[9]

It was with a sense of relief that Henry Stanton removed his impressionable young wife from such company at the end of the convention. He took her to Paris, toured the north of England, and climbed Ben Nevis with her in Scotland. Although he had objected to her imbibing Lucretia Mott's ideas on the subject of female rights he showed himself to be an enlightened husband, never for one moment wishing Elizabeth to subscribe to the feminine stereotype of the day. He didn't mind her wearing a dress to the knee or men's boots to climb in and he was proud of her hardihood in enduring a twelve-hour descent (they got lost in the mist) better than he did. He was already realizing that the spirit he had admired in his wife was even greater than he had guessed. Elizabeth wrote home mockingly, "I hope cousin Nancy will write me one of her long serious letters often. Henry often wishes that I were more like her. I console him by telling him that cousin Nancy was quite gay and frolicsome once."[10] In November, after a brief trip to Dublin where they dined with Daniel O'Connell, the newly-weds returned to Boston by steamer. From there they returned to Johnstown where Judge Cady had bowed to the inevitable and agreed to take his new son-in-law on as a law student.

For a year the Stantons lived in the Cady family home while Henry read law and political economy. Elizabeth was very happy. She had grown to feel for Henry what she had once felt for Edward (who was still, uncomfortably, in the same house but careful never to be on his own with her). She wrote to a friend in England, "It may be that my great love for Henry may warp my judgement in favor of some of his opinions . . ."[11] To all outward appearances she had become a loyal wife and in the process forgotten the rebellious thoughts discussed with and agreed to by Lucretia Mott. But she had not quite forgotten. Happiness had indeed made her passive, but she still corresponded with Lucretia, saying things like, "The more I think on the present condition of woman the more I am oppressed by the reality of her degradation. The laws of our country how unjust they are! Our customs, how vicious! What God has made sinful in both man and woman custom has made sinful in woman alone."[12] It was thoughts of organizing any proper, public protest which had vanished not the thoughts themselves. Her husband and then her first baby took precedence.

In March 1842 she gave birth to her first son named Daniel after her delighted father, and was absorbed in motherhood. She had time for nothing else – motherhood completely engrossed her and required all her attention. It was, she said pompously, "the most important of all professions, requiring more knowledge than any other department of human affairs."[13] It struck her as extraordinary that this being the case and the world teeming with new mothers "there was no attention given to this preparation for office."[14] She engaged an experienced nurse but immediately came into conflict with her over whether her baby should or should not be tightly bound in shawls. Elizabeth thought she would feel uncomfortable wrapped like that so the baby must too and she took them off. The nurse threatened disaster. The doctor threatened it also when his treatment for a collarbone twisted during birth was rejected. Elizabeth went ahead formulating her own theories on babycare based on commonsense and observation and came to think of herself as an expert in no time at all. For the rest of her life no baby was safe from her good intentions – she was liable to approach any baby she saw, undo its clothes, give it water and march it into the fresh air whatever its state of health and whatever the weather. Those around her found it all rather trying and it was perhaps fortunate that in 1843, when Henry was admitted to the bar, the Stantons moved to Boston.

In Boston, Elizabeth was for the first time mistress of her own house. She loved it. Her theories on housekeeping quickly became second only to those on motherhood and were put into practice with the same energy. The Stanton house was a new house overlooking Boston Bay. "It is a proud moment," wrote Elizabeth solemnly, "in a woman's life to reign supreme within four walls."[15] Her approach to the job was as analytical as usual. "I studied everything pertaining to housekeeping and enjoyed it all . . . Even washing day . . . had its charms . . ."[16] Her natural passion for orderliness now became her greatest asset. She tried not only to keep the whole house "from front to back" clean and tidy but to give it "an artistic touch". She had a particular fondness for freshly laundered cotton tablecloths upon which she arranged bowls of carefully chosen flowers. In later years she blushed to remember how far she had taken her pride in the appearance of her house confessing that she had once paid a man "an extra shilling to pile the logs of firewood with their smooth ends outward"[17] so they would look more attractive. A second son, Henry, was born in 1844 and a third, Gerrit Smith, in 1845 but still Elizabeth enjoyed housekeeping even though it was not as easy.

What finally removed much of the charm was moving from that first house. In 1846, for the sake of Henry's health, the Stantons moved to Seneca Falls, another small New York State town. It was situated on a river at the head of the Finger Lakes but was no pretty Boston Bay type village. Industry boomed there. There were seventeen new mills, five factories, and a distillery. The town itself was in a raw state as it expanded to cope with the influx of workers. There were no pavements and the roads were clogged with enough mud to make them quite frequently impassable. The house the Stantons bought was isolated, stood in five acres of rough ground overgrown with weeds, and had been empty some years. There was an enormous amount of work to be done as Judge Cady, who owned the house, knew. "You believe in woman's ability to do and dare – now go ahead and put your own house in order,"[18] he instructed Elizabeth. With three small children, only one inadequate servant girl, neighbours who leaned on her rather than helped her (they were mostly Irish immigrants) she had a hard time trying to do so. Her exacting standards were impossible to maintain. The boys were more interested in pulling off rather than admiring the pretty tablecloths she so loved and as for washday, that was first to become a chore. "The novelty of housekeeping had passed away," she wrote, "and much that was once attractive in domestic life was now irksome."[19] What made it all worse was Henry's absence.

From the moment Henry had started to practise in Boston he had warned Elizabeth that he would have to work hard. He was not an established figure like her father with the same salary to go with the job. "Do not expect to see me getting great fees yet. I must get under weigh first,"[20] he wrote to her in his first year. It proved even harder than he had envisaged. There were, he told his wife, queues of "hungry young lawyers" like him. She misunderstood him if she imagined for one minute that he chose to be away from home – quite the contrary. He hated leaving her and his children. His letters were full of anxiety that the boys might forget him and he envied her being with them. If she was sad when he left he assured her he was sadder – "You have the sweet little kiddy to play with and embrace and so you forget all about the poppy, but reflect, where would the kiddy have been but for me?!"[21] It worried him that Elizabeth would give full rein to her cranky ideas without him. "Do not let the kiddy catch cold," he wrote. "See that he is not held by the window in the evening. He must get older before you toughen him. We must take great care of our precious treasure."[22] But what upset him most of all was how few letters he received from his wife compared to how many he sent. True, she had three small children and a big house to organize but he had long, hard days and evenings working and yet still found time to write before he fell asleep. "Dear Lizzie, think of me often, pray for me often, write to me often,"[23] he begged. But she did not. "Do write me immediately," he would instruct her, the words heavily underscored. "I say, immediately" . . . "Write at once" . . . "*Write*". He suggested that Daniel might even write a few lines if she guided his hand, but none was forthcoming. She wrote once to his four times and at half the length. "I long to see you, my lovely Lee. I am lonesome, cheerless and homeless without you,"[24] he confided and told her that if her silence was due to any "coldness and unkindness" he had displayed towards her when they were together he was sorry and would she forgive him.

Elizabeth's apathy extended not just to Henry but to everything. She was suffering, she wrote, from "a general discontent". Nobody could love their children more but being virtually alone with three babies under five years of age for long stretches of time exhausted her. There were no close friends near with whom to share the burden – all her friends were left behind in Boston, there was no one congenial to talk to. "I suffered from mental hunger," she wrote, "which, like an empty stomach, is very depressing."[25] It was also very common. She was merely experiencing the usual confusion of all young, intelligent mothers who find, guiltily, that although they ought to be satisfied they are not. "It is not in vain that in myself I have experienced all the wearisome cares to which woman in her best estate is subject"[26] Elizabeth later wrote to Susan Anthony. She felt often that she had been elected to suffer "in double measure" what the vast majority of women suffered without complaint, and yet she knew she was by no means the worst off. She was never poor and she had a loving if often absent husband who did his best to understand. But after two years in Seneca Falls the real dilemma of women seemed to her clear and sharp: it was a conflict between self-development and self-abnegation in the cause of motherhood. She believed firmly that women should not sacrifice their own individuality for the sake of the family but how could she do otherwise? In practice, she saw she subdued herself all the time, constantly giving precedence to the needs of her husband and children. She became more and more convinced that "some active measures" should be taken to make the lot of women easier but she could not think what these should be or how they should be secured.

It is quite possible that she never would have done so either if her old friend Lucretia Mott had not come to visit her sister Martha Wright in nearby Waterloo and invited Elizabeth to come and have tea. Elizabeth went over, excited at the thought not just of the outing but the assurance of stimulating conversation. She and Lucretia took up where they had left off eight years before. The need for women's rights was greater than ever and now that Elizabeth had gone through the mill of motherhood she spoke with even more passion and conviction. This time, something would be done. There and then the five women taking tea – Elizabeth, Lucretia, Martha, and Mary Ann

McClintock and Jane Hunt – decided to call a convention to discuss woman's rights. (Calling a convention was the accepted pattern of the day and meant to them no more than arranging a meeting – but it sounded better.) On July 13th 1848 they drafted an advertisement to appear in the *Seneca Court Courier*, a local newspaper, which read as follows:

> "A convention to discuss the social, civil and religious condition and rights of woman will be held in the Wesleyan Chapel of Seneca Falls, New York, on Wednesday and Thursday, 19th and 20th July current; commencing at 10 a.m. During the first day the meeting will be exclusively for women who are earnestly invited to attend. The public generally are invited to be present on the second day when Lucretia Mott of Philadelphia and other ladies and gentlemen will address the convention."

On Sunday, Elizabeth again went over, this time to Mary Ann McClintock's parlour, and sat round a table with her four Quaker friends to plan the convention. They all looked at each other "as helpless and hopeless as if they had been asked to construct a steam engine."[27] Lucretia Mott was by far the most experienced, with a long history of attending and addressing anti-slavery meetings behind her, but even she was at a loss. What exactly was their aim? Other declarations and reports from anti-slavery, peace and temperance literature were looked at but none of them seemed to provide the appropriate form to follow. They were breaking new ground and there were no guidelines of the kind they were looking for. But then Elizabeth had the brilliant idea of using the style of the Declaration of Independence of 1776. America had wanted independence from Britain by whom she felt unjustly treated and exploited: women wanted independence from men by whom they felt unjustly treated and exploited. The analogy was surprisingly apt. The more the women tried it out, the better it fitted – it was just a matter of substituting "all men" for "King George". Only the eighteen grievances did not correspond exactly so they set themselves to formulate their own. The finished document was called a Declaration of Sentiments, and pleased them all highly. Every one of the grievances listed (the final tally was fifteen) was felt to be justified.

Afterwards, they went home to prepare for the great day and to work on the resolutions they meant to propose. Henry Stanton at that time was at home and at first amused and encouraging. He was pleased to see his wife so animated once more. But then, when he came to cast his eye over her draft of the resolutions, his sympathy evaporated. One resolution in particular caught his eye. It had been proposed by Elizabeth herself and read "It is the duty of the women of this country to secure to themselves their sacred right to the elective franchise." It was, Henry said, quite absurd and must be crossed out – the whole idea was ridiculous and he would be smeared with the ridicule too. If his wife read such a proposal out he would have to leave town. Very well, replied Elizabeth, he should feel free to leave town if he wished.

The more she thought about it the more important it seemed to her to stand by her demand that women should be given the vote, and she would not be moved. But her resolution wavered when it came to standing up in a public meeting and saying this out loud. She was extremely nervous when she set out on the first morning of the convention for the hall where it was to be held and almost relieved to find that the doors had been locked and the meeting looked as if it would have to be cancelled. But the enthusiasm of the waiting women – astonishing numbers, many of whom had travelled long distances to be there – encouraged the organizers to push a small boy through an open window and effect entry. James Mott, Lucretia's husband, took the chair because neither his wife nor any of her friends had quite the courage to break that particular convention. Elizabeth, in a quavering voice which gained strength as she went on, then gave an address. "I should feel exceedingly diffident to appear before you at this time," she began, "having never before spoken in public were I not nerved by a sense of right and duty." It was no good, she said, men speaking for women any longer. They must stand up and speak for themselves because only a woman understood "the height, the depth, the length and the breadth of her own degradation." Women had allowed themselves to be made martyrs "early schooled to self denial and suffering." Their rights had been ignored and the time had come "to declare our right to be free as man is free, to be represented in the government we are taxed to support . . . we now demand our right to vote." She warned her audience that gaining this right would not be easy – "We do not expect our path will be strewn with the flowers of popular applause but over the thorns of bigotry and prejudice will be our way and on our banners will beat the dark storm clouds of opposition from those who have entrenched themselves behind the stormy bulwarks of custom and authority . . ."[28]

With these stirring words to inspire them, the meeting then debated the proposed resolutions which followed Elizabeth's reading of the Declaration of Sentiments. The debate was calm and orderly. Lucretia, Martha and Mary Ann were in Quaker costume and presided gravely over the proceedings and Elizabeth herself was the epitome of feminine respectability. She stood up on the platform, the very opposite of the harridan her enemies were to imagine. Only five feet three inches, she had black, curly hair, small delicate hands and feet and a general air of softness and warmth. Her dress was spotless and fashionable, her grooming immaculate. She was pretty, lively and dainty and not in the least masculine. The mere sight of her puzzled the opposition.

The discussion on the resolutions was animated, with Elizabeth's demand for the vote arousing, as expected, the most controversy. But it was passed. At the end of the meeting one hundred women present signed the Declaration of Sentiments and Resolutions. Elizabeth and her friends went home well pleased with their first efforts, looking forward to the next meeting they had already arranged, and quite unprepared for the publicity which followed. The press gave them extensive coverage of an unwelcome sort. Elizabeth was astonished and dumbfounded by the way in which the Seneca Falls meeting was so "extensively published, unsparingly ridiculed."[29] She did not recognize the gathering she had taken part in from the lurid and downright ridiculous descriptions given. Only the *New York Tribune* gave a fair and accurate account – the rest made vicious attacks on herself and the other speakers which were quite unsubstantiated. Within hours of these reports appearing many of those who had signed the Declaration withdrew their signatures: they did not wish to be associated with what was now branded as a dangerous and ludicrous movement. But another convention in nearby Rochester had already been arranged and it went ahead with equal success. It was also equally mis-reported.

By the end of August 1848, Elizabeth had no doubt that something important had been started and that there was no need to fear malicious newspaper reports seeking to distort the truth. The truth was that all over America conventions on Woman's Rights were now being held. In Ohio, Indiana, Pennsylvania and Massachusetts women were getting together to discuss what should be done and there was a uniformity of appeals and resolutions quite impossible to explain. At Ohio, the women even ran the convention themselves – "not a man was allowed to sit on the platform, to speak or to vote . . . for the first time in the world's history men learned how it felt to sit in silence when questions in which they were interested were under discussion."[30] Natural orators were springing up everywhere. Sitting at home in Seneca Falls, Elizabeth Cady Stanton was no longer depressed. She realized that unwittingly she had tapped a river of resentment already running strongly underground. She could not travel to these other conventions, surrounded as she was by small children, but she wrote letters of encouragement and endorsement to them all and the valuable habit grew up of such letters being read out at the start of each convention. In this way, links were made and maintained and women reassured that their particular protest, wherever it was made, was no isolated occurrence. The time was right. This was warily being acknowledged by the state legislatures who had begun to grant women their property rights. In that very year, the Married Woman's Property Bill passed the New York legislature and Elizabeth noted "The reception of the Bill showed unlooked for support."[31] The problem now was how to harness that support, how to organize it.

During the next decade, from 1848 to the outbreak of civil war, this was what pre-occupied the new Woman's Rights movement. No permanent organization was set up in the fifties, no ideology formally adopted. Instead, conventions were held on a regular basis and ideas disseminated through sympathetic newspapers and magazines. If this seems amateurish there were good reasons for it. The fifties was a period of exploration during which all concerned were tentatively trying out ideas not only on what should be done to change the condition of women but on what that condition was in the first place. What did being a woman mean? How many of women's grievances were unavoidable, due to "nature"? As everyone felt their way carefully, Elizabeth Cady Stanton formulated ideas which seemed to express, in a logical and forceful way, what women felt. At first, these ideas were spread through articles in the *Lily*, a newspaper started in 1849 by Mrs Amelia Bloomer, the sub-postmistress of Seneca Falls. Elizabeth had simply walked in one day and asked if she might contribute under the pen name Sunflower. She wrote on general topics, mostly on the duties of a woman bringing up children, but gradually the content of her articles became more openly feminist and they were taken up in other newspapers, like the *New York Tribune*, in whose pages lively discussions would follow. But of course the effect of Elizabeth's writings and of all the conventions was limited. It was still a case of preparing the ground only. And then, in 1852, Susan B. Anthony began to work in close partnership with her.

Elizabeth Cady Stanton had by then a fourth son, born in 1851, and was even more housebound. It was quite impossible for her to do anything but write letters and articles and she did not for one moment delude herself into imagining this was sufficient. It was only sufficient for the moment. Soon, if the impetus was not to be lost, all the women speaking and writing and thinking along the same lines must be brought together and positive action taken. Once Elizabeth met Susan Anthony her work became twice as important. "I forged the thunderbolts," said Elizabeth, "and she in the early days fired them."[32] They met in 1851 at an anti-slavery convention held in Seneca Falls and struck up the most significant of partnerships although they seemed so unalike. Susan was a schoolteacher who had originally worked for Temperance in the valley of Mohawk. She was a spinster with no ties, able to travel around bringing like-minded people together. She could literally hold the baby while Elizabeth wrote one of her splendid speeches. Through Susan, Elizabeth extended her range and without her she would have continued to experience the agony of that conflict which bedevils life for all feminists – the conflict between domesticity and career. To the Ohio convention of 1850 Elizabeth had written grandly of woman, "By her own efforts the change must come. She must carve out her future destiny with her own right hand. If she have not the energy to secure for herself her true position neither would she have the force or stability to maintain it if placed there by another."

But energy and force were strictly limited in her own case. Her own right hand was strong metaphorically but weak in reality. She could only do her bit at night when the children were asleep. The rest of the time, during each hectic day, she could only think. "You see," she explained to Susan, "while I am about the house surrounded by my children, washing dishes, baking, sewing etc I can think up many points but I cannot search books for my hands as well as my brains would be necessary for that work."[33] Instead of things getting easier they got harder: she had more children. By 1856 she had six and although she wrote vigorously, "The woman is greater than the wife or mother and in consenting to take upon herself these relations she should never subscribe one iota of her individuality to any senseless conventionalisms or false codes,"[34] she knew it was not as simple as she made it sound. The woman in her was subordinated all the time to being a wife and mother. Her children came first, often to Susan's fury. Once, when she had almost left her brood in the charge of a housekeeper while she went to a convention, she felt faint at what might have happened because during the time she would have been away, if she had followed her own desire, one of the boys shot an arrow into her baby's eye – "imagine if I had been in Rochester when it happened!" Imagine indeed: the mother would never have forgiven the woman. But with Susan's cooperation her domestic concerns were not entirely all-consuming. She managed to achieve a great deal without betraying her own high ideals as to what a mother should be. As her work gathered momentum she was not so fortunate in her relationship with her husband.

On the evidence available it is difficult to decide when exactly things began to go wrong between the Stantons and also how wrong they actually did go. There was no split on the surface. Henry was away a lot in Boston or New York but then he always had been. When he was at home the Stanton family life seemed happy. They all played games together (Elizabeth being by far the most fiercely competitive) and musical instruments. They appeared both close and affectionate. But when Henry was away his wife did not seem to miss him unduly. The days of leaning on him for support and of being influenced by his opinions were over. "A true conjugal union is the highest kind of human love,"[35] wrote Elizabeth authoritatively but like many women she found later in her marriage that she was closer to her children. Alice Stone Blackwell was bold enough to cast doubts on Elizabeth Cady Stanton's own fidelity, writing in a letter that she was shocked because Mrs Stanton had said "that a woman's obligation to be faithful to her husband extended only to that period while she was having children. After that it was none of his business what she did . . . Of course we don't proclaim these things about publicly for the sake of the cause . . ."[36] But whatever the true nature of the Stantons' marriage there were visible signs of friction right from the beginning of Elizabeth's involvement with the Woman's Rights movement even though Henry basically supported her work.

One of the biggest causes of this friction was the amount of time this work took up. Already competing with the children for Elizabeth's time, Henry found that when he was at home he was also competing with the writing and composing of articles and speeches. Competing and losing. He was proud of Elizabeth but also resentful that she appeared to care more about the cause than about him. Then there was the embarrassment he had to endure. "Woman's degradation is in a man's idea of his sexual rights,"[37] thundered Elizabeth, and Henry understandably squirmed. Unlike George Butler, Henry was no saint and thought the inference people might draw distinctly unpleasant. There is no doubt that he had a great deal to put up with and that many friends sympathized with his position. It was not easy, for example, to have a wife wearing the new Bloomer costume while he was running for the New York Senate. It exposed him as well as her to ridicule and he is to be admired for being willing to walk with Elizabeth while she was wearing it without ever trying to persuade her not to. When she returned to ordinary dress it was because her sons begged her to, not Henry, and because she herself had decided the "cup of ridicule" was too great to make it worth bearing.

By the end of the fifties Elizabeth felt that great strides had been made in advancing the idea that changes should be made to give women rights that were theirs in the first place, but she was also taken aback at the realization of how much further there was to go. In the field of legal rights it was possible to point triumphantly to actual reforms in a large number of northern states but politically not one legislature had given an inch. Votes for women, after ten years of agitation, were nowhere in sight. Elizabeth was puzzled by this lack of real progress and inclined to put it down to women themselves. Women seemed only responsive to matters concerning changes in marriage and were hard to rouse on political affairs, not appearing to appreciate that through political power everything that eluded them could be gained. There were cheers if she stood up and said, "Let them fine a woman 50 dollars for every child she conceive by a Drunkard,"[38] but tepid applause if she spoke on anything whatsoever to do with the vote. The plain truth was, as she observed at every convention, women were politically uneducated. "We shall never get what we ask for until the majority of women are openly with us," she concluded "and they will never claim their civil rights until they know their social wrongs."[39]

By 1861, when these social wrongs had been thoroughly exposed, the Civil War was beginning and the next stage could hardly be embarked on. All activity on the Woman's Rights front had to be suspended. But Elizabeth Cady Stanton and Susan Anthony were both quick to see that the war might actually turn out to be useful to the cause. Women, because of their desire to help, organized themselves on a national level and involved themselves in national politics by doing so – all excellent experience and practice for the future. The women formed a sanitary commission and a Women's Loyal League. There was every reason to believe that having proved themselves women would get their thanks after the war was over.

It came as a great shock to Elizabeth Cady Stanton to discover her trust was misplaced. The men in power had no intention of giving women the vote. They could go back to the position they had occupied before the war and wait their turn – the negro must come first. Once he had been enfranchized women would be considered. Elizabeth's rage was real and deep. She remembered with bitterness the praise for the women's war efforts and wrote, "All these transcendent virtues vanished like dew before the morning sun. And thus it ever is so long as woman labours to second man's endeavours and exalt *his sex* above her own."[40] She would not listen to the plea of the male liberal leaders who argued that, if women were included in the proposed 14th Amendment to the Constitution, the negro would not get the vote and that was surely more important. She denied that it was. Not caring about the implications of her reasoning she maintained that women who had "wealth, education and refinement" were more valuable as voters than many ignorant black men. Well-known anti-slavery leaders like her own cousin Gerrit Smith, who wanted suffrage to follow quickly after emancipation, told her firmly that "the removal of political disabilities of race is my first desire, of sex my second." He expected her to agree but she refused. She found this attitude contemptible. The willingness of women humbly to agree maddened her. "If all the women . . . had stood firm woman would have been enfranchised with the negro. But few could withstand the persecution, the ridicule, the pathetic appeals to keep silent . . ."[41] Nobody would listen to her or to Susan who warned that "in purging the constitution of all invidious distinctions on the grounds of colour" new distinctions were being created on the grounds of sex. If, said Elizabeth, the word "male" was inserted into the constitution it would take a hundred years to get it out. But it was inserted. The 14th Amendment passed into Congress in 1866 and a new phase began in the woman's suffrage movement.

Up to 1866, Elizabeth Cady Stanton had always been convinced that eventually reason would prevail and women would be given their rights. After 1868, when the 14th Amendment was finally ratified, she lost that faith (although never the greater faith that women would in the end secure the vote even if it was not handed to them). She became tougher and cynical. She saw that the time was over for developing and expounding civilized arguments. "There are no new arguments to be made . . . our work today is to apply ourselves to those so familiar to all,"[42] she commented, but agreed that it was important to keep them at the forefront of people's minds. To that end she and Susan began a newspaper, the *Revolution*, with George Train, financier, speculator and a decided eccentric, as their backer. They produced a wholly Woman's Rights paper with the stirring banner "Principles, not policy; justice, not favor; men, their rights and nothing more; women, their rights and nothing less." Elizabeth hoped she was helping to inaugurate a new era and when a friend soothed her disappointment over the 14th Amendment's failure to include women with the assurance that in another twenty years the vote would certainly be theirs she replied, "Twenty years! Why, every white male in the nation will be tied to an apron string by that time while all the poets and philosophers will be writing essays on the sphere of man."[43] There was a new urgency about her work and instead of being disheartened she was more determined than ever. She was also more able as well as willing to devote her prodigious energies to working for the vote. For the first time, the prospect of leaving home for weeks at a time was considered. She had seven children by then but the youngest, Robert, born in 1859, was nearly ten and more than capable of being left in the care of a housekeeper and his father. There were no babies to tear at her heart strings, no small children barely tottering about to give her nightmares if she did not supervise them herself.

For the next twelve years, 1868 to 1880, Elizabeth Cady Stanton intermittently travelled the country lecturing on woman's rights issues. "It makes me shudder," she wrote when this period of her life was over, "to think of my weary lecture tours from Maine to Texas . . ."[44] Her father was appalled at the vulgarity of this "tramping about" and Henry objected but she was past caring what either thought. Nothing was going to stop her. Off she went to California, Iowa, Missouri, Illinois and Nebraska, becoming more and more radical as she went. Although she asserted, "I do not believe there was ever a woman who esteemed it such a privilege to stay at home,"[45] she proved herself curiously suited to the life. When male lecturers pronounced themselves unable to fulfil engagements because of weather conditions she gloried in getting through the snow and ice. She slept in cabins and huts, on floors and porches, in carriages and trains. She revelled, too, in the barracking of the lecture hall and was quick and witty in response. One small, skinny man once shouted out didn't she think his wife was doing more good bearing him eight children than anything she might do otherwise and Elizabeth retorted to the delight of the crowd, "I have met few men worth repeating eight times."[46] But she learned, all the same, to beware of men like that questioner when she was distributing leaflets and never offered one to "a man with a small head and high heels on his boots, with his chin in the air, because I know in the nature of things that he will be jealous of superior women."[47] She knew arousing jealousy was no way in which to proceed. It was even more a waste of time to offer a leaflet to a woman whose mouth had "the prunes and prisms expression for I know she will say 'I have all the rights I want.'"[48] Again, antagonism was not to be desired. She learned to be forbearing and not to let opposition rile her. She learned too to snatch time off when she could and not to fuss if plans were upset. And although she swore frequently that she felt "like a squeezed sponge" she clearly thrived on her exacting itinerary (as well as making a good deal of money which she used to put her two daughters through college).

Everywhere she went Elizabeth Cady Stanton saw more and more the true circumstances of women's lives. She saw that they were hard and understood better than most Woman's Rights leaders the burdens women endured. The birth of her last two children had to a great extent changed her own outlook on maternity. Even childbirth itself, once spoken of by her so lyrically, had come to take on a new and dreaded aspect. She was forty-one when Harriet was born in 1856 and forty-four when she had her last child, Robert. She wrote after Robert's birth, "My labour was long and severe . . . I am through the siege once more."[49] There were no more boasts of bouncing up and writing letters minutes after "that beautiful, natural act." She loved all her children passionately but saw how too many could drain a woman of energy and pull her down, especially if she was not protected, as Elizabeth knew herself to be, by the benefits of money. She also knew that not even money could protect a mother from guilt about neglecting her children if she did anything for herself. She could write with anguish, "I feel guilty when I have a sick child," and also, "once in a while, in thinking what I might have done for my children, I feel suddenly depressed . . ."[50] It was hard to impress upon audiences containing women who were much more aware of these problems than she was that they must not allow themselves to be subjugated by husbands or children, that they must assert themselves and retain their individuality. In spite of all her work and her fame she was never sure that she was doing so herself. But she held firmly to her extremist views and continued to believe that obtaining the vote would change everything. Women would not only get rights but adopt different attitudes and be treated differently – a wonderful circle of beneficial effects would be started.

There was still, after another ten years, no sign of it. The Seneca Falls Convention had been in 1848; by 1858 the signs that female suffrage would be granted were there; then came the Civil War and by 1868 no woman in the United States of America yet had the vote. Furthermore, although the ranks of those agitating for female suffrage swelled all the time, there was dissension among them.

Elizabeth and Susan began to think it was time they should have their own organization, formed specifically to achieve woman's suffrage, instead of merely being a part of the all-embracing Equal Rights Association. In May 1869, tired of being what they called betrayed by men, the National Woman Suffrage Association was set up for women only. Naturally, there were many who up to then had supported Elizabeth and Susan who now decided they did not like this development and could not join the new Association. One of them was Lucy Stone, herself by then almost as powerful as Elizabeth and Susan. In the following November she set up the American Suffrage Association. For the next twenty years the two rival associations operated independently, which seemed a ridiculous waste of resources. The ASA concentrated on practical work for the franchise and nothing else: they wanted suffrage to be a straightforward, "clean" issue not tarnished by controversial other questions like the divorce question. They also wanted to work for suffrage at state level, converting each state legislature as it went along. The NWSA, on the other hand, had no desire to separate suffrage from other issues affecting women. Indeed, Elizabeth herself thought this attitude cowardly. She wanted to engage battle on every front and not only win the vote but have a programme of reform ready for when it was won. "It is puerile," she said scornfully, "to say 'no matter how we use the ballot the right is ours.' "[51] Nor did she have any intention of working away humbly at state level. It was all part of the plot to try to make female suffrage tame and respectable when in her opinion it could never be that and ought not to try. "Society as organised today under the man power is one grand rape of womanhood,"[52] thundered Elizabeth. It was exactly language like that which alienated those who joined the ASA. When, in addition to this kind of provocative statement, Elizabeth also started attacking religion and claiming that "bibles, prayerbooks, catechisms and encyclical letters" were all simply instruments used to oppress women, even her own followers shuddered. The vote would never be won by such attacks.

It seemed, by the mid-seventies, that it would never be won anyway. The women of Wyoming had thrilled everyone involved in the Woman's Rights movement by gaining their vote in 1869, followed by those in Utah in 1870, but there were special reasons why they had been able to manage such a victory in those far off, outlying Western Frontier territories. Elsewhere, campaign after campaign failed even when hopes ran high. *The History of Woman Suffrage* records how the Woman's Rights ladies felt as they watched the new voters, enfranchised by the 14th and 15th Amendments, go to the polls. "It was a sight to be remembered to behold women crowned with honour standing at the polls to see the freed slave go by and vote, and the newly naturalized fellow citizen, and the blind, the paralytic, the boy of 21 with his newly fledged vote, the drunken man . . . the man who read his paper upside down." Everyone, it seemed, except women. It disgusted Elizabeth Cady Stanton. More and more it seemed to her that in allowing this state of affairs the constitution had been violated. It began, after all, with the words "We, the people of the United States of America . . ." Were women not people? Why should women even need a special amendment to enable them to vote? Why did those words not secure this right to them? But a test case introduced into the Supreme Court arguing this failed in 1875. A special amendment was after all going to be necessary.

By this time Elizabeth Cady Stanton was sixty years old, white-haired and stout but mentally as alert and sharp as ever. Her family were all grown-up and her relationship with Henry cordial but no longer close. In many ways, she was at the height of her powers, freed at last from those domestic ties – which even when they had loosened still bound her until Robert went to college – and hardened by experience. She was ready for one more mighty attempt on Congress when, in 1878, a committee was appointed to receive a deputation from the NWSA asking for a 16th Amendment. Excitement ran high; this time enough senators had promised support. But Elizabeth said she had never, ever, been so humiliated as she stood before the committee pleading the woman's cause. Her anger grew greater every minute as "standing before a committee of men many years my juniors, all comfortably seated in armchairs, I pleaded for rights they all enjoyed though in no respect my seniors, denied me on the shallow grounds of sex. But this humiliation I had often felt before. The peculiarly aggravating feature of the present occasion was the studied inattention and contempt of the chairman, Senator Wadleigh of New Hampshire . . . He . . . took special pains not to listen. He alternately looked over some manuscripts and newspapers before him then jumped up to open or close a door or window. He stretched, yawned, gazed at the ceiling, cut his nails, sharpened his pencil, changing his occupation and position every two minutes, effectually preventing the establishment of the faintest magnetic current between the speakers and the committee. It was with difficulty I restrained the impulse more than once to hurl my manuscript at his head."[53] The petition for a 16th Amendment was of course rejected. More humiliation followed. In 1882 both Houses appointed Select Committees on Woman's Suffrage which reported favourably but no bill resulted. In all the vital votings after debates senators always let the women down. It was not until 1887 that an actual bill struggled onto the floor and it was promptly defeated by thirty-four to sixteen votes with twenty-six abstaining. Was there really any point in going on?

Elizabeth Cady Stanton never doubted that there was. She realized it was all taking too long – "we reach the women too late with the new gospel and then it requires great labour to plant the seed"[54] – but she never doubted for one moment the final outcome. When Colorado carried woman's suffrage in 1893 she wrote, "My soul rejoices, but how slowly the world moves."[55] She was seventy-eight years old but although her eyes grew dimmer her intellectual vision grew brighter. She never despaired. There was a kind of exhilaration present during her old age which continued to inspire as well as amaze all with whom she came into contact. It did not matter that "our movement is belated and like all things too long postponed now gets on everyone's nerves."[56] The thing to do was what she herself did: she rose above the dreariness and tedium and kept plugging away against all the vested interests deliberately scheming to stave off the inevitable. They would not be able to stop progress forever – the dam simply could not hold. To her joy, there was a whole new generation of women, twice as vociferous as she and Susan had been, clamouring to carry on the work. In 1890 the two rival suffrage organizations had been re-united as the National American Woman Suffrage Association and Elizabeth had become president but in 1892 she felt she could safely take a back seat and she resigned. The movement, with the younger Susan at its head, could manage without her. Coming up to succeed her was Carrie Chapman Catt – there were no worries that without Elizabeth Cady Stanton or Susan Anthony leadership would vanish. Their active contribution was finished.

Elizabeth enjoyed old age as few are able to do. Unlike the majority of early active feminist leaders she had never complained of constant ill-health or threatened imminent death. Tiredness was her only problem and even then none of her correspondence or diaries breathe quite the same sense of exhaustion as the others'. Her weight, which others thought excessive, never troubled her nor does it seem to have caused her any of the health problems that might have been expected – she really was fat and happy, with a great love of food. In France she once complained she missed muffins, cream, butter and powdered sugar, all items of which an eleven stone elderly lady of only five feet three inches ought to have been glad to be deprived. But, as she wrote on her eighty-eighth birthday, "I enjoy life more and more."[57] Her one regret was that she had not married a dentist because her teeth were paining her. Henry had died in 1887. They had never come to any official parting of the ways nor had they openly had liaisons with anyone else but his death was no tragic event in Elizabeth's life in spite of forty-seven years of marriage. She heard of his death while she was in England staying with her daughter Harriet at Basingstoke and was quiet for a while and generally sad but by no means distraught. Henry had faded in her life long ago – it was her children who preoccupied her, especially her two daughters and her fourth son, Theodore, and her grandchildren – Nora, Harriet's daughter, was her great delight. Nora came to America to go to Cornell to study architecture and engineering and stayed with her grandmother in her apartment on West 94th Street in New York. She was one of those younger volunteers who read to Elizabeth when cataracts deprived her of this greatest of pleasures.

But as well as the love and support of her family Elizabeth Cady Stanton's last years were illuminated by her strong sense of universal sisterhood. She never felt lost or lonely, never felt isolated or cut off even when technically she was for short periods. On the contrary, she had a highly developed spiritual feeling of companionship. "Through suffering we have learned the open sesame to the hearts of each other," she wrote. "There is a language of universal significance . . . by which with a sigh or a tear, a gesture . . . we know the experiences of each

other in the varied forms of slavery."[58] That was more important to
her in her declining years than anything else. Until she was too old to
travel she also loved to visit other countries and immediately became
aware that her feelings of identification with all other women because
they were women were not flights of fancy. In both France and
England she felt "at one" with others and she loved it. Whether she
was having breakfast with Josephine Butler or tea with Elizabeth
Blackwell she would feel excited, too, by an additional sense of
common destiny: they had all been born to start things off, to fight for
all women. There was nothing vain or egocentric about this feeling of
being chosen – she was no megalomaniac – but rather a humility and
deep happiness. Her life meant something. It was not conceit to say so.
There seemed no harm in relishing her own fame because she had
earned it and because it meant something significant had been achieved
for her cause. It did not seem to her a tragedy that she was not going to
live to see women enfranchised – she accepted this philosophically,
saying, "I should feel that I had not lived in vain if faith of mine could
roll off the soul of woman that dark cloud, that nightmare, that false
belief that all her weaknesses and disabilities are natural . . ."[59] And it
had. The vote, which she had absolute faith would come, would be the
culmination of all her efforts, and the efforts of all the hundreds of
others who had joined her after her brave stand at Seneca Falls, and at
last women would move forward to take their true place in society.
She died on 26 October, 1902 quite confident.

★   ★   ★

"I wish you and I had been beautiful," Elizabeth Cady Stanton wrote
to Susan Anthony in 1864, "then we could have carried all men with us
to heights divine and entrenched them on principle."[60] Even as a joke
this carries the unmistakable stamp of her particular brand of feminism. She was always proud to be a woman and she enjoyed her
womanhood. The only time she ever wanted to be male was when she
was a child for her father's sake and she came, very quickly, to pity
him for his misguided reverence for the importance of gender.
Throughout her career Judge Cady continued to upbraid his daughter
for behaving in an unwomanly fashion but she continued to resist his
efforts to make her conform to any feminine stereotype. It often
pained her deeply to do so. "I cannot tell you how deep the iron
entered my soul," she commented after one such battle. "To think

that all in me of which my father would have felt a proper pride had I been a man is deeply mortifying to him because I am a woman."[61] She herself valued her own femininity highly and never thought of it as being in the least diminished by anything she wrote, said or did. Nor did she feel any shame in exploiting it where and when it was useful, although her attitude was in fact dangerous for feminism. On the one hand, Elizabeth Cady Stanton denied the existence of any weakness in woman which might prohibit them from sharing fully in the governing of their country but on the other hand she urged women to stress this very weakness to use against men.

She gives an account in her memoirs of a friend who longed to buy a new stove to heat her house properly but did not dare to do so because she feared her husband's anger at such expense. Elizabeth advised her to buy it when her husband was away. When her friend looked frightened and asked what she would then do when her husband came back and raged Elizabeth said, " . . . sit and gaze out of the window with that far away sad look women know so well how to effect . . . men cannot resist beauty and tears."[62] Feminine wiles, in short, were always to be kept in reserve when rational argument failed. Elizabeth Cady Stanton saw nothing inconsistent in this. "Our trouble," she wrote, "is not our womanhood but the artificial trammels of custom under false conditions."[63] It was the conditions which must change. There was no need, in the process, to eradicate femininity. A woman was as entitled to use this as a man was to use his greater physical strength just so long as that was not *all* she was allowed to use. This was why the vote was so important: political responsibility must not be denied women because of their femininity. When she told her friend to use tears and sighs on the domestic front she did not mean her to use them exclusively. Tears and sighs, those cunning feminine wiles, were no good at all in weightier matters than new stoves. She only had contempt for those women who believed in exerting power over men by "managing" them in such a way.

These women, who asserted they had all the rights they wanted and achieved what they wanted by subtly controlling men behind the scenes, earned her greatest scorn. They were, she said, "the mummies of civilisation," exhibiting in their complacency "the strongest possible argument against it . . . a woman insensible to such indignities needs some transformation."[64] She wrote an article entirely on the subject called *I Have All the Rights I Want* in which she savagely exposed the wickedness as well as the folly of women who said such a thing, and she attacked, too, the idea that working for Woman's Rights was "unfeminine". "For those who do not understand the real objects of our conventions," she wrote ". . . I would state that we do not meet to discuss fashions, customs or dress, the rights or duties of man, nor the propriety of the sexes changing positions but simply our own inalienable rights, our duties, our true sphere . . ."[65] Any idea that Woman's Rights supporters were either unfeminine or automatically hated men was nonsense. "I have never been a man hater,"[66] she stated emphatically. It was only one of the lies people used to misrepresent the entire movement.

Elizabeth Cady Stanton had a very clear idea of what might happen to the history of the movement she belonged to. Misrepresentation was only one of the problems. It was more than likely that no accurate account of what had happened would survive. Because of this she sat down in 1880 and embarked on *The History of Woman Suffrage* with the help of Susan Anthony and Matilda Gage. It was a measure of her confidence that one day suffrage would be granted and, when it was, women would want to know how. She and Susan were determined to provide a record. "My large room with a bay window is the literary workshop," she wrote. "In the middle is a big library table and there Susan and I sit vis-à-vis, laughing, talking, squabbling day in and day out, buried in illegible manuscripts, old newspapers and reams of yellow sheets. We have the sun pouring in on all sides and a bright wood fire in the grate while a beautiful bouquet of nasturtiums of every colour stands on the table with a dish of grapes and pears."[67] It was a happy scene and happy work not in the least shadowed by the knowledge that during the writing of these three first volumes of the eventual six-volume history there was no concrete evidence that it would remain anything but unfinished. But the job was done because Elizabeth Cady Stanton wanted a fitting memorial for all those who had contributed to getting women the vote. She thought her own sex too modest, too likely to underestimate themselves, too afraid of seeming pretentious and she wanted to cure them. The plan of a gigantic history was a grand one but she was determined to accomplish it. "We are only the stone that started the ripple," she wrote to Susan at the end of her life, "but they are the ripple that is spreading and will eventually cover the whole pond."[68] The "pond" was the world. It thrilled her to include in her history book a letter from Harriet Martineau written after the 4th annual Woman's Rights convention in Cleveland. This described how a direct result of the American action

had been a letter to the *Westminster Review* by Harriet Taylor supporting it, which had in turn been the starting point for John Stuart Mill's
The Subjection of Women, that overwhelmingly important handbook of
the nineteenth-century women's movement. There was no doubt that
she and Susan had been "the stone" and that their aim was devastating-
ly sure. Letters (many of them included in the *History*) came to them
from all over Europe acknowledging that they had been the inspiration for other women deciding to act. Theodore Stanton wrote, "To
an American . . . European woman's rights is rather tame; it is like the
play of Hamlet with Hamlet left out." But Europe was moving and all
records of this movement were promptly encouraged and included in
the *History* which expanded gradually to include accounts of the
international conferences begun in 1878.[69]

Although Elizabeth Cady Stanton did not live to see female suffrage
granted throughout her own country she did survive long enough to
hear that New Zealand had become in 1893 the first entire country to
grant it, followed by most of Australia, and Norway in 1901 (although
with an age limit). By 1920, when America finally capitulated, a large
number of European countries had already enfranchised their female
populations. But the response of women to gaining something for
which some of them had struggled so long was not what Elizabeth
Cady Stanton had expected. It would have puzzled her extremely. She
knew she was not an average woman ("Such pine knots as you and I
are no standard for judging ordinary women,"[70] she once wrote to
Susan) but she thought nevertheless that *all* women, once they had the
vote, would awaken to their responsibilities. She expected older
women to participate in politics in considerable numbers. Until they
were fifty (which she thought "the heyday of a woman's life") she
acknowledged that most women were too bound up in marriage and
motherhood to enter politics, but at, and after, fifty years of age she
thought women were able, and would be willing, to come forward
and take their place with men. They have not.

Women form a very small proportion of the elected governing
representatives in all Western countries (except Iceland).[71] They form
an even smaller proportion of those holding cabinet and similar posts.
If it is true that a political career proves incompatible with motherhood
for all but the exceptional few, that still leaves a puzzle. What about all
the Susan Anthonys? What about the Elizabeth Cady Stantons over
the age of fifty? Where are they all? But even more significant for
feminism, why has the so-called "feminine influence" failed to alter in

any substantial, measurable way how we are governed? Elizabeth Cady Stanton was emphatic that, when millions of women voted, the world would be a better place. It is not. Either the feminine influence does not exist (which is perhaps something feminism should be glad about) or it is failing to make itself felt. Either way, things have not turned out as she predicted and hoped.

It is perfectly possible that so far as feminism is concerned this does not matter. It only seemed to matter. If feminism is fundamentally concerned with making sure no woman is denied self-fulfilment solely because of her sex does it matter that, presented with every opportunity, she chooses to reject some? But then there is the worry which began to appear as woman's rights were being triumphantly won in every sphere: perhaps this rejection was forced upon women, perhaps the choices secured for them were not choices at all. Even Elizabeth Cady Stanton, with her seven children, had no real choice, not if she wanted to be a wife and mother as she did. The choice was false. The next stage of feminism was to make it real, to give women such control over their own bodies and over their own fertility that choice meant something. If the thought of what the vote would do for women was exciting, the thought of reliable contraception in female hands was stupendous in its implications for feminism.

BIRTH CONTROL

Margaret Sanger
(*Courtesy of the Library of Congress*)

Margaret Sanger
1879–1966

The strongest argument used by anti-feminists throughout the nineteenth century to keep women in their existing place in society was the biological one. Nature decreed that women should bear and suckle children. This being so women were going against nature if they did not fulfil their natural function. How, it was asked, could women have careers, with all that this entailed, and still be mothers? It was a question the feminists themselves found virtually unanswerable which was why the notion of "choice" had been built into feminism. Women must choose. Either they were mothers or they had careers or they started to have careers after their mothering days were over. For a long time feminists encouraged women to believe that devoting themselves to work, rather than to men or children, was a more worthwhile and self-fulfilling way to spend their lives. If you had the right temperament and talents they even argued it was your *duty* to choose not to be a wife and mother. Elizabeth Blackwell, Florence Nightingale and Emily Davies were adamant that great happiness could be found in a life of work. But for the vast majority of women the cruelty inherent in the so-called choice available to them made it unacceptable. They found they could not suppress the urge to mate and reproduce and that, once they had done so, any thought of a career was out of the question. The feminists did nothing to help them. The idea that, if women could control their own fecundity, "choice" might have some meaning was not a feminist one in the nineteenth century. Freedom from constant childbearing was not in the forefront of feminist demands, not part of that familiar cry for either protection or justice and, when the first attempts at publicizing efficient contraception began, the feminists were suspicious. Their reaction was to assume men were trying to make the sex act "safe" so that they could make even freer with women's bodies. The consequences of safe sexual intercourse would be to remove all restraint and that carried frightening moral implications for the future of marriage.

But, as the nineteenth century progressed, the consequences of *not* trying to limit the number of children being born became even more terrifying. In England, the birth rate soared and the problem grew. Malthus gained ground with his doctrine on over-population but his suggestions for controlling it – late marriages and abstinence for long periods within it – were not popular. In 1823 Francis Place entered the controversy by denouncing Malthus' suggestions as out of harmony with human nature. What was needed, he thought, were better contraceptive methods available for everyone. He had handbills printed with simple instructions for the use of a sponge "as large as a green walnut or small apple" inserted into the vagina before intercourse and pulled out afterwards. His chief justification for contraception was economic. People were consuming their own incomes and impoverishing themselves and their children by having too large a family. Prosperity lay in a small family. Place was called a monster ". . . a nasty old man . . . corrupting the youth of both sexes of this country . . . making catamites of the male portion of the youth and of the female PROSTITUTES."[1]

Beastly or not, Francis Place had become the world's first birth-control campaigner long before the term was coined. He was not, of course, the first to be interested in contraception. Ever since the very earliest societies there had been a preoccupation with controlling pregnancies. All primitive societies show evidence of crude attempts at contraception – there are hundreds of methods documented – but it was not until the days of the Greeks and Romans that definite advances were made. The greatest gynaecologist of antiquity, Soranos of Ephesus (98–138 BC) lists an elaborate number of suppositories and vaginal plugs which destroyed male sperm. These were widely used and were the most efficient form of contraception available until, in the sixteenth century, the rapid spread of syphilis across Europe produced the invention of the linen sheath for the male. Efforts then became concentrated on improving the sheath. The word "condum" first appears in print in 1706 (Dr Condum is believed to have been a physician at Charles II's court). The materials used for the sheath varied but the principle was the same and it became the most widely used contraceptive in the eighteenth century together with the sponge for women. But in 1840, when rubber was vulcanized, the condom became much more reliable and much more acceptable. In London and other big cities condoms were for sale in the streets but this was not much good to the population at large, nor was it much good to women whose men could not be bothered with cumbersome precautions. It was women who needed a reliable method for themselves. Until they were given one, abortion and infanticide had to be resorted to.

And they were, by rich and poor alike. Coroners throughout England recorded the dismal details of dead babies and aborted foetuses found in privies, canals and fields. Lady Stanley of Alderney who had nine children in seventeen years showed herself as desperate and as ignorant as the most wretched servant girl when at the age of forty she believed herself once more with child. She wrote to her husband that "a hot bath, a tremendous walk and a great dose have succeeded" but that she felt "not too well."[2] Her husband replied he shared "the same horror" at the thought she might not have managed the miscarriage. Men and women alike wanted to limit their families. There was no doubt at all that the demand for knowledge about efficient contraception came from both and that it came, as it were, from below, that it was not superimposed on society. If proof of this was needed it was found in the colossal sales of any literature whatsoever to do with contraceptive methods. Francis Place's handbills had initiated a long line of pamphlets and books all of which were snapped up by a public desperate for knowledge. Richard Carlile's pamphlet *What is Love?*, later entitled *Everywoman's Book*, sold ten thousand copies in 1828 simply because it contained some basic contraceptive advice. It was followed in 1832 by Charles Knowlton's highly important *Fruits of Philosophy* first published anonymously in New York (then suppressed). The *Daily Telegraph* said of Knowlton's book when it appeared in England the following year, "There is no difference between this vile book and poisoned food" but it was in fact an excellent book and for feminism much more important than any which had gone before, although this was not recognized at the time.

Knowlton was the first *doctor* since Soranos to attempt to give contraceptive advice. He wrote his book in answer to all those people in his Massachusetts practice who had begged him to show them how they could prevent pregnancy and he did so conscious that he was providing a service which would alleviate the hardship and suffering he had encountered in the course of his work. Far from being either scandalous or licentious *Fruits of Philosophy* was a most sober volume, merely a lecture on the workings of the body and the sex act, with advice on how to prevent conception limited to four pages out of the total fifty-four. Knowlton's approach was humanitarian. "Owing to his ignorance," he wrote, "a man may not be able to gratify a desire without causing misery (wherefore it would be wrong for him to do it) but with knowledge of means to prevent this misery he may so gratify it that more pleasure than pain will be the result of the act, in which case the act to say the least is justifiable. Now, therefore, it is virtuous, nay, it is the duty of him who has a knowledge of such means to convey it to those who have not; for by doing so he furthers the cause of human happiness."[3] What Knowlton conveyed was not just information about the condom but precise instructions for women to protect themselves. He advocated not only the sponge soaked in a chemical solution which he specified but syringing the vagina *after* intercourse with a solution of sulphate of zinc, alum, or pearl ash – any salt in fact which would act chemically on semen – or a vegetable astringent of white oak bark or red rose leaves. He advised two applications within five minutes after intercourse and not later than ten. The correct syringe was available at any apothecary's for one shilling.

For his contribution to furthering the cause of human and especially female happiness Knowlton was sentenced to three months' hard labour. While he served them, his book became a best seller in America and when it crossed the Atlantic the first edition sold 125,000 copies in a few weeks. But the authorities everywhere did everything possible to hinder the publication and distribution of contraceptive literature believing that it attacked that bedrock of Victorian society, the institution of marriage. It went on all the same, but underground. In 1855 Charles Drysdale's *Physical, Sexual and Natural Religion* had six pages on Preventive Sexual Intercourse giving prominence to the safe period (incorrectly calculated) but stressing the use of the sponge as the best method; but nobody improved on Knowlton. By 1875 the birth rate in England had begun to decline and there was clear support for the view that people were discovering contraception for themselves. This was still frowned on by the medical establishment. When in 1886 Henry Allbutt produced *The Wife's Handbook* (price 4 pence) mentioning the Dutch cap, he was struck off the medical register. His book went on to sell 390,000 copies.

Yet there was still no *movement* either in America or England. All attempts at spreading contraceptive advice were isolated and unco-ordinated, even if remarkably successful within their limited scope. If you had not access to the information that existed on contraceptive methods you went on relying on old wives' tales and hoping for the best. It was Margaret Sanger who decided this was wrong. She did not create female contraception, nor was she the first even in her own day to advocate it, but what she did was organize it into a movement and a movement primarily for women. She did this in the first quarter of the twentieth century in the face of both feminist apathy and hostility: she *made* it a feminist issue. To her it was no use women demanding the vote or better education or equal rights at law if they could not control their own bodies which gave them "the key to the temple of liberty."[4] Endless childbearing was "tyranny" and "the feminine spirit" must reject it. Contraception, she stated unequivocally, was *women's* busi-ness, not men's. Furthermore, it was not just going to free women from unwanted pregnancies it was going to free them from all fear about sex. Behind the advocacy of continence, she declared, lay "a loathing of sex" and women had come to believe themselves actually superior if they were indifferent to it. Efficient contraception in their own hands was going to enable women to enjoy sex as much as men had enjoyed it for centuries.

It is not surprising that with these views, loudly voiced, Margaret Sanger was more hated and feared than any of the other feminist activists. Josephine Butler's attack on the double standard was a feeble slap compared to this powerful punch. What Margaret Sanger threatened to do was free even those who did not wish to be freed by turning completely upside-down women's own attitude to sex. No longer was it simply to be a duty, a means of procreating children as the marriage service decreed, something quite unavoidable. It was to become something done *for its own sake*. By presenting women with such a prospect Margaret Sanger challenged their very function as women.

★　　★　　★

Margaret Higgins was one of the few feminist activist leaders to come from a working-class background. She was born on September 14th, 1879 (a date carefully concealed as she always made herself four years younger) in Corning, a factory town near New York. She was the

sixth of eleven children and realized very early what being part of a
large, poor family meant: going without. Yet, in spite of the material
deprivation she suffered, she valued the love she had been given by her
parents and remembered with gratitude the closeness of her family.
There was respect and affection among them in the midst of all the
hardship. The family was dominated by the father, Michael Higgins,
born in Ireland and once a drummer boy in Lincoln's army. He was a
large, red-headed, free-thinking man, a stonemason by trade, and his
one rule in life was that people should "say what they mean." He was a
member of the Knights of Labour and organized visits from other
free-thinkers which often ended in fights. Margaret was, she said,
neither ashamed nor frightened on these occasions and was in fact
quite proud of being called, with her brothers and sisters, "children of
the devil". Her father represented power to her. Her mother, Anne
(also of Irish descent), worked hard to keep the family and the house
clean and tidy even though she was not physically strong. She always
had a cough and was always recovering from or about to undergo
childbirth. But there was no friction between these parents – "no
quarreling or bickering" – and they each idolized the other. Michael
Higgins was a great believer in woman's rights, supporting female
suffrage and even the wearing of the Bloomer costume, but this
"never evidenced itself in practical ways."[5] He would sit "when he
had nothing on hand" laughing and joking while Anne worked
incessantly around him.

Outside her home, the young Margaret was conscious of different
lives going on. Corning was an unattractive place and the poor, like
the Higgins family, lived in the most unattractive part, on the
crowded river banks near the factories. The rich lived literally above
them, on the hill tops above all the noise, dirt and overcrowding.
Margaret envied them. She noticed in particular the contrast between
her mother's way of life and that of the women who lived up there:
"mothers . . . played croquet and tennis with their husbands in the
evening . . . (they were) young looking . . . with pretty, clean dresses
and they smelled of perfume."[6] Margaret's own mother usually
smelled of milk as she produced and fed baby after baby, all delivered
by Michael Higgins himself. He would never allow a doctor anywhere
near his wife, not even to attend to her cough. After every birth she
was weaker and coughed more but he dosed her with whisky and
eventually she would be on her feet again. None of this put Margaret
off childbirth. She loved the babies and looked forward to having her

own. She liked to look at pictures of the Virgin Mary and fantasized herself looking like that after she had had a baby. "Sex knowledge," she wrote, "was a natural part of my life."[7] She always knew how babies were made and how they arrived and there seemed nothing repugnant or scaring about either process. Babies were always welcome in the overcrowded Higgins household and if one died the grief was real. Margaret remembered vividly the death of Henry, aged four, and her mother's inconsolable distress which her father tried to soothe. He took Margaret with him in the night to the cemetery where he dug up Henry's coffin, opened it, took a plaster cast of his face and next day made a bust of the dead child for his wife. She was greatly comforted.

But if she loved her family, Margaret hated Corning. She wanted to get out. Her two older sisters, Mary and Nan, recognizing that she had talent and ambition deserving something better than they had had, saved up to send her away to school. Both of them had worked from the age of fourteen as companions and maids to supplement the family income and they wanted Margaret to escape this likely fate. Entirely through their self-sacrifice, Margaret was sent to Claverack, one of the first co-educational schools in the East, at the age of thirteen, supplementing her board by helping as a domestic assistant. At home, she had had no background of learning although her father was an intelligent man and a great reader of political tracts. The entire family library consisted of the Bible, *Aesop's Fables*, a medical book, a general history of the world, a book on phrenology and Henry George's *Progress of Poverty*. She had a great deal of background to make up but did well, although causing some problems as the ringleader in various escapades.

When her schooldays ended, she found a job in a new public school in Southern Jersey as a student teacher but she was called home after a few months. Her mother was dying. The TB from which she had clearly suffered for a decade at least, even if it did go undiagnosed, had flared up after the birth of her eleventh child and not even Michael Higgins's all-purpose whisky cure worked. Her death was a long drawn out affair during which she tried desperately to protect her children from witnessing the full horror of it. One by one they were sent off on "holidays" to stay with friends and relatives in the surrounding area while she battled to prepare her husband for the inevitable end. But he remained wilfully blind and unprepared. When Anne Higgins died, aged only forty-eight, Michael Higgins became an embittered, unpleasant, belligerent man. Grief made him violent and tyrannical. Margaret began to hate him. She was expected to look after the smaller children and require no life of her own. If she went out with her sister Ethel to a dance they were quite likely to come back and find the door bolted against them. Margaret stood this for a year but then she had had enough. She managed to find a place for herself at White Plains Hospital, near New York, where she could train as a nurse. It was not what she wanted, which was to be a doctor so that she could save people like her mother, but it was the best escape route she could find.

White Plains, which she entered in 1898 aged eighteen, was not a modern hospital run on any kind of Nightingale lines. The building was old, a three-storey manor house set in overgrown grounds which gave it a "spooky" air to the young nurses. There was no resident intern. The probationers not only made and fixed dressings but also did a great deal of heavy domestic work. They also assisted at operations and Margaret was pleased to find she could do so without feeling squeamish. The hardest part of her job was night-duty which she hated. All sorts of emergencies, with which she was not equipped to deal, tended to happen at night and she found it frightening to have to cope with them. In addition, since the supply of registered nurses in the White Plains catchment area was limmited, the probationers there were in any case always being pushed out into situations for which they were not ready.

Most of these were maternity cases. They would arrive to find neither qualified midwife nor doctor present and would just have to go ahead and deliver the baby themselves. Naturally, this gave Margaret valuable practical obstetric experience, which she found exciting, but it also plunged her into a world she had never encountered before. Most of the mothers were not ecstatic with joy at giving birth and new babies were not greeted with the rapture which had awaited them in the Higgins household. The circumstances in which they arrived were often not just poor but desperate. The most common question Margaret was asked by the mothers whose confinements she attended was "Miss, what should I do not to have another baby straight away?" She did not know. When she referred the question to the doctor on the case, if there was one, he would brush it aside and remonstrate with the mother for asking it of a young nurse. She grew used to seeing not just women but men, too, driven nearly insane with worry about having more children. Something, clearly, was wrong. "To see a baby

born is one of the greatest experiences that a human being can have,"
she wrote. "As often as I have witnessed the miracle, held the perfect
creature with its tiny hands and tiny feet, each time I have felt as
though I were entering a cathedral with prayer in my heart."[8] But the
mothers into whose arms she put these scraps of perfection were
uninspired by her emotion.

The last six months of Margaret's three-year training were spent at
the Manhattan Eye and Ear Hospital. While there, she met a young
architect called William Sanger at one of the hospital dances. He was
eight years older than Margaret and the first serious suitor she had had.
His mother was German and his father had been a wealthy sheep
farmer in Australia. He was, wrote Margaret, "a dark young man
with intense, fiery eyes"[9] who was very romantic and ardent. He
proposed marriage very quickly but Margaret says she was adamant
she did not want to marry. It was, she said, "a kind of suicide". But
Bill Sanger was "impatient of conventionalities, intense in his new
love" and she was deeply attracted to him. He admired her
tremendously, writing that he thought her "really heroic" for putting
up with the hours she did and he didn't know how she could stand it –
"I must have at least six hours sleep," he wrote, "and you have none at
all at night!"[10] He wanted her to "give up this strenuous life" and
promised he would soon be able to provide her with "a real home
. . . a little house nestling under the trees – we shall build it, of course
we shall."[11] His confidence was infectious. When he not only professed undying love but promised "we shall soon be in easy street . . .
you will be able to have all the leisure you want"[12] Margaret began to
envisage a future as Mrs Sanger in which her fantasy of being one of
those hill top mothers of her childhood would be fulfilled.

In the last week of her training she capitulated and married him. Bill
whisked her off to a secret wedding ceremony. "That beast of a man
William," she wrote to her sister Mary, "took me for a drive last
Monday and drove me to a minister's residence and married me. I
wept with anger and wouldn't look at him for it was so unexpected
. . . I had on an old blue dress and looked horrid . . . He was afraid this
precious article would be lost to him . . . I am very, very sorry to have
the thing occur but yet I am very, very happy."[13] To her sister Nan she
gave a simpler explanation. Bill was, she wrote, "beastly, insanely
jealous." He insisted on marriage and, since she did not want to lose
him and he would not wait, she married him. But even then Margaret
was a strong character. She would never have married Bill Sanger if

she had not thought she loved him and certainly not out of fear of losing him alone. The fact was, she was not just attracted to him but irresistibly drawn to the way of life he could offer her.

The marriage was at first happy, in spite of Margaret's poor health. She had been ill off and on throughout her nurse's training with "gland trouble" and when she became pregnant soon after her marriage this flared into TB. She was sent to a sanatorium outside New York where she was acutely miserable and determined to leave. In November 1903 she returned home to her apartment in New York and gave birth to her first son, Stuart. It was, she commented, "agonizing" and made worse by the inexperience of the doctor who attended her. She was sent back to the hated sanatorium but quickly rebelled against the régime imposed there. Deciding that if she was going to die she'd rather do it at home she discharged herself and once more returned to New York. There she doctored herself and against all expectations the outbreak of TB began to subside (although she was never free from such outbreaks for the rest of her long life). Meanwhile, intent on fulfilling his wife's dream and also moving her to somewhere healthier, Bill had designed and begun to build a house at Hastings-on-Hudson, a pleasant suburb outside New York. It took a long time to complete but in 1907 the Sangers moved in and early the next year Margaret gave birth to her second son, Grant. She then found herself happily in the position she had always wanted to be. She, too, played tennis and wore pretty dresses and smelled of perfume. She had a husband who was both attentive and generous, regularly bringing her presents home and taking her to the theatre and to concerts. There was nothing demanding about her domesticity and Bill even helped with shopping and was willing to be involved in all household chores. In 1910, when a daughter, Peggy, was born, everything seemed perfect.

But it was not. Margaret was far too honest to pretend her dream life satisfied her. She became restless and critical not just of the life she was living but of the people among whom she was living it. She saw that "this quiet withdrawal into the tame domesticity of the pretty hillside suburb was bordering on stagnation."[14] It bored her. She had no great love for cooking or dressmaking or any of the other hobbies with which her neighbours filled their time and although she maintained she had "a passion for motherhood" it did not prove an all-consuming one. If Bill was disappointed he did not show it. He said he did not particularly like Hastings-on-Hudson either and was perfectly agreeable to moving. So the Sangers sold their dream house and moved back into New York, into Greenwich Village. There, they joined the local Socialist party, Labour Five, and instantly became involved in recruiting new members from the clubs of working women in the area. It beat genteel games of tennis any day. "Our living-room," wrote Margaret proudly, "became a gathering place where liberals, anarchists, socialists and IWWs could meet."[15] Modestly, she added that her role was to make the cocoa. Very soon, other jobs were found for her within Labour Five and she had also resumed her career as a nurse. Among the wives of Hastings-on-Hudson careers were rare and frowned upon but in Greenwich Village any self-respecting socialist wife wished to justify her existence. Bill's mother came to stay to look after Peggy and Grant while Stuart was enrolled in a progressive local school and Margaret took on obstetric cases (because these were short term).

Her work took her more and more frequently to the lower East Side of New York where she came across misery far worse than any she had found during her training. She was called to cases in tenements where families were living ten to a small room, where women had neither the food nor the money to support the babies she was delivering, where both men and women alike were prematurely aged by the struggle to survive. But what was even more of a shock to her was her involvement in botched abortions. She would be called out to what she thought was a birth and arrive to find some terrified woman bleeding to death. She passed queues on Saturday nights outside well-known (but not to the authorities) abortionists and found herself the next morning dealing with the effects of what the women had been given to take. What disturbed her most was that the women who tried to abort their babies were so very often "good" mothers. They were not the feckless or wanton type, nor were their husbands blackguards or brutes. It was simply cause and effect. Marriage meant sex, sex meant babies, babies meant increased poverty. The only solution was abstinence but even having sexual intercourse only once a year produced a baby a year. To Margaret's disgust she heard doctors tell one distraught husband to "go and sleep on the roof" if he wanted to avoid his wife becoming pregnant again. It was this brutal indifference to genuine suffering that made Margaret determined to do something to help.

She was by this time not the inexperienced young girl of the White Plains days. As a married woman, who after the birth of her third child had been advised not to have any more children, she had practised

contraception herself. But when she came to pass on to her patients the
"secret" of not having any more babies she found that her wonderful
information was virtually useless to them. "I resolved," she wrote,
". . . to do something to change the destiny of the mothers whose
miseries were as vast as the sky."[16] She discovered that explaining
about *coitus interruptus* and condoms changed no destinies among the
mothers of the lower East Side. What they needed was *female* contraception which was efficient and above all easy to use. They wanted
the responsibility in their own hands. They also wanted to understand
more about the workings of their own bodies and it was this demand
for knowledge that led Margaret to give health talks for the Women's
Commission of the Socialist party and to write short articles on health
matters for the New York paper *Call*. Out of all this came a series of
articles in 1912 originally entitled *What Every Mother Should Know* then
changed to *What Every Girl Should Know*. These at first simply gave
information about sex and facts about reproduction which mothers
were advised to tell their daughters, but then the articles became
bolder, including more detailed notes on human physiology and also
trying to stress that the sex act was normal and healthy and not
something to be feared or shunned by women. Finally, the last article
touched on venereal disease, its causes and effects, and how to avoid it.
The Post Office immediately banned *Call* under the 1873 Comstock
Law which made it illegal to send obscene matter through the US
mail.

As far as Margaret Sanger was concerned this was flinging down the
gauntlet. She determined to pick it up. Bill encouraged her, urging her
to write up her articles into a pamphlet for distribution by hand. "You
go ahead and finish your writing," she quotes him as saying, "and I'll
get the dinner and wash the dishes."[17] This he would then do
"drawing the shades so no one would see him." The children were not
so co-operative. She describes her sons hating to come home and find
her writing. But a sense of mission had begun to inspire her and she
began trying to find out all she could about every form of contraception available. Her quest took her to various libraries, where she
missed a lot of valuable information apparently through not knowing
how to look for it, and to talk with socialists like Bill Haywood who
had a great interest in the subject of limiting families through judicious
use of contraception. Emma Goldman, whom Margaret also met, had
already included the subject in her lectures. But as she went about her
enquiries, interrupted by helping to organize picket lines during the

Paterson silk-workers' strike of February 1913, Margaret began to doubt whether even those advocating contraception were doing so for the reasons which inspired her. Were any of them really thinking about the women, or were they just influenced by political and economic considerations? "I was enough of a feminist," she wrote, "to resent the fact that woman and her requirements were not being taken into account in reconstructing this new world about which all were talking. They were failing to consider the quality of life itself."[18] This, she became convinced, was for women intimately bound up with being able not only to *choose* to have babies but also to enjoy the act which produced them. But where was the simple, safe contraceptive which even an illiterate woman could use? She might find it, Bill Haywood said, in France.

There was really no sense in going to France in person (and perhaps no real need at all if only Margaret could have tapped existing American sources) but both the Sangers became wildly enthusiastic about such a venture. Bill was tired of being an architect, and was not in any case doing very well even though Margaret says she was told he was one of "the best eight draftsmen in New York." He said he had always wanted to be "a real artist" and Paris was his natural home. So in October 1913 the entire Sanger family sailed for Europe. (How they paid for the trip Margaret never revealed – she said such questions were "irritating".) First they went to Glasgow, where a youth from the Municipal Corporation, one Willie MacGuire, was employed to look after the children while the parents went sightseeing; then they travelled by cattle boat to Antwerp and from there by train to France. They ended up on the Left Bank in Paris. Bill immediately plunged himself into the art world, where he met Matisse and was "aglow" with pleasure, while Margaret followed up Bill Haywood's introductions to people who would help her find out about contraception. What she discovered was that although there was no actual movement there was a large body of individual knowledge about family limitation in existence. "I went into shops and bookstalls," she wrote, "and purchased all the devices of contraception available."[19] She was shown pamphlets which were in circulation and talked to women who possessed "recipes" for suppositories passed down from generation to generation. It amazed her that in a Catholic country it should prove easier to learn about contraception for women than in New York, where the Comstock laws had made the circulation of information impossible.

When the three-month trip was at an end it was Margaret and not Bill Sanger who was ready to go home. She was full of enthusiasm for her cause, eager to return to New York with samples of all kinds of contraceptives and ready to put into practice what she had learned. Beside the thought of this mission the fun of being in Paris was nothing. But Bill did not agree. He loved Paris, felt he was making progress as an artist, and had no desire at all to return. Far from causing conflict in the Sanger marriage this difference of opinion was faced by both Bill and Margaret with equanimity. He would stay, she would go. In fact, Margaret was glad to go back just with the children. She wanted a return to America "to stir up a national campaign"[20] and Bill would just get in the way. But of course there was more to it than that. After twelve years of marriage Margaret was beginning once more to view the institution as "a kind of suicide". She felt stifled by being married. Although Bill was the most understanding and accommodating of husbands she still wanted to be on her own and free of the emotional obligation under which he placed her. Nobody mentioned the phrase "trial separation" but it is clear Margaret thought that was what she was embarking on when in December 1913 she sailed for home.

As soon as she arrived she rented an apartment in upper Manhattan and set about planning the production of her own newspaper in order to spread contraceptive advice. At once she came up against those laws with which she was already familiar, the Comstock laws. These proved far more all-embracing and obstructive than she had ever realized, especially since Anthony Comstock himself was still in office as Special Inspector of the Post Office. He had been responsible personally for 700 arrests, 333 sentences and the seizure of 34,836 articles classed as "for immoral use." Margaret raged against him – "his stunted, neurotic nature and savage methods of attack had ruined thousands of women's lives"[21] – but she was not quite so silly as to doubt that any direct challenge to Comstock would invite certain prosecution and probable imprisonment.

For a while, she cast about trying to find ways of getting round the Comstock laws, as many had done before her, and seeking help for her general mission. Naturally, she approached influential feminists, among them Charlotte Perkins Gilman. They advised her (so she said) to join them in helping to win the vote and then all would be well – women would vote for the right to information on contraception. Margaret did not believe them, nor did she have any intention of waiting until the millennium dawned. It made her angry that the avowed feminists were not giving priority to the release of woman from her biological subservience which in her opinion was a far greater obstacle to progress than not having the vote. The Socialists were of more use to her (and of course a great many of them were also feminists) because they gave her hints on how to set about publishing a clandestine newspaper, which they had great experience in doing. But Margaret was determined to accept only advice from her political friends and nothing more: her newspaper would not be part of any general political propaganda but specifically feminist in purpose. She said she wished to make it "as red and flaming as possible" in order to bring to everyone's notice the problems affecting women.

She called her newspaper *The Woman Rebel*. The first issue, on eight pages of cheap paper, came out in March 1914 and was a very serious-looking publication. Bill Sanger had sent over some cartoons to enliven the pages but Margaret scorned them – she *was* serious and was not going to dress up what she had to offer. The whole tone of her paper was strident and belligerent, full of startling statements like "The marriage bed is the most degenerating influence of the social order." It was sent by mail to a list of 2,000 subscribers obtained from socialist friends. There was no precise contraceptive advice given but it was made clear that contraception was approved of and known about. Meanwhile, Margaret was working hard to provide this very information. A pamphlet she was writing called *Family Limitation* was going to be absolutely explicit.

Family Limitation was written in plain, strong, fearless language. It was outspokenly feminist, stating women's right to enjoy sex as much as men and even asserting that if they did not it was usually because men were "clumsy fools". It tried to rouse women to help themselves, speaking scornfully of women who were lazy or sentimental – "of course it is troublesome to get up to douche, it is also a nuisance to have to trouble about the date of the menstrual period . . . it seems inartistic and sordid to insert a pessary or a suppository . . . but it is far more sordid to find yourself several years later burdened down with half-a-dozen unwanted children . . . yourself a dragged out shadow of a woman . . ." What to do to prevent yourself becoming a shadow was starkly set out. The importance of keeping a calendar of monthly periods was stressed, the existence of any "safe" period emphatically denied, *coitus interruptus* condemned as well as all douches labelled as cleansing but not preventative in themselves. Advice on condoms was

thorough (what they were made of, which were best, where to buy
them, how to make sure they were used properly) but the real
emphasis was on female contraceptives.

Crude, and rather alarming, diagrams (Marie Stopes found them
"prurient") illustrated how to use a pessary and fears about the use of it
were banished – it was "silly" to think this object might "go up too
far" and mysteriously get lost – "It cannot get into the womb nor can it
get lost." Nor was there any need to worry about it spoiling a man's
pleasure (though the pamphlet made it quite clear what it thought on
that subject). Sponges, if used with the right chemical solution, were
recommended and if all else failed suppositories were better than
nothing. A recipe was given for a vaginal suppository for those quite
unable to get them – "take 1 ounce of cocoa butter, 60 grains quinine,
melt the cocoa butter, mix the quinine with it, form it into supposithor-
ies by letting the mixture harden into a cake and then cutting it up into
ten pieces – insert one into the vagina 3 minutes before the act." An
address was given for mail-order goods in case anybody lived far from
a chemist. At the end of the pamphlet fourteen of the most common
queries about contraception were printed (eg "Does nursing a baby
prevent pregnancy?") and dealt with. Women were urged to tell other
women how to avoid pregnancy – "spread this important knowledge!" – and to help the movement towards birth control (a term she
had coined and now used for the first time) which it was prophesied
"will shortly win full acceptance and sanction by public morality as
well."

Naturally, once Margaret finished her pamphlet she then found it
difficult to get it printed. She touted it round various socialist printers,
who all "turned deadly pale" and told her the risks were too great,
until she found Russian-born Bill Shatoff who was prepared to do the
job on his own after hours so that it could be kept completely secret
and nobody else would risk imprisonment. But, as soon as the
printing of 100,000 copies had been arranged in the summer of 1914,
events began to move too fast. Within days of the first issue of *Woman
Rebel* coming out in March letters started to arrive asking for specific
information, but by that time the Post Office had sent word to say the
newspaper was breaking the Comstock Law. Margaret ignored the
communication and went ahead with the April issue. There were no
objections to that one. In May, July, August, other issues appeared
and then at the end of August Margaret received a visit from two
officials. They told her the last three issues broke the law on nine

counts. They refused to say how but announced they had orders to arrest her. She received the news calmly, but was instantly aware that she must move very fast to exploit her arrest as much as possible.

Margaret was told she would have plenty of time to prepare her case but in October she was "suddenly informed" that it would be in two days' time. Considering she had had six weeks since August 25th when she was told a trial would take place she was perhaps unreasonable to find this "sudden" but she seems to have been genuinely startled. In any case, although thrilled at the thought of hearing the words "The People v. Margaret Sanger", and longing to stand up in open court and proclaim her beliefs, she had no intention of going to battle over the _Woman Rebel_. She wanted to do so over _Family Limitation_. It seemed to her foolish to risk losing the chance to fight over this much more important document so she decided to take the drastic step of leaving the country, having _Family Limitation_ released as soon as she was safely away, then returning after an interval with a case prepared specifically on the birth control issue. In one way, this made obvious sense, but it was fraught with problems. The most important one was the fate of her children. Stuart, then ten, was at camp and could stay there until he returned to his boarding school where he had been for some years but Grant was only five and Peggy three. Bill Sanger was still in Paris and for the first time Margaret found that her long-suffering sisters were not disposed to be surrogate mothers. She had banked on the ever-obliging Nan taking them in and was stunned when a shocked Nan said she would not be party to this flight from maternal responsibility. She refused pointblank to have them. Mary, in Buffalo, was too far away to be of immediate use and so was Ethel.

What Margaret then decided to do is very difficult to understand. Grant and Peggy were sent on holiday to the Catskills with a friend and extremely precarious arrangements made for their return – a network of friends and neighbours with nobody in actual control except Mary in Buffalo and Bill on his way back (she hoped). She wrote years later that what she did in leaving her small children to this kind of care was "a spiritual crucifixion" but it calls into question her own strangely conflicting notions on motherhood and her relationship with her children. She seems to have convinced herself that she had made the "supreme sacrifice" a mother could make. She claimed to be "passionately maternal" and yet thought sending children away, to school or anywhere else, "the most unselfish act . . . because it shows a selfless consideration for the child's good rather than an egoistic self-indulgence in sentimentality."[22] Any consideration for her own children's good seems nevertheless to have been entirely lacking when she decided, the day before she was due to appear in court, to take the train for Montreal. This can either be seen as heroic or as incomprehensible but either way it puts Margaret Sanger's attitude to motherhood in a different category from most women's.

In Montreal, Margaret was put up by some friends until a place was found for her on the RMS *Virginian*, sailing for Liverpool on November 1st, 1914. She selected the pseudonym "Bertha Watson", which she said was a name so "atrociously ugly" that it robbed her of her femininity every time she answered to it. Unable to produce a passport she had no idea how she would get herself into England, especially in wartime conditions, but she says she made friends with an official on board who managed to arrange her entry. She stayed in Liverpool for a few "dreadful bleak weeks" suddenly feeling not quite so brave and noble and miserably conscious that her children, especially Peggy whom she had left with a sore leg, might be missing her as much as she was missing them. Then she went to London where she rented a room in Torrington Square. From there, she went every day to the British Museum to do research on birth control methods.

She was not friendless, arriving in London with several useful introductions to leading exponents of birth control in England. The Drysdales asked her to tea and through them she received an invitation to visit Havelock Ellis whose books she had just read and admired. She took a bus to Dover Mansions in Brixton and had tea and toast with him in front of the fire. Afterwards, they met in the British Museum where Ellis showed himself keen to direct the studies of this young and attractive student. Very soon they were close friends, though never lovers technically if Ellis is to be relied upon. "On me this first meeting simply left a pleasant impression," he wrote, "aided by sympathy with her lonely situation in a strange city,"[23] and after the second he found himself brought into "a relationship of friendship, I may say of affectionate friendship . . ."[24] Within two weeks they were on kissing terms which for Ellis, says his biographer, counted as "near rape by anyone else." Even if, as Ellis maintained, the friendship with Margaret merely had a touch of "sweet intimacy" about it he records himself, after a kiss on New Year's Eve, as "like a drunken man . . . all of a rapture . . . I was aching and beaten and sore."[25] Perhaps in kissing as in all else Margaret Sanger was a powerful lady. But for her part, although pleased with Ellis' attention, she was hardly swept off her feet. Her relationship with her husband she now regarded as finished and was about to write him "an epoch making letter" telling him so. Starting another such relationship was no part of her plan. She had work to do.

It was Ellis who suggested to her a visit to Holland where, he had been told, birth control clinics were in existence teaching the use of the comparatively newly invented diaphragm. England was of course at war and the idea of going to Holland a dangerous one but Margaret set off in January 1915 with introductions to Dr Rutgers of The Hague. Dr Rutgers was elderly and harassed and his English was poor but he was very welcoming. He took Margaret to his clinic, showed her the Mensinga diaphragm and demonstrated with several of his patients how to use it. The diaphragm had been invented by a German, Dr Wilhelm Mensinga (sometimes known as C. Hasse) who had published details of his invention in German medical journals in 1882. Birth control was a field in which German physicians were for some reason prolific – popular pamphlets were on sale to the general public in the last quarter of the nineteenth century and as well as Mensinga's treatise on the subject there were forty others published at roughly the same time. Dr Rutgers had read about Mensinga's device and had gone to visit him the following year, bringing back with him the new contraceptive. The diaphragm was *not* a cervical cap of the type Margaret Sanger and others had publicized but a much simpler and more efficient cap which fitted longitudinally in the vagina, secured by the pubic bone. It amounted to the greatest advance since the condom and had the additional advantage of being for women. At his clinic, Dr Rutgers showed his fascinated visitors fourteen different sizes of the German diaphragm which, since its use in Holland, had become known as the Dutch cap, and he emphasized that accurate fitting was vital. It was, he stressed, a medical matter and decidedly not something women could do for themselves although once fitted and taught they could certainly manage to use it much more easily than a pessary. Margaret was at first disappointed. Her vision had been of women taking matters into their own hands and helping each other until a chain of self-help existed everywhere. But she accepted Dr Rutger's verdict quickly and turned to examining how his clinics worked.

A network of birth control clinics was already in existence in

Holland under the direction of Dr Aletta Jacobs, a great feminist as well as the country's first qualified woman doctor. Unfortunately, Dr Jacobs was not as friendly or helpful as Dr Rutgers. She was deeply suspicious of this young, non-medical American woman and refused either to meet her or to take her round her clinics. Brusquely, she said birth control was not a matter for lay-people. Offended and annoyed, Margaret had to make do with visiting other doctors. She also discovered that, in spite of the insistence by them that this was a medical matter, women could actually go into shops throughout Holland and be fitted up. She went into several herself and found ". . . there was a small, adjoining room, containing a reclining chair and a wash basin. The woman, if she so desired, was taken into this room, examined, and fitted by the shop attendant."[26] It seemed to her that this being so there must be room for some sort of compromise. Nurses, for example, like herself, were surely medical – perhaps it would be possible to run clinics with specially-trained nurses in charge. What she wanted was a system whereby women went to places specifically designed for this one purpose and where they would find other women specifically catering for this purpose without doctors necessarily being in control as Dr Jacobs insisted they must be. Besides that, pamphlets paled into insignificance. What she wanted to do now was return to New York, face her trial, then put her energies into opening clinics. But first she extended her trip to Spain, where she found women in a state of "oriental seclusion", and then went back to London where she sat down and wrote three more pamphlets, setting out very clearly what she had learned in Holland (and also gave a lecture which Marie Stopes attended. They had tea together after-wards when Maries Stopes gave Margaret a copy of *Married Love* and told her of her own ambition to open a clinic.) The pamphlets were printed and sent on to America but the ship carrying them was torpedoed. It seemed an ominous sign: perhaps if she went herself the same would happen to her. For a while, she hesitated. In her autobiography she goes over the alternatives: should she bring Grant and Peggy over to join her, leaving Stuart at school, and take them to Paris to write a book? But that was as risky as returning herself. Which risk ought she to take?

While all this agonizing was going on Bill Sanger, back in New York, had been arrested by Comstock's agents for possessing one of Margaret's *Family Limitation* pamphlets. He wrote telling her what had happened and assuring her that he was proud to be standing trial for her sake. Offered a free pardon by Comstock if he revealed where his wife was Bill boasted that he had replied he would "Let hell freeze over first."[27] If he expected Margaret to be impressed or touched he was greatly mistaken. She was extremely angry, commenting "Bill had to get mixed up in my work after all and of course it made it harder for me."[28] She saw his stand as showing-off and an attempt to ingratiate himself with her. But at least it brought her to a rapid decision: she must return at once before Bill grabbed any more of the limelight. In September 1915 she sailed, via Bordeaux, through the torpedo-threatened Atlantic to New York, arriving safely only to find Bill had already been released after serving a nominal jail sentence and that, ironically, his trial had been the occasion of Anthony Comstock catching a chill which had killed him. She also found that in other ways the birth control scene had significantly changed. Other people were now interested and trying to take control of a movement she had regarded as hers to head and lead. One of these "other people" was Mary Ware Dennet who infuriated Margaret by explaining that she envisaged, now that Comstock was dead, an orderly campaign staying strictly within the law aimed at repealing those statutes blocking the advance of birth control. This Margaret rejected. What *she* wanted was direct action, challenging the law flamboyantly, and starting with her own deferred court case for which she desired maximum publicity. As far as she was concerned ". . . the whole issue is not one of a mistake, whereby getting into jail or keeping out of jail is important, but the issue is to raise . . . birth control out of the gutter of obscenity and into the light of understanding."[29] To attract even more "light" she intended to conduct her own defence at her trial.

Before this was to take place, Margaret Sanger had a trial of a different sort to go through. On November 6th, 1915, five-year-old Peggy died of pneumonia. Margaret was never able to write about it, as Josephine Butler later managed to, nor was this normally expressive woman able to express her grief. "The joy in the fullness of life went out of it on that morning," she wrote, "and has never returned."[30] As well as grief there was also guilt to confront – guilt that of Peggy's short life she had robbed herself of almost a quarter by leaving her to go to England and that during the remainder she had very often indeed put her second to work. But there was no breakdown. The horror of Peggy's death seemed to freeze all emotion in her. Her only way of dealing with it was to block it out by redoubling her efforts for the birth control cause. She longed passionately for her trial to begin and was bitterly upset when told that instead the case against her was to be dropped. She *needed* that trial, needed to make it the focus of her damaged life, needed to stand up and show she had left Peggy for something that mattered. But pressure had been brought to bear upon the government to prevent them making fools of themselves. As George Bernard Shaw put it, "Comstockery is a world joke at the expense of the US" and the laughter was growing uncomfortably loud. The New York *Sun* commented accurately, "The Sanger case presents the anomaly of a prosecutor loath to prosecute and a defendant anxious to be tried." But on February 18th, 1916 the government finally entered a *nolle prosequi*.

Margaret's immediate reaction was to go off on a speaking tour for three months. She made the same speech 119 times, first practising it from the roof of her hotel in Lexington Avenue. In it, she went over seven sets of circumstances in which birth control should be used, including the first two years of any young couple's marriage "to give them a chance to grow together." She began in New Rochelle by reading her speech but by Pittsburgh she had memorized it and become less nervous. She presented a curious spectacle wherever she went because of her apparent fragility. For a while, conscious that she might not look "serious", she wore "severe suits" but soon gave up because they made her feel constrained and uncomfortable. In any case, she quickly realized that there was in fact an advantage in looking frail and feminine – it made audiences protective and that was an asset. She was described by one reporter as "a rather slight woman, very beautiful, with wide apart eyes and a crown of auburn hair . . ."[31] This appearance, and her low, soft voice disarmed those who, as usual when any woman spoke in public on any woman's rights issue whatsoever, expected a battleaxe. Wherever she went she was a great success. People packed the halls in which she spoke and supporters marched the streets with banners proclaiming such slogans as "Poverty and large families go hand-in-hand." The atmosphere everywhere on this issue was highly charged and Margaret delighted in inflaming passions. She wrote that "my flaming Feminist speeches . . . scared some . . . out of their wits."[32] When the opposition took action by arresting her or locking her out of halls she was pleased and said, "I see immense advantages in being gagged. It silences me but it makes millions of others talk about me and the cause in which I live."[33]

But Margaret Sanger's avowed purpose in returning to America had been to open clinics and once her tour was over she began to consider how and where she could start. She had already been quoted in *Tribune* as saying, "I have the word of four prominent physicians that they will support me in the work . . . There will be nurses in attendance at the clinic and doctors who will instruct women in the things they need to know. All married women, or women about to be married, will be assisted free and without question."[34] As she herself added, "A splendid promise but difficult to fulfil." For a start, which "prominent physician" when it came to the bit would put his professional head on the legal block? The answer, as she found, was not one of them. Carefully, she went over and over the two sections of the 1873 Comstock Law, under which she would be prosecuted if she opened a clinic, looking for a loophole. Section 1142, the one most often cited, said *no one* could give information to prevent conception to *anyone* for *any* reason, but Section 1145 did say that doctors could give advice "to cure or prevent" sexual diseases. This had been squeezed in to cover venereal disease but Margaret saw how it might be used if the prevention of disease was interpreted as covering lives endangered through too many pregnancies. But she did not, of course, really imagine that such a specious line of argument would be accepted. Obviously, as soon as she opened a clinic it would be closed and she would then face arrest and trial. She knew this, and accepted her fate not just with resignation but with positive relish.

This decided, she set about finding premises and helpers. "I preferred a Jewish landlord," she wrote later, "and a Mr Rabinowitz was the answer."[35] The point of him being Jewish was that she had the idea "Jewish people were more interested in health." The obliging Mr Rabinowitz lived in Brownsville, a poor but perfectly respectable immigrant district of New York. "He was willing to let us have No. 46, Amboy St. at 50 dollars a month, a reduction from the regular rent because he realized what we were trying to do."[36] He spent hours cleaning the rooms they were going to use and even insisted on white-washing all the walls so that the atmosphere would be "more hospital looking." This amused Margaret but she saw the point. A house-to-house canvas of local inhabitants was then made. Five thousand handbills were distributed in English, Yiddish and Italian saying:

MOTHERS!
Can you afford to have a large family?
Do you want any more children?
If not, why do you have them?
DO NOT KILL, DO NOT TAKE LIFE, BUT PREVENT.
Safe, harmless information can be obtained of
TRAINED NURSES at
46 Amboy St.
nr. Pitkin Ave, Brooklyn.

Tell your friends and Neighbours.
All Mothers Welcome.
A registration of 10 cents entitles any mother to this information.

On the morning the clinic was due to open, October 16th, 1916, there was a long queue outside – "halfway to the corner they were standing in line, at least one hundred and fifty, some shawled, some hatless, their red hands clasping the cold, chapped, smaller ones of their children."[37] It was a pathetic and moving sight. By seven in the evening, they were still arriving, standing patiently and hopefully in line, many of them accompanied by men. It was impossible to see them all. When the doors were regretfully closed at the end of that first exhausting day a hundred women had been seen – but not one by a doctor. Margaret had failed to recruit a single qualified doctor. She had to run the clinic herself with the help of her sister Ethel, also a nurse. Another friend, Fania Mindell, helped by keeping the records and looking after the children while Ethel and Margaret lectured batches of seven to ten women each, in separate rooms, on contraception in general. It had not escaped Margaret's notice that in Holland no records were kept. She had rightly concluded that if there had been records, which could be collated and published, they might be of great value for research purposes and so she was determined from the beginning to adopt this business-like approach – it was all part of her greater design and indicated the scope of her ambition. She knew quite well that her Brownsville clinic would in itself be insignificant but that was not the point. The point was to make a positive beginning from which all else would flow.

And it did, remarkably rapidly. The clinic was only open nine days, packed to bursting all the time, before it was raided in a gratifyingly spectacular fashion. Black marias, screeching sirens, fully armed policemen, and all to herd three perfectly willing women to the local police station. If the authorities had been trying to attract sympathy for Margaret Sanger and publicity for her cause they could not have managed it better. By the time the first case was called, against Ethel, a committee of a hundred prominent women had been formed to work for the reform of the Comstock Law. On the day of Ethel's trial, fifty of them took Margaret to breakfast at the Vanderbilt Hotel before proceeding with her to the courtroom. Ethel, sentenced under Section 1142 as expected, was given thirty days' imprisonment. She went on hunger strike, refusing liquid as well as food. Margaret, still awaiting her own trial, was genuinely concerned for her sister's health but determined to exploit the situation, as indeed Ethel wished her to do. She kept Ethel's suffering in the public eye, in spite of attempts by the authorities first to keep it secret and then to play it down. By the time she herself went on trial, a month later, public opinion was widely alerted to what was going on. When she took the stand, she was impressive. Every allegation the prosecution made was fiercely contested, especially that of wishing "to do away" with Jewish people by preventing them breeding. Birth control, she said, was nothing to do with doing away of any sort, nor was it a way of making money as was also alleged. She itemized the cost of her clinic and invited those in court to do their own sums.

After half of the fifty Brownsville mothers who had attended the clinic had given evidence, Judge Freschi said, "I can't stand this any longer," and adjourned the court – he was overwhelmed by the endless recitation of miscarriages, illnesses and childbirths. When it met again, a compromise was quickly offered: if Mrs Sanger would promise to agree not to break the law again she would get a free pardon this time. She refused, standing up and saying, "I cannot respect the law as it stands today."[38] She was sentenced to thirty days, like Ethel. This was more of a shock than she had thought. Whenever she had thought of going to prison she said she had somehow always imagined that at the last minute she would be saved – "I believed fully and firmly that some miracle would happen and that I should not go to jail."[39] But no miracle happened, and she went to jail, quite amazed to find the indignities of which she had heard actually coming to pass. Even so, she was given preferential treatment (not, for example, being strip-searched) and knew she had an easy time compared to others. Nobody stopped her giving birth control talks to the other prisoners and she enjoyed herself. What she enjoyed even more was coming out to the strains of the Marseillaise being sung at the gates by a crowd of her friends. "No other experience in my life has been more thrilling,"[40] she wrote triumphantly.

Yet when she took stock of what opening a clinic and going to prison had gained her she was depressed to conclude very little indeed. She was particularly disappointed at the response from the women of New York whom she described as sitting "with folded hands" and keeping "aloof from the struggle for women's freedom."[41] She had, she felt, sounded the call to action but "American women were not going to use direct action." The next few years, 1917 to 1921, were "leaden years". She had resolved, after prison, on a four-part campaign: agitation, education, organization and legislation, but it was hard to be the driving force behind all four. Most of her energies went into launching a magazine again, the *Birth Control Review*, which she herself helped to sell on street corners. "Street selling was torture for me," she said, "but I sometimes did it for self discipline and because only in this way could I have complete knowledge of what I was asking others to do."[42] She soon found that selling the magazine was an unsatisfactory business anyway. Those who bought it were aggrieved and disappointed when they found it contained no practical contraceptive advice. However hard she tried, it seemed impossible to give people what they undoubtedly wanted without promptly landing back in prison again and again. Not only did her work make her unhappy at this time but so did her personal life. She had been a woman on her own since her return in 1915. Her two sons were at boarding-school, and she was lonely. She had always thought she liked to be on her own but the reality of "not a cat, dog or bird to greet this homecoming, the fire dead in the grate"[43] was too much. Work was not, after all, enough. Her health was poor again in the winter of 1917–18 so she went to California, uprooting Grant and taking him with her for company. There, she spent three months recuperating and writing a book.

The book was *Woman and the New Race* finally published in 1920. In it, Margaret Sanger expounded with great fervour and passion her belief that the most important force in the remaking of the world was "a free motherhood". Legal and suffrage rights were utterly unimportant beside birth control because "these don't affect the most vital factors of her existence." But "free motherhood" was not going to be given to women – she stressed repeatedly it was something they had to claim for themselves. Women had to stop accepting their inferior status. They had to realize they had power of their own because it was only through them that the future generations could be born. The "new woman" so in vogue thought the ability to earn her own living a great victory and perhaps it was but "it is of little account beside the untramelled choice of mating or not mating." Only by using contraception could women make the most of this "untramelled choice". The "new woman" must look after herself and not be stupid enough to leave it to men. As for any idea that using birth control was immoral – that was absurd. All that was immoral was having unwanted babies, or leading oneself to believe that governments were right to encourage large families. This was "the most serious evil of our times" especially as the modern woman was not as suited as other generations to motherhood because of the tension of modern life. There were some graphic descriptions to illustrate this, and to show what it meant "to be a broken drudge of a woman" through endless childbearing. All that marred this visionary tract from the feminist point of view was the outline given of a new great race in America – the feebleminded, the prostitutes, the very poor, and those with any history of serious illness were not to be allowed the right to breed. Margaret saw nothing wrong in advocating birth control as a means of controlling breeding. She wanted strong, healthy, fit mothers not just willing ones.

When she returned from California (and put Grant back into school as quickly as she had snatched him out) she felt rejuvenated. She had also decided to try new tactics to get clinics opened. Aware that certain prominent medical men, such as Dr Robert Dickinson (who was one of America's most eminent gynaecologists) were beginning to feel uneasy about their profession's attitude to birth control, Margaret Sanger decided to set about suggesting her movement could be put into the hands of doctors. In 1923 she opened a Clinical Research Bureau on Fifth Avenue in New York and then asked Dickinson if he and his newly formed Committee on Maternal Health (composed of New York obstetricians and gynaecologists and privately financed) would like to take the bureau over and develop it. She herself, of course, would still control it but she would be more than happy to involve Dickinson and his colleagues in the running of it. If they wanted to, they could man it completely. For seven years of constant argument Dickinson tried to get doctors to do this but he failed. The stumbling block was always Mrs Sanger herself. The doctors neither liked nor trusted her. They suspected her motives, doubted her competence and feared her interference. Yet in spite of this setback, Margaret was more hopeful and buoyant than she had been since her imprisonment. She had failed to get any "Doctors only" legislation through state legislatures and failed to get medical co-operation for her research bureau but everywhere she saw her movement making headway.

The post-First World War world *was* different. Contraceptives were being used without any changes in the law. The judiciary was making itself ludicrous with cases like United States of America v. One Packet of Japanese Contraceptives. Judges were being educated to changed mores and their jobs made impossible. What was even more significant were the signs that the birth control movement was becoming world-wide. Although she wrote, "I had an uncanny dread of social organisations" Margaret had in fact inaugurated world conferences on birth control (even though many of these were principally occupied with eugenics). In 1925 she organized the Sixth International Birth Control Conference in New York and had the immense satisfaction of accepting Dr Aletta Jacob's apology for her brusque treatment of ten years before. Mrs Sanger, said Dr Jacobs, had done what she herself would have liked to do but had not succeeded in doing which was making birth control into a movement. In 1927 another triumph was the holding of a World Population conference in Geneva.

It seemed, in the twenties and thirties, that Margaret Sanger was everywhere, endlessly travelling and lecturing and preaching for her cause. Her personal life was also happier. In 1920 she had been quietly divorced from Bill Sanger for whom she still felt affection but nothing more. He irritated her, he was in the way. In the way of what she did not quite know, and when she got her official freedom she describes in her autobiography how she went through a period of slight panic during which she attempted to form closer relationships with her sons, then seventeen and twelve. Grant, the younger one, was easier for her to woo. He was always the more original and still young enough for her to dominate. In 1921 she once more took him out of school, against the advice of the headmaster who strenuously objected on the grounds that Grant's studies were continually interrupted to serve as his mother's companion, and took him with her to Japan. He was "a tall, dark, rather gawky youth," very affectionate and demonstrative. Margaret was extremely proud of him, referring to him as "Exhibit A".[44] She was rather hurt when, during the last part of this Far Eastern tour, he announced he was fed up and wished he could get to see some decent tennis. She let him go home ahead of her but missed him dreadfully.

When she arrived home herself she amazed her friends by marrying again, in 1922. Noah Slee, her new husband, was a business man twenty years older than she who had courted her with presents of filing cabinets and date stamps. Hearing that although she was a formidable career lady she was frivolous enough to enjoy dancing he had also taken ten lessons at Arthur Murray's Dancing School so that he could partner her. Once again, Margaret succumbed to the prospect of a way of life put before her. Noah Slee was a rich widower. He was only too willing to put considerable amounts of money and his business organization at the service of birth control. So, at the age of forty-three, Margaret married him, on the understanding that she would not be tied down by the marriage. Noah kept his word. He rented a villa between Nice and Monte Carlo so that Margaret would have a base for her European conferences and meetings, and he obligingly imported Mensinga diaphragms from Germany through his oil plant in Canada as well as giving large sums of money (amounting to 56,000 dollars between 1921 and 1926) to fight legal battles for the birth control movement. For her part, Margaret respected and loved him rather more than people knew. Everyone assumed it was a marriage of convenience, and it bore all the signs of it, but there are letters which show that even ten years later Margaret did love Noah – "Dearest Noah – darling – it is really always lonely to be away from you even one day,"[45] she could write. She never wrote like that during her marriage to Bill Sanger.

The same year that she married Noah Slee, Margaret had also published another book – *The Pivot of Civilization*. In it she had a great deal to say about the importance of sex. "Woman," she wrote, "must elevate sex into another sphere." To do so, she must reject the present teaching that sex was merely a means of procreating children. This was "a superficial and shameful view of the sexual instinct." Birth control carried with it, she argued, "a thorough training in bodily cleanliness and physiology, and a definitive knowledge of the physiology and function of sex." She attacked the Catholic church for saying birth control was "unnatural" when what was in fact unnatural was being forced to thwart or subdue the sexual instinct. Mankind had gone forward to "capture and control the forces of nature" and this should be a matter of rejoicing. No longer need fear inhibit women – "women can attain freedom only by concrete, definite knowledge of themselves, a knowledge based on biology, physiology and psychology." Using birth control was the means to all this, she claimed. Margaret Sanger called this book her "head" book, full of reasoned argument she hoped, while her earlier one, *Woman and the New Race*, was her "heart" book, full of passion and emotion. In fact, they were both similar, setting out the same arguments and only differing in the emphasis on sex and in the examples she chose to illustrate her points. They both sold well and established her more firmly as a figure on the international birth control scene. But she was not a secure figure in her own country. From the day she founded the American Birth Control League (in 1921) Margaret Sanger was involved in internal power struggles and in 1928 she resigned as its president. She also gave up the *Birth Control Review*, and Noah withdrew his financial support. From then onwards, she confined herself to the research bureau and to a new organization she set up, the National Committee on Federal Legislation for Birth Control.

In 1937, the Committee on Contraception of the American Medical Association agreed that physicians now had the right to give contraceptive advice and that the subject should be taught in medical schools. By then, the anti-contraception laws had been side-stepped for nearly a decade anyway and the birth control movement had become respectable. But Margaret Sanger saw this victory as only the first official one of the many more needed. The next battle was to get the government to make birth control a Public Health programme. "Birth control must seep down until it reaches the strata where the need is greatest; until it has been democratised there can be no rest."[46] A visit to India in 1936 had made her see the true evils of overpopulation and she was haunted by the sight of the "unspeakable poverty . . . the poorest women of Bombay, sober faced and dull looking . . . lived in the grubby and deadly 'chawls', huts of corrugated iron, no windows, no lights, no lamps, just three walls and sometimes old pieces of rag or paper hung up in front in a pitiful attempt at privacy."[47] It made her determined not just to establish a whole, world-wide system of birth control clinics but to continue to seek a better, simpler, cheaper female contraceptive. The rest of her life remained devoted to this quest. From her winter home in Tucson, Arizona, and her New York estate, Willow Lake in Dutchess County, she sallied forth agitating for more money to spend on research and contributing a good share of her own from the inheritance Noah left her on his death in 1943. It was her research bureau which financed Dr

Ernst Graefenberg, pioneer of the IUD, and began work on hormonal contraceptives which led to the development of the Pill. In 1959, Dr Gregory Pincus inscribed the report on oral contraceptives "to Margaret Sanger with affectionate greetings – this product of her pioneering resoluteness." By then, she was living full-time in Arizona, on her own, feeling very much out of contact with what was going on in the movement to which she had dedicated her life. "I would hesitate to go anywhere to speak on birth control these days,"[48] she said. There was no need to do so. By the time she died in 1966, it looked as though the Pill had solved the whole birth control problem, at least in the Western world, and with it many of the problems feminism had been unable to overcome.

★   ★   ★

Margaret Sanger had many enemies, both feminist and anti-feminist. In the course of her career she provided all of them with plenty of ammunition. One of her slogans, "More children from the fit, less from the unfit – that is the chief aim of birth control"[49] was particularly unfortunate having as it did both elitist and racist implications. It was hardly surprising that feminists should accuse her of losing sight of her feminism in her conversion to eugenics. She had been accused of robbing feminism of its ideology and she has been depicted as a megalomaniac with no concept of democratic leadership.

Many of these and similar accusations are true. To her, the end always justified the means – she did not much care how or why birth control was spread so long as it *was* spread as far and wide as possible. She did indeed wish the movement she had organized to remain under her own personal direction and she was certainly guilty of leaving unacknowledged debts to all kinds of people who had worked as hard as she had and often in a more altruistic fashion. Like Marie Stopes[50] (whom she first met in London in 1915) Margaret Sanger liked the limelight. It was never an evil necessity. Her relish for public controversy was despised by contemporaries. They liked modesty and humility in their women and she was neither modest nor humble. She went out and grabbed headlines and faced cameras with confidence. She was thought of as a publicity seeker whose values were suspect and whose thinking was not quite sound. She lacked intellectual depth and her writings and speeches were too often glib, a hotch-potch of ideas culled from other people. Her outlook was often blinkered – she failed completely, for example, to understand what were really the dilemmas for the Roman Catholics.[51] Again and again she oversimplified issues and antagonized people by her scorn for their difficulties. Yet in spite of these truths Margaret Sanger ought not to be underrated, nor ought she to be condemned by feminists. The whole starting point of her original campaign was "concern for the suffering of women" and a passionate desire to change the lives and status of all women. It is simply perverse to doubt her sincerity. Her feminism may have been different from the accepted feminism of her day, but it was just as valid and every bit as tenable.

Those who sneered at Margaret Sanger for what they thought of as her melodramatic and mawkish stories about the conditions on the East Side which had inspired her forgot how well acquainted she was with life there. There was a distinct failure of the imagination to visualize what she had experienced and to recognize its cumulative effect. Unlike many of her detractors, Margaret Sanger was no theorist – she had had a practical working knowledge of everything she described. This made her truly compassionate, and compassion is at least as praiseworthy as a starting point for feminism as anger or resentment or ambition. She viewed the women who came to her first clinic with something very close to real anguish – ". . . these puzzled, groping women; misled and bewildered in a tangled jungle of popular superstitions, old wives' remedies and back fence advice – all the ignorant sex teaching of the poor, an unguided fumbling after truth."[52] She genuinely wanted to solve their problems and rescue them from the nightmare of unwanted pregnancy. She wanted to give them back their health and make them cherish instead of dread sex. She was familiar with bad housing, poor diets and the whole joyless nature of many women's lives. She knew what a botched abortion looked like, what suffering in childbirth was when it took place in an atmosphere of hopeless fear. In the early days of her movement the memory of all this haunted her and even in the mid-1920s when she was far removed from it she never forgot. She was overwhelmed with depression on her visit to China at the suffering she saw – "Pestilence, famine and war are the loathesome substitutes for contraception,"[53] she wrote. If anyone could argue against birth control in those circumstances she thought there was no hope for them.

But Margaret Sanger's feminism showed itself not just in her compassionate concern for women less fortunate than herself – which was, after all, not much different in essence from the outlook of the nineteenth-century philanthropists – but in her determination that sex should be enjoyed by women purely for its own sake. Mabel Dodge Luhan wrote of Margaret Sanger that "she was the first person I ever knew who was openly an ardent propagandist for the joys of the flesh." This was what really frightened the feminists. Loudly and clearly Margaret Sanger announced that birth control would increase the *quality* of sexual intercourse for women not just that it would make it safe. Sex was, she also said, a thing of the spirit not just of the body, and love of it should not be suppressed. She wanted women to glory in the beauty of sex and this, in feminist eyes, brought her dangerously near to advocating that free love doctrine they saw as a trap. Carrie Chapman Catt wrote to Margaret Sanger that she could not possibly sponsor the American Birth Control League because "your reform is too narrow to appeal to me and too sordid. When the advocacy of contraception is combined with as strong a propaganda for continence (not to prevent conception but in the interest of common decency) it will find me a more willing sponsor . . ."[54] The same suspicion of sexual pleasure for women made many more feminists wary of Margaret Sanger who they saw as destroying the family which was, they thought, women's protection. There was open confusion about how birth control would affect sexual morality and whether this would work against women or not. In the midst of all the worry and debate, the sound of Margaret Sanger proclaiming from the rooftops that sex was "glorious" and should be "enjoyed by women as much as men had enjoyed it for centuries" was too much. Feminism, at that stage, was not prepared to endorse such an inflammatory doctrine.

Yet by the end of Margaret Sanger's work it was forced to do so. There was no going back. Women, through the use of birth control and that knowledge Margaret Sanger had given them of their own "biology, physiology and psychology," did look upon sexual pleasure as their right. In that region, as in others, gender was not to be tolerated as preventing self-fulfilment. The woman as the passive partner, ashamed to admit she desired sex and was ready for it, had been banished even if lip service was still paid to the old image – the reality was that women no longer needed to pay the penalty they had always had to pay. Women had done with blaming men for unwanted pregnancies or if they had not they no longer had justification. Margaret Sanger had taught them to look after themselves. They must, she said, expect *nothing* from men, birth control was "not men's business" and she would listen to no nonsense about joint responsibility for it. Women had to bear the babies if birth control was not properly managed, therefore it was their responsibility. It was also their responsibility to assert their rights within marriage. The church, with its notion of conjugal rights, sanctioned "lawful rapes" and women should not put up with it. They should never simply service men under some mistaken belief that this was their duty, that a man's "natural urge" had to be accommodated. If a woman did not also feel the urge then she should decline to satisfy a man's. Yet women should not regard, at the other extreme, all sex as lust. This was wrong. When she met Gandhi in India and he described the sex act as merely lust which should be gratified no more than three or four times in a man's life, and otherwise conquered and subdued, Margaret Sanger was horrified. It distressed her beyond measure to hear this view of sexual relations.

But, although her arguments for enjoying sex make it sound as if this was to be birth control's finest gift, this was not all she intended her movement to do. It was her contention that for feminism to have any future at all women must be able to plan their families. Otherwise, nothing else could be planned. Birth control, to Margaret Sanger, was the logical starting point for, not the product of, self-fulfilment. At the Sexual Reform Congress in 1921 Naomi Mitchison put the problem well: "Intelligent . . . women want two things: they want to live like a woman, to have masses of children by the men they love, and leisure to be aware of both lovers and children; and they want to do their own work, whatever it may be. The two things are not compatible, except in very rare cases. So, even if they live violently, twice as hard as men, fitting things in, wasting no time on anything of less importance than the fundamentals (and this is all very difficult and only the very healthy can keep it up indefinitely) yet they cannot make two hours out of one. They insist, as I think they should, on having both worlds, not specializing like bees or machines, but they must give up something of both, not necessarily all the time, but sometimes the work and sometimes their full sex life. It is very unfortunate but there seems to be no way out of it. Adequate contraceptive methods are an essential part of this compromise." Margaret Sanger gave women the means to make this kind of compromise and thought that in doing so she had solved the last great problem feminism faced. No longer would nature dictate terms. As in so many other respects, man had learned to bend nature to his will. For the first time a woman's right to choose had real meaning. There was no need for martyrdom any more. A woman could have a career *and* have a family and all she had to do was a little planning.

Unfortunately, it turned out that this was *not* all she had to do. As ever with feminism, the situation was more complex than that. The post-First World War woman had the vote, she was highly educated if she had the will and ability to wish to be, she had some legal protection, she could enter most professions and now she had access to birth control: one by one difficulties in the way of self-fulfilment caused by gender had been overcome. Yet immediately a new and much more sinister dilemma emerged. The women who "chose" everything found themselves appreciating nothing, and the women who "chose" one or the other were miserably aware that they were doing so. The longed for, at last realized thing called "a proper choice" began to wreck the life of the feminist woman in very many cases. She began to curse the necessity for making her choice, to long for the days when fate or nature or even men decided her destiny. She had to learn how to use her options for her own benefit and not so that they worked against her, and in the process she came to learn a great deal about herself which until then had been obscured.

Concern about that "feminine spirit" of which Margaret Sanger was so fond of talking (and so bad at defining) emerged as a powerful factor. What was "feminine", what was not? How much of "femininity" was innate and how much conditioned? Was "femininity", if it existed as separate from female, desirable? Or was it a curse? How much should be retained and how much discarded? Was it illogical to be both feminine and feminist? Had progress gone far enough, as far as it could go in all essentials, or even too far? There were a great many questions still to sort out and if possible to answer before feminism, for the time being, could rest on its laurels. It had come a long way in a hundred years, shaping and redefining woman's role in society with great thoroughness, but it still lacked a final sense of direction. Nobody quite knew any more exactly what to aim for. Hundreds and thousands of important details still needed to be filled in on the Grand Design but in the feminist writings of the inter-World War period, even while Margaret Sanger was assuring everyone all problems were solved through birth control, there was the pressing urgency of deciding exactly what this Grand Design was: what did feminism want? And did this conflict with what it might have? Once more, there was no single hypothesis.

IDEOLOGY

Emma Goldman
(*Courtesy of the Library of Congress*)

Emma Goldman
1869–1940

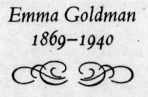

The 1920's proved a dangerous era for active feminism. On the one hand, there was so much at which to rejoice but on the other so much about which to worry. There was no doubt at all that by the time the vote was won there had also been a great loosening of all those social restrictions which had handicapped women as much, if not more than, their lack of political power. From the 1890s onwards the effects of the bicycling rage and of the dress reform that went with it had produced a new female image which was decidedly easier to conform to than any that had gone before. It was also easier for women to work. Working-class women had always worked but those legions of "respectable" middle-class daughters, who had been kept idle at home, found it acceptable to become typists and secretaries in the thousands of offices which began to emerge following the invention of the typewriter and the huge growth in those business activities using cheap female labour. The working middle-class girl was not yet the norm but she was no longer the exception. And her movement out of the home was part of a general movement away from nineteenth-century attitudes which was felt throughout the Western world. Yet all was not well with feminism. There was only one certainty: the old, narrow interpretation of woman's rights would not do. A wider, deeper ideology was needed and needed quickly before feminism floundered in a sea of complacency.

There was no doubt that winning the vote did produce complacency and that it weakened feminism. It was not just the feeling that there was nothing more to do – the natural result of having promised the vote would achieve everything – but the dangerous belief that there was nothing that *could* be done. Everyone expected women to use the vote to further their own interests. When they did not, it was a shock. "Modern young women," as one English feminist of the time put it, "know amazingly little of what it was like before the war, and show a strong hostility to the word 'feminism' and all which they imagine it to connote."[1] In the equal rights days it had been so easy to see the targets. In the 1920s it became impossible. It was in this atmosphere of ambiguity that Emma Goldman made her distressing announcement that women now needed emancipating from emancipation.

Emma Goldman gave voice early to the fear that others soon began to feel about the position of the "new" woman. True, hordes of women had by the 1920s been liberated from the home but to what? A new bondage? Women who had jobs did not find that what they had to do in the home was in any way decreased. The burden was now often double and different. Emma Goldman observed the women who came to a massage parlour she once ran in New York and felt sorry for them. "Most of the women claimed to be emancipated and independent," she wrote, "as indeed they were in the sense that they were earning their own living. But they paid for it by the suppression of the mainsprings of their natures . . . the emancipation of the women was frequently more of a tragedy than traditional marriage would have been."[2] It was, to her, simply no good pretending the "new" woman was a happier being. Independence was a pathetic farce. "Glorious independence!" she wrote sarcastically. "No wonder that hundreds of girls are so willing to accept the first offer of marriage, sick and tired of their 'independence' behind the counter . . ."[3] It was not that she thought the Woman's Rights movement had achieved nothing – on the contrary, she was well aware that it had "broken many old fetters" and she wholeheartedly approved. Her point was that in the process it had forged new ones unwittingly. Emancipation had never really been understood, that was the trouble. The emphasis on suffrage had been "absurd". Woman had been duped into thinking political power would solve everything. "In her exalted conceit she does not see how truly enslaved she is not so much by man as by her own silly notions and traditions. Suffrage cannot ameliorate that sad fact; it can only accentuate it, as indeed it does."[4] It was only a means of strengthening woman's basic subordination. Not having the vote had only been one of woman's external handicaps. Removing that handicap was good but actually irrelevant. *Real* emancipation was to do with abolishing *internal* tyrannies. "Artificial stiffness" and "narrow respectabilities" were the chief enemies. And how would these be overcome? By women changing themselves from within. "True emancipation," said Emma Goldman firmly, "begins neither at the polls nor in the courts. It begins in a woman's soul."[5]

It was a shocking thought, but then Emma Goldman's whole life was dedicated to shocking people into thought. It took courage to proclaim that the new Jerusalem, far from having been gained, as the feminists like Margaret Sanger boasted, was a mirage. Women, thrilled by their new independence, excited by their new status, hated to have this attacked. They also hated to be told they were betraying their own natures. It looked like simply another, uglier, side to the old anti-feminist argument that a woman's natural place was in the home being a good little wife and mother. But Emma Goldman thought no such thing. Through her own experience she had discovered the trap posed by so-called emancipation and she struggled heroically to make a way out of it towards a quite different liberation. In doing so, she heralded the later feminist movement of the 1970s, sowing seeds that were to germinate only very slowly indeed. But they were there, and eventually they provided feminism with the ideology it needed.

★ ★ ★

Emma Goldman liked to date her "birth" as the day she arrived in New York City at twenty years of age. It was on that day that she felt that everything which had gone before was "cast off like a worn garment." But, in fact, Emma Goldman carried the history of her youth slung round her neck like an albatross, hating the memory of it and yet unable to forget. It was the whole experience of those twenty pre-natal years which made her into the kind of feminist she became – a kind quite distinct from any that had gone before.

She was actually born on 27th June, 1869 in Kovno (now Kaunas) in what became modern Lithuania. The province had been given to Russia in the land division of 1795 so technically she was a Russian. Prior to 1795, Kovno had been in Poland and the inhabitants went on regarding themselves as Polish, especially the large Jewish population. Russia did nothing to welcome them. Work was difficult to get and discrimination against Polish Jews quite open. Emma's father, Abraham, an unhappy man, frustrated by his bad luck, managed to get a job as an innkeeper in the small Baltic town of Popelan soon after her birth. Emma he saw as part of his misfortunes since he had passionately wanted a son. His wife Taube already had two daughters, Lena and Helena, from her first marriage. She had married very young to a man she adored and after his sudden death her arranged second marriage to Abraham had not brought her the happiness she had once enjoyed.

The Goldmans were dissatisfied with each other and, even after the birth of the longed-for son (and then another) a few years later, their bitterness continued. Their marriage prejudiced Emma against that institution from the start. Her father's "harsh treatment of Mother . . . ending in Mother's fainting spells"[6] distressed and angered her. When she discovered that her father had swindled her half-sisters of their rightful inheritance her disgust grew. She began to hate and despise him, seeing him as a brute who dominated and punished the whole family. As she grew up, she was confused to discover that mixed with her hatred was a strong measure of physical attraction. Abraham was "the nightmare" of her childhood but there was something about his sheer strength and his strong good-looks which aroused in her a secret admiration. Outwardly, though, she was all challenge and rebellion. She argued and fought with him over every conceivable issue and he exerted his power over her by beatings and blows.

Emma was not compensated by having a better relationship with her mother. The birth of two brothers put Emma in the unenviable position of being in the middle of the family between two daughters born of a much loved husband and two welcome sons. Taube Goldman was always tired, depressed, overworked and resentful. Most of all she resented the way Emma caused so much trouble. Sensing that in adolescence the situation could only grow worse she dreaded the onset in Emma. When her daughter began to menstruate at eleven she was unable to control her fears. "Early one summer morning," wrote Emma, "I woke up in great agony. My head, spine and legs ached as if they were being pulled asunder. I called for Mother. She drew back my bedcovers and suddenly I felt a stinging pain in my face. She had struck me. I let out a shriek, fastening on Mother's terrified eyes. 'This is necessary for a girl,' she said 'when she becomes a woman as a protection against disgrace.' "[7] With this elliptical comment Emma had to be content. It shocked her so much that it was no good her mother afterwards trying to take her in her arms to comfort her. She rejected the embrace. Being a woman was branded on her mind as being something to be ashamed of, like all the other natural instincts she experienced.

The strongest of these instincts was sex. Emma maintained she could remember clearly erotic sensations at six and she was always contemptuous of how parents treated any such feelings in children. By the age of fifteen she had been seduced by a hotel clerk with whom she had been secretly going out for several months. She did not enjoy the experience much – "not until after the violent contact of our bodies and the excruciating pain he caused me did I come to my senses."[8] She began to see sex between men and women as something not necessarily as pleasurable as the urge which led to it. At any rate, she became wary. "After that," she wrote, "I always felt between two fires in the presence of men. Their lure remained strong but it was always mingled with violent revulsion. I could not bear to have them touch me."[9] This suited Abraham whose plans for her were an early, decent marriage, arranged by him to his own profit. He was furious when Emma refused to entertain such a notion and showed signs of wanting to educate herself more. He threw her French grammar in the fire on one well-remembered occasion and yelled at her, "All a Jewish daughter needs to know is how to prepare gefülte fish, cut noodles fine and give the man plenty of children."[10] Determined though she was to escape this fate, Emma was ill-equipped to do so. Her prospects were poor. She had never managed to get to the German Gymnasium in Königsberg, where the family had moved in 1876, although she was undoubtedly bright enough (her way was blocked by a teacher's refusal to give her the required good-conduct certificate). Her only real education had been the last six months of her schooldays, spent in St Petersburg because her family had again moved in 1881. There, she had been on the fringe of intellectual and political activity, coming into contact with students who had loaned her works like Turgenev's *Fathers and Sons*. But none of this helped her when she began to look for work. All she could find was a low-paid job as a seamstress in a corset factory.

There Emma might have been obliged to stay, forced eventually to submit to her father's authority and marry a man of his choice, if her half-sister Helena had not in 1885 announced she was going to emigrate to America. Her sister Lena was already there and sending home good reports. This news put Emma into a panic. She had never cared much for Lena but adored Helena who had been very nearly the only comfort of her childhood. If she lost Helena she would not only lose her only source of affection but also the only buffer between herself and her father whose matrimonial designs loomed nearer every day. She determined to accompany Helena. Her father would not hear of it. For weeks the Goldman house echoed to the roars and screams of threats and counter-threats as Abraham and Emma engaged in their most vicious battle yet. When her father would not given an inch, Emma played her final card. She threatened suicide. So convincing was her promise to throw herself in the river that Abraham for once was frightened and capitulated. She could go, get the hell out and never darken his door again. He gave her the princely sum of twenty-five roubles and off she went, triumphant. The two girls, one sixteen, the other twenty, left St Petersburg in December 1885 for Hamburg where they boarded the *Elbe*. Emma was utterly happy. She was with the person in the world she loved best and leaving behind the person she hated most. Nothing could spoil her happiness, not even being packed like cattle into the steerage quarters of the ship. Throughout the long journey to America which everyone else found so frightening and tedious she remained in a barely controlled state of intense excitement.

When the Statue of Liberty loomed ahead out of the New York dawn mist her eyes filled with tears – "Ah, there she was, the symbol of hope, freedom, opportunity! She held her torch high to light the way to the free country, the asylum for the oppressed of all lands."[11] Agonizing disillusionment came almost immediately. When she and Helena were taken to the clearing house for immigrants, then Castle Garden, they were pushed about brutally by the guards and treated with contempt by the officials. The atmosphere was horrible, "charged with antagonism and harshness". The whole of their first day on American soil was "a ghastly shock". In haste, she and Helena completed the formalities and were allowed out to go to Lena's home in Rochester. Although they were warmly welcomed this too was a shock. Rochester was supposed to be The Flower City but the impression on a cold, raw January morning was grim, and in spite of Lena's ready hospitality both the new arrivals caught the unmistakable whiff of poverty. The rooms in which she and her husband lived were already overcrowded and a baby was due. The only income was the husband's twelve dollars a week he earned as a tinsmith and on that he also supported an elderly relative who lived with him. Clearly, Lena's could only be a temporary refuge. They must both find jobs at once.

Helena found work first, retouching negatives, then Emma got a place in Garson and Mayer's factory sewing vests ten and a half hours a day for two dollars fifty cents a week. She was told she was a very lucky girl to be so privileged. The friend of Lena's who had found her the job expressed the opinion that she wouldn't need it for long anyway as with her red cheeks and pretty blue eyes a man would soon snatch her up and keep her in silk and diamonds. He gave her "the sense of standing naked in the market place because he even came over and tried to feel my arms."[12] Nor did she find the job he had fixed for her so marvellous. At first, it was true she was impressed. Unlike the premises back in St Petersburg, the Garson and Mayer's factory was "large, bright and airy" and it didn't smell. But on the debit side there was the discipline which was rigid and made the already monotonous nature of her job worse. She missed the camaraderie of the dirty, dark St Petersburg factory. The only bright spot in her existence was Stella, Lena's newborn baby. Otherwise she was as wretched as ever, endlessly yearning to escape to better things. Goaded by feelings of guilt at how little she was able to contribute to Lena's household expenses Emma finally nerved herself to ask for a raise. It was refused so she left and found a place, with difficulty, in a less modern factory for four dollars a week. It was here that, at the next machine, she met a young man called Jacob Kershner. He was a Russian who had arrived from Odessa in 1881 and had become a cloakmaker. He was attractive and kind to her, "the only human being I had met since my arrival"[13] outside the family. Within four months he had asked her to marry him.

If Margaret Sanger had thought of marriage as a kind of suicide Emma Goldman thought of it as murder – a monstrous act a man committed against a woman. She had set her face steadfastly against it all her short life. Every married woman of her limited acquaintance was a helpless drudge, a pathetic warning of what "love" led to. And she did not in any case love Jacob. She was merely attracted to him. She did not want to marry him only to go to bed with him. But he was the one who wanted, who insisted, on marriage. So she refused his proposal at first. Jacob ignored her refusal. Day after day, week after week he walked to work with her, stayed at her side all the long hours they spent there and afterwards walked her home keeping up his courtship all the time. When she agreed at last to become engaged to please him, he thought the battle won. Halfway through their engagement the rest of the Goldman family arrived from Russia and in order to support them Emma and Helena left Lena's and took rooms with them. Jacob came as a lodger to eke out their income. He slept on a couch in the living room and Emma found his close proximity torture.

"I suffered from sleepless nights, waking dreams and great fatigue at work."[14] The sexual frustration was so exhausting that it sapped her willpower. In February 1887 she finally capitulated to Jacob's endless pleas to marry him, miserably aware that her motives were wrong. "He filled a void in my life," she wrote, "and I was strongly attracted to him."[15] The awful irony was that having married Jacob primarily to satisfy her sexual urges she discovered on their wedding night that the reason he had been able to be so principled about marriage first was that he was impotent. Just as securely as Caroline Norton, and with far less reward, Emma Goldman was caught in the trap she had always been able to see.

At first, she tried to make the best of it. Jacob was persuaded to go to the doctor. He returned with the charming news that if he was to be cured it was up to his wife "to build up his manhood." Depression made her incapable of doing so even if she had known how. "The material anxiety of making ends meet," she wrote, "excluded everything else. I had stopped work: it was considered a disgrace for a married woman to go to the shop."[16] They lived on Jacob's fifteen dollars a week which would have been enough, with judicious management, if he had not taken to gambling. The talks about literature and the outings to dance halls stopped. The man Emma thought she had married disappeared. It was the kind of situation from which there was no possible escape and Emma saw herself being dragged further and further down. She recovered enough of her innate determination to put a stop to it the only way she knew – by insisting on a divorce. Her family were appalled. A divorcée in their community was a social leper. They begged her to stay with Jacob and threatened her with ostracism if she left him. But she was adamant. The same rabbi who married her divorced her and she promptly left Rochester for New Haven where she took another factory job. She made some congenial friends but unfortunately fell ill and had to take refuge with Helena who had just married.

Almost as soon as she returned to Rochester she met Jacob in the street. He began to plead with her to marry him again, swearing things would be different. Dramatically, he produced a bottle of poison and said he would drink it if she did not agree. So she took the astonishing step of remarrying him, simply commenting, "I could not be responsible for his death."[17] She did not imagine he had really changed ("I was not naïve enough to think that a renewed life with Kershner would prove more satisfactory or lasting than the first"[18]) but she did not care. Marriage was a sham anyway. This being so, she might as well treat it as such. She was simply expressing her contempt for the institution. And yet, when she came to write about this episode in her autobiography, Emma was uneasily aware that her remarriage was hard to explain away. She did not usually plead indifference as a reason for positive action and her insistence that she was saving Jacob Kershner from suicide is curiously unconvincing. But at least she went into marriage for the second time more prepared than the first. Secretly, she took a course in dressmaking and saved to buy her own sewing-machine so that she could make her living without resorting to factory employment. What she intended to do, when she was ready, was to go off on her own to New York (presumably no longer worried about her husband's suicide threats).

Nowhere does she mention if Jacob remained impotent but since, soon after their remarriage, she refers to "the futility of a patched life" it seems likely that he was. After only three months she had had enough. There were "bitter recriminations" from her husband and parents when she announced she was leaving and that this time she would never come back. Only Helena was kind and loaned her money for her fare to New York. Off she went, swearing that "if I ever love a man again I will give myself to him without being bound by the rabbi or the law and when that love dies I will leave without permission."[19]

August 15th, 1889, the day Emma Goldman arrived in New York, aged twenty, was a very hot day. The city was oppressive and stifling. But Emma, although suffocated by the atmosphere, felt a return of that same exhilaration which had buoyed her up on the original voyage from Russia. There was no rational basis for her excitement and optimism, considering that behind her she left a broken marriage and hostile parents and that nothing had gone right for her in the country from which she had expected so much, but she felt on the edge of "something new and wonderful." She had discovered in herself "a great ideal, a burning faith, a determination to dedicate myself . . ." To what? To anarchism. She was to say later that she was an anarchist "of the Topsy variety – I was just born so" but in fact there had been specific reasons for her interest and also a specific starting point. It had all begun when she went with Helena on Sunday afternoons to meetings in a hall in Rochester. They had gone to alleviate boredom, to give themselves something to do apart from sit at home hearing "the ever lasting talk about money and business." One day, Johanna Greie, a well known anarchist, came to speak about the case of the eight Chicago anarchists who were being tried for allegedly throwing a bomb which had killed six policemen. Emma had read about the case and was already passionately interested in what would happen but Johanna Greie convinced her not only that the eight men were innocent but that their work – calling for a strike among the steelworkers to secure an eight-hour day – must be continued. When, soon after this meeting, she heard that five of the anarchists had been hanged, her mind was made up. She would go to New York City, the centre of anarchist activity, and learn more about this movement to which she felt so irresistibly drawn. It was this mission which made her feel so expectant.

For a girl of twenty to arrive in New York City virtually penniless announcing she wished to dedicate her life to anarchism, which she really knew nothing about, was nothing short of madness. But Emma Goldman had done with convention. She had tried to behave and live as a girl of her age and class was expected to and she had been repelled by the process. She had tried making her living the only way she was equipped to do so and had discovered it was nothing more than a form of slavery. She had tried marriage and discovered it was another. She saw clear evidence that her sex penalized her, that it disabled her so that she was fit for nothing but drudgery. She felt she had nothing to lose because it was absolutely plain that in her circumstances everything had been lost the moment she was born. What had been instinctive in her was not anarchism but feminism. She rejected outright her fate as a woman and by her decision to go to New York City and stand on her own she completed the first stage of her feminist education. It looked very much, on that day, as if it might end disastrously. She only had five dollars, a small bag with a few clothes and her precious sewing-machine, symbol of her independence, which she left in a locker on 42nd Street. She also had three addresses of people with whom she might stay while she found her feet. One was that of a married aunt, another of a student she had met during her short stay in New Haven after her divorce, and the third was that of the *Freiheit* offices (the German anarchist newspaper). She had no knowledge whatsoever of the layout of the city and could not speak more than a few words of English at that stage. Naturally, she had great difficulty locating any of the addresses. The aunt, when tracked down, gave her such a frigid welcome that Emma proudly rejected the grudging offer of a bed but the student restored her spirits by giving her a warm and genial invitation to stay as long as she wanted. More important, he took her that very evening to Sach's café on Suffolk Street, the headquarters of the East Side radicals. There, he introduced her to the Minkin sisters, who were providentially looking for someone to share a flat, and also to Johann Most, the editor of *Freiheit*. The last introduction of significance was Alexander Berkman.

This rapid acquaintance with such a different environment left Emma almost too happy to speak. Her instinct had been right – she was going to be among people who thought like herself, who shared her barely formed ideals and principles. The next day was even better. Alexander Berkman called on her, inviting her to visit the *Freiheit* office with him. She had greatly taken to this young man the night before and now liked what he told her about himself. He had been born, like her, in Russia, in 1870, but unlike her had gone to the St Petersburg Gymnasium. There he had been a brilliant student but was expelled for writing an essay entitled *There is no God*. He had arrived in New York in 1888 and instantly established himself in the anarchist circle. He took her along with him to the *Freiheit* office where Johann Most suggested that if she wanted to she could come along the following week and help to bring the paper out. Emma went, proved diligent and a quick learner, and was taken out to dinner as a reward. Meanwhile, she had started work (which she hoped would only be temporary) in yet another corset factory and found a place to live with the Minkin sisters not far from Sachs's café. Life was moving almost too fast. It hardly mattered that she was still working a long, monotonous, poorly paid factory day because of what there was to look forward to in her free time. She had real friends, endless stimulating discussions with them, the social life she had dreamed of in Sachs's café, and a niche in the *Freiheit* office doing "real" work which might lead to other worthwhile things. One of the things it did lead to was an affair with Johann Most. He was her idol and she was completely under his influence. He valued her, she believed, for her mind. The fact that she was a girl was irrelevant. He took her to the Opera and gave her meals with wine but assured her it was her ideas that attracted him. She could be his protégée, he told her. She had "great talent" and must begin to use it. He would teach her how to become a great public speaker in the anarchist cause.

Emma began in a small way, making speeches (in Russian and German but not as yet English) on topics like the necessity for an eight-hour day at various Trades Union gatherings. They were not at first a success. She felt sick, had to grip a chair to keep her upright, couldn't see her audience for the haze suddenly clouding her vision, and was unable to control her trembling voice. Whenever she stumbled to a halt she found herself bathed in a cold sweat. But Johann Most pushed her on. He told her that nobody could tell she was suffering from the signs of nervousness she said she experienced, and that these would gradually diminish as she gained more experience. Her confidence grew a little but she found speaking a terrible strain and Johann Most's insistence that she should speak more and more did nothing to help. The love of Alexander Berkman, whom she called Sasha, did. Together, they found an apartment and invited an artist friend, known as Fedya, and Helen Minkin to share it to meet the costs. At last, Emma felt secure in a way she had never done before. She loved Sasha deeply – "we were engulfed in a wild embrace . . . deep love for him welled up in my heart"[20] and he very obviously loved her. Their little commune was her ideal, based as it was to be on mutual trust and respect with everyone's personality allowed expression.

Unfortunately, this domestic idyll showed signs of strain almost from the beginning due to the different interpretations all four partners put on what it was actually necessary for the household to spend out of their communal earnings. Sasha's idea of necessary things was uncompromising: the minimum of plain cheap food, heating only if it was freezing, no new clothes and absolutely no luxuries. It was the luxuries which caused the most disagreement. Emma was disturbed to discover that she could not reject so-called luxuries as Sasha did. She liked flowers, for example, and since they lived in a city without a garden these had to be bought if she wanted them. Surely if she passed a flower seller in the street and bought some violets very cheaply that was not forbidden? But it was. Sasha was furious when he saw the offending violets in a jug on the table. He demanded to know how she could pretend to care about the starving millions in the world if she spent money on violets. Emma was ashamed and yet resentful. All she wanted was a little fleeting beauty. "I did not believe that a cause which stood for a beautiful ideal," she wrote, "for anarchism, for release and freedom from conventions and prejudice, should demand the denial of life and joy . . . I want freedom, the right to self-expression, everybody's right to beautiful, radiant things."[21] Nor did she want to hear Sasha despise her "feminine" yearnings to make their apartment look attractive and to make meals more than just a means of keeping alive.

But at least Sasha survived a bigger test: he accepted Emma having

Fedya as a lover as well as himself and also accepted, though less easily, her more casual relationship with Johann Most. Emma herself had been first put to the test: her belief since her disastrous marriage had been that love should not be bound by rules and restrictions. When love was felt, it should be expressed fully and reciprocated joyously. She loved Sasha but in an entirely different way she loved Fedya. He was an artist whose sensitive nature kindled quite other fires in her (though later she confessed that she endowed Fedya with romantic qualities that perhaps were never in him). Why should loving Sasha mean excluding Fedya? "Could one love two persons at the same time? . . . I felt Sasha had left something untouched in me, something perhaps Fedya could waken to life . . ."[22] But did she dare have two lovers living so closely together? She decided to tell Sasha how she felt. "His response was bigger and more beautiful than I had expected."[23] Sasha acknowledged he felt possessive about her but that he hated this side of himself and wanted to overcome it and share Emma's interpretation of love. When Fedya came home that night Sasha embraced him. Emma was triumphant – she had broken out of the hideous convention which said a woman could only love one man at a time and could only secure him by marriage. She had made "free" love work. "The days and weeks that followed were illuminated by the glorious new light in us."[24]

The only thing that dimmed the light was the thought of Johann Most. Here, Emma was not so sure of herself. Sasha, on the contrary, was perfectly sure. He told her she was being a fool if she believed for one moment that Most treated her like this because he valued her mind. He was notorious – "didn't I know that he only cared for women physically?" Emma refused to accept this cynical judgement although she acknowledged that Most was interested in her as a woman as well. When she was with him he called her his "blue-eyes" and his "little girl-woman" and she could not deny she responded sexually to him. She was secretly appalled to find that Most seemed so *manly* compared to the boyish Sasha and Fedya and that it was this strength and force to which she was drawn. When he kissed and embraced her "years of suppressed intensity crushed my body . . ."[25] She always felt "limp" in his arms and to her horror found that she enjoyed her own helplessness. Most had the uncanny knack of making her want to serve him – "he was hungry for affection, for understanding. I would give him both." She did not want to examine what kind of relationship this resulted in but Sasha was there to point it out: she was Most's dupe, used by him as women had been used by men for centuries, every bit as enslaved as the bourgeois little wives she despised and thought herself above.

Emma angrily denied this, but felt the first stirrings of doubt about her success in handling her own nature. She also began to query what that nature was, whether there was an innate predisposition in her as a woman, *because* she was a woman, which caused her to act as she did with Most. When he ordered her to leave her "blissful nest" and go on a lecture tour speaking on the futility now of the struggle for the eight-hour day she was reluctant – but she did what he asked. He took her to Grand Central Station in a cab to see her off (to Sasha's disgust). She did well in each town but felt all the time as if she was Most's puppet. On her return she wanted to discuss this feeling but he told her not to worry and cuddled her. She flared up and declared she refused to be treated "as a mere female." Passionately, she attacked a great deal of what he had told her to say and pointed out she had enough mind of her own, a mind he said he respected, to be able to think for herself and that what she did think was not the same as he did. Most broke out in "a storm of abuse" and said she was "just like the rest" and he was going to cut her out of his heart. Exhausted, miserable and extremely confused Emma crept back to her flat and the comfort of Sasha and Fedya.

For a while she was ill and depressed. Partly, the trouble was physical. She had suffered ever since she began to menstruate from excruciatingly painful periods which always obliged her to stay in bed for at least a day, usually more, every month. When she first came to New York she had confided her problem to her medical student friend and he had arranged for her to see a specialist who had told her she had a retroverted womb and that she would never be free from pain, nor would she ever experience full sexual release, unless she had a minor operation to correct the condition. Nor, the specialist had said, would she ever be able to conceive and bear a child without such surgery. He had offered to perform the operation, a very simple one, but she had refused. Now, as she lay jaded in bed, feeling that she could not go through this pointless suffering for another thirty years, she wondered if she should after all have it.[26]

The thought of a child of Sasha's tempted her. She had always "loved children madly". As a child what she had most wanted in life (but never got) was a doll and when her brother Leibale was born she was filled with "ecstatic joy" to have in the family a living doll. Her mothering instincts, at six, were so strong that she continually put the baby to her non-existent breasts in an attempt to feed him and only gave up when he turned blue and began choking at having his nose squashed against her bony rib cage. But remembering this, she also remembered her own awful childhood and the hunger in her lessened. She knew her own experience was quite commonplace and was determined that "no child of mine should ever be added to those unfortunate victims." She could neither support a child nor guarantee it stability. The love and affection she would give it in abundance were not enough – she had a most realistic appreciation of how inadequate these qualities might prove to be. But her decision not to have the operation, which would effectively remove the in-built form of birth control she mistakenly thought her retroverted womb provided her with was also based on other reasons. At that moment, she was tired and sick of working for anarchism. She only wanted to stay at home. If she had a baby, she would have to stay at home. It would be a form of voluntarily dropping out and when she thought about what that meant sacrificing it was too much. She was only temporarily fatigued – ambition still burned strongly within her. It was essential to remain "unhampered and untied" if she was to fulfil the mission she felt she had. So, stifling her desire for a child of her own, a desire which grew stronger rather than weaker as she aged, Emma decided to endure her monthly torture and "pay the price." Her need for children as she said in her autobiography and in letters to her friends, must find its outlet in loving all the children in the world already in existence. Her decision was, in essence, exactly the same one as feminists had always had to make. Birth control instead of simplifying it in fact only complicated the decision.

The care of Sasha and Fedya restored Emma to health, and Most sent her flowers. He appeared to have forgiven her for her little rebellion. She went on a New England tour with him and her admiration for him again overwhelmed her. He was very pleased with how she was developing as a speaker and said he was grooming her to be his successor as leader of the anarchist cause. Her life was developing as she wished it to. Back home in New York City she was the centre of various activities – organizing education groups, arranging and giving lectures, holding socials and dances and all the time working hard as a dressmaker to support herself. At twenty-one she was more fulfilled than she had ever thought it possible to be and yet there was no hint of complacency. Every day brought new evidence of the world's outrages which called for anarchist involvement and

Emma felt each one personally. In the winter of 1890 she was particularly moved by news of the indiscriminate killing of "politicals" at Yakutsk in Russia and decided, with Sasha, that they must return at once to help. Johann Most was against this. Certainly Sasha could go but not Emma who was "too valuable" where she was. Suppressing her desire to ask why she was too valuable Emma went with Sasha to New Haven where he was going to train as a printer so that when he got to Russia he could bring out a newspaper. She had not decided if she would disobey Most and go with Sasha but she wanted at least to help him prepare. She went back to factory life as well as increasing her private dressmaking work to raise money for his voyage. She also opened an ice-cream parlour where the sandwiches and "dainty dishes" she made sold so well that in no time at all she was a proper little capitalist making a handsome profit. She invested part of the profits in a soda-water fountain and some coloured dishes she was unable to resist. The money needed for both of them to go back to Russia in the anarchist cause was suddenly within her grasp.

The only problem was Most, who told her that she would have to choose between him and Sasha. This enraged her. Remembering that Sasha had not asked her to choose she began to look at Most's "love" more critically and to suspect he was not so much advanced as retarded in his thinking. Once, he had laughed in her face and said, "Love, love, it is all sentimental nonsense, there is only sex!" Even if he was right, why did sex need to be exclusive? And yet there was this pull towards Most which could not be denied. Again and again Emma tried to analyse her feelings but it was useless. She behaved in Most's company like a typical female, a species she herself endlessly denied existed. Her response seemed to her sexually instinctive, having nothing to do with her personality or mentality, but what could she do about it? What ought she to do?

She was saved from deciding on that occasion by the imprisonment of Most (he was always in and out of prison for his anarchist activities) and by an event that drove all thoughts of going to Russia out of her head. At Homestead, near Pittsburgh in Pennsylvania the chairman of the Carnegie Steel Company, Henry Clay Frick, had ordered hired thugs to open fire on his workers who had demanded higher wages. Some of the workers had been killed in the resulting fracas. The minute he heard this Sasha had felt inspired. He felt "a blow aimed at Frick would re-echo in the poorest hovel, would call the attention of the whole world to the real cause behind the Homestead struggle."[27]

He would go to Pittsburgh and kill Frick then himself. It would be Emma's job to live on and "articulate" the meaning of his act to the workers of the world. Overnight, the ice-cream parlour was sold. Sasha and Emma caught the first train to New York, talking non-stop about their plan. There was no danger of being overheard because neither of them spoke good enough English to use it as their first language. Sasha was wildly excited and Emma hardly less so but for different reasons. Once more, she was confused. Something in her – was it that wretched femaleness? – was protesting against Sasha's proposed death. Even if it could be proved that this self-sacrifice would greatly advance the anarchist cause she still did not want it to happen. "Message, cause, duty, propaganda . . . what meaning could these things have compared with the force that had made Sasha flesh of my flesh . . ."[28] She loved him too much to want him to die for whatever worthy reason. He said he loved her too but how could he if he was prepared to separate them. Did it mean her love was stronger, or that women loved in a different way from men? "Is not love, not ordinary love but the love that longs to share to the uttermost with the beloved, is it not more compelling than aught else?" she asked herself. The only solution seemed for her to die with Sasha. They would both assassinate Frick then kill themselves. But this made Sasha angry – that, it seemed, would ruin half the point.

On and on they argued, with Sasha conceding that she could at least accompany him to Pittsburgh when they had made the bomb that was to kill Frick. This proved harder than they had thought. Sasha accidentally exploded the bomb he made (without harm to anyone) and that changed matters. There was no more money to buy materials for another bomb – all that was left was enough for a pistol and one train fare. Emma saw Sasha off, equipped with a cheap revolver and came back to their flat. She had so little time to raise the money to follow him. Unless she could do it within forty-eight hours, the time it would take Sasha to organize the assassination, the deed would be done and Sasha dead and she would be alive without him. It seemed to her that desperate measures called for desperate solutions. She would go on the streets and in one night buy her passage to her lover's side and her death with him.

Emma never doubted for one moment the rightness of what she proposed to do. She would be selling her body to gain the money to help Sasha – there could be no more worthy reason. Since time began women had been reduced to exploiting their femaleness in this way, to offering sex to gain some advantage for themselves and others. It was wrong that society so arranged things that this should be sometimes necessary but the deed itself although terrible for the woman, was not wrong. Emma aligned herself with Sonya in Dostoyevsky's *Crime and Punishment* and was just as sure as Sonya that the end justified the means. What she suddenly found herself not so sure about was whether she could go through with it. Was her body just a body? Could she persuade it "to do it with strange men?" Despising herself for her own cowardice she began preparing herself on the morning of Saturday, July 16th, 1892. First of all she assessed her market value. "I stepped over to the mirror to inspect my body. I looked tired but my complexion was good. I should need no make-up. My curly blond hair showed off well with my blue eyes. Too large in the hips for my age, I thought. I was just twenty-three . . . I would wear a corset and I should look taller in high heels (I had never worn either before)".[29] Clothes were another problem. With surprisingly romantic ideas of a prostitute's dress Emma thought "dainty underwear" imperative. She bought some soft flesh-coloured material and made some.

Then, as it began to get dark, she put herself on 14th Street. After only an hour she was in tears. As soon as any man approached her she found herself walking away. If he got hold of her, she shook him off. The vulgarity of her prospective customers, their crude remarks and leers, aroused in her an automatic rejection she was unable to control. A body was not after all just a body. Again and again she tried to force herself to accept the advances she invited but loathed and again and again she failed. Convinced she would have to give up she made one last effort, promising herself that the very next man who wanted her should have her. It happened to be "a tall distinguished looking person" with white hair who took her to a café, bought her a drink, said he could tell she was a novice and advised her to go home because she would never have the knack. He gave her ten dollars. She was "too astounded for speech." It was proof of something she had always wanted to believe in: that there existed a class of men who did not see women as sex objects and who practised what they preached.

Emma now had half the money she needed to follow Sasha but before she could raise the rest the news came that Frick had already been shot. Unfortunately for Sasha he had bungled his hasty attempt. Frick was only wounded and Sasha had failed in his own suicide bid. He was in prison facing what would undoubtedly be a long prison sentence if not the death penalty. Emma's prodigious energy now went into canvassing support for him. She immediately organized and chaired a large public meeting at which she was correctly described as being "possessed by a fury". When Johann Most, now out of prison, publicly sneered at Sasha's action and called him a misguided fool who had damaged the anarchist movement Emma went to a gathering he was addressing, stalked up onto the platform and proceeded to whip him in front of his audience with a horsewhip she then broke over her knee. Neither this touch of melodrama nor all her speeches helped. Sasha was moved to Murderer's Row in prison and she herself was put on the wanted list. She was hunted by the police and spent her days hiding and her nights riding the Bronx streetcar wearing a blue and white striped dress and long grey coat which gave her some protection because she was taken for a nurse. As soon as Frick's survival was assured Sasha was brought to trial: he got twenty-two years. Horror at the savagery of such a sentence at first blinded Emma to her own tragedy. Her happy life was smashed. Estranged from Johann Most and without her beloved Sasha she was confronted with the need to rebuild her own world. It was not that she was a helpless, dependent female who could not function without a man to direct her – far from it – but it could not be denied that she desperately needed the kind of strong supportive love and respect both Most and Sasha (though not Fedya) had given her. There was a terrible fear in her mind that she could not manage without them. It seems not entirely fortuitous that at this crucial stage a new man called Edward Brady entered her life.

At one of the many meetings she held to rouse support to get Sasha's sentence commuted, Emma became aware that a man in the audience was staring fixedly at her. She noted he was tall, broad, well-built and that he had soft blond hair and blue eyes. He was fiddling with a box of matches which irritated her. After she'd finished speaking she walked over to him and said he shouldn't play with fire. "I love fire," he said. "Don't you?" With this promising opening he began pursuing her. He told her he had just arrived from Austria after serving a ten-year sentence for publishing illegal anarchist literature, that he was forty-years'-old and a scholar. He also said he greatly admired Sasha for what he had done. Gradually, says Emma, a "beautiful comradery matured between Brady and me."[30] It rapidly matured even further into a love affair so passionate Emma wondered if she had ever known what passion was before. Within weeks, Ed was indispensable to her. She discovered that sexual love could be "ecstatic" and her flat became "a temple of love". Her regained happiness frightened her – "so much peace and beauty could not last; it was too wonderful, too perfect."[31]

She was right in her estimation. Her work soon got in the way of her personal relationship. In 1892 the industrial crisis of that year had thrown thousands out of work and Emma saw her main job as helping the unemployed. When she told Ed this, "his mood changed." He said he did not want her to tire herself, especially as she had been ill again. She was, he said, his to hold and protect and watch over. Alarmed, Emma asked him if he actually meant she was his property, "a cripple who had to be taken care of by a man?" He said no, it was merely concern for her health that had prompted his words not any desire to stop her doing what she wanted to do. Relieved, Emma threw herself into committee sessions, collecting food and feeding the homeless. Ed helped. Her biggest effort was a mass meeting in Union Square which she led carrying a red banner. She made a brilliant speech which the newspapers claimed was "just what the ignorant mob needed to tear down New York."

From then on she was known as Red Emma. New York detectives followed her wherever she went and finally arrested her in Philadelphia in August 1893 for inciting revolution. She was tried and sentenced to a year in prison on Blackwell's Island. She withstood the hardships this entailed very well except for being deprived of cigarettes which, since she smoked forty a day, she found torture. She was put in charge of the sewing shop where she refused to slave drive the women to satisfy the matron. When she fell ill and spent some time in the prison hospital one of the doctors, noticing her concern for the sick, suggested she might help out when she recovered. This she did, finding nursing congenial. It consoled her to be looking after "those derelicts on the social dung heap."

When she came out of prison she felt derelict herself. She was only twenty-five but felt tired and ancient. There was a meeting called to welcome her back to the anarchist movement at which she planned to speak to express her gratitude but she could not find her voice. Ed, at her side, said she simply needed looking after. He urged her to go away with him somewhere quiet and peaceful. On the way home they happened to discuss a very pretty newcomer who had spoken at the meeting and Emma confessed how depressed the woman's beauty had made her feel. Ed said this woman wouldn't stay beautiful long, so not to worry – she was Italian and "Latin women mature young, they grow old with their first child, old in body and spirit." Emma said in that case the woman shouldn't have any children if it was going to wreck her. Ed replied, "No woman should do that. Nature has made her for motherhood. All else is nonsense, artificial and unreal."[32] They had a blazing row about this then and there in the street. Ed tried to end it by embracing Emma but she pushed him off and ran away. Next day, Ed came round and asked her to go for a walk on Manhattan beach with him so that at least they could talk things over calmly. She went and as they walked on the beach, the sun bright even though it was November, he tried to explain what he really meant. He said he could not help it, he did want her to give up speaking and devote herself to something less exhausting and time-consuming like writing. He begged her not to be angry about his opinions on motherhood. "You are a typical mother, my little Emma, by build, by feeling." In spite of herself, Emma was "profoundly stirred" and tried to examine her own reaction to what Ed had said more honestly. What he was really suggesting was that all women, even she herself, wanted to be mothers and that they were thwarting their own natures and instinctive desires if they tried to suppress this. Was this true? Was Ed right to imply that her work for anarchism, in all its various demanding forms, was simply a substitute for motherhood? As she thought about this, it occurred to her that this kind of charge was never levelled at men – fatherhood was never seen as in any way incompatible with work fulfilment. The reason why was clear: "Man's physical share in the child is only a moment's; woman's part is for years . . ." If she acknowledged, as she did, that she would indeed like children and that yes, she was indeed subduing her instinct, this did not solve the problem. What Ed failed to realize was that, motherhood and work being incompatible, it did not necessarily follow that a woman must automatically choose motherhood or she would suffer. Either way there would be suffering. Either way, one half of her must be denied. In her own case, work was the more important. Ed was wrong, it was not a substitute but her whole reason for living. But since she did love him, and did want to be with him, she suggested that they should move in together and try to make it work. He would have to accept she was going to continue her work, that nothing would stop her, that there was not the faintest chance not only of her becoming a mother but of becoming a wife or any other version of the standard female role. Ed accepted.

Emma and Ed moved into a four-room flat together on Eleventh Street and bought a brand new double-bed. To Ed's annoyance, Emma insisted that one of the rooms should be her own private sanctum. Long before Virginia Woolf had ever thought of it she saw a room of her own as essential for her own well-being. She also began working as an auxiliary nurse at the new Beth-Israel Hospital on East Broadway. Ed was earning good money at the time (as an Insurance Agent) and protested there was no need for her to work at all, but she insisted. Women supported by men were "parasites" and anyway she was growing more and more interested in nursing. What she really wanted to do was train properly. Surprisingly, since he was so possessive, Ed agreed that she should go to his native country and train in Vienna. He liked the idea of her sharing his heritage and he was "willing to let me go knowing it was for my own good." In August 1895, Emma sailed for Europe feeling "rich" because she had "experience, a name . . . friends . . . the love of a beautiful personality."[33] Only the thought of Sasha in prison spoiled her pleasure at leaving America so much happier than she had arrived ten years before.

She was away a year. In Vienna, she took a course in midwifery as planned and another in children's diseases, earning two good diplomas. She also attended Freud's lectures which fascinated her. Although later she was to say too much weight was given to family inhibitions she found many parts of her own family life were illuminated and she was glad of it. Socially and intellectually Vienna enriched her and she returned to New York reluctantly. Ed met her carrying a bunch of red roses and took her back not to their old flat but to a new one where the rooms were more spacious. He had furnished it with "lovely old mahogany" and put prints on the walls. There was a large kitchen with a big window overlooking a garden. Emma was thrilled because she was now living for the first time in a place that had "atmosphere and taste". Ed made her an elaborate dinner and toasted her return with good wine. He told her he was well-off (but only by anarchist standards) and that they were going to have a wonderful life together now that she was back. Emma, not ungrateful for his efforts, would have liked to believe it, but was suspicious. She now had a proper profession and intended to enter it with dedication and enthusiasm. Not only would she be a working woman, but she was if anything even more zealous in the anarchist cause than she had been before she went to Vienna – every spare minute of her non-working time would be devoted to it. Did Ed know what he was welcoming back?

Time quickly showed that nothing had changed. He might continue to say he did not want to get in the way of anything she wanted to do but in fact he was intensely jealous of all the hours she spent away from him, treating with equal contempt her work as a midwife (bringing all these "unwanted, squalling brats into the world") and as a leading anarchist agitator. He accused her of having "no thought for anything else – your love has no thought of me or my needs . . . you are simply incapable of deep feeling . . . you will have to choose."[34] Emma had heard those words before. Men, it seemed, were obsessed with dictating choices to women, choices they never saw themselves as needing to make. "It is me or work," men said. Which women ever said the same and did not expect to be ridiculed?

When Emma refused to choose, Ed stormed out of the flat. Left alone, Emma struggled with conflicting emotions. She saw perfectly clearly how Ed was trying to make her feel guilty and she rejected completely his rationale, but at the same time she missed him. A life of work *was* barren – worthy, certainly using her many talents to the full, but barren. There seemed no point in all her daily labours if at the end of them there was no Ed. It was not just that she craved him physically (although she did) but that she had a great emotional hunger that only he could satisfy. It seemed to her that learning to do without Ed was a pointless sacrifice, so she took the extraordinarily humiliating step of writing to him begging him to return. He came, and they had a joyful reunion. In the following weeks Emma tried to achieve a new balance in her life. She cut out some of her evening meetings and spent the time at home with Ed. In a way, this did help but the trouble was that it did not help enough. The more she gave Ed, the more he wanted. She was heavily involved at the time in birth control work but her commitment to this particular cause was limited by Ed's increasing monopoly of her leisure. What was even more disastrous for her own self-esteem was the way in which worrying about Ed's resentment spoiled her concentration. He had no faith in the value of her work so she began to doubt herself. The strain of fighting his disapproval produced "strange nervous attacks" during which she would fall to the ground, not unconscious but suffering from some sort of temporary paralysis. Ed triumphantly diagnosed overwork. He told her he wanted to care for her, that if she stayed at home and gave in to being a woman for a change he would soon restore her to health.

For a while, because she felt so weak, Emma tried to do things Ed's way. She stayed at home – no work, no anarchist activities. The weeks slipped by "happy and peaceful". Ed went out to work every day and when he came back there she was, rested, ready to be kissed and cosseted. They read together (Racine, Molière, Corneille) went to concerts (their favourite composers were Wagner, and Beethoven) and took trips into the country. It could, Emma reflected, go on forever. It was an easy life, she wasn't in the least bored. Then one day they had an argument about Nietzsche whose philosophy meant a great deal to her. Ed thought Nietzsche was a fool. As the argument grew more heated Ed suddenly drew back and begged her to stop. There was no point in spoiling their happiness by a silly row over Nietzsche. "It isn't Nietzsche it is you," Emma burst out. "Under the pretext of a great love you have done your utmost to chain me to you, to rob me of all that is precious to me in life. You are not content to bind my body, you want also to bind my spirit! First the movement and my friends – now it is the books I love . . . You are going to clip my wings . . . I'll free myself even if it means tearing you out of my heart."[35] Ed was devastated. He did not even try to reply.

Next day, knowing her love was now "like a cracked bell", Emma rushed off to Philadephia to make a speech again and to begin lecturing. Her lectures, to her distress, somehow lacked inspiration but she kept going, to Washington, Pittsburgh and Detroit, where a long, loving letter from Ed awaited her. After that, still feeling disorientated and upset, she went on to Rochester where her father was dying (Helena had sent her a telegram earlier to which she had replied HE SHOULD HAVE DIED LONG AGO). Now, seeing him so old and ill, she felt compassion for him too. He had been the first of many men who had tried to dominate her and to make her conform to his idea of the feminine stereotype and she had truly hated him for it, but now she saw him as someone to be pitied, just "one of the mass of the exploited and enslaved for whom I was living and working."[36] When she returned to New York she took her brother Yegor with her. Both of them were welcomed by Ed as though nothing had happened.

But of course it had. Emma had made the "choice" which Ed had imposed upon her. She had chosen to follow the dictates of her own conscience, to reject her soft life as the little woman at home. She had made her bid for freedom and was never again to be sucked into the domestic cocoon. Very soon she was off on another speaking tour, this time to California. In San Francisco she had a strange experience, highly relevant then to her troubled thoughts on how women were treated by men. A "Mr V." offered to be her manager. Because he was "a fine Jewish type" and "a likeable person" she accepted. He reserved a luxurious room in the best hotel for her and when she entered it there were roses to greet her. There was also a black velvet dress. "Is this going to be a lecture or a wedding?" she asked sarcastically, but she put it on and was pleased at how she looked. The next day, there was another new dress provided for her, this time black chiffon. Emma waited cynically for the catch and sure enough it came. "Mr V.", although assuring her he had been motivated only by the desire to help the cause, declared his passion for her and proposed marriage. He did not in the least object to her working but she must give up her "free love stuff". Emma took great pleasure in telling him that the only love she was interested in was the free variety. In fact, she could think of no other sort that was not a contradiction in terms: *all* real love was free. That was the end of "Mr V".

Once back in New York, Emma continued to live with Ed but uneasily, feeling all the time that she ought to "have it out" with him. Before she could do so, Ed fell dangerously ill with pneumonia. She was terrified he would die and abandoned everything to nurse him back to life. Her relief and gratitude when he did survive were balanced by her horror at the realization that she might have been stupid enough to leave him. Once more, she was back to confronting the ugly truth that she could not pretend work of any kind meant she did not need Ed. She went out to the first meeting she had attended since Ed fell ill feeling she had no right to go. While she was away, the convalescent Ed made what looked like a suicide bid, taking a large dose of morphine from which he was only saved by Emma's prompt action on her return. Unfortunately, he eventually confessed he hadn't intended to kill himself at all, merely to frighten her into stopping her "mania for meetings". The revelation of this cruel attempt at blackmail shocked Emma into once more reassessing her already complex feelings for Ed. She loved him but he was destroying her. She had to get out while she was still capable. So she left him, quickly and without more exhausting discussion.

When next year she met him, a year and a trip to Europe later, he had married and was the proud father of a daughter. He commented that their love had "never been much of a success." This made Emma bitter. "Is love ever?" she managed to reply. It occurred to her that perhaps love with men was a lost cause – they might not understand what love was really about. Perhaps what she needed was the love of her own sex, a friend "to share feelings I could not express to men." But although she had many female friends she never quite found what she was looking for and was never remotely sexually attracted to any female. It seemed her fate was to have unsatisfactory love affairs with men whether she chose to or not.

Emma was by this time (1899) thirty years of age. She felt, after she left Ed, that she had learned everything there was to learn about what part love played in a woman's life but in fact she still had a long way to go. As with Sasha and Johann Most so it was after leaving Ed – she could not do without a lover. Immediately after leaving Ed she had "an exhilarating companionship" with an anarchist called Max Baginski. He left her for another woman and she was extremely hurt – "I laughed aloud at the folly of my hopes. After the failure with Ed how could I have dreamed of love and understanding with anyone else? . . . I felt robbed by life, defeated in my yearning for a beautiful relationship."[37] During her second trip to Europe (from November 1899 to the summer of 1900), she had a violent argument with Peter Kropotkin about women and sex in which she tried to rationalize her own feelings. Kropotkin's view was that equality had nothing to do with gender. When women became men's intellectual equals, through at last sharing their much privileged education and training, and when they also began to share men's ideals instead of being content with the domestic ones imposed upon them by circumstances, then they would be free. He did not believe women's sex made them intrinsically different. Emma disagreed. She maintained this was faulty thinking on the part of both feminists and socialists. Sex was a problem which no amount of equality would alter. In sexual relations women could not be made equal. Although she called the idea that women need love more than men "a stupid romantic notion, conceived to keep her ever dependent on the male"[38] she nevertheless thought women were affected differently by sex and that this had to be allowed for in any vision of true emancipation. For herself, she had decided to make an attempt to "live and work without love."

It was an attempt that failed. By trying to live without love Emma discovered that she became only half a person and that even that half person was stunted and diminished by this enforced deprivation. She was intensely miserable after her second European visit. Partly this was due to being suspected of provoking the assassination of President McKinley on 6th September, 1901. The young man who committed the crime had attended one of her meetings and though Emma had done no more than shake hands with him she was hounded by the police and press as being party to the assassination. Her innocence was established but her depression at the treatment meted out to her deepened into a more serious and lasting disillusionment with the anarchist movement itself. Many of its adherents, she wrote, filled her with loathing. They bore no resemblance to herself and Sasha and all the other hopeful, inspired East Side Radicals of ten years ago. So she effectively dropped out. She lived incognito as Miss E. G. Smith in a flat on 1st Street which she shared with her brother Yegor. Her days were spent as a semi-recluse. She did some nursing to support herself but otherwise she stayed at home, abiding by her self-imposed rule that love should be cut out of her life in all its many forms. Love, anyway, "seemed a farce in a world of hate."

She was rescued from this existence by a young friend of Yegor's called Dan. Dan was nineteen, "naïve and unspoiled." He said he didn't care for young girls. His "pleading voice" was like music to Emma's ears which suddenly opened once more to "the seductive whisperings of love." She and Dan became lovers and she at once felt alive. She came out of her seclusion and with a return of her former energy and vitality joined in the anarchist action yet again. Her lesson had been learned: no matter how painful and difficult, love and sex were essential to her and she would never again be ashamed of this or try to pervert her own nature. She still had not found the way to absorb her emotional needs into the framework of her life without wrecking it but she was now dedicated to doing so. There must, surely, be a way of finding total self-fulfilment.

Ironically, just as she had recovered her equilibrium, everything she had resolved was threatened by the reappearance of Ed Brady. He came to see her and confessed he had made a mistake – he, too, had underestimated the force of real love. He now recognized that he and Emma *had* known real love and that his marriage had been a sham, not based on love at all. He was bitterly sorry for the pain he had caused her. On Christmas Eve 1901 he showered her with presents – "a wonderful coat with a real astrakhan collar, muff and turban to match . . . a dress, silk underwear . . . stockings and gloves." Emma dolled herself up in this finery and Ed exclaimed, "That's the way I have always wanted you to look." Seeing her expression change he added, "Some day everybody may be able to have beautiful things like these"[39] but he had missed the point. It was not so much the economics of the gifts which worried Emma as the implication that the way he wanted her to look was feminine in the accepted sense and that what went with that was the same old desire to constrain her as a person. But their affair was resumed even though this time Emma made no concessions about work. She was deep in birth control lecturing and she kept it up.

In the spring, Ed said he was leaving his wife and running away with his daughter to Europe. Would she come with him? Emma said she would certainly go with him but not if he took the child. She would not have another woman robbed of her child on her account. Ed accused her of being "like all feminists who rail against man for the wrongs he supposedly does to woman without seeing the injustices that the man suffers."[40] He adored his daughter, she was much more precious to him than to his wife and he would give her a far better life. All Emma was doing was reasoning subjectively "like a woman". But Emma stood fast, even though she had always believed the act of physically bearing a child did not necessarily make a woman a "true" mother. Motherhood was more subtle than that, to do with caring and responding. She would even be prepared to admit that theoretically a man could "mother" as well as a woman. Yet in the case of Ed she felt an instinctive revulsion to being party to what he proposed. She was frightened that her uncharacteristic display of female solidarity for the sake of it would scare Ed off but it did not. His constant visits went on being "beautiful Events". Then in April 1902 Ed died with brutal suddenness of a heart attack. Emma's shattering grief was tinged with guilt. She felt that if she had given in to love and put it first and gone off with Ed to start a new life together he might not have died. Her confidence in her new philosophy – that love should be listened to but not allowed to dominate everything else – was shaken. She saw herself as having "this hunger for love" but "an inability to hold it for long". Something always went wrong, her life was always being wrecked by personal disasters.

The antidote for remorse was, as ever, work. There was nothing to stop her giving all her time to it and she did. Her niece Stella, Lena's daughter, came to live with her, and Emma gave up nursing in order to run her own beauty parlour, specializing in head-and-neck massage, on Broadway. It was her clients there who were the ones that aroused her compassion for the "emancipated" woman and made her begin to formulate the thoughts which were eventually expressed in her essays. What she realized she wanted to do was not only try to live her life as she wanted to, and not as society dictated, but also to help other women do so. This was what brought her to the idea of starting a magazine specifically feminist as well as anarchist in content which she could use as a platform. It was to be "not just a venture but an adventure".[41] The money for what she referred to as her "child" came from a Russian actor she had helped. She called it *Mother Earth*. The first issue came out in March 1906 carrying the motto "The Earth free for the free individual". Right from this issue an uncompromising feminist tone ran through the magazine reflected in almost every article, story and poem. No. 6 for example carried an attack on modesty – "let us go on in the good old modest way, sick and ailing all our lives but not sacrificing one shred of the precious conventions that we have collected about us at such a terrible cost, let us live maimed, deformed, decrepit ignorant half-sexed caricatures of women – but let us be modest." No. 5 had a stirring tale about the dangers of subscribing to what the world called morality entitled "In the Tread-mill" and Emma herself wrote strong pieces on prostitution and related topics in almost every issue. Anthony Comstock, that guardian of American morals, was a constant target for jokes and ridicule.

Within six months, *Mother Earth* had established itself as a leading voice among feminist agitators even though many of Emma's ideas ran counter to prevailing attitudes in the feminist "movement" as a whole. At that time, many feminists thought it essential to shut men out if women were to make any real progress – men were enemies, even the sympathetic ones. Emma rejected this. She agreed there was a great deal wrong with the male sex as a whole but her vision of a better future for women included a better relationship with men. She saw no future in a state of hostility between the sexes. Nor did she like the notion that feminist and feminine were contradictory. Just as she hated anarchism being thought of as excessively puritanical so she hated feminism being branded as equally rigid. She saw nothing wrong in frivolity and even acknowledged the importance of making yourself as beautiful as you wished. "Physical attraction always has been and no doubt always will be a decisive factor in the love life of two persons,"[42] she once wrote. This being so, the power of beauty should not be denied and women ought not to be taught that making the most of their beauty was in any way letting themselves down as feminists. Similarly, having fun was not anti-feminist. She herself held regular *Mother Earth* parties at which she danced with great abandon (even inventing a dance called the Anarchist Slide). Women, she warned, were simply going to be alienated if feminism became equated with joylessness. What feminism was about was self-fulfilment *as a woman* not as some kind of neutered species. She would not go along with the so-called radical feminists of her day who were busy trying to get women to reject the traditional role as wives and mothers, nor with the woman's rights feminists who accepted woman's basic position in society so long as it was better safeguarded. Her own feminism, which first found public expression in *Mother Earth,* was original. She was determined to acknowledge the differences in being female and find a way that these could be retained without making of woman a subordinate creature.

All the time she was working on *Mother Earth* Emma was looking towards an important event: the release of Sasha from his long imprisonment. She had never stopped writing to him and campaigning for his release and she knew she still loved him in spite of all the years which had passed. But Sasha coming back into her life was also an ordeal she dreaded. He would not be the same, she was not the same, the world was not the same. Another challenge to love was undoubtedly going to be issued. In May 1906 Sasha came out and Emma faced him. Of the two of them, Sasha had the greater shock. He himself was grey, pitifully thin, old-looking and exhausted but then that was how it had been expected he would look after fourteen years in prison. The change in Emma was unexpected. She was self-assured and authoritative. She was a mature woman and not his "little sailor girl" looking to him for advice. Things could never again be the same between them. Sasha had had no other woman in his life, obviously, and Emma had had several lovers. Strangely, it was Emma who no longer had any sex appeal for Sasha, not the reverse – "whatever physical appeal I had for you before you went into prison was dead when you came out"[43] she alleged years later. But even more distressing than the realization that although they still loved each other they were no longer *in* love was the embarrassing fact that Sasha no longer occupied a central position in the anarchist movement as Emma now did. He could not return to his old position because it did not exist. The group to which he had belonged was broken up. He was, of course, a hero to most anarchists but not a hero with a role clearly defined. The strains and stresses of becoming aware of all this produced a nervous collapse which Emma feared at one point might end in suicide. It was to help Sasha that in 1908 she made him editor of *Mother Earth.* She hoped that having a proper job would help him reorientate himself.

To a large extent her hope was fulfilled. Sasha changed the balance of _Mother Earth_ into being more anarchist than feminist and in the process once more became involved in quite an important way in the direction of the movement. It was just as well because Emma was moving away from him personally and he would have found her new love affair hard to tolerate without the security his editorship gave him – to have been drifting and feeling unwanted just as Emma began her most passionate love affair yet would have finally wrecked any chance of rehabilitation. As it was, Sasha still found the new lover difficult to endure as did all Emma's friends.

He was called Ben Reitman, known as Chicago's King of the Hobos, and Emma met him when he helped her organize a meeting in his town against great opposition. She was immediately attracted to him but most people found him repulsive. He was described by her as "a tall man with a finely shaped head covered with a mass of black curly hair which had evidently not been washed for some time. His eyes were brown, large and dreamy. His lips, disclosing beautiful teeth when he smiled, were full and passionate. He looked a handsome brute . . ."[44] The appeal this character had for Emma was so strong that she was unable to sleep. His sexual attraction overwhelmed her – she was "caught in the torrent of an elemental passion I had never dreamed any man could rouse in me."[45] Yet she did not approve of Ben as she had of Sasha, Most and Ed Brady. He was an intellectual light-weight, and even worse what she had always called contemptuously "one of those reformers of social evils" for whom no anarchist could have any time.

Born in 1879, and therefore ten years younger than herself, he had an exotic background quite unlike that of any other man with whom she had had a love affair. His family came from Galicia in Poland (then Russia) in 1877. As soon as Ben was born, his father, a pedlar, deserted his mother and Ben by eight years of age was virtually fending for himself. At eleven, he finally ran away and became a vagabond until he was twenty when he got a job as caretaker in a hospital. Here he was befriended by some doctors who encouraged him to believe he could enter medical school himself. This he did and duly qualified (although Sasha always doubted it and sneered at the "Dr" Ben put in front of his name). He became a personality in Chicago not only because of the flamboyant way he dressed – "with a large black cowboy hat, flowing silk tie and huge cane" – but for the way he made himself champion of the unemployed whom he led around the city in large and slightly menacing gangs. Ben solemnly defined his problem as "what the psychologists call Immediacy – I just got to do things fast."[46] He suffered, he said, from "weakness of the body, an inferiority complex, and unmanageable balls."[47] Perhaps it was this brutal honesty which made Emma love him in spite of the fact that she said, "my reason repudiated the man but my heart cried out for him." Apart from sex the truth was they had not a thing in common.

The alliance between the King of the Hobos and the Queen of the Anarchists naturally caused a sensation. Margaret Anderson who edited the influential *Little Review* said "the fantastic Ben R . . . wasn't so bad if you could hastily drop all your ideas as to how human beings should look and act." (Ben, when he heard of this, was very hurt, maintaining Margaret Anderson had always been friendly). Sasha was shocked and disgusted and never missed an opportunity to expose Ben's worthlessness. His intellectual crudity and social naïvety jarred on everyone's nerves and his endless boasting about his pathetic exploits was nauseating. He talked sheer nonsense half the time and had not the faintest understanding of what anarchism stood for. Even worse, he was a liar and a cheat and had hordes of camp followers without a principle between them. Yet Emma, aged almost forty, had taken him as her lover. It seemed scarcely credible. What made her infatuation even harder to comprehend was that she was not blind to Ben's many faults. She admitted all the allegations made against him were true. He lacked true social feeling, had no rebel spirit (beyond a schoolboy desire to cause mischief) and embarrassed her with his "love of swagger". But she loved him. He was, she said, "the first man who would love the woman in me and yet who would also be able to share my work."[48] The way he shared it was to become her superbly effective and efficient manager. He went with her on tour and under his adroit handling of publicity her audiences greatly increased and arrangements went more smoothly. In the autumn of 1908 after she met Ben, Emma visited thirty-seven cities in twenty-five states and spoke in universities for the first time. Her lectures, especially on morality, went down well. Ben looked after her tenderly as well as master-minding the tour and she found herself more relaxed than she had ever been in her life. Sasha might ask what the awful Ben knew about anarchism but she had faith that in time he would learn and meanwhile his contribution to the movement was practical and solid. Furthermore, for the first time she found herself the dominant partner. Ben shared *her* work: the difference was vital.

By this time, Emma was an important figure in America. Everyone had heard of her even if they were not quite sure what they had heard. In 1910 she consolidated her position as a leading anarchist and feminist with the publication of a book of essays, *Anarchism and Other Essays*. This made available to a wider public those ideas upon which she had been lecturing for over a decade and established her not just as an agitator but as a thinker of some stature. The feminist content of the essays was considerable, pointing women as they did towards a different sort of equality than that symbolized by the vote and legal rights. Marriage, she said in more than one essay, was women's greatest enemy. It made parasites of women. Women should not enter into such a ruinous legal arrangement but on the other hand they should not hold themselves back from love itself. "I believe," wrote Emma, "when woman signs her own emancipation her first declaration of independence will consist in admiring and loving a man for the qualities of his heart and mind and not for the quantities in his pocket."[49] She wanted women to make such declarations of real, fearless independence and not to repress their natural instincts. Again and again she emphasized the dangers of women being misled into imagining that any part of true feminism must involve antagonism to men. Nor must they imagine that, if they were given an equal share in political power, it was up to them to change the world. To expect them to do so was monstrous. It was "absurd" to think that woman "will accomplish that wherein man has failed."[50] If woman tried to take on this impossible role she would be "wasting her life force." The targets were all wrong: what woman ought to be attacking were conventions and traditions which, "in her exalted conceit," she was not recognizing as much more her enemy than man was. Puritanism was what made woman's life insufferable. The Calvinistic idea of life was her true curse, making her "repudiate every natural impulse." What women must do was to liberate themselves from this stranglehold while at the same time holding onto their femininity.

Emma was pleased with the reception her book received and not at all put out by the disapproval of many feminists. It seemed to her that she ought not to be afraid to draw from her own experience lessons which could be applied generally and which called doubt upon some of the more extreme feminist attitudes. Over the next eight years she was learning the hardest lesson ever taught her by experience which reinforced many of her earlier suspicions about the nature of women. Ben Reitman was her teacher. At first, she was "like a schoolgirl in love for the first time," basking in Ben's adoration and admiration. He thought she was "easily the greatest woman in the world . . . you've got a great brain and soul and remarkable courage and Jesus what a wonderful lover . . ."[51] Gradually, he began to behave more naturally with her friends and it was grudgingly admitted by them that at least he was a hard worker and that he was prepared to suffer for the cause even if he still did not wholly embrace it. (Once, in San Diego, he was tarred and feathered and badly beaten by vigilantes who had gathered to stop Emma speaking, and on several other occasions he fought off those who tried to attack her with convincing determination.) Nobody doubted any longer that whatever existed between Ben Reitman and Emma Goldman could not be described as a passing emotion. But then it was noticed that Ben was also having other women without telling Emma.

Eventually, she found out and was more devastated by his deliberate deceit, which ran counter to all anarchist principles, than by the affairs themselves. Ben swore none of them meant anything to him, that he could not help it, that he hadn't even known the names of those with whom he had had brief liaisons. But the lies went on – silly lies about where he had been or how he had financed his secret trips. Emma wrote that when she discovered the full extent of his duplicity the "depths of my woman's soul" were appalled. She found her feelings slowly changing. By "free" love she had not meant this, by giving herself fearlessly without need of marriage she had not expected to be betrayed. She pondered long and hard on this feeling of betrayal, wondering what new aspect of love she had now humiliatingly learned. It seemed that love did not work unless the love given and received was the same on both sides.

Though they carried on as before, after each showdown over other women, she saw now that Ben "did not really live in his work or in our love." They rented a large house together on East 119th Street, with a basement big enough to house the *Mother Earth* office, and took on a housekeeper and a secretary. Ben's mother also moved in with them, which precipitated the breakdown of their now shaky relationship. Emma became bored with Ben's ridiculous mother complex. One day "something snapped" in her and she picked up a chair, threw it at Ben, and ordered both him and his wretched mother out of her house. Though he moved out, he still came each day to work with her; but then he met a girl with whom he had an affair and began to develop "a conscious feeling for fatherhood." The time had come for Emma to put an end to what was rapidly disintegrating into a farce – what she called "the height of tragi-comedy." She brought down the curtain in 1916, leaving herself feeling "lonely and unutterably sad."

But there was still Sasha in the background, as close as ever to her. She felt she had crushed him, but now turned to him. If her connection with Ben had been "mainly erotic", as she put it, that with Sasha was both cerebral and emotional – their lives, she never doubted, were "inextricably entwined" even if each of them became involved with others. After news of the Russian Revolution they began to work together closely again, touring America and speaking out on behalf of the revolutionaries and explaining the significance of their struggle. They also organized a No-Conscription league when America entered the First World War and for this both of them were arrested, tried and imprisoned in the summer of 1917.

Soon after their release they were deported. On December 21st they were despatched on the *Buford* to Finland from where they travelled under military guard to Russia. At first, it was exhilarating to be home, although right from her arrival Emma felt "an undercurrent of uneasiness". She saw too many glaring contradictions around, too much fuss about permits, too much evidence that cities like Moscow were nothing more than armed camps. The awful hunger and the brutal treatment of the poor begging in the streets distressed her. People tried to convince her that she had become "a pampered bourgeoisie [*sic*]." They told her "grey, dull spots" were inevitable at first and she must start working to help to eradicate them. She had interviews with Lenin and Alexandra Kollontai and then set about nursing, establishing camps for deportees, and finally collecting archive material for a Museum of the Revolution. This meant touring the whole vast country and brought her to what she called her Calvary. She determined to leave Russia and speak out against the terrible perversion of a wonderful idea. The old, cruel régime had simply, in her opinion, been replaced by a new, equally cruel one.

In December 1921 she and Sasha managed to get a visa for Lithuania. From there they went to Estonia and then by boat, on January 2nd, 1922, to Sweden, and finally to Germany. There, she managed to extend her visa long enough to write *My Two Years in Russia* about her disillusionment; but she was restless and longing to return to America. Absence had made her heart grow very fond indeed but she could not return. Instead she went to England (in 1924) where she was unhappy. The English were not like the Americans. In spite of the warm friendship of Rebecca West she was miserable. The weather, the lack of any real anarchist movement and the apparent impossibility of earning her living depressed her. All England gave her that she valued was a new passport. Joseph Colton, a staunch Scottish anarchist whom she had met in the 1890s, married her to provide her with one. She used it to go to Canada, hoping to smuggle herself into America from there, but failed in her attempt.

Meanwhile, her many friends had raised enough money to buy a cottage (Bon Esprit) among the vineyards on the hills above St Tropez. There she wrote her magnificent memoirs. Yet her active life was still not over. She toured Germany in the early 1930s, denouncing Hitler and the Nazis, and then during the Spanish Civil War she was invited to Barcelona. At sixty-seven she endured the daily bombardment of that city side by side with her comrades for seven weeks before going to London and then Canada to enlist support. On 14th May, 1940 she died there after a stroke. Her dead body was allowed back into America where she was buried in Chicago near the graves of those anarchists whose deaths had inspired her.

★   ★   ★

Sasha always said of Emma that she had "a squelching effect" on other women. She was too strong for them and they felt it, especially younger women. She was dictatorial, outspoken and mercilessly direct. She was not afraid to condemn women harshly and would not tolerate uncritical solidarity. Once she had lost her youthful plump blond prettiness and become a stout, squat figure, careless in appearance, she was an unattractive character to meet. Other women understandably were frightened of her. Her chain-smoking, apparent lack of any attention to her dress and her rather grim expression made her seem formidable. They also made her seem unfeminine, and yet she was deeply feminine and made the defence of femininity one of her basic aims. But, although she acknowledged the importance of staying attractive, she rejected the notion that femininity depended upon it. She criticized Margaret Anderson for looking "chic" and Alexandra Kollontai for having "such beautiful clothes." Femininity, she felt, was an emotional quality, an internal state unaffected by external disguises. And yet she herself fretted about those external manifestations even when she was old. When she was in her sixties she wrote to a friend in London asking her to send "a sweater coat of very fine wool either mauve or beige with some coloured border, collar and cuffs. I look so sombre in plain colours, I must have some gay strain in it."[52] She didn't want light blue whatever happened because she said it made her look awful. Another time she requested "nice soft ruching for the wrists of my black dress." It was not in fact true that she despised clothes and other frivolities as much as she appeared to.

What she did despise wholeheartedly was any inhibitions about sex. Sex was overwhelmingly important in her life and led her to query the nature of her own femaleness. She was quite, quite sure that sex affected women in a way it did not affect men. After Ben Reitman her sex life was by no means over. In Sweden, she took a young lover called Arthur Swenson, thirty to her fifty-three, who accompanied her to Germany before telling her she did not attract him any more. Then in 1934, when she was sixty-five, she had an extraordinary affair with Frank Heiner, a young, blind American osteopath. Frank, she wrote to her niece Stella, was all she had ever longed for – "primitiveness, tenderness, a complete harmonious blending of intellect, spirit and body . . . the capacity for supreme passion and the tenderness of a child."[53] She was decidedly not, she wrote, "an old fool in love." Frank had given her what love had never given her before – "it is strange, isn't it dearest, that at sixty-five I should wake up to the realisation that with all the men I have known intimately my love has never been fulfilled." His letters made her weep – "In your lips, in your breasts, in the sweet maddening intimate ecstasy of you all the anxiety, all the sordidness of the world vanishes and the golden age of legend is once more. My own precious woman, dearest Emma, I love you."[54] But Frank was married and they had only a brief two weeks alone together – Emma could not bring herself to wreck his marriage. She cared nothing for what she knew would be the sniggers of the world at large, a world which thought it acceptable for an elderly man to have a young mistress but disgusting and ludicrous for an elderly woman to have a young lover. But Frank's wife loved him, too, and there was his future to think about, so they parted. She regarded the affair with him as the highlight of her life and rather scorned Sasha for *his* last love affair with Emmy Eckstein. By comparison, it was nothing. Emmy was a Hausfrau type, obsessed with getting Sasha to marry her if she could. "What I need in life is affection," she wrote plaintively to Emma, and even more strangely, "I would not want Sasha at all if you were not in his life."[55] What did either of them know about love, or even sex? "It seems to be my fate," commented Emma bitterly, "to prepare my lovers for other women and then act as confidante of the women."[56]

But she never regretted any of her love affairs. They had shown her secrets about herself she would never have learned otherwise. "Sex is like a double-edged sword," she wrote, "it releases our spirit and binds it with a thousand threads, it raises us to sublime heights and thrusts us into lowest depths."[57] For a woman it was more important than for a man because "it creates a greater storm in her being and lingers on when the man is satisfied and at ease."[58] As well as sexual fulfilment women needed with it affection, devotion and tenderness and as they aged they needed it even more. This was where nature, that old enemy of feminism, was cruel to them, making them far less likely to attract what they needed than men. What she called "a new medium" had not yet been devised to deal with this. There was "a longing for fulfilment" in love as in all other spheres and it could not yet be realized. "The modern woman cannot be the wife and mother in the old sense, and the new medium has not yet been devised, I mean the way of being wife, mother, friend and yet retain one's complete freedom. Will it ever?"[59] Her own experiences had led her to doubt it though not in the end to regret the existence of "modern" woman.

She never intended her searing criticisms to be interpreted as meaning she did not think anything worthwhile had been gained. She was proud of modern women, especially the American variety. "The fact is," she wrote in 1929, "the only woman who stands out today as an entity is the American woman, not only in her independence but in her eagerness to assert herself in creative forms . . . Granted that the modern American woman is running after effects – that does not seem to me any reason why she should swing back to the days of half a century ago when women lived and died in the kitchen and behind the washtub."[60] In short, Emma Goldman had faith. "I confess I prefer the modern woman," she wrote, "the modern mother too . . . she knows that the child is not brought into the world for her pleasure . . . she knows that in order to be of any help to her child she herself must grow and develop – to give her own life purpose and meaning."[61] However much she berated "so called emancipation" she also praised it. "I do insist," she wrote, "that there is in America a large minority of women, advanced women if you please, who will fight to the last drop of their blood for the gains which they have made, physical and intellectual, and for their rights to equality with the man."[62] All she asked them to do was beware the direction they took: she wanted feminism to stop and consider what was being lost as well as what was being gained and in the process to decide to preserve those differences between men and women which were valuable and unharmful.

Emma Goldman re-orientated feminist ideology. In her own life she tried to combine her anarchism and her belief in sexual liberation and it was through achieving this difficult combination that she was able to point women in a new direction. But for a long time her voice was not heeded. In the 1930s, and for three decades afterwards, feminism appeared to languish, resting on its laurels. When it emerged again in the late sixties it was to concern itself with that "true emancipation" Emma Goldman had envisaged. It was the soul that was now fought for, just as she had predicted. In the first big public demonstration of the "new" Woman's Liberation movement in New York on August 26th, 1970 a group calling itself the Emma Goldman Brigade marched down Fifth Avenue with a banner bearing her name and as they marched they chanted, "Emma said it in 1910/Now we're going to say it again . . ." What they said was what she had said in her speeches and essays. The link was direct and proclaimed as direct yet the world at large acted as if it were new, as if feminism had only just been discovered, as if it had no history, as if nothing had already been achieved. "There is only one thing that is stronger than armies," said Victor Hugo, "and that is an idea whose time has come." Emma Goldman quoted this in the fourth issue of *Mother Earth*. She thought then the time for women to liberate themselves from themselves had come. The marchers in 1970 thought it again. Some of the feminists of today are afraid it will still be necessary in the future for yet another generation to repeat what has gone before. Feminism seems to progress only by a method of two steps forward, one step backwards. "I hold," wrote Alexander Berkman in 1919, "that ultimately it's the ideal that conquers and having conquered it mounts to still higher and further visions. As to the individual – he is the stepping stone of man's progress . . ."[63]

So is the woman to woman's. Caroline Norton, Elizabeth Blackwell, Florence Nightingale, Emily Davies, Josephine Butler, Elizabeth Cady Stanton, Margaret Sanger and Emma Goldman were stepping-stones too important for any water, especially the brackish water of ignorance, to wash away. Without them, feminism would have been nothing.

Conclusion

What the history of feminism has always appeared to lack is continuity and also development. The tendency in the 1970s was to imply that no matter how heroic the struggles of the nineteenth-century pioneers had been, and no matter how much these struggles *appeared* to have achieved, nothing had really changed. This conclusion was both stupid and inaccurate. The study of active feminism shows clearly that there has been a continuous if not easily identified development which has succeeded in substantially redressing the balance between the sexes. It is quite absurd to maintain that women are as grossly disadvantaged in the western world as they were at the beginning of the nineteenth century. They are not. On the contrary, in historic terms the changes in women's status in society has been both violent and swift. It would be a salutary experience for those who sneer that a century and a half of strenuous effort has made no real difference to compare, say, Barbara Bodichon's list of laws regarding women with any contemporary list. What, *by comparison*, have women now to complain of?

The short answer would seem to be: themselves. The women in this book changed lives for future generations of women dramatically. What they could not change was how women themselves approached their own problem (because not even the most ardent feminist would deny a problem remains and that its existence is not entirely due to men). At first, the obsession was with justice. Women "only" wanted men to admit they were penalized in the existing social system and to put it right. But Caroline Norton and the many like her proved naïve. Justice, after all, was not enough. It was no good asking men to protect and look after women if, in all essentials, their role remained as subordinate. Women, however cherished and safeguarded by "rights" in law, were always going to remain stunted beings if they had to conform to the feminine stereotype of that era. Justice must surely give way to choice or there was no real justice at all.

When Elizabeth Blackwell and Florence Nightingale claimed the right to do real work instead of staying within the proscribed domestic sphere they took feminism onto a new stage. It was no wonder that feminism then seemed exciting – the possibilities before girls were suddenly thrilling. If they wished, there was a respectable and attainable alternative to marriage and motherhood (or to penurious servitude for the legions of unfortunate spinsters). Not all girls could, or would, choose careers but those who did no longer believed their lives were poorer. There was something noble about actually *choosing* not to marry or have children. Instead, one dedicated one's life to others. This was no philanthropic drudgery: one used one's talents and got paid for doing so and this added up to making a career which was highly satisfying. But it was also dangerous. There was no doubt that, from the mid-nineteenth century onwards, feminism was asking for and getting martyrs. The traditional path of marriage and motherhood began to look soft – how much better to take the hard road, to choose a worthwhile career, than to succumb to the desires of the flesh and the luxury of materialistic security. Choice, even then, began to look like a trick although it was not until the twentieth century that the full extent of the trickery became evident.

This was the point in its historical development at which feminism approached its most dangerous corner. Feminists had done with the quest for justice and then the demand for choice. By the third quarter of the nineteenth century they had realized that the entire role of women needed reappraisal and with it the very concept of femaleness. They saw that the old stereotype had indeed gone, or at least been seriously undermined, but that in its place was – what? With the new rights and privileges came new responsibilities which in turn created a very confused image of how a woman saw herself. If she no longer claimed to be purer, feebler, more delicate and modest than her male counterpart where did that leave her? There was the fear that a great deal that was valuable had been lost through the gaining of so-called emancipation. Margaret Sanger tried to convince women that actually, through birth control, they were now for the first time stronger than men. But women did not feel strong. On the contrary, in the first quarter of the twentieth century they felt particularly vulnerable.

Instead of less being expected of them they found twice as much was. They were glad to be educated, to have careers, to keep their own earnings, to vote, to control their own bodies but for most of them the result of all this was not salvation but exhaustion. The promised land may have been reached but only for them to work twice as hard in it. Was this what feminism had intended? Was this the desired destination towards which the women in this book, those who initiated radical change, had been travelling for so long? And if not, what had gone wrong?

Nothing. What the nineteenth- and early twentieth-century active feminists had done was forge all the right keys to woman's genuine emancipation. They had fitted them to the appropriate locks and turned them successfully, if with difficulty. But what they had failed to do was make sure all the now opened gates were used – and therein lies the basic difficulty still confronting feminism. "The woman is greater than the wife or mother; and in consenting to take upon herself these relations she should never sacrifice one iota of her individuality . . ." said Elizabeth Cady Stanton. Unfortunately, few women find themselves agreeing. They may *wish* to agree, but come the testing time and the woman is rapidly submerged by the wife and mother sometimes never to reappear. It may be that feminism will always have to face this fact and adapt accordingly. Certainly, there is a great deal which could still be done to make the chances of the woman surviving marriage and motherhood more likely, particularly when it comes to every kind of working-condition. But what the history of feminism shows is that, in spite of this basic and very important difficulty, real progress *has* been made. The challenge is to hold on to it. Women, said Caroline Norton, believe themselves isolated. They are not. They have a joint purpose – never to accept artificial limitations imposed upon them solely through reason of their gender – and a joint investment in the future. Feminism is not something new that sprang up fully armed in the 1970s: it has a long and worthy history. If it were recognized for what it is, a force purely for the good of both men and women, its future would be assured, and the enmity shown towards it might cease.

Appendix

List of publications by

CAROLINE NORTON

1829   *The Sorrows of Rosalie and Other Poems* (John Ebers & Co.)

1830   *The Undying One & Other Poems* (H. Colburn & R. Bentley)

1835   *The Wife, and Woman's Reward.* Two prose tales. (Saunders & Otley)

1836   *A Voice from the Factories.* A poem. (John Murray)

1837   *The Separation of Mother and Child by the Law of Custody of Infants Considered.* A pamphlet. (Ridgway)

1839   *A Plain Letter to the Lord Chancellor on the Infants Custody Bill* by Pearse Stevenson (*nom de plume*). Printed by Ridgway for distribution to MPs.

1840   *The Dream and Other Poems* (Henry Colburn)

1845   *The Child of the Islands* (Chapman and Hall)

1851   *Stuart of Dunleath.* A Novel. (Hurst & Blackett)

1854   *English Laws for Women in the 19th Century* (Privately printed)

1855   *A Letter to the Queen on Lord Cranworth's Marriage and Divorce Bill* (Longman, Brown, Green & Longmans)

1859   *Verses on Burns*

1862   *The Lady of la Garaye.* A Poem (Macmillan)

1863   *Lost and Saved.* A Novel (Hurst & Blackett)

1867   *Old Sir Douglas.* A Novel (Hurst & Blackett)

Caroline Norton also wrote fifty-one songs, most of which are now impossible to trace. Some of her sketches and poems for magazines were published in collections:

1832–4   Poems and Sketches in *The Belle Assemblée and Court Magazine* for 1832–4 (J. Bull)

1845–8   *Fishers Drawing-Room Scrapbook*

1847   *Aunt Carny's Ballads for Children*

Several of her letters to newspapers were also published in a collection:

1848   *Letters to the Mob* (first published in the *Morning Chronicle*)

ELIZABETH BLACKWELL

1852   *The Laws of Life, with Special Reference to the Physical Education of Girls* (Putnam, NY)

1856   *Address on the Medical Education of Woman* (Baker & Duyckinck, NY)

1870   *How to Keep a Household in Health* (Ladies Sanitary Association)
1871   *Lectures on the Laws of Life with Special Reference to Girls* (Samson Low & Co.)
1878   *The Religion of Health* (John Menzies & Co.)
1880   *The Human Element in Sex* (McGowan's Steam Printing Co. Ltd)
         Counsel to Parents on the Moral Education of their Children (Brentano's Literary Emporium, NY)
1881   *Medicine and Morality* (W. Speight & Sons)
         Rescue Work in Relation to Prostitution and Disease: an address (T. Danks)
1882   *Christian Socialism* (D. Williams)
1883   *Wrong and Right Methods of Dealing with Social Evil* (D. Williams)
1887   *Purchase of Women: The Great Economic Blunder* (John Kensit)
1888   *A Medical Address on the Benevolence of Malthus* (T. W. Danks & Co.)
1889   *The Influence of Women in the Profession of Medicine*. An Address (G. Bell & Sons)
1891   *Erroneous Method in Medical Education* (Women's Printing Soc.)
         On the Humane Prevention of Rabies (J. F. Nock)
         Christian Duty in Regard to Vice. A Letter (Moral Reform Union, London)
1892   *Why Hygiene Congresses Fail* (G. Bell & Sons)
1895   *Pioneer Work in Opening the Medical Profession to Women* (Longmans, Green & Co.)
1898   *Scientific Method in Biology* (Elliot Stock)
1899   *Essays in Medical Sociology* (privately printed until 1902 2 vols. Ernest Bell)

Elizabeth Blackwell also wrote numerous articles for magazines on a large variety of subjects some of which were later extracted and printed (for a complete list see Nancy Sahli).

FLORENCE NIGHTINGALE

1851   *The Institution of Kaiserworth on the Rhine for the Practical Training of Deaconesses* (printed by Inmates of the London Ragged Colonial Training School)
1854   *Letters from Egypt* (privately printed)
1858   *Notes on Matters Affecting the Health, Efficiency and Hospital Administration of the British Army* (privately printed by Harrison & Sons)
         Subsidiary Notes as to the Introduction of Female Nursing into Military Hospitals in Peace and War (privately printed by Harrison & Sons)
1859   *A Contribution to the Sanitary History of the British Army During the Late War with Russia* (Harrison & Sons)
         Notes on Hospitals (John W. Parker & Sons)
1860   *Suggestions for Thought to the Searchers after Religious Truth among the Artizans of England* (privately printed in 3 vols by Eyre & Spottiswoode)
         Notes on Nursing: What it is and What it is not (Harrison & Sons)
1862   *Army Sanitary Administration and its Reform under the Late Lord Herbert* (M'Corquodale & Co.)
1863   *Observations on the Evidence Contained in the Stational Reports Submitted to the Royal Commission on the Sanitary State of the Army in India* (Edward Stanford)
1871   *Introductory Notes on Lying-in Institutions. Together with a Proposal for Organising an Institution for Training Midwives and Midwifery Nurses* (Longmans, Green & Co.)
1876   *On Trained Nurses for the Sick Poor* (Metropolitan & National Nursing Association)
1878–82   *Florence Nightingale's Indian Letters* (Ed.) Priyaranjan Sen (not published until 1937)
1872–1900   *Miss Florence Nightingale's Addresses to Probationer Nurses*. Printed for private circulation.

There are also some unpublished proofs on Indian matters in the Nightingale Papers together with various printed statements about voluntary contributions received by Florence Nightingale.

EMILY DAVIES

1860 *★Letters to a Daily Paper, Newcastle-on-Tyne*
1861 *★Report of the Northumberland & Durham Branch of the Society for the Promotion of the Employment of Women*
1862 *★Medicine as a Profession for Women* (Social Science Association)
1863 *★The Influence of University Degrees on the Education of Women*
1864 *★On Secondary Instruction as Relating to Girls* (Social Science Assoc.)
1865 *The Application of Funds to the Education of Girls* (Social Science Assoc.)
1866 *The Higher Education of Women* (Strahan)
      Letters to the Morning Post (Women's Suffrage Leaflet)
1868 *★On the Influence upon Girls' Schools of External Examinations* (The London Student)
      ★Some Account of a Proposed New College for Women (Social Science Assoc.)
1869 *The Training of the Imagination* (First in *Contemporary Review*, then reprinted as a pamphlet)
1878 *★Home and the Higher Education* (Birmingham Higher Education Association)
1896 *★Women in the Universities of England and Scotland* (Macmillan & Bowes)
1897 *Speech at the Conference on University Degrees for Women* (Spottiswoode)
1905 *★The Woman's Suffrage Movement* (Girton Review)
1906 *A Plea for Discrimination* (Woman's Suffrage leaflet)
1907–8 *★Letters to* The Times *and* Spectator *on Women's Suffrage*
1910 *Thoughts on Some Questions Relating to Women* (Bowes & Bowes). (★This brings together all the above asterisked papers.)

There are also articles in the *Englishwoman's Journal* for 1862 and the *Victoria Magazine* for 1863 by Emily Davies.

JOSEPHINE BUTLER

1868 *The Education and Employment of Women* (Macmillan)
1869 *Woman's Work and Woman's Culture* Introduction to (Macmillan)
      Memoir of John Grey of Dilston (Edmonston & Douglas)
1870 *An Appeal to the People of England on the Recognition and Superintendence of Prostitution by Governments* (Banks)
      The Duty of Women (Hudson Scott)
1871 *Sursum Corda* (Brakell)
      The Constitutional Iniquity of the CD Acts (Bradford)
      Vox Populi (Brakell)
      The Constitution Violated (Edmonston & Douglas)
1872 *The New Era* (Brakell)
      A Few Words Addressed to True-Hearted Women (Personal Rights Association)
1874 · *Some Thoughts on the Present Aspect of the Crusade* (Brakell)
1875 *Une Voix dans le Désert* (Sandoz)
1876 *State Regulation of Vice* A Pamphlet
      The Hour Before the Dawn (Trübner)
1877 *The Paris of Regulated Vice* (Methodist Press)
1878 *Catherine of Siena* (Dyer Brothers)
1879 *Government by Police* (Dyer Brothers)
      Social Purity (Morgan & Scott)
      Souvenirs des Réunions à Vevey (Fontaines)

1881   *A Call to Action* (Hudson)
       Letters to the Mothers of England (Brakell)
1882   *Life of J. F. Oberlin* (Religious Tract Society)
1883   *The Salvation Army in Switzerland* (Dyer Brothers)
       Dangers of Constructive Legislation in Matters of Purity (Arrowsmith)
       The Bright Side of the Question (Arrowsmith)
1885   *The Principles of the Abolitionists* (Dyer Brothers)
       The Work of the Federation (Federation Offices)
       Marion, Histoire Véritable (Neuchatel?)
1886   *Rebecca Jarrett* (Morgan & Scott)
1887   *Our Christianity Tested by the Irish Question* (Fisher Unwin)
       The Revival and Extension of the Abolitionist Cause (Doswell)
1892   *Recollections of George Butler* (Arrowsmith)
1893   *St Agnes* (J. Cox)
       The Present Aspect of the Abolitionist Cause in Relation to British India (Federation Offices)
1896   *A Doomed Iniquity* (Federation Offices)
       Personal Reminiscences of a Great Crusade (Horace Marshall)
       Truth Before Everything (Dyer Brothers)
1898   *Some Lessons from Contemporary History* (Friends Assoc.)
       Prophets and Prophetesses (Mawson)
1900   *Native Races and the War* (Gay & Bird)
       Silent Victories (Burfoot)
1901   *In Memoriam Harriet Meuricoffre* (Horace Marshall)
1903   *The Morning Cometh* (Grierson)

In addition there are numerous printed letters and addresses, both in English and French, mainly for the period 1871 to 1882; also contributions to the *Stormbell* and the *Dawn*. These are listed in the Fawcett Society Josephine Butler Collection.

ELIZABETH CADY STANTON

1881   *History of Woman Suffrage* Vol. 1 (Fowell & Wells, New York)
1882   *History of Woman Suffrage* Vol. 2 (Fowell & Wells, NY)
1886   *History of Woman Suffrage* Vol. 3 (Fowell & Wells, NY)
       (all with Susan B. Anthony and Matilda Joslyn Gage)
1898   *Eighty Years and More: Reminiscences 1815–1897* (T. Fisher Unwin London – reprinted 1975, Schocken Books, NY)
1898   *The Woman's Bible* (with the help of a Revising Committee) (reprinted 1978, Coalition Task Force on Women and Religion, Seattle)

These few titles represent all Elizabeth Cady Stanton's work published in book form. Most of her writings took the form of articles or speeches. Extracts from some of these are to be found in *Elizabeth Cady Stanton/Susan B. Anthony – Correspondence, writings and speeches* – edited, with a critical commentary, by Ellen Carol DuBois – Schocken Books, New York, 1981.

A complete list of published articles, speeches, and letters to newspapers and magazines is available from the Manuscript Division of the Library of Congress processed by Audrey Walker in June 1979.

MARGARET SANGER

1914   *What Every Mother Should Know* (Rabelais Press, NY)
       Family Limitation
1915   *Dutch Methods of Birth Control*
       English Methods of Birth Control   pamphlets
       Magnetation Methods of Birth Control

1916   *What Every Girl Should Know* (M. N. Maisel, NY)
1917   *Voluntary Motherhood* (NY National Bookclub League)
1920   *Woman and the New Race* (Brentano's, NY)
1921   *Appeals from American Mothers* (NY Woman's Publishing Co.)
      Sayings of others on Birth Control (NY Woman's Publishing Co.)
1922   *Woman, Morality and Birth Control* (NY Woman's Publishing Co.)
      The Pivot of Civilization (Brentano's, NY)
1924   *Hygienic Methods of Family Limitation* A Pamphlet
1926   *Happiness in Marriage* (Brentano's, NY)
1928   *Motherhood in Bondage* (Brentano's, NY)
1931   *My Fight for Birth Control* (Faber/Farrar Straus, NY)
      The Practice of Contraception (ed. with Hannah M. Stone)
1938   *Margaret Sanger: an Autobiography* (W. W. Norton & Co.) (Reprinted Dover 1971)

There is also a complete (and very long) list of published articles, speeches and letters to newspapers prepared by the Manuscript Division of the Library of Congress (March 1976, Michael J. McElderry).

EMMA GOLDMAN

1911   *Anarchism and Other Essays* (Mother Earth Publishing Association)
1914   *The Social Significance of Modern Drama* (Mother Earth Publishing Association)
1921   *My Disillusionment in Russia* (changed to *My Two Years in Russia*) (Doubleday, Page & Co.)
1922   *Voltairine de Cleyre* (Oriole Press)
1931   *Living My Life* (2 Vols) (Knopf, NY) (reprinted Dover 1970)

Emma Goldman's published books were few. Her main contribution was through essays and articles printed in magazines, newspapers and sometimes as pamphlets. They are not all brought together or listed in any one place. Many of them exist in manuscript form among the enormous, but as yet imperfectly catalogued, Goldman papers in the anarchist section of the International Institute of Social History, Amsterdam.

Notes

The principal sources for this book are the letters, diaries, autobiographies, private papers and writings of the eight women concerned. These are both unpublished and published but even the published books are difficult to locate. Fortunately, the situation is changing all the time due to the immense interest within the last decade shown in the history of feminism. Every month seems to bring the publication, usually by enterprising feminist publishers, of long-lost texts. I have therefore tried, whenever possible, to give page references for these new paperback editions in preference to the original first editions. I have also included, in a separate Appendix, a list of all the books and most of the pamphlets published by the women written about.

Secondary sources are listed in these notes and require no separate bibliography. I have given page references only to letters or documents they contain which are now either unobtainable in the original or difficult of access. Manuscript sources are referred to in greater detail. The government reports are referred to in the text and not usually repeated in these notes.

Introduction

1. There are now as many definitions of the word feminism as there are feminists. Some are quite ludicrous and meaningless. The word "femina" is of course Latin for "woman" but the word "feminism" was first used in France and denoted simply "qualities of woman." In the early and mid-nineteenth century feminism was not used at all to describe any of all the various emerging movements for a fairer position in society for women. The terms used were Woman's Rights, especially in America, and Equal Rights and even the Woman Movement. It was not until the 1890s that the word "feminism" started to appear and quickly came to mean simply anything to do with trying to advance the position of women. It has become a blanket word covering a multitude of meanings, some of them contradictory.

2. There were a few extremely important women who had a firm foot in several camps but were never the acknowledged leaders in any of them. The most obvious example was **Barbara Bodichon** (*née* **Leigh-Smith**) 1827–91, first cousin to Florence Nightingale. She was behind the drive for the Married Women's Property Bill; helped finance the *Englishwoman's Journal*; was Secretary of the Suffrage Committee in 1867; greatly assisted Emily Davies in founding Girton, and in general was both the inspiration and focal point for feminist agitation in England for forty years. But because she kept herself in the background, and also because she spent half the year in Algiers with her French husband, she never became a household name in her own time and is now barely remembered. The other woman who connected together many separate causes was **Harriet Martineau** (1802–76), the journalist and political

economist whose articles in the *London Daily News* from 1852 to '66 were vitally important to feminist propaganda. She supported the Married Women's Property Bill in them, campaigned for employment for women, raged against the Contagious Diseases Acts and backed Higher Education for girls. Her role as mouthpiece for the active feminism of her day was crucial, not least because so few women had available access to the reading public.

Law – Caroline Norton 1808–77

1. *A Letter to the Queen on Lord Cranworth's Marriage & Divorce Bill* (1855).
2. Appendix to above *Letter to the Queen*, etc.
3. *Letter to the Queen*, etc.
4. *Ibid.*
5. *The Separation of Mother and Child by the Law of Custody of Infants Considered* (1837).
6. *The Life of Mrs Norton*, Jane Perkins (pub. John Murray, 1910) p. 149.
7. *Letter to the Queen*, etc.
8. *The Life of Mrs Norton*, Jane Perkins (pub. John Murray, 1910) p. 8.
9. *Letters of Caroline Norton to Lord Melbourne*, ed. James O. Hoge and Clarke Olney (Ohio State Univ. Press 1974) p. 3 (from letters in the University of Georgia Libraries).
10. Perkins p. 12.
11. *Letters of Caroline Norton to Lord Melbourne*, p. 56.
12. *Ibid.* p. 53.
13. *Ibid.* p. 60.
14. Perkins p. 49.
15. *Ibid.* p. 29.
16. *Ibid.* p. 41.
17. *Ibid.*
18. *Ibid.*
19. *Ibid.* p. 46.
20. *Ibid.* p. 31.
21. *Ibid.* p. 154.
22. *The Wife, and Woman's Reward* (1835).
23. Microfilm of Norton correspondence in BM (original possessed by Berg Collection, NY).
24. *Ibid.*
25. Perkins p. 63.
26. *Letters of Caroline Norton to Lord Melbourne* p. 64.
27. Perkins p. 102.
28. *Ibid.* p. 91.
29. *Letters of Caroline Norton to Lord Melbourne* p. 73.
30. *Ibid.* p. 75.
31. *Ibid.* p. 138.
32. *Ibid.* p. 83. (This was exactly the kind of remark that got Caroline into such trouble. She equates herself with Melbourne's wife and mistress making it look as if she too had a sexual relationship, though she did not. Melbourne swore on his deathbed that Mrs Norton had always been innocent and Caroline herself most passionately swore the same even in her most private and intimate correspondence. The "place" she refers to is that of being a loved one – she knew Melbourne had loved her as he had his wife once and Lady Brandon also. "God forgive you," she once wrote, "for I do believe no one, young or old, ever loved another better than I have loved you.")
33. Microfilm BM (letter to her nephew William Cowper).
34. *Ibid.* (1832 letter to Melbourne).

35. Sheridan papers Vol. V: BM Add. MS 42, 767.
36. *Ibid.*
37. *Ibid.* (the emphasis is Caroline Norton's own).
38. *Ibid.*
39. *Ibid.*
40. *Ibid.*
41. *Letters of Caroline Norton to Lord Melbourne* p. 96.
42. Perkins p. 99. .
43. Microfilm BM.
44. *Ibid.*
45. Perkins p. 133.
46. Microfilm BM.
47. Sheridan papers Vol. V. BM Add. MS 42, 767.
48. *Ibid.*
49. *Letters of Caroline Norton to Lord Melbourne* p. 107.
50. *Ibid.* p. 108.
51. *Ibid.* p. 65.
52. *Ibid.* p. 142.
53. Sheridan papers Vol. V. BM Add. MS 42, 767.
54. *Ibid.*
55. *Ibid.*
56. *Ibid.*
57. Perkins p. 146.
58. *Ibid.* p. 109.
59. *Caroline Norton* by Alice Acland (Constable) p. 131.
60. Sheridan papers Vol. V. BM Add. MS 42, 767.
61. *Ibid.*
62. *Ibid.*
63. *Ibid.*
64. *Ibid.*
65. *Ibid.*
66. *Ibid.*
67. *Ibid.*
68. *Ibid.*
69. *Ibid.*
70. *Ibid.*
71. *Letters of Caroline Norton to Lord Melbourne* p. 20.
72. *Stuart of Dunleath* by Caroline Norton (1851), in Dedication to Queen of Netherlands.
73. Peel Papers (312) BM.
74. Perkins p. 144.
75. *Ibid.* p. 230 (also *The Times*, August 19 for account of trial).
76. *Ibid.*
77. Caroline Norton always believed Queen Victoria was sympathetic to her particular plight but the Queen's *known* sentiments on any kind of Woman's Rights were that they were "mad" and when, in 1870, Lady Amberley expressed sympathy with them she said, "Lady Amberley ought to get a *good whipping*." But receiving Caroline at court after the Melbourne trial was taken as a sign that she was at least not hostile. She never replied to Caroline's *Letter to the Queen* but then she was never expected to.
78. Perkins p. 248.
79. Microfilm BM.
80. *Ibid.*
81. *Separation of Mother and Child* etc.

82. *Stuart of Dunleath* Vol. II, p. 102.
83. *Ibid*. p. 76.
84. *Ibid*. p. 31 (Vol. II).
85. Gladstone papers: BM Add. MS 44, 379 (March 27, 1854).

The Professions – Elizabeth Blackwell 1821–1910
  1. *History of Woman Suffrage* (ed. E. Cady Stanton, Susan B. Anthony, Matilda Gage – Vol. 1 – Letter NY May 27th 1852).
  2. *Pioneer Work in Opening of the Medical Profession to Women* – Autobiographical Sketches by Dr Elizabeth Blackwell (pub. 1895 Longmans); Schocken Books 1977 (this edition used) p. 178.
  3. *Ibid*.
  4. *Ibid*.
  5. Nancy Ann Sahli, "Elizabeth Blackwell: A Biography" – PhD Dissertation Univ. of Pennsylvania 1974 (authorized facsimile produced by Univ. Microfilms Ann Arbor, Michigan USA). My debt to this brilliant work is enormous. Sahli's detailed footnotes were an indispensable means of locating Blackwell papers in the Library of Congress, to whom I am also greatly indebted for providing me with photostats.
  6. Sahli p. 9.
  7. Diary of EB March 21st 1837 (photostat LC).
  8. *Ibid*. March 23rd.
  9. *Ibid*. April 5th.
 10. *Ibid*. May 29th.
 11. *Ibid*. July 18th.
 12. *Ibid*. July 7th.
 13. Sahli p. 20.
 14. *Ibid*. p. 21.
 15. *Ibid*. p. 22.
 16. Diary Oct. 10th (photostat LC).
 17. *Ibid*. Dec. 19th.
 18. *Ibid*. Jan. 16, 1839.
 19. *Ibid*. Mar. 9th.
 20. *Ibid*. Feb. 27th.
 21. *Pioneer Work* etc. p. 15.
 22. *Ibid*. p. 18.
 23. *Ibid*. p. 17.
 24. *Ibid*. p. 28.
 25. *Ibid*. p. 27.
 26. *The Lancet* (1873). There is a useful essay ("The Conspicuous Consumptive: Woman as Invalid" by Lorna Duffin) in *The Nineteenth-Century Woman – The Cultural and Physical World* ed. Delamont and Duffin (pub. Croom Helm) which led me to these amazing statements in *The Lancet*.
 27. Sahli p. 48.
 28. *Pioneer Work* etc.
 29. *Bulletin History of Medicine* 1947 Vol. XXI (prints 2 letters and has an article on the subject) Wellcome Institute.
 30. *Pioneer Work* etc. p. 72.
 31. *Ibid*.
 32. *Ibid*. p. 83.
 33. Sahli p. 80.
 34. *Ibid*. p. 83.
 35. *Ibid*. p. 83.

36. *Ibid.* p. 87.
37. *Ibid.* p. 111.
38. *Pioneer Work* etc. p. 197.
39. Sahli p. 123.
40. *Kitty Barry's Reminiscences* (photostat of microfilm LC).
41. *Pioneer Work* etc. p. 198.
42. *K.B.'s Reminiscences.* For Kitty's place in rest of Blackwell family and her relationship with Elizabeth see Sahli, Chapters IV, V and VI.
43. Sahli p. 202. The baby became Sir Henry Paul Harvey, British diplomat and editor of the *Oxford Companion to English Literature.* He arrived at the Blackwell home in 1870 when his parents went abroad.
44. Letter to Mme Bodichon in Fawcett Library, City of London Polytechnic.
45. *Ibid.*
46. *Ibid.*
47. *Ibid.*
48. Sahli p. 168.
49. *Ibid.* p. 200.
50. *Ibid.* pp. 247–8.
51. *Ibid.* p. 90.
52. *Ibid.* p. 288.
53. *Ibid.* p. 448.
54. Address given at opening of winter session of London School of Medicine for Women, London 1889.
55. These are figures for the United Kingdom provided by the General Medical Council from the Register of Medical Practitioners. In the USA 4,970 female students entered medical colleges out of a total of 17,204, which was 28.9% (figures from *Professional Women and Minorities* – A Manpower Data Resource Service, Scientific Manpower Commission, 4th edition, 1983).

Consultancies do not exist in the USA but 10.1% of physicians were female in 1980–81. Interestingly, Pediatrics (27%) was the leading specialist field for women but Obstetrics was well down (11.4%).
56. Letter to Lady Byron, April 1851 (in Wellcome Institute).

Employment – Florence Nightingale 1820–1910
1. Miss Nightingale to Mme Mohl, April 1868 (quoted p. 477 *Florence Nightingale* by Cecil Woodham-Smith, Constable 1950).
2. FN to Sir John McNeill, Feb. 7, 1865 (Nightingale Papers Vol. LIII BM).
3. FN to Harriet Martineau, Nov. 30, '58 (Nightingale Papers Vol. I. Add. MS 45, 788 BM).
4. FN to J. S. Mill, Aug. 11, 1867 (Add. MS 39, 927 BM).
5. *Ibid.*
6. *Ibid.*
7. Appendix to *Notes on Nursing: What it is and What it is not* by FN (1860).
8. FN to Mme Mohl, Dec. 13, 1861 (quoted C. W-Smith p. 385).
9. *Ibid.*
10. *Cassandra:* Vol. II *Suggestions for Thought to Searchers after Religious Truth among the Artizans of England* (3 Vols privately printed 1860). Also printed as Appendix in *The Cause* by Ray Strachey (Virago 1979) – this version used – p. 399.
11. *Ibid.* p. 400.
12. *Ibid.* p. 403.
13. *Ibid.* p. 416.
14. *Ibid.* p. 409.
15. FN – Private Note 1842 (Nightingale Papers – hereafter NP).

16. *Reminiscences – Julia Ward Howe (1819–99)*, (pub. Houghton, Mifflin & Co., NY 1900).
17. C. Woodham-Smith p. 76.
18. FN – Private Note 1842 (NP). I share Cecil Woodham-Smith's interpretation of the reason why FN's handwriting varies so remarkably both in formation of the words (wavering to very strong) and the pressure applied to the pencil. Nobody could doubt the extreme agitation of the writer.
19. *Ibid.*
20. *Ibid.*
21. Cecil Woodham-Smith: *Florence Nightingale* – quoted in letter 1897 p. 91.
22. FN to mother Oct. 8, 1850 (NP Vol. LII. Add. MS 45790).
23. Oct. 25, 31 (*ibid*).
24. FN to mother July 16, 1851 (*ibid*).
25. *Ibid.*
26. *Ibid.*
27. *Ibid.*
28. FN to mother Aug. 31, 1851 (*ibid*).
29. *Ibid.*
30. Private Note 1851 (quoted CW-S p. 93).
31. FN to father Aug. 13, 1853 (quoted CW-S p. 116).
32. FN to father Dec. 3, 1853 (*ibid* p. 121).
33. FN to Sidney Herbert Jan. 4, 1855 (quoted CW-S p. 176).
34. FN to Dr Bowman Nov. 14, 1854 (quoted E. Cook – *The Life of Florence Nightingale* Vol. I p. 185).
35. FN to Sidney Herbert Feb. 1855 (quoted CW-S p. 209).
36. FN to Hilary Bonham Carter Nov. 24, 1871 (Joyce Prince unpublished PhD thesis Univ. of London (1982) "Florence Nightingale's Reform of Nursing 1860–1887").
37. *Ibid.*
38. *Ibid.*
39. *Miss Florence Nightingale's Addresses to Probationer Nurses* (1872–1900).
40. *Ibid.* (for 1873).
41. *Ibid.*
42. FN to mother March 7, 1862 (NP Vol. LII BM. Add. MS 45, 790). Sir James Paget was surgeon to Queen Victoria.
43. FN to mother Feb. 23, 1863 (*ibid*).
44. FN 1889 (quoted CW-S p. 577).
45. *Ibid.*
46. FN to mother March 1862 (NP Vol. LII BM. Add. MS 45, 780).
47. Parthe to Mrs Gaskell Aug. 4, 1862 (NP Vol. LVIII BM. Add. MS 45, 796).
48. FN to Fred (?) April 1896 (NP Vol. LVIII. Add. MS 45, 791).
49. FN to father March 19, 1868 (NP Vol. LII BM. Add. MS 45, 790).
50. FN to father Nov. 4, 1850 (*ibid*).
51. FN to father Oct. 12, 1867 (*ibid*).
52. FN to Aunt Mai (quoted CW-S p. 562)
53. Notes on Register 1892 in NP Vol. LIII.
54. FN to father April 22, 1861 (NP Vol. LII BM. Add. MS 45, 790).
55. FN to Louis Shore Oct. 1897 (quoted CW-S p. 588).
56. Memoir of Caroline Fox (NP LVIII Add. MS 45, 796).
57. FN to Mme Mohl June 1857 (quoted CW-S p. 288).
58. FN to father April 22 1861 (NP Vol. LII Add. 45, 790).
59. FN to Cardinal Manning 1852 (NP Vol. LVIII Add. MS 45, 796).
60. FN to Mary Jones 1867 (quoted in *A History of the Nursing Profession* Brian Abel-Smith, Heinemann 1960 p. 25).

61. FN 1892 (quoted in "Mrs Bedford-Fenwick and the Rise of Professional Nursing" by Winifred Hector, Royal College of Nursing 1973) Intro. p. ix.
62. The total number of nurses (male and female) on the UKCC Register was 817,243 on 30th March 1981, of which 13,838 were male. (Figures from UK Central Council for Nursing, Midwifery and Health Nursing.)
63. FN to Harriet Martineau Feb. 8 1860 (NP Vol. L. Add. MS 45, 788).
64. 1899 (quoted Hector – Intro. p. ix).

Education – Emily Davies 1830–1921

1. *Life of Frances Power Cobbe. As Told by Herself* (1904).
2. Schools Inquiry Commission 1867–8 (Vol. VII – 13 – Pt VI – Mr C. H. Stanton's report on Counties of Devon and Somerset).
3. *Ibid.* Mr H. A. Giffard's report on Surrey and Sussex.
4. *Ibid.*
5. *Ibid.* Mr D. R. Fearon, Metropolitan District.
6. *Ibid.*
7. *Ibid.* Appendix on submitted documents on educational background (No. 23).
8. *Emily Davies and Girton College* by Barbara Stephen (pub. Constable 1927) p. 25.
9. "Family Chronicle" – ED's handwritten memoir – Girton College Library.
10. "Family Chronicle".
11. "Family Chronicle". (The chronicle breaks off in the middle of the story of William's disgrace and is not resumed for 100 pages. Girton College has made every effort to trace this missing section but has failed. Barbara Stephen's biography which was heavily based on the chronicle makes no mention of what happened to William.)
12. "Family Chronicle".
13. *Ibid.*
14. Report on the Northumberland and Durham Branch of the Society for Promoting the Employment of Women 1861. (Reprinted in *Thoughts on Some Questions Relating to Women.*)
15. "Family Chronicle".
16. Stephen p. 71 (letter to Jane Crow Jan. 1864).
17. "Family Chronicle".
18. In America the first endowed institution for the education of girls was the Troy Female Seminary opened by Emma Willard in 1821. The first free school for girls opened in Worcester (Mass.) in 1824. Thomas Woody (*A History of Women's Education in the USA*, NY Science Press, 1929) traces the development of women's education in all its aspects.
19. Stephen p. 73.
20. Stephen p. 83 (letter quoted ED to Miss Richardson).
21. *The Influence of University Degrees on the Education of Women* (*Victoria Magazine*, 1863).
22. *Feminists and Bureaucrats* Sheila Fletcher (Cambridge Univ. Press, 1974).
23. *Ibid.*
24. Stephen p. 100 (quotes letter ED to Mr Tomkinson).
25. "Family Chronicle" Jan. 1868, Emily Davies wrote "By and by, when the colleges at Oxford and Cambridge are open to women, we will open ours to men."
26. Stephen p. 103 (quotes Mr Hutton to ED).
27. *Frances Mary Buss* by Annie E. Ridley.
28. Stephen p. 149 (quotes ED to Miss Richardson, Oct. 1866).
29. *Ibid.* p. 189.
30. *Ibid.*

31. *Ibid.* p. 194.
32. *Ibid.* p. 168.
33. *Ibid.* p. 169 (ED to Mme Bodichon, March 1868).
34. *Ibid.* p. 208 (ED to Mme Bodichon, March 1869).
35. *Ibid.* p. 219.
36. *That Infidel Place – Short History of Girton 1869–1969*, Bradbrooke (quotes Mrs Townshend).
37. Stephen p. 220 (ED to Anna Richardson, Oct. 20 1869).
38. *Ibid.* p. 224 (account given by Miss Dove).
39. *Ibid.* (account given by Miss Maynard).
40. *Ibid.* p. 221 (Miss L. I. Lumsden, *Girton Review*, 1907).
41. *Ibid.* p. 232 (Lumsden on ED).
42. *Ibid.* p. 239 (ED to Anna Richardson from the Examination Room, Dec. 1870).
43. *Ibid.* p. 262 (ED to AR Jan. 1872).
44. *Ibid.* p. 295 (ED to Mme Bodichon).
45. *Ibid.* p. 276.
46. *Ibid.*
47. *Ibid.* p. 278 (ED to Mr Tomkinson).
48. *Ibid.* p. 302 (ED to Mme Bodichon).
49. *Ibid.* p. 303.
50. *Ibid.* p. 304 (ED to Miss Manning).
51. Stephen p. 355.
52. *That Infidel Place* Bradbrooke.
53. Josephine Butler to Albert Rutson May 28, 1868 (JB Fawcett Library). (Josephine Butler had just become president of the North of England Council for Promoting the Higher Education of Women when ED formed a committee Girton in 1867. She later resigned to concentrate on fighting the Contagious Diseases Acts.)
54. Stephen p. 132.
55. *Ibid.* p. 293.
56. "Family Chronicle" (1864).
57. Stephen p. 109 (ED to Mr Tomkinson Nov. 1865).
58. *Ibid.* p. 249 (ED to A. Richardson).
59. *Ibid.* p. 108.
60. *Ibid.* p. 112.
61. "Family Chronicle".
62. The figures for 1981 for university entrance show that 34,613 girls registered compared with 52,214 boys (CSO Annual Abstract of Statistics 1983). Ten years earlier there were 21,199 girls as opposed to 44,618 boys. In America, there is no exact equivalent of British university entrance, but in 1980 the percentage of women in full-time higher education was 49.9% of the total.

Sexual Morality – Josephine Butler 1828–1906

1. Introduction to *Personal Reminiscences of a Great Crusade* by Josephine Butler (pub. Horace Marshall, 1896).
2. *Ibid.* p. 42.
3. *Memoir of John Grey of Dilston* (Edmonston & Douglas, 1869).
4. JB Feb. 17, 1868 Fawcett Library Josephine Butler Collection (hereafter FL).
5. JB Jan. 1894 (FL).
6. *The Hour Before the Dawn* by Josephine Butler (Trübner, 1876) p. 96.
7. JB Feb. 18, 1890 (FL).
8. *Recollections of George Butler* by Josephine Butler (Arrowsmith, 1892) p. 64.
9. *Ibid.* p. 232.
10. JB to father 1853 (FL).

11. *Recollections* etc. p. 94.
12. *Ibid.* p. 90.
13. *Ibid.* p. 155.
14. Arthur Butler Jan. 4, 1907 (FL).
15. JB to Stanley, June 3, 1891 (FL).
16. *Recollections* etc. JB's diary for Oct. 30, 1864 p. 159.
17. JB to Miss Priestman Jan. 24, 1873 (FL).
18. *Recollections* etc. p. 182.
19. *Ibid.*
20. *Ibid.* p. 183.
21. JB (1867 FL). The reference to Dr Moore is contained in the Notebook of Edith Leupold (daughter of JB's eldest sister).
22. Poem in JB collection filed with notebook above.
23. In spite of their unanimity on the necessity of employment opportunities keeping pace with education for girls Josephine Butler and Emily Davies did not get on well. JB was President of the North of England Council for the Promotion of Higher Education for Girls when Emily Davies set up a committee to found Girton and was seen by ED as a dangerous rival offering, in the Ladies Lectures scheme, a "lesser" alternative which would harm her own aims. (See E. Davies chapter.)
24. GB to JB Dec. 3, 1867. (There are many such instances, of George looking after the children, in the JB papers.)
25. JB May 22, 1868 (FL).
26. *Ibid.*
27. JB to mother-in-law Feb. 1869 (FL).
28. *Recollections* etc. p. 218.
29. *Ibid.*
30. Quoted in a letter from JB to an MP in *Flame of Fire* by E. Moberley Bell (Constable 1862).
31. *History of Woman Suffrage* (see E. Cady Stanton chapter) Vol. 3 appendix – EC-S's reminiscences of a visit to England in 1882.
32. *Personal Reminiscences* etc. p. 27.
33. *Ibid.* p. 48.
34. The Harriet Hicks case is described by J. and D. Walkowitz in *Clio's Consciousness Raised – New Perspectives on the History of Women* ed. Mary Hartman and Lois Bamer (Harper Colophon Bks).
35. JB to Miss Priestman Jan. 24, 1873 (FL).
36. JB to Mr Wilson Feb. 26, 1873 (FL).
37. JB to Mr Wilson April 1, 1873 (FL).
38. JB to Miss Priestman July 4, 1874 (FL).
39. *Ibid.* Sept. 20, 1874 (FL).
40. *Recollections* etc. p. 237.
41. *Ibid.* diary for Aug. 14, 1876 p. 303.
42. JB to Mr Martineau May 27, 1873 (FL).
43. JB Feb. 17, 1883 (FL).
44. Account of repeal in JB's letter to sister Harriet, April 1883 (quoted in *A Singular Iniquity* by Glen Petrie pub. Macmillan 1971 p. 208).
45. *Recollections* etc. p. 225.
46. JB to Eliza (her eldest sister) July 12, 1885 (FL).
47. JB to Stanley April 1891 (FL).
48. *Rebecca Jarrett* by Josephine Butler (Morgan & Scott, 1886).
49. *Ibid.*
50. *Ibid.*
51. *Ibid.*
52. *Ibid.*

53. Quoted in *Josephine Butler, a Life Study* by W. H. Stead (Morgan & Scott, 1887).
54. JB to Stanley Oct. 1, 1886 (quoted in Petrie p. 266).
55. JB to G. W. Johnson Feb. 18, 1891 (quoted in Petrie p. 266).
56. JB to ? Jan 17, 1883 (FL).
57. JB to Stanley June 3, 1891 (FL).
58. JB to Stanley Dec. 23, 1901 (FL).
59. JB to Stanley transcribed by Mr Burfoot after the new Liberal administration had taken office in 1906 (FL).
60. (FL the last letter).
61. Quoted in *Facts are Stubborn Things; a Selection of Cases Illustrative of the Working of the Contagious Diseases Acts* by Alfred Dyer (a contemporary of JB's).
62. Quoted in *Josephine Butler: Flame of Fire* by E. Moberley Bell.
63. JB to Mr Wilson June 14, 1873 (FL).
64. JB to Mrs Wilson Nov. 18, 1873 (FL). It has been stated that Josephine Butler had "absolutely no interest whatever in the question of female suffrage" (Petrie p. 63). This is utterly untrue. Over and over again in her letters Josephine Butler stresses the need for suffrage.
65. JB to B. Jowett 1860 (FL).
66. JB to Miss Priestman April 28, 1883 (FL). I have been unable to find "massinian" in any dictionary although its meaning is easy enough to guess in this context.

Politics – Elizabeth Cady Stanton 1815–1902

1. From "The Solitude of Self", a speech made by ECS in 1892 (printed also in *Elizabeth Cady Stanton, Susan B. Anthony – Correspondence, writings & speeches* ed. Ellen Carol Dubois (Schocken Books, NY). ECS thought it was the best she ever made.
2. Lydia Maria Child Letters p. 74 (quoted in *Century of Struggle – the Woman's Rights Movement in the United States* by Eleanor Flexnor p. 62. This is the best book for the background to woman's rights in America and immensely readable).
3. *Elizabeth Cady Stanton as Revealed in her Letters, Diaries and Reminiscences* edited by Theodore Stanton and Harriot Stanton Blatch Vol. 1, p. 3. This is the main source for all information on ECS's early life and all quotes come from it unless otherwise stated. Hereafter Stanton & Blatch (S & B).
4. Diary Sept. 6, 1883 (Stanton & Blatch Vol. 2 p. 210).
5. Quoted in *Created Equal: Elizabeth Cady Stanton* by Alma Lutz.
6. Henry Stanton to ECS (photostat of letter dated only "Tues. 5 pm" in manuscript collection of ECS papers in Library of Congress).
7. ECS to Rebecca R. Eyster, Stanton & Blatch Vol. 2 p. 15.
8. Stanton & Blatch Vol. 1 p. 93.
9. Stanton & Blatch Vol. 1 p. 79.
10. Lutz.
11. ECS to Elizabeth Pease 1840 (Lutz).
12. ECS to Lucretia Mott 1841 (Lutz).
13. Stanton & Blatch Vol. 1 p. 109.
14. *Ibid.*
15. Stanton & Blatch Vol. 1 p. 133.
16. *Ibid.* p. 134.
17. *Ibid.*
18. *Ibid.* p. 141.
19. *Ibid.* p. 143.
20. Henry Stanton to ECS June 1843 (photostat from manuscript div. Library of Congress).
21. HS to ECS 1843 (photostat L of C).
22. HS to ECS 1843 (photostat L of C).

23. HS to ECS 1843 (*ibid*). All three of these photostated manuscript letters bear only the year in Henry's writing and the day of the week but not the month or date.

24. *Ibid.*

25. Stanton & Blatch Vol. 1 p. 144.

26. ECS to Susan B. Anthony, June 10, 1856 (S & B Vol. II p. 67).

27. *History of Woman Suffrage* (ed. ECS, Susan B. Anthony, Matilda Gage).

28. ECS. Address delivered at Seneca Falls July 19 1848 (printed in Dubois).

29. *H of WS* Vol. 1 (In her autobiography ECS also said "If I had had the slightest premonition of all that was to follow that convention I fear I should not have had the courage to risk it . . .").

30. *H of WS* Vol. 1.

31. Between 1839 and 1850 most states in America passed some kind of legislation giving married women property rights. This swift movement for legislative reform contrasted with the slowness of England to follow suit. After J. S. Mill's great suffrage speech of 1867 drew attention to women's property disabilities, bills were introduced in 1868, 1869 and 1870 (for the agitation that preceded them see chap. 1 Caroline Norton) but it was not until 1882 that the Married Women's Property Bill finally secured to married women not just property they had *at* marriage but property and earnings acquired *after*.

32. Stanton & Blatch Vol. 1 p. 154. (Susan B. Anthony was introduced to ECS by Amelia Bloomer. Susan later confessed she was disappointed not to be asked to dinner, or at least into her home, by ECS, who maintained her mind was full of what her "three mischievous boys" would have been up to while she was at the meeting.)

33. ECS to Susan B. Anthony Dec. 1, 1853 (Stanton & Blatch Vol. II p. 55).

34. *H of WS* Vol I. ECS to Lucy Stone 1856.

35. ECS to Lillie Devereau Blake Jan. 6, 1879 (Stanton & Blatch Vol. II p. 156).

36. Alice Stone Blackwell to Kitty Barry Dec. 24, 1882 (quoted Nancy Sahli p. 451).

37. ECS to SBA June 14, 1860 (Stanton & Blatch Vol. II p. 82).

38. ECS to SBA March 1, 1853 (Stanton & Blatch Vol. II p. 48).

39. ECS to Lucy Stone (*H of WS* Vol. 1).

40. *H of WS* Vol II (and Gerrit Smith's comment).

41. *Ibid.*

42. *Ibid.* (National Convention 1869).

43. ECS to Theodore Tilton, *H of WS*. Vol. II. 1869.

44. ECS Diary Dec. 25, 1880 (Stanton & Blatch Vol. II).

45. ECS Diary Nov. 15, 1880 (*ibid*).

46. Stanton & Blatch Vol. I p. 249.

47. *Ibid.*

48. *Ibid.*

49. ECS to SBA April 2, 1859 (Vassar Coll. Lib. quoted Dubois p. 68).

50. ECS to Nov. 12, 1880 (her 65th birthday) Stanton & Blatch Vol. II.

51. Quoted Dubois (p. 182) from ECS unpublished manuscript Library of Congress on "What Should be Our Attitude Toward Political Parties".

52. Quoted Dubois (p. 119) from *The Revolution* Jan. 14, 1869.

53. *H of WS* Vol. III.

54. ECS Diary May 3, 1894 (Stanton & Blatch Vol. II p. 303).

55. Stanton & Blatch Vol. II p. 300.

56. ECS Diary Feb. 10, 1902 (Stanton & Blatch Vol II p. 363).

57. Stanton & Blatch Vol. II p. 345 (daughter Harriot's footnote).

58. Quoted Dubois p. 208 from "Report of the International Council of Women" 1888.

59. Quoted Dubois p. 137 from ECS's speech Home Life (ECS papers, Library of Congress).

60. Stanton & Blatch Vol. II p. 100.
61. ECS to SBA Sept. 10, 1855 (Stanton & Blatch Vol. II p. 59).
62. Stanton & Blatch Vol. I p. 177.
63. ECS Diary Dec. 27, 1890 (Stanton & Blatch Vol. II p. 270).
64. Intro. to Vol. I *H of WS*.
65. Appendix to Vol. I. *H of WS*.
66. ECS Diary Aug. 28, 1884 (Stanton & Blatch Vol II p. 220).
67. ECS Diary Oct. 28, 1881 (Stanton & Blatch Vol. II p. 187).
68. ECS Diary Feb. 25, 1883 (Stanton & Blatch Vol. II p. 283).
69. ECS was critical of the slowness with which the suffrage movement in Europe moved and particularly so of England, where it was not until 1903 (with the formation by Mrs Emmeline Pankhurst of the Women's Social & Political Union) that she felt a proper attack was being at last launched. She approved of the militant tactics but, interestingly, considered Mrs Jacob Bright "unquestionably stands at the helm of the woman suffrage movement on this side of the ocean."

    Women's suffrage in England was always most likely as part of general parliamentary reforms. John Stuart Mills' speech in 1867 first brought the possibility of female suffrage into the centre of the political stage; hopes ran high in 1884, 1911 and 1912 but were always dashed, sometimes dramatically at the last minute. In January 1918 the Representation of the People Bill with Clause IV giving women the suffrage finally passed both houses.
70. ECS to SBA April 5, 1879 (Stanton & Blatch Vol. II p. 160).
71. Britain and America have fared badly in the political stakes (in contrast with the Scandinavian countries for example). In Britain only 19 women were elected in the 1979 election. Never at any time since the vote was granted to women has the percentage of women in Parliament been higher than 4.6%. The number of women holding Cabinet office at the moment (1983) is 2. It has never been higher than 2.

    In America, in 1983, there were 24 women in Congress – 4.5% of the total (*Congressional Quarterly*, Oct. 1983). In 1981 women held 11.8% of appointed positions in state governors' cabinets (there have been only 5 female state governors and there were none in 1983). Between Jan. 1981 and Aug. 1983 President Reagan appointed and had confirmed by Senate 134 women to office. This was 9.5% of the total – a fall of 4.8% from the number President Carter appointed.

Birth Control – Margaret Sanger 1879–1966

1. From *The Bull Dog* (quoted in *The Birth Controllers* by Peter Fryer pub. Secker & Warburg 1965 p. 83).
2. *Victorian Women: A documentary account of women's lives in nineteenth century England, France and the United States* ed. Hellerstein, Hume & Offen (pub. Harvester 1981) p. 200.
3. *Fruits of Philosophy* by Charles Knowlton (1832) p. 2.
4. *Woman and the New Race* by Margaret Sanger (Chapter I).
5. *Margaret Sanger: an Autobiography* (Dover Books edition) p. 16.
6. *My Fight for Birth Control* by Margaret Sanger (Faber ed. 1932) p. 11.
7. *Ibid.* p. 19.
8. *Autobiog.* p. 55.
9. *My Fight for Birth Control* p. 38.
10. William Sanger to Margaret Sanger ?1902 (photostat of manuscript letter in Manuscript Division of Library of Congress, Container No. 2).
11. *Ibid.*

12. *Ibid.*

13. Quoted in *Margaret Sanger* by Emily Taft Douglas (NY Reinhart & Wilson 1970).

14. *My Fight for Birth Control* p. 42.

15. *Autobiog.* p. 70. (*IWW*: Industrial Workers of the World, known as "Wobblies".)

16. *Ibid.* p. 92.

17. *Autobiog.* p. 66.

18. *Ibid.* p. 85.

19. *My Fight for Birth Control* p. 72.

20. *Ibid.* p. 74.

21. *Ibid.* p. 79.

22. *Ibid.* p. 277.

23. Quoted in *The Sage of Sex: A Life of Havelock Ellis* by Arthur Calder-Marshall (Hart-Davis 1959).

24. *Ibid.*

25. *Ibid.*

26. *My Fight for Birth Control* p. 107.

27. *Ibid.* p. 117.

28. Quoted in *Birth Control in America* by David Kennedy (Yale 1970) p. 33.

29. Margaret Sanger to "Friends & Comrades" Jan. 5, 1916 (quoted Kennedy p. 78).

30. *Autobiog.* p. 82.

31. Henry Pratt Fairchild in *Nation* May 7, 1955 (quoted Kennedy p. 35).

32. *Autobiog.* p. 199.

33. Margaret Sanger's speech, Boston, April 16, 1929 (quoted Kennedy p. 82).

34. *Autobiog.* p. 191.

35. *Ibid.* p. 215.

36. *Ibid.*

37. *Ibid.* p. 216.

38. *Ibid.* p. 237.

39. *Ibid.* p. 239.

40. *My Fight for Birth Control* p. 177.

41. *Ibid.*

42. *Autobiog.* p. 257.

43. *My Fight for Birth Control* p. 278.

44. *Autobiog.* p. 332.

45. Quoted Emily Taft Douglas.

46. *Autobiog.* p. 494.

47. *Ibid.* p. 467.

48. Margaret Sanger to Clarence Gamble Feb. 8, 1943 (quoted Kennedy p. 270).

49. Margaret Sanger in *Birth Control Review* May 1919 p. 12.

50. Marie Stopes and Margaret Sanger were at first friends. (Marie invited Margaret to tea at 14 Well Walk in Hampstead.) Their ideas, particularly on the need to give women not just adequate contraception but joyous sexual lives, were very similar. It was Marie who organized a petition to President Woodrow Wilson when Margaret faced prosecution in 1915. But after Margaret opened her Brownsville Birth Control Clinic in 1916 they became rivals – especially when Marie feared Margaret might open another in London and rob her of the glory of doing so. In fact, Marie did manage to open the first British clinic in Islington in March 1921 and her two books *Married Love* and *Wise Parenthood* (both 1918) had much greater sales and wider appeal than Margaret Sanger's. But Marie Stopes never became quite the international power Margaret Sanger did, nor was her vision as feminist: she wanted sexual activity confined to the married and was against abortion, masturbation and lesbianism.

51. Margaret Sanger's hatred of the Roman Catholic church blinded her to the fact that there might actually be something in their argument. She saw the RC

outlook as part of a plot against women: to her, there *was* no moral problem. (Birth control, she said, was no more against nature than the Pope shaving was against nature and neither was a moral problem.) For a full discussion and the RC attitude and how it hindered the spread of birth control in America see Kennedy Chapter 6.

52. *My Fight for Birth Control* p. 150.
53. *Woman and the New Race* (1920).
54. Carrie Chapman Catt to Margaret Sanger 1920 (quoted p. 238 Birth Control in America: *Woman's Body, Woman's Right* by Linda Gordon, Penguin 1977).

Ideology – Emma Goldman 1869–1940

1. Ray Strachey (quoted in *The Feminists* by Richard J. Evans pub. Croom Helm 1977 p. 210).
2. *Living My Life* by Emma Goldman Vol. I p. 371. (This two-volume autobiography is the basis for almost all that is known of Emma Goldman's early life. It is a brilliant piece of work showing far more honesty and frankness than the usual autobiography and, in so far as it has been possible to check by reference to other contemporary sources, it seems remarkably accurate.) Hereafter referred to as EG I or II (Dover edition page references).
3. *The Tragedy of Woman's Emancipation – Anarchism and other Essays* by Emma Goldman (1911). (Also reprinted in *Red Emma Speaks* – The Selected Speeches and Writings of Emma Goldman ed. Alix Kates Shulman, Wildwood House edition p. 136.)
4. *Anarchism and Other Essays – Woman Suffrage*, Chapter 4.
5. *The Tragedy of Woman's Emancipation* (Shulman p. 142).
6. EG I p. 36.
7. EG I p. 21.
8. EG I p. 22.
9. *Ibid.*
10. EG I p. 12.
11. EG I p. 11.
12. EG I p. 12.
13. EG I p. 20.
14. EG I p. 21.
15. *Ibid.*
16. EG I p. 23.
17. EG I p. 25.
18. *Ibid.*
19. EG I p. 36.
20. EG I p. 44.
21. EG I p. 56.
22. EG I p. 45.
23. EG I p. 61.
24. EG I p. 62.
25. EG I p. 65.
26. EG's belief that her retroverted womb prevented her being able to conceive and caused her period pains was mistaken. In about 15% of women the womb is retroverted and neither causes pain nor prevents conception. EG's pain was more likely to have been caused by muscle cramps of the uterus due to stimulation by the hormone progesterone, and her apparent infertility by early pelvic inflammation which went undetected.
27. EG I p. 87.
28. EG I p. 88.

29. EG I p. 91.
30. EG I p. 118.
31. EG I p. 120.
32. EG I p. 151 (and following pages for EG's account of this important argument).
33. EG I p. 162.
34. EG I p. 183.
35. EG I p. 195.
36. EG I p. 209.
37. EG I p. 244.
38. *Ibid.*
39. EG I p. 333.
40. EG I p. 340.
41. *Mother Earth* editorial March 1917 Vol. 12 No. 1.
42. *Voltairine de Cleyre* by Emma Goldman (pub. Oriole Press 1922). In this memoir of her friend and fellow anarchist EG went even further, saying that "most men prefer beauty to brains". She did not criticize them for this but said "therein lies the tragedy of many intellectual women".
43. *Nowhere at Home: Letters fr. Exile of Emma Goldman and Alexander Berkman* ed. Richard and Anna Maria Drinnon (pub. Schocken 1975) p. 148. Hereafter Drinnon.
44. EG I p. 416.
45. EG I p. 420 (long after her affair with Ben was over and she had grown to despise him EG said "Ben was for 10 years a great and elemental force in my life which I would not have missed for worlds" – May 14, 1929 in manuscript collection International Institute of Social History, Amsterdam, File XVII C. This immense collection of EG's letters is at the moment being more efficiently catalogued and will undoubtedly reveal much new material).
46. Ben Reitman to EG May 22, 1929 File XVII C (II Amsterdam).
47. Ben Reitman to EG Dec. 1934 File XVII B.
48. EG I p. 433.
49. Shulman p. 44.
50. Woman Suffrage, Chap. 4 in *Anarchism & Other Essays.*
51. Ben Reitman to EG Aug. 7, 1932 File XVII C (Ben reminiscing about his hero-worship of her nevertheless accused her of having demanded "unreasonable" sexual fidelity).
52. EG to Nellie Harris Oct. 28, 1931 File XVII B (II Amsterdam). (She also added that her bust was 110 and her hips 123 – presumably centimetres which equals 43 ins. and 48½.)
53. EG to Stella (her niece) Sept. 9, 1934 File XVII A (II Amsterdam).
54. Frank Heiner to EG (undated) File XVIII A (II Amsterdam).
55. Emmy Echstein to EG (undated) File XVIIIA (II Amsterdam).
56. EG to Henry Alsberg June 27 1930 (quoted Drinnon p. 163).
57. EG to Stella July 18, 1931 File XVII B(2) (II Amsterdam).
58. EG to Frank Harris Aug. 7, 1925 (Drinnon p. 129).
59. Drinnon p. 125.
60. EG to Max Nettlau Feb. 8, 1935 File XVIII A (II Amsterdam).
61. *Ibid.*
62. EG to Max Nettlau Feb. 8, 1935 File XVIII A (II Amsterdam).
63. Drinnon p. 9.

Index